SCHOOLS THAT WORK

SCHOOLS THAT WORK
WHERE ALL CHILDREN READ AND WRITE

Richard L. Allington
The University at Albany, SUNY

Patricia M. Cunningham
Wake Forest University

HarperCollins*CollegePublishers*

Executive Editor: Chris Jennison
Project Coordination and Text Design: Electronic Publishing Services Inc.
Cover Designer: Amy Trombat
Art Studio: Electronic Publishing Services Inc.
Electronic Production Manager: Mike Kemper
Manufacturing Manager: Helene G. Landers
Electronic Page Makeup: Electronic Publishing Services Inc.
Printer and Binder: R.R. Donnelley & Sons Company
Cover Printer: Phoenix Color Corp.

Schools That Work: Where all Children Read and Write
Copyright © 1996 by HarperCollins College Publishers

Library of Congress Cataloging-in-Publication Data

Allington, Richard L.
    Schools that work : where all children read and write / by Richard L. Allington,
Patricia M. Cunningham.
       p. cm.
    Includes bibliographical references and index.
    ISBN 0-673-99881-9
    1. School management and organization. 2. Language arts
(Elementary) 3. Reading (Elementary) I. Cunningham, Patricia Marr. II. Title.
    LB2805.A449   1995
371.2—dc20
                                         95–15798
                                             CIP

9 10 11 12 -DOC- 01 00 99 98

Contents

Preface

WHY WE WROTE THIS BOOK

Both of us have focused our professional careers on understanding how schools might organize instructional resources so that all children become readers and writers. In our earlier book, *Classrooms That Work: They Can All Read and Write* (HarperCollins, 1994) we offered a framework for classroom instruction to achieve that end. However, in the closing chapter of that book we noted that there were forces outside the classroom that could foster or hinder progress in achieving classrooms that work for all children. In this book we address, primarily, those factors most typically outside the control of classroom teachers.

We wrote this book because, with the best of intentions, many schools are organized in ways that hinder creating effective classrooms. Having worked with numbers of schools, we have found that many of them use the extraordinary financial resources offered by local, state, and federal education agencies (e.g., funds that support developmental kindergartens; bilingual, remedial, and special-education programs; dropout-prevention efforts; family-involvement programs) in ways that literally cannot work to accelerate participating children's achievement.

We have found that many schools are "stuck," unable to create more effective programs, because historical policies and practices constrain the visions of how schools might change. Too often, schools add more of the "same old, same old," and often increasing these efforts interferes with enhancing classroom effectiveness. For instance, 1992 marked the year when schools first employed more adults who were not classroom teachers than adults who were. Fifty-two percent of those working in schools are not classroom teachers! The addition of these "special program personnel"—resource room teachers, speech therapists, counselors, psychologists, reading teachers, and so on—has created an environment in many schools where scheduling at-risk children for self-esteem workshops or articulation therapy has taken precedence over ensuring access to intensive and effective classroom instruction. As we have tried to squeeze more special services into the school day, we have often squeezed effective instruction out.

But it is not just special programs that need restructuring in the schools we have. We need to rethink curriculum standards to meet the expanded literacy demands of a technological society. We need to rethink the very notion of the school day and school year as more and more children—now the majority—come from families where parents are employed and often not at home until after 5:30, several hours after most children have ended their traditional school day. The compelling evidence that traditional in-service education offerings are largely ineffective should cause us to rethink the nature of professional development across the career-span for teachers and administrators. Likewise, assessing students and evaluating programs must change; so, too, must family-involvement policies and initiatives.

Already we see a rethinking of the traditional management model for schools. We see whole-scale shifts toward decentralization of decision making in the advent of the site-based management teams, federal schoolwide projects, shared decision-making mandates, and so on. But for schools to achieve the change they will need—to develop all children as readers and writers—better ideas will be more important than increased funding. We are not arguing that schools are well funded but rather that we can get more bang for the buck than we are now.

This book is a practical text for those wanting to create elementary schools where all children become readers and writers. In this book we describe the critical features of school organizational plans (e.g., professional roles, organization of time, curriculum, student assessment, professional development, parental involvement) that can support or impede developing more effective educational settings.

In writing this book, we have drawn on our combined fifty years of experience as teachers, curriculum coordinators, administrators, researchers, reformers, evaluators, and consultants in schools. We have tried to make the book readable and practical while grounded in proven practices. We describe exemplary efforts in real schools across the country and offer a variety of activities for taking stock of the educational effort in your school. We offer you information on where to obtain specific materials that will support changing your school for the better—even providing toll-free telephone numbers for many suppliers. As school systems move toward greater use of site-based decision making, there is a need for clear, effective resources such as this book. The shared decision-making teams of teachers, principals, parents, and community members need a source they can all read and where they can find both research-based information and a vision for schools that work.

Schools That Work offers a clear view of how schools must change if they are to meet the increased demands of education for the twenty-first century. Still, because schools differ substantially, no single strategy will work in every location. Thus, we provide information and examples and hope that you will develop your own vision of what your school might become. Take a moment and scan the table of contents. We have tried to label each chapter so that you will be able to easily locate information on specific topics or issues. In chapters 2 and 10, we have attempted to offer snapshots and portraits of schools that work better for all children.

We know that schools can be created where every child reads and writes. We have seen these schools! Elementary schools have but one overriding mission: to foster the development of independent literacy in all students so that each becomes literate for a lifetime. Our aim is for this book to move us a little closer to creating schools where all children are readers and writers.

This book could not have been written without the assistance of a number of school administrators, teachers, and university colleagues across the country. It is to these devoted and innovative professionals that we dedicate this book. We might have tried to list all the folks that invited us to schools to observe programs and talk with the professional staff and parents. However, that would be a very long list, and we would never remember everyone. So, instead, we will provide a short list of some of the folks who offered support that went above and beyond the normal course of events. First, there are the professionals who read and commented on chapters of the book as we wrote and revised them. Steve Pavone, principal of Park Terrace School in Gloversville (New York) Enlarged City Schools; Sandi Schwartz, reading and language arts director in the Rochester (Michigan) Public Schools; Marguerite Radencich, curriculum director in the Dade County (Florida) Public Schools; Helen Stuetzel, director of instruction in the Ballston Spa (New York) Public Schools; Marcie Brown, federal programs staff in the Adrian (Michigan) Public Schools; Dottie Hall, curriculum coordinator in the Winston-Salem/Forsyth (North Carolina) Public Schools; and Kathleen Jongsma, curriculum supervisor in the Northside (Texas) Public Schools. We must also thank the parents, children, and professional staffs of the Park Terrace School in Gloversville (New York), the Beall and Alta Vista Elementary Schools in the El Paso (Texas) Independent School District, the Cash and Clemmons Elementary Schools in Winston-Salem (North Carolina) for the use of the photographs we took while visiting. Finally, both of us are indebted to the many others—our colleagues, including especially our spouses, Anne McGill-Franzen and Jim Cunningham, and our students—who have helped us shape the ideas offered in our two books.

Richard L. Allington
Patricia M. Cunningham

SCHOOLS THAT WORK

CHAPTER 1

The Schools We Have— What Doesn't Work

N
o matter how smart or how cute or how wonderful a child might be, parents should hope that their child finds learning to read and write easy. For it is the children who have difficulty learning to read and write alongside their peers that are most often at risk in our schools. Delays and difficulties in learning to read and write are the most common reasons given for retaining children, labeling them, placing them in a special track, group, class, or program. In the schools we have, children who do not experience early school success too often experience no success at all. The longer children experience failure, the greater the level of risk they face.

It is the children who arrive at kindergarten with a history of few home experiences with print, book, story, and pencil activities who are most likely to occupy the desks in the basic skills and special education classrooms in high school ten years later. Early school achievement, especially in reading and writing, is a terribly reliable predictor of later school achievement. It is these children who are least likely to experience success in kindergarten or first grade. These at-risk children often then continue to struggle throughout elementary, middle, and high school. The schools we have are better at sorting and labeling at-risk children than at accelerating their academic development (Allington, 1994). Of course, some schools have created programs that work better than others. But, generally, the schools we have do not work well for at-risk children.

We must admit at the outset that we are uncomfortable with describing children as being at risk. The term is but the most recent label for those children who have difficulty fulfilling their academic learning potential. In the past we have had other popular labels ranging historically from "laggards," to "slow learners," to "disadvantaged," to "dyslexics." Perhaps the notion of *risk* is a more appropriate concept than those previously popular labels for children who fail to profit substantially from the usual instruction offered in the schools we have. Being *at risk* does not suggest the same sort of inevitability that the label "slow" seems to suggest, for instance. Being at risk does suggest that some sort of intervention may be necessary to reduce or eliminate whatever one is at risk of experiencing.

We always seem to be searching for the single quick fix that will solve the problems of American schools. We mandate, bandwagon, proselytize, and alienate and continue our ever-reforming educational innovations. Perhaps it is time for us to realize that:

1. There is no quick fix.
2. We have actually learned quite a lot about schooling and teaching reading to all children.
3. Achieving literacy for all children isn't such a simple matter that we can blame the method of teaching or the type of curriculum, though those are about all we ever debate.

The risk faced by some children is that they will not successfully negotiate the demands of our schools. These are the children who leave our schools underprepared for the demands of adult life in our modern technological society. Some of these children leave school before completing any course of study—those children we call dropouts. Others complete a course of study and graduate with a local diploma, a special education diploma, an attendance diploma, but they leave school ill-equipped to fully participate in our modern American society. These underprepared or underachieving children are less likely now than ever before to find permanent employment in a position that offers occupational and social security. Today we can identify these children with horrifying accuracy after they have completed but a year or two of schooling. Some children we identify as being at risk of school failure and having limited life chances do, of course, beat the odds. But many more attend school for 10 to 13 years only to have their destiny largely unaltered. Far too many of the children we identify early as being at risk never overcome the factors that placed them at risk. Despite good intentions, the schools we have often increase the risk that some children face.

In this book, we hope to offer educators a vision of elementary schools that reduce the risks for children—schools that do not perpetuate the type of traditional practices that actually increase the risk that some children face in attending school. American society has changed, but our schools have remained largely static in their organization and predictable outcomes. The elementary school of today mirrors the basic design of the graded elementary school that was laid out at the turn of the last century. Those schools were designed to sort children into three worker groups—laborers, craftspeople, and professionals—with most children sorted into the laborers group. But agriculture and factory work were the primary occupations of most workers during much of this century. Today, few people work in agriculture, and the number who work in factories or at the traditional skilled trades is rapidly declining. Today, information, management, and technology jobs dominate the marketplace. Hardly anyone is satisfied that our schools are producing young adults with the knowledge, experiences, and skills needed to be successful in modern society. Recent projections for the year 2000 are that the shifting American economy will require a workforce whose median education level is 13.5 years. The average worker, not the bosses, will need some college or other postsecondary education just to bring home a paycheck (Smith & Lincoln, 1988).

We need schools that educate children—not schools that simply sort children into worker groups. We need schools that help children exceed their destiny—schools where *all* children are successful, not just those lucky children who find schooling easy. We need schools that develop in all children the knowledge, skills, and attitudes that have historically been reserved for just a few children. We need elementary schools that break the gridlock of low achievement that stymies efforts to educate all children further along the schooling process. We need elementary schools where virtually all fifth graders are on track to complete a traditional college-preparatory degree and prepared to participate in postsecondary education.

"America entered the 1990s with more than three times as many lawyers as firefighters." So went the opening line of an Associated Press news story (January 29, 1993) that summarized a Census Bureau report showing that the United States had more white-collar workers in 1990 than blue-collar workers—for the first time in this nation's history. The shrinkage in the number of workers who make their living making or transporting goods continues unabated while the expansion of the executive, professional, and technical workforce has exploded. No one is predicting that the American economy will ever again be dominated by manufacturing.

To accomplish this will require elementary schools to be quite different from the schools found in most communities. To accomplish this in schools that serve large numbers of children historically considered at risk will require substantial rethinking of the school day, the curriculum, and the allocation of the educational resources available. After nearly a century of increasing centralization of educational decision making there seems, finally, a realization that perhaps teachers and principals, those professionals closest to the children, are best equipped to plan effective schools.

The shift away from centralized decision making is emerging as, perhaps, the major educational innovation of the nineties. Terms such as site-based management, shared decision making, total quality management, and school development teams are now found throughout the educational reform literature and are heard at conferences, in legislatures, and at school board meetings. Reorganizing and restructuring of school systems and the traditional centralized decision-making processes will require hard work and, we expect, a fit of starts, stutters, stops, and restarts across this decade.

School-based decision-making teams will struggle with decisions that have to be made. In this book, we attempt to provide administrators, supervisors, and teachers with information and ideas that will be useful in making decisions about organizing and delivering reading and writing instruction. We draw upon what we have learned while working in elementary schools. We emphasize creating schools where all children become readers and writers because (1) that has been the primary focus of our own work in schools and (2) learning to read and write are fundamentally essential to success in school and in society. We focus on at-risk children because it is a substantial accomplishment to create schools where these children—where *all* children—become readers and writers.

Too often, educational reformers have failed to learn from the past. Instead, schools reform again and again and again—returning after a few years to practices found lacking in the past but seemingly lost from our institutional memory (Cuban, 1990). If our schools are to survive and succeed, the past cannot be forever repeated. It is possible to create elementary schools where all children become readers and writers alongside their friends. However, these schools will necessarily look different from most schools of today.

In this book, we focus on the children who have historically been placed at risk by our educational programs. We focus on these children because when schools work well for these children, schools work better for all children. We begin by exploring which children are placed at risk in schools today.

■ WHO IS AT RISK IN OUR ELEMENTARY SCHOOLS?

The 1980s was not a good decade for children in the United States. The number of children living in poverty rose from 16 percent at the start of the decade to 20 percent at the end. The majority of these poor children were white, but a greater proportion of minority children live in poverty in this country. Today, fifteen million children are being raised in single-parent households with incomes within $1,000 of the official poverty levels. The average incomes of these single-parent families hover about the poverty level and are well below the average incomes for two-parent families ($11,400 versus $34,000). Eleven million workers are currently employed at or near minimum wage; the majority of these workers are women over age 25 with dependent children (Hodgkinson 1993). Forecasters predict that by the year 2000, 25 percent—one out of every four children in our schools—will come to us from a family living in poverty. Forty percent of all children will live in a household receiving Aid to Families with Dependent Children for at least one year before they reach age 18. Nearly two-thirds of all children can be expected to have lived in a single-parent household for at least part of their childhood.

Poverty and Risk

It is the children whose families are poor (including children of the working poor) whom our schools serve least well. It is poor children who risk school failure most commonly. School performance has been, unfortunately, quite predictable from student social-class data. When schools enroll large numbers of children from poor families, student achievement is routinely ranked among the lowest performing schools (Cooley 1993). Conversely, when schools enroll few poor children, achievement typically ranks much higher. It is not only achievement that varies but also school attendance, high school completion rates, and college attendance after graduation. In fact, most measures of school quality vary as a function of poverty levels among the families in the community. Education spending also varies along with student poverty. Ironically, American society currently concentrates educational funds on those schools with the fewest children from poor families. More money is spent per student in our relatively stable, relatively wealthy suburban schools than in schools that serve large numbers of poor children in rural or urban communities (Kozol, 1991). In addition, we spend more on high school educational programs than on elementary school educational efforts.

Poverty is not the only factor that places a child at high risk of academic failure, but it is the most pervasive one. With childhood poverty on the rise, more of the children who arrive at our schools will be at risk for school failure. The central role of family poverty can be seen by examining the data on minority-student achievement. For example, the academic achievement of African-American and Latino students from middle-class homes substantially exceeds the achievement of white and Asian students whose families are poor. Nearly a quarter of African-American and Latino students from middle-class families achieved advanced levels of mathematics performance compared to only 7 percent of the white students from poor families (Hodgkinson 1993). This is not to suggest that minority status is unimportant but rather that family poverty increases the likelihood that children are placed at greater risk in our schools.

Parents' Education and Risk

Parental educational attainment influences the level of risk that children experience in schools. Of course, parent educational attainment is also related to family income. Better-educated parents generally earn more money than less-well-educated parents. This added income allows parents to purchase various sorts of educational support for their children (e.g., tutorial assistance, home educational materials, or summer educational experiences). Parents who are better educated themselves have resources other than additional family income available to support their children. These parents often have more time, energy, education, and schedule flexibility to assist their children in school-related activities. It is the minimum-wage worker who works the longest hours with the least flexibility for the smallest paycheck. It is the children of working poor who are most likely to be latchkey children. These are the children whose parents can least afford private tutors and who are least able to provide their children with needed instructional support themselves. All parents care about their children, but parents have different sorts of resources for acting upon that caring and concern.

Better-educated, middle-class parents share many of the values common to schools. This should not be surprising because most teachers hold middle-class values as important to school success and it is teachers who set the values considered important in school. But middle-class parents also see teachers as their social equals and feel far freer to raise questions about school policies and school experiences than other less-advantaged and less-well-educated parents. The better-educated parent has a broader range of school experiences to draw upon and knows more about what is important for school success. Less-well-educated parents are often intimidated by schools and school personnel and avoid confrontations or meetings where they might be asked to do what they cannot. These parents more often entrust the school to address the difficulties their children have in school. These parents are more likely to defer to the school's authority and ask the fewest questions when they do come to school. Often schools expect these parents to intervene in the same ways that middle-class parents might, but we cannot expect parents to do that which they are unable to do, either because of limited financial resources or limited educational experiences.

All parents cannot help with homework. All parents cannot read to their children. All parents cannot attend parent conferences. Some parents struggle just to get their children fed, bathed, and to school each day. Many parents, especially poor and less-well-educated parents, feel that by regularly sending clean, healthy children to school they have fulfilled their parental obligations. Often though, schools expect more from parents (Lareau, 1989).

Oddly, schools seem to expect more from parents today, an era when more children live with one parent and when both parents work (in the majority of families with school-aged children). Schools are expecting more just at time when more families have fewer parents available and when those parents have less discretionary time than ever before. Besides, not all parents hold the same beliefs about parental responsibility. Blue-collar and white-collar parents' views of what parents should do often differ. Parents with white-collar jobs more often have beliefs about their roles that match those of the white-collar teaching profession. Parents with blue-collar occupations often hold different beliefs about the roles of parents and teachers. These differences seem related to differences in the careers of the different groups of parents.

Educators often overestimate the educational levels of the average American citizen. It is important to remember that only 20 percent of the adult population has earned a BA/BS degree, while 25 percent of the adults failed to complete a high school degree program (or an equivalent). Our nation still has more adults who were high school dropouts than adults who are college graduates.

(*Source: Current Population Reports,* no. 428 [series P-20])

Imagine a widget manufacturing plant. As the factory whistle blows at 3:30 ending the workday, the foreman calls out to the assembly-line workers, "I'll go punch everyone out on the time clock. Let's all stay and put in another hour to finish out this order of widgets." The workers quickly agree and continue building widgets until 4:30, donating the last hour without pay.

This image will strike anyone familiar with blue-collar work as rather ludicrous. Whether it is factory workers, carpenters, grocery store cashiers, or city public works employees, the workday is bounded by time. Extra time at work means extra wages, generally. However, this is not typically the situation for white-collar workers. Teachers, store managers, city department heads, lawyers, plant managers, financial planners, and other white-collar workers earn a salary less often tied explicitly to a fixed-length workday. White-collar workers often stay late, take work home, and work on weekends, usually without earning extra pay.

This difference in work patterns may explain why some parents see homework as useful and, indeed, necessary while others view it as an unwarranted intrusion on home life. Parents with white-collar occupations often support their children's homework, while other parents more often believe that schoolwork should be confined to the school day. White-collar parents view supporting children's homework as part of parenting responsibilities, but not all parents hold this view. As long as such differences in beliefs exist, some children will be more likely to do their homework and receive parental assistance completing it. We cannot simply assume all parents adhere to the same beliefs about school and parent roles.

Parents are important in children's school careers. Ideally, though, schools would neither reward nor penalize children for the parents they have. Schools must be designed so that children who lack parental supports are not placed at risk. Parents are better educated today than ever before, but only one in five is a college graduate. Schools cannot change the parents the children have, but schools can change in ways that make the lack of parental educational resources less likely to place children at risk.

Gender, Immaturity, and Risk

Gender also plays an important role in children's school careers. Boys, more often than girls, are retained in grade, placed in remedial classes, identified as handicapped, and suspended from school. Boys seem to experience more risk in elementary schools today regardless of other factors. However, when children accumulate multiple characteristics of risk status, the level of risk they experience increases. For instance, poor children are more likely to be retained in grade than middle-class children. Poor boys are much more likely to be retained than middle-class students generally. Poor minority boys are most at risk for retention in grade and for being identified as handicapped or suspended or placed in remedial classes (Smith-Burke, 1989). Schools cannot change children's gender, but schools can change in ways that make gender less important in terms of school success.

"Immaturity" is a tag hung more often on boys in schools. This supposed immaturity is viewed as one source of the academic difficulties boys experience. But boys in elementary schools today are older than boys of only a few years ago. There are several reasons for this. First, and probably most important, is that middle-class parents are now more likely to hold younger boys out of school for an additional year (Mergendoller, Bellsimo, & Horan, 1990). These parents seem to recognize that schools are sometimes not well-adapted to young boys, and holding them out is seen as one way of reducing the risk for those boys. A second factor is that the eligible entering age for kindergartners seems to be moving up. While January 1 was a common birthdate cutoff for school entry twenty-five years ago, today August/September/October cutoffs are more common. Finally, boys are more likely to be retained in grade or placed in a transitional grade program (e.g., pre-first-grade classes) than are girls (Shepard & Smith, 1990). This delays the entry of some boys into the primary grades thereby raising the average age of children in those grades. Nonetheless, even though boys are now older, in many schools "immaturity" is the most common reason teachers give for academic difficulties children experience.

This is an odd situation for several reasons, beyond the fact that elementary school boys are now older. The reported immaturity involves reports of short attention spans, wigglyness, lack of small motor coordination, small size, and expressive language difficulties. At the same time, studies show that boys tend to favor activity over inactivity and large motor activity over small motor activity and are less likely to engage voluntarily in print and language play (especially when active alternatives are available). Boys, it seems to us, are often considered immature when they prefer the activities that most boys prefer. Schools can have a balance of large motor and small motor activity—schools where dance and creative dramatics are as valued and as common as penmanship and coloring assignments. Schools can be developed where Lego and block activities are as common and as important as cutting, coloring, and pasting. Schools can be designed so that movement is encouraged and sitting passively in desks for long stretches is uncommon. Schools where boys do as well as girls are possible. There is no need to perpetuate the current mythology that many boys are not ready for school. Instead, schools can be made more ready for boys.

Being a boy increases the risk faced in elementary school. Being a "young" boy, or a boy considered "immature" because he acts on his boy preferences for activity, also increases the risk faced in our schools today. Being a "young" poor minority boy from a single-parent family places a child at enormous risk, unfortunately. But schools create risk, not boys acting like boys.

Is Your School Biased?

In the ideal school, all children would have similar opportunity to become literate. But today, in many schools, the odds seem stacked against some children. It may be useful to examine the patterns of success and failure in your school. In the chart below we collected information on first graders who had been retained in one school.

	Poor	Male	Minority
Max	x	x	
Minh	x	x	x
Randy		x	
Miriam	x		x
Jonah	x	x	x
Harish	x	x	x
Candace	x		x
Ereno		x	x

In this school, 35 percent of the children were poor, 48 percent were male, and 20 percent were minority-group members. We found a bias, or overrepresentation, in this school on each characteristic: family poverty, gender, and minority-group membership. In other words, six of the eight (75 percent) children retained were poor, male, or members of a minority group. We concluded that poor children, boys, and minorities face greater risks in this school than children who had none of these characteristics.

This evaluation activity can be applied to any number of educational outcomes. For instance, schools might examine similar patterns in the identification of gifted children or learning-disabled children or children selected for safety patrol. Reducing the risk some children face begins with locating biases that exist in a school.

WHAT DOESN'T WORK? WHY NOT?

Schools have long used a number of tired responses when children exhibit difficulty learning to read and write. These responses have long histories of offering little of benefit to children. Many common school responses do not typically accelerate literacy development, and at-risk children remain at risk even after participating. Schools must begin to more adequately respond to the risks faced by some children and begin to respond as soon as children arrive.

The Gift of Time Is No Gift at All

When five-year-olds come to school with little or no reading and writing experience, they often appear uninterested in learning to read and write. This may lead to the suggestion, "Perhaps we should wait for that interest and readiness to develop."

Observing what has happened in kindergarten programs in the seventies and eighties will make the "to wait or not to wait" dilemma clear. Kindergarten was, for most of its existence, "a world of its own." Children were expected to learn to socialize and to become accustomed to the world beyond their home. In many states, kindergarten children came for only a few hours each day, and most of that time was spent in "play and discovery."

Two changes brought about huge differences in the kindergarten curriculum. As more mothers entered the workforce, more children, especially middle-class children, spent many years in preschools and prekindergarten classes. These schools often assumed the socialization roles formerly assumed by kindergartens. When children arrived at kindergarten after having had many years of socialization, sand and water play, and so on, kindergarten teachers and parents began to expect kindergarten to be "more academic." Many schools began full-day kindergarten programs, and the "extra time" was often allotted to academics. With the establishment of these academic goals came kindergarten retention. The rapid rate of change from a "play" to an "academic" kindergarten can be demonstrated by the reactions of the "over-30 generation" who hear about kindergarten retentions and remark in disbelief, "You can flunk kindergarten?"(Martin, 1988).

Not all kindergartens made these changes. Rifts developed within schools and communities. Some parents complained that their children would "fall behind" if they were allowed to "play all day." On the other side, some parents objected to the "worksheet, sit down" curriculum they found in their kindergartens.

Along the way, many people became alarmed by the high rate of kindergarten retention, and two new entities appeared in many schools—developmental kindergartens and transitional-grade classrooms. Developmental kindergartens were a sort of prekindergarten and usually added an extra year of schooling to the child's school career. These developmental kindergartens emphasized socialization and play. To determine who should be placed in developmental kindergartens, children were often given a test. The test, of course, usually identified children with little preschool experience and few home experiences with books, stories, and print as developmentally unready. Based on the test results, these "unready" children were assigned to the developmental kindergarten.

While it was theoretically possible to go from developmental kindergarten directly to first grade, this rarely happened in practice. Most children assigned to developmental kindergarten spend two years in kindergarten—one in the developmental kindergarten and one in the normal kindergarten (which, since the less developed children were not there, became even more academic/first-grade-like than it had been).

Developmental kindergartens tried to solve the problem of unready children by sorting them out ahead of time and giving them an extra year to develop. However, these programs often denied children involvement in the very literacy learning activities that fostered the development in more advantaged children. Too often these classrooms were not designed to immerse the children in a print-rich language and literacy environment. Too often these developmental programs had no story circles, no big books, no scribbling tables, no drawing and labeling activities, and none of a host of other activities that characterize the book, story, and print experiences of more advantaged preschool children (McGill-Franzen, 1992).

Waiting for development to occur rarely fosters development. For children to develop concepts about print, stories, and literacy, they need to be immersed in literate activity and literate environments. This does not mean that these "unready" children need worksheets and drill. But they need the chance to develop the same understandings that their more advantaged peers developed in their homes or in emergent-literacy-oriented preschools.

McGill-Franzen (1992) traces the traditional view of readiness for reading, dating it back more than a century. Amiriah Brigham, a nineteenth-century physician, warned that "cultivating intellectual faculties of children before they are six or seven" would harm both body and soul. Early schooling, it was argued, would lead to "imbecility and premature old age." This theme was extended in the work of Arnold Gesell and Carleton Washburne in the 1930s when it was argued that a mental age of 6½ was needed before reading could be successfully taught. Many such ideas live on today, a half-century of research debunking such ideas notwithstanding. Very simply, Gesellian and even Piagetan notions of readiness as biologically fixed are wrong. Walking on balance beams, hopping on one foot, and size have nothing to do with cognitive development. Instead, as Vygotskyian developmentalism explains, experience and instruction foster development of language and literacy learning. Waiting for development to emerge from biological readiness fosters only further delay in literacy and language learning.

Transitional-grade classrooms (e.g., pre-first) were created for children who had been to kindergarten but who were judged not ready to be promoted to first grade using the same rationale as was used in developing other "gift of time" programs. Instead of being retained in kindergarten, these children were "promoted" to the transition room! (Does this bring to mind the "rose by any other name" analogy?) When transitional-grade classes wait for development, when they slow the instructional pace as they inevitably seem to do, there is no reason to expect that learning or development will be accelerated. Participation in a transitional-grade class increases the risk children face in school (Meisels, 1993).

Children who arrive at school with few book, story, and print activity experiences are those most likely to become candidates for these *gift of time* projects. These are most often children of low-income families but not always. A lack of experiences with books, stories, and print should signal the need for placement in a literacy-rich classroom that immerses these children in the sorts of literacy activities that abound in most middle-class homes. These are the children who need classrooms with many books at hand, with markers, pencils, crayons, and paper, along with Legos, charts and labels, rhyme, rhythm, movement, and song.

Retention Retains Risk

Retention in grade increases the risk that children face in our schools. Retention as practiced today arrived with the advent of graded schools at the turn of the century. It was a hot topic in the thirties and forties, and the research pointedly noted the lack of positive effects, either educational or social/emotional, on retained children. The fifties and sixties emphasized social promotion and ungraded schools. Educators talked about "teaching the whole child" and respecting "individual differences," and children moved from grade to grade along with their peers regardless of their academic development.

Accountability was the watchword of the late seventies and the eighties, and with the press for public accountability, retention once again became a common response to the problem of failing to learn to read along with your peers. States passed laws mandating minimum standards, and in some cases, tests determined who could move to the next grade. In some schools, you could once again see nine-year-olds in the first grade. In fact, currently it is estimated that about half the children in the United States are retained before grade nine even though research evidence still indicates that positive effects of retention are hard to find (Allington & McGill-Franzen, 1995).

Many educators find it difficult to believe that nearly 50 percent of children have been retained. What is at work is the "cumulative effect" of years of retention practices. What happens in most schools is that small numbers add up over time. For instance, retaining only 5 percent of the children each year in grades K–8 results in 45 percent of all children retained by the end of eighth grade (5 percent $\times$ 9 years = 45 percent). If each teacher retains just one child each year, almost half of all students will be retained before they arrive at high school.

The rise of high-stakes assessment, testing where the results are publicized and school performances are compared, seems to have fostered an increase in both retention practice and special-education placements. A recent study (Allington & McGill-Franzen, 1992) found that significantly more primary-grade children were being retained and/or placed in special education now than 15 years ago, before high-stakes testing was popular. Some schools seemed to use retention in grade and special-education placement to inflate artificially the scores on the standardized tests implemented as part of the accountability agenda. As one principal said, "We used to try and do what was good for kids. Now, my neck is on the block" (McGill-Franzen & Allington, 1993).

Placement in a transitional-grade classroom (e.g., pre-first class) has the same negative effects as simple retention. The original concept of transitional classes was that through intensified instruction, low-achieving children could be "caught up" to their peers during the transitional-grade year. The notion was that smaller classes and more intensive teaching would accelerate learning and children would move from a transitional first grade into second grade. In practice, however, this intensive instruction did not occur. Without intensive instruction, learning acceleration did not occur. Instead, transitional-grade classes became much like repeating a grade with a different teacher.

Even if retention and transitional-grade classes were effective, and they are not, they would be expensive options for attempting to meet the needs of low-achieving children. The extra year of schooling adds the full cost of that year to the educational expenses. Currently, that cost will range from $3,500 to $7,500, depending on which district in which state the child attends school. Most remedial programs and summer-school programs cost less than $1,000 per child, and a semester of one-to-one daily tutorial instruction costs $1,500 to $2,000. Each of these options is not only less expensive but also more likely to actually serve the children well (Allington & McGill-Franzen, 1995).

Perhaps retention is popular because costs are hidden in the general school budget and so it seems a no-cost option. A recent study of retention in California schools, however, estimated that current retention rates there created the need for an additional 60 elementary schools, each with 20 classrooms! We spend billions of educational dollars each year on retention, a failed solution. We spend that money on a symptom of the real problem, low-achievement in reading. We spend the money on a response that does not address the root of the problem—inadequate instruction. Do we spend these billions on retention because retaining children is easier than creating more effective schools?

Ultimately, retained and transitioned children become older underachievers. In adolescence, two factors, older than classmates and low-achievement, are powerful predictors of who will drop out of school. Retained children are four times more likely to drop out of high school than other students. Obviously, the odds are stacked against retaining any child. However, everyone knows someone—a cousin, a nephew, a neighbor—who was retained and seemed to do just fine. But even here we do not know that the child would have not been similarly successful if promoted. Unfortunately, most retained children do not catch up. In fact, retained children commonly do better during the retention year but again fall behind in the years to come.

Decades of research on retention was recently summarized by Shepard and Smith (1989, 1990). Their syntheses indicate that, on average, (1) retained children perform more poorly than they would if they had been promoted without repeating a grade, (2) children view retention as punishment for being bad or failing to learn (3) retained children have lower levels of self-esteem than those promoted, and (4) almost any alternative, including remedial help, summer school, and peer tutoring, is more effective than retention.

The gap between research and practice is currently quite large, although many schools do seem to be rethinking the practice of retaining low-achieving children. We think the current gap between research and practice can best be explained by noting that retention effects are often examined quite differently by teachers (and administrators/supervisors) than they are by researchers. Basically, it seems, school personnel tend to examine short-term effects of retention while researchers examine longer-term effects. School personnel often see a modest improvement in performance in the year following retention. Researchers see retained children dropping out ten years later. The achievement of retained children gradually slips downward as they continue in school. Four or five years after retention, most retained children are again among the lowest achieving students in their grade. This result is quite predictable, and the impact on retained children seems devastating.

In making the decision to retain, the appropriate question is, Will retention benefit the child more than the school? We think the evidence is so consistent and so powerful that we do not believe retention can be justified as benefiting children. The evidence gathered in study after study over sixty years (1930–1990) clearly indicates that the best policy keeps children with the peers they enter school with (Shepard & Smith, 1989).

While we are quite convinced that retention does not benefit children, we need to note that the answer is not simply social promotion. Social promotion has fewer negative effects on children than retention but social promotion alone does little to address the problem of

Examine the cumulative record summary depicted below. The six-year school careers of ten children are illustrated. Half the children completed fifth grade on schedule. But notice the histories of the five who failed to complete fifth grade on schedule. Billy, Tarika, Ricardo, Wonder, and Mars illustrate the most common experiences of children who fall behind their peers. Even though they were retained or placed in transitional grade programs, their achievement remains significantly behind their peers who entered school at the same time. The records depicted below represent ten real children whose records we collected. Perhaps school systems should be required to collect and analyze routinely the experiences of children they have retained. Perhaps examining the effects of established practices would produce more interest in replacing ineffective practice with alternatives that benefit children. In any event, examining the performance of groups of children who enter school together is simply the most straightforward method for evaluating the long-term effects of decisions we make about how to respond to children who find learning to read difficult.

| | School Year | | | | | | | | | | |
| | 1988–89 | | 1989–90 | | 1990–91 | | 1991–92 | | 1992–93 | | 1993–94 | |
Student	Gr.	G.E.	Gr.	G.E.	Gr.	G.E.	Gr.	G.E.	Gr.	G.E.	Gr.	G.E.
Tommy C.	K	1.2	1	2.1	2	3.0	3	4.2	4	5.1	5	6.4
Billy	K	K.2	Pre1st	1.1	1	1.8	2	2.3	2	2.7	3	3.3
Wonder	K	1.1	1	2.0	2	2.8	3	3.4	3	4.0	4	4.7
Ricardo	K	K.9	1	1.5	1	2.1	2	2.5	3	3.1	4	3.9
Helena	K	1.5	1	2.5	2	3.4	3	4.5	4	5.3	5	6.1
Tarika	K	K.6	Pre1st	1.5	1	2.1	2	3.0	3	4.1	4	5.0
Julius	K	1.2	1	2.2	2	3.2	3	4.3	4	5.3	5	6.2
Kaiping	K	1.3	1	2.1	2	3.3	3	3.8	4	4.7	5	5.6
Mars	K	K.7	1	1.8	2	2.2	2	2.5	SPED	2.8	SPED	3.2
Julie	K	1.4	1	2.6	2	3.8	3	4.9	5	6.2	5	6.5

Notes: *Gr.* is the grade level placement for the academic year indicated; *G.E.* is the end of year grade equivalent score on a group standardized reading achievement test; *SPED* indicates student was classified as handicapped during that year.

low achievement. Low-achieving children who are simply promoted continue the pattern of low achievement.

Children who find learning to read difficult need some educational intervention that gives them access to sufficient instruction to accelerate their literacy learning (Slavin et al., 1993). When social promotion is coupled with access to an extraordinary educational intervention, achievement is enhanced. The intervention might provide extended instructional time through an after-school program or a summer-school program. It might provide short-term tutorial assistance designed to accelerate development. While few studies report on programs that combine social promotion with intensive intervention, those available suggest that increasing the intensity of instruction works far better than either retention or social promotion by themselves (Shepard & Smith, 1989).

Tracking Does Not Get At-Risk Children Back on Track

Tracking has been a common school response to the problem of children who do not achieve and move along as fast as average children. But tracking may also increase the risk for children placed in the bottom tracks. Tracking occurs in the elementary school when children of similar achievement levels (achievement in reading, most commonly) are assigned to the same teacher. Such tracking began in the forties and was prevalent in most elementary schools through the sixties. Its popularity waned during the seventies and eighties but is currently on the rise in some school systems. While some schools track as early as kindergarten, tracking is most commonly seen from grade three on through high school.

Tracking is based on a flawed logic. The argument is made that not all children will learn at the same rate and that if the slow learners (or the fast learners) are put together with one teacher, that teacher can teach them on their level and provide the instruction they need to progress to higher levels. Furthermore, tracking proponents suggest, the teacher can devote all of his/her time to planning for and directly teaching the assigned children without having to provide seatwork activities to keep another group of children busy. The tracked children will spend less time in seatwork activities (which don't contribute much to achievement) and more time in direct instruction on the skills and at the level needed. Finally, tracking proponents argue that by separating the slow, the average, and the fast, the average children will not have to be held back while the slow ones are taught, and the fast children will have a chance to excel.

Presented in this logical way, tracking seems like a reasonable solution. In practice, however, children placed in the bottom track achieve less than similar children placed in untracked classes (Gamoran, 1986). This occurs primarily because children placed in the low tracks are simply taught less. These children are offered a "slow it down" curriculum. The problem with tracking is that it purposely creates classrooms that produce low achievement. Tracking programs assume that some children cannot learn and then creates instructional programs that deliver that very result. Tracking does not typically create classroom environments for low-achieving students that offer richer and more intensive instruction than that offered in the classrooms for the other students. Tracking perpetuates the problem of low achievement and increases the risk some children face.

There are other problems with tracking. Often the children in the various tracks have actually been sorted by social class. Thus the low-track class is filled with poor children. In addition, class-achievement patterns are not nearly as homogeneous as is often assumed. This happens for two reasons. First, all low-achieving students are not low achieving in all subject areas. Thus, some children having difficulty with reading and writing do just fine in mathematics. Others do fine in reading but have difficulty in math. These differences in performance in different academic areas increase the heterogeneity such that there is no real possibility of offering a single curriculum and having it be appropriate for all children. In addition, tracking models incorrectly assume an equal distribution of high-, middle-, and low-achieving children. If we recall the bell-shaped curve that is supposed to express the distribution of individual differences, we note a big hump in the middle range. There are simply far more middle-track students than either high- or low-track students. Thus, the low-track classes invariably contain many children who would be more appropriately placed in the middle track, as do the high-track classes. The end result of tracking is that both the low and high tracks still include many middle-track students. However, teachers tend to see the tracks as homogeneous and do not provide much differentiated instruction.

The standard bell-shaped curve places about 70 percent of all students' achievement in the average range leaving only 15 percent of students in the below-average and above-average ranges (or one standard deviation above or below the mean). Thus, with 100 third-grade students we would need high- and low-achievement classes each with 15 students and two average achievement classes with 35 students in each to distribute children appropriately (or we could add additional staff and create three average classes with 23 students or four such classes with 17 students). Any other system results in inappropriately placing average-achievement students in both the high- and low-achievement classes or tracks.

Tracking can take other forms. The most common arrangement is for teachers to have heterogeneous homeroom groups to whom they teach science, social studies, physical education, and so on, and then to track the children for math and reading. This Joplin Plan (after Joplin, Missouri, where the plan originated in the fifties) solves some of the problems of all-day tracking. While many of the low math children would also be in the low reading group, it is possible with this arrangement for a low math child to be in the average-reading or even the high-reading track. The problems, however, of how to assign children accurately and objectively, the disproportionate numbers of children who really would belong in each track, and the self-fulfilling prophecy still remain. Unfortunately, some new problems are created.

Time is lost whenever the children have to pack up and change classrooms (and even when the teachers change classrooms). It takes children a minimum of 10 to 15 minutes to pack up to leave one class, exit the room, get to the next class, unpack, and then get started at academic work again. If children switch for math and reading, this will take 30 to 60 minutes each day (or 2.5 to 5 hours weekly), which is 10 to 20 percent of the actual instructional time available in most elementary schools. Children must also adjust to perhaps three different teachers, and teachers could conceivably teach 75 to 90 different children each day. It is hard for teachers to maintain a level of commitment and concern for each child's education when each teacher has this many children to worry about. It is harder for teachers to know 75 to 90 children well—to know their strengths and weaknesses and individualities. It is also hard to schedule this many children into that many different sections according to achievement and maintain any sort of balanced class size—so again we get classes not nearly as homogeneous as first assumed.

Finally, today we hear calls for increased integration of curriculum areas. These calls are for linking reading and writing strategies to social studies, math, and science to present a more coherent course of study. But when children switch teachers for different classes, opportunities for the integration of instruction across curriculum areas, which might occur naturally in most elementary classrooms, are lost.

George (1988) summarized the research on tracking and concluded that "tracking is an idea whose time has passed." Regardless of the form it takes, homogeneous achievement grouping does not enhance the academic learning of higher- or lower-achieving children. Segregating children by achievement for instruction increases the risk children face in school.

Ability Grouping Has Little to Do with Ability

Related to tracking is the age-old practice of creating "ability groups" within classrooms. Of course the groups created are really *achievement groups,* not ability groups, because children are placed in them based on some estimate of achievement, usually reading achievement. We think it is important to clarify this point because the term *ability* connotes some relatively fixed trait. Achievement, on the other hand, seems more amenable to change. Because achievement is often confused with ability, or intellectual capacity, children placed in the bottom group are often perceived and labeled as slow learners. Mistakenly assuming these children are of low ability is one reason these children have been offered a "slow it down" curriculum.

Children are often placed in such groups while still in kindergarten. In this case the basis for grouping is often preschool experiences with print, stories, books, and pencils. Children with many such experiences are labeled as high-readiness learners, and those with few are labeled low-readiness. Too often, then, the limited-experience children are considered "slower" and offered a "slow it down" curriculum. In our view, the most appropriate intervention for low-experience children would involve immersing them in rich and intensive experiences with print, stories, books, and pencils. The goal would be to accelerate literacy development through broad holistic experiences with language and literacy activities. This design is quite different from the traditional focus on presenting small parts of the literacy process with much repetition and at half the pace of instruction offered those lucky children considered to be of average "ability." Conceiving of early school differences as primarily experiential differences would undoubtedly result in more appropriate educational practices.

> "Common sense tells you to rank people. Beware of common sense."
> —Total Quality Management guru W. Edwards Deming

As children move into first- and second-grade classrooms, researchers have compared the reading instruction experienced by children in different reading groups in the same classrooms. The researchers typically collected information on the amount of time children spent on different activities and tasks (for example, oral reading versus silent, workbook versus summary writing, drill versus independent reading). In these studies researchers concluded that usually children placed in high groups received more and better instruction than children in low groups (Stanovich, 1986). This has been called the Matthew Effect after the Gospel of Matthew passage about the rich getting richer and the poor getting poorer.

More specifically, these studies report that children placed in the higher-achievement groups have more actual opportunities to read (especially silent reading opportunities), their instruction is more often comprehension focused, they cover more of the designated curriculum material, the lessons foster independence, and so on. Children in lower-achievement groups are occupied with more round-robin oral reading, more isolated skills and drills, fewer comprehension activities, and more dependency-creating instruction, and they do less reading and writing (Allington, 1983). In other words, the instruction traditionally offered in different groups literally created different kinds of readers. Children in top groups received instruction that facilitated developing independent comprehending readers. Children in low groups read less and had their attention focused on oral reading accuracy. They also covered less of the planned curriculum, and as a result, they remained low-achieving readers.

Achievement grouping increases the risk faced by low-achieving children. It is not an adequate response to the differences that children present us as learners. On the other hand, some schools have responded to the reported negative effects of ability grouping by mandating whole-class instruction with little or no modification of instruction for children who are finding learning to read difficult. We cannot simply mandate away real differences that children have for literacy learning. Moving to whole-class instruction with little or no extraordinary support for children having difficulty also increases the risk for those children.

Compare the reading and language arts instructional experiences of higher- and lower-achieving students in your school by observing what each group of children does during their lessons and then completing the checklist below.

	High	No Difference	Low
Which children read more?	_____	_____	_____
Which children write more?	_____	_____	_____
Which children spend more time on skill and drill work?	_____	_____	_____
Which children are interrupted more often while reading?	_____	_____	_____
Which children are more often expected to figure things out by themselves?	_____	_____	_____
Which children are most likely to be reading books?	_____	_____	_____
Which children have the largest array of "easy for them" books to select from in the classroom?	_____	_____	_____

Special Programs Aren't Special Enough

In the past thirty years, a proliferation of special programs has been created in an attempt to address the needs of children who find learning difficult (Allington, 1994). These are the remedial reading and math classes, the resource room classes for the learning disabled, the speech and language therapy sessions, and the migrant and bilingual programs that operate in many schools. Unfortunately, there is little evidence that these efforts substantially alter the academic futures of the children served (Johnston & Allington, 1991).

Simply put, most children who participate in these special programs do not become good readers. They do not catch up with their peers. Far too many are "lifers," children who continue to qualify year after year because of continued low achievement. When the most common designs of these programs are examined, however, it becomes clearer that such an outcome is exactly what one might reasonably expect. Several key features of these programs lead to the typical lack of any substantial positive effect on achievement.

First, the very presence of such programs undermines the responsibility of the regular education program to educate all children. Another way of considering these programs is to note that each child who participates represents the failure of the classroom reading program to adapt to the instructional needs of all children. Adding these special programs has led classroom teachers to believe that teaching some children is not their responsibility and often suggested that they are insufficiently expert to teach them. In some schools we have studied, as many as three out of four classroom teachers told us that the reading/language arts instruction of remedial and mainstreamed learning-disabled children was not their responsibility! Even though the children spent 80 to 90 percent of their day in the regular classroom, the classroom teachers assigned responsibility for their literacy lessons to the reading teacher or special education teacher.

A second common feature of these programs is that they have been scheduled into the school day. Thus, "special" instruction replaces some part of the regular instruction offered. Children participating in special reading programs leave the classroom during some part of their regular reading instruction. Thus the classroom teacher has less time to teach these children than others without difficulties, even though one would think these children would benefit from increased instruction. Because transitions from the classroom to the reading or resource room (or hallway) take time, children who participate have less time available to learn to read.

Additionally, when the children leave the classroom, they are more likely to experience curriculum fragmentation. Low-achieving children benefit from a rich, organized, and consistent curriculum plan. However, these are the children who hop from material to material, from lesson to lesson, from teacher to teacher, across the school day. These are the children who find it difficult to keep up with their classwork but who are offered lessons from more different materials than anyone in the school (Johnston & Allington, 1991).

These are also the children most likely to spend time with the least well-trained school personnel—teacher aides. The use of minimally trained paraprofessionals is one reason that children in these special programs have the lowest quality instruction (Allington & McGill-Franzen, 1989). Heavy use of paraprofessional staff in special programs has been linked to limited effects on student learning. The schools relying most heavily on paraprofessional staff are those schools that enroll the largest numbers of at-risk children. Assigning relatively poorly trained professionals to work with children experiencing difficulty learning to read and write is unlikely to accelerate learning (Allington, 1994).

Do classroom teachers and special staff share knowledge of each other's practice? If two teachers, each working with a child, know little of the other's instructional activities, it is unlikely that the instruction they offer the child is coherent and consistent. You may want to use a strategy employed in a classic study (Johnston, Allington & Afflerbach, 1985) to examine shared knowledge in your school. Select a few children who participate in special programs. Interview the teachers who work with the children and ask:

What work was _____ doing with you today?
What work did _____ do in his/her classroom (special program) today?

You might also ask which curriculum materials were used and what each teacher sees as the primary difficulty the children are having. In some schools little knowledge is shared, while in others teachers not only share knowledge but share plans, goals, and instructional emphases. When classroom and support teachers exhibit higher levels of shared knowledge of each others' activities, we are likely to find higher levels of achievement.

So, when these special programs are examined carefully, they are found to be not very special. If special programs are designed in ways that (1) lead classroom teachers to believe that children who participate are not really their responsibility, (2) the time available for literacy learning is reduced, and (3) the children who find learning to read difficult are the children most likely to work with minimally trained paraprofessionals, then it should not be surprising to find that few children have their reading difficulties resolved in special programs. Unfortunately, current special programs may increase the risk faced by the children who participate in them.

If special programs (remedial reading and math, resource room classrooms for the children labeled learning disabled or language impaired, migrant education, bilingual education, and so on) do not substantially expand children's opportunity to learn, if they do not substantially enhance the quality and intensity of instruction, then these programs may increase the risk participating children face in schools. If special programs do not routinely accelerate literacy development and allow children to return to the classroom and experience success, then the programs need restructuring. Schools need to explore an array of program designs when considering how best to respond to the instructional needs of children who find learning difficult.

Perhaps the first question that needs to be asked is, Do special programs enhance the quality of classroom instruction? In our view, special programs must have a positive impact on the quality of classroom instruction to justify continuation. We argue this because no matter how good the special program, consistently high-quality regular classroom instruction is the key feature of schools where all children become readers and writers. The second question is, How do these programs expand the opportunity to learn for participating children? Finally, What evidence do we have that children substantially benefit academically as a result of this program?

SUMMARY

Some children arrive at school and are placed at risk of school failure simply because of their families, their parents, their gender, or their experiences (or lack of experiences). Our schools were largely designed to sort children by perceived intellectual capacity in an era when it was felt that just a few children could be educated very completely—an era when just a few needed to be educated very completely. While our society has changed dramatically, the schools we have are still organized primarily to sort children and to educate fully only some.

The paradox is that while there exists good evidence that more children read and write and add and subtract better today than ever before, public confidence and political support for public schools is waning. Our schools today successfully educate more children to higher levels of proficiency than ever before. But it is hard to convince even educators of that. Someone suggested that "our schools are doing pretty well at what we used to want them to do. But we don't want them to do that anymore." Society has changed dramatically since we restructured our schools around the turn of the last century. The schools we have must change to accommodate those societal changes. Our schools must change to sustain public support. Our schools must change if all children are to have an opportunity to lead fulfilling lives as adults.

Believing that those who don't learn from history are doomed to repeat it and convinced that there is no time to pull out and dust off the old solutions that didn't work, we have begun this book by describing what won't work and why not. Children who arrive at school at risk for failure will not have that risk eliminated by waiting for their literacy skills to develop, retaining them, tracking them, or putting them in special programs. The conclusion that these "solutions" are really part of the problem is based on decades of research and experience. What we need most is consistently high-quality classroom instruction that better addresses the needs of all children (Cunningham & Allington, 1994). We will also need responsive extraordinary interventions that actually meet the needs of children who find learning to read difficult. Unlike past efforts, however, we must create a broader array of interventions, efforts that are more personalized, more intensive, and more coherent than most that have been found in the schools we have.

Having begun this book in the negative world of what won't work, we now leave this morass behind and move to the questions around which this book is focused. How can we create those schools where all children become readers and writers? How can we use the expertise of specialized staff to respond to the instructional needs of at-risk children? How can special-program funds be allocated to ensure that children have access to more and better instruction when it is needed? How can the quality of classroom lessons be enhanced? What can schools do to foster parental support for learning? None of these are easy questions.

We are fortunate to have, in a few communities across this country, models of successful schools. We are sure that we can create schools where virtually all children are successful because we have worked in such schools, studied such schools, and visited such schools. However, we do not underestimate the difficulty of creating schools where all children learn to read and write alongside their peers. We are especially mindful of the difficulty of changing a school compared to creating a school. While we want everyone to recognize that change takes time and hard work, we also want to convey a real sense of possibility. Schools can reduce the risk that children face.

The most sensible strategies reduce risks gradually and over time (although everyone wants instant improvement). It has taken a century to develop the school traditions of today, and these traditions cannot be undone easily or quickly. Creating schools that better respond to the difficulties that some children face when learning to read and write will require substantial institutional and individual learning. But that learning must begin with recognizing the mistakes we have made. Change can be fostered, but the changes in classrooms matter most. Good schools are primarily collections of good classrooms.

In the next chapter, we will transport you into some schools where all children become readers and writers. Once you have a vision of what can be accomplished, future chapters will provide the nitty-gritty details you need for "getting it done."

2

The Stories of Schools Where All Children Become Readers and Writers

I n this chapter, we will tell you how one elementary school that serves many high-risk children has restructured so that all children become readers and writers. We will also provide sketches of several larger efforts to restructure elementary schools—efforts to create schools that work for all children. The restructuring we describe did not come easily, and in fact, the folks in these schools will tell you they are "not done yet" but are still "becoming" schools that work.

> "Change has no constituency. People like the status quo."
> —Jack Welch, CEO of General Electric Co.
> *Source: Fortune,* January 25, 1993, p. 88)

THE STORY OF A SCHOOL IN TROUBLE

Once upon a time in a small city in the southeastern United States, there was an elementary school that didn't work very well for children (Hall, Prevatte, & Cunningham, 1995). Approximately 75 percent of students were members of a minority group, mostly African-American. About 80 percent of the children were poor, qualifying for free or reduced-price meals. Many of the students came from homes with limited book experiences. Before the restructuring, most students finished both first- and second-grade reading below grade level. Although the teachers were working hard, their instruction was often not developing children who were readers and writers. Behavior problems consumed valuable teaching time. Many students had tuned out learning and turned instead to disruptive behavior. The students consistently scored lower on achievement tests than those from other elementary schools in the district, and they had the worst attendance record. Parents did not actively participate in the school, and some viewed the school with belligerence and hostility.

Even though the school's status seemed bleak and the needs too great, the faculty became determined to initiate change that would impact upon the education of its children. The common instructional model used by classroom teachers had been quite traditional: a skills-driven basal reader with students assigned to one of three achievement groups. The bottom groups were usually the largest of the three groups, and students tended to maintain their place in this group throughout the elementary grades. Grouping necessitated large quantities of seatwork, which turned into a discipline nightmare. Many students found it difficult to complete assigned seatwork independently as expected. Worse yet, these students could not afford the luxury of nonproductive time even when they were working on this seatwork.

In addition to classroom instruction, many students also received support in a Title 1 remedial reading program (see box, page 27). Students experiencing the least reading success were pulled out of the classroom for 30 minutes of remedial reading instruction each day. They were expected to assimilate back into the classroom upon their return. They rarely did! Many of the students resented being singled out as problem readers and accounted for many of the discipline problems. Little growth in reading was measured for children in Title 1, and children remained in remedial program as they progressed from grade to grade.

Upon looking closely at the instructional model in use, the school faculty determined that neither the use of reading groups nor the pull-out remedial programs were facilitating learning to read and the special programs were not having positive impacts on classroom performance or classroom instruction. At year's end, 40 percent of the first-grade students were struggling at the preprimer level and having little or no success. In second grade, one in five students were virtual nonreaders—unable to read anything but the very simplest text.

A team of several teachers and a curriculum coordinator newly assigned to the school decided to change the situation and began to explore alternatives. They read everything they could find on providing success-oriented instruction for at-risk children. They attended local professional meetings and picked the brains of presenters and others. When they heard about successful programs, they arranged to go "see for themselves."

One visit led them to another local elementary school with a smaller proportion of at-risk children. This school had implemented a multimethod, multilevel instructional program for reading/language arts instruction (Cunningham, Hall, & Defee, 1991). In this program, the 120–130 minutes of reading/language arts time was divided into four 30–35 minute blocks. These blocks—writing, self-selected reading, guided reading, and working with words—represented the four major competing approaches to reading instruction. All children were included in all four blocks and thus provided multiple "methods" through which they could learn to read and write.

The instruction in each block was multilevel, but the children were not placed in separate achievement level groups. During the writing block, children wrote on whatever level they could and all writing was accepted and encouraged. But minilessons on writing strategies were routinely offered to small, flexible groups of children. Books in the book baskets for self-selected reading included easy, predictable books along with informational books and chapter books. Material read during the guided reading block included new and old basals along with multiple copies of trade books on a variety of levels. Teachers made the guided reading block multilevel by varying the difficulty of the material read and ensured the success of all children by using a variety of partner and flexible small-group reading formats. Phonics and spelling activities included during the working with words block were also multilevel (Cunningham, 1995).

This multimethod, multilevel instruction had achieved good success in the visited school, so the faculty in search of improvement decided to try to adapt the model. The staff committed to implement the new model fully until Christmas. If unsuccessful, the staff agreed they would not return to their previous model but would continue the search.

Fifteen years ago, Ron Edmonds (1981) asserted that:

1. We can, whenever and wherever we choose, successfully teach all children whose schooling is of interest to us;
2. We already know more than we need to do that;
3. Whether we do it must finally depend on how we feel about the fact that we haven't so far.

Staff development began for everyone the week before school started and continued all year long, as the curriculum coordinator supported the teachers in this change. The teachers saw the need for multiple methods through which children could learn, as well as the need to eliminate achievement groupings. They agreed that their pull-out programs were not effective, but they still felt that their children needed some intensive small-group instruction. The curriculum coordinator worked out a plan called FROG, *F*acilitating *R*eading for *O*ptimum *G*rowth, which provided for the additional support of some daily small-group instruction for all first- and second-grade students.

FROG was designed to provide the daily small-group instruction needed to assure the success of all students. The role of existing personnel in the school was redefined. Remedial reading teachers and other special teachers formed FROG teams, which converged upon each classroom for 45 minutes each day. The students in each class were divided into small heterogeneous groups, which included one higher-achieving student, two or three average students, and one low-achieving student. These groups received daily intensive instruction with one of the FROG teachers or the classroom teacher. This instruction included those components of the four blocks that the teachers felt could better be carried out in small groups. Each FROG session included four 10- to 12-minute components.

All children participated in the self-selected reading block as part of their classroom multimethod, multilevel instruction. The FROG time began with a literary discussion based on these self-selected books. This discussion focused on a particular literary element, such as author, character, plot, setting, mood, style, theme, or illustration. Children read or discussed parts of their own book related to the literary element.

The second component of FROG, shared reading using predictable big books, strengthened and supported the students' reading in the guided reading block. The students were taught to use a variety of reading strategies including semantic, syntactic, and graphophonic cues. Punctuation, vocabulary, predictions—all teachable elements found in a particular book—became a part of the instruction as the teacher led the students to read a predictable big book.

The third component included in each FROG session supported the working with words block. Children were given letters and instruction on how to manipulate those letters to make a variety of words. The emphasis was on learning that words are made up of predictable letter patterns.

The final component of FROG supported the classroom writing block. In the classroom, all children wrote on self-selected topics. During the FROG time, the predictable big book provided a model for teacher-directed writing instruction, allowing the children to make the reading-writing connection. There was a pre-writing activity, followed by writing, revision, editing, and sharing.

When the 45 minute FROG time ended, the FROG teachers leapt to another classroom and the classroom teacher continued instruction with the whole class. Reorganizing the special teachers into FROG teams provided the small-group support needed by many of the children to assure their success in the four blocks.

Here is a typical classroom schedule showing how FROG time and the classroom four blocks worked together.

8:45	Opening Activities
9:00	FROG
9:45	Guided reading block
10:15	Self-selected reading block
10:45	Working with words block
11:15	Lunch
11:45	Writing Block
12:15	Math
12:45	Teacher Read Aloud
1:00	Music/Library/Art
1:30	Integrated Science/Social Studies
2:00	Physical Education
2:30	Computer Technology
3:00	Dismissal

At the end of this first year of restructuring, informal reading inventories given to all children indicated that more than half the children were reading at or above grade level—a remarkable improvement over previous years. The multimethod, multilevel model was making a difference. But, other—as meaningful—changes occurred at the school. Parents who had been reluctant to be part of the school began to trickle in. Membership in the parent-school association increased 120 percent. Parent volunteers increased dramatically, from 5 to 80. Behavior problems decreased dramatically, although they were not eliminated. The school no longer had the poorest attendance in the school system, with attendance rising to near average levels. But most significant was the change observed in the students. Chaotic classrooms had been replaced with classrooms filled with excited children involved in reading and writing activity. Adding the FROG component to the multimethod, multilevel

During guided reading blocks, teachers actively demonstrate effective reading strategies to their students.

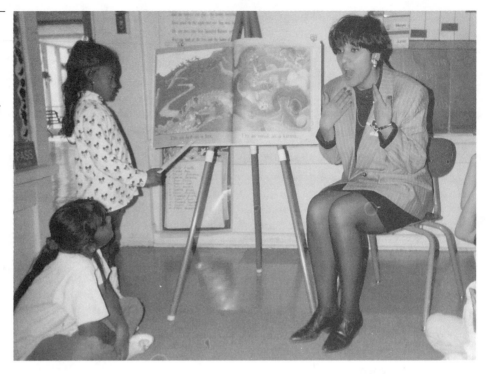

instruction gave at-risk students some small-group instruction. Making the FROG groups heterogeneous allowed at-risk children to read, write, and share with others who were good models.

While the first year of restructuring had begun with determination mixed with fear and uncertainty, the second year began with enthusiasm and positive anticipation. The teachers had a successful year behind them and were anticipating the implementation of several additional innovations. Students exhibited the same confidence and enthusiasm. This year, the school became a Title 1 Schoolwide Project (see informational box below). The building leadership team elected to use much of the federal Title 1 funding to reduce class sizes in the primary grades. Thus, school opened with fewer remedial reading teachers but with class sizes that averaged about sixteen students (compared to the twenty-five students previously).

In another important and difficult decision, primary-grade teachers decided to stay with their classes for two years (grades one to two). Teachers and parents felt this would contribute to a stronger "family" atmosphere (parents can request children be moved to another classroom in the second year). This shift moved classroom teachers away from thinking of themselves primarily as a particular grade-level teacher and gave them the responsibility for and the opportunity to provide the same children with high quality lessons over a two-year period.

Classroom instruction in the four blocks continued, as did FROG instruction. Smaller classes meant fewer interruptions during the day, and teachers who had developed more instructional expertise contributed to accelerated learning in the classroom. The students were on task and involved in reading and writing. Learning was their primary concern, leaving little time for discipline problems. Teachers had to work hard to keep the students supplied with books.

Results were indicative of the growth that occurred during the second year with multimethod, multilevel instruction and FROG and the first year with smaller classes. In May, 82 percent of first-grade students were reading on or above grade level and 18 percent read at the primer or preprimer level. There were no children who could not read at the preprimer level. In second grade, 83 percent of the students were reading on or above grade level—a dramatic increase from previous years. There were no nonreaders.

The largest federal eduation program provides funds for schools serving disadvantaged children. The program originated as Title 1 in the 1960s, was retitled Chapter 1 in the 1980s, and is once again known as Title 1 in the 1990s. When the number of Title 1 eligible students exceeds 50 percent of a school's enrollment, that school may elect to become a Schoolwide Project. That means, basically, that a parent/faculty building leadership team prepares a plan for using the Title 1 funds to meet better the needs of all children, not just the Title 1 eligible children. The most common uses of the funds have been to reduce class sizes in some or all grades and to extend the school day or school year for some or all children.

As this story is being told, the school is halfway through its fourth year of restructuring. The schoolwide achievement no longer occupies the bottom slots in the district, and performance continues to improve. Teachers in upper grades are beginning to reap the rewards of the restructuring done at the primary grades. The vast majority of their children read at grade level and those still below grade level have developed independent reading and writing abilities. These teachers are now able to move the children into more sophisticated reading and writing and focus more of their energies on content subjects such as science and social studies. Such differentiation is easier now that classrooms have a wider array of materials. Teachers can elect to take the funds that would be spent on workbook and copying expenses and use that money to purchase books for classroom libraries. In addition, teachers can now use federal Title 1 funds to purchase books for classroom libraries. Thus, each year, classroom libraries grow, providing children with increased access to books they can read.

Some businesses have also provided funds to enhance classroom libraries, as has the Junior League. Other community efforts have resulted in every child having his or her own book bag and the supplies needed to complete work at home. Every few weeks, each class is transported to the public library where children check out books and learn to use the resources there for home and summer projects.

A variety of minigrants support purchasing books for children themselves—usually from book clubs. This puts books into children's hands and into their homes. An additional benefit is the increased numbers of books in the classroom as children bring these books to school to read and share. Recently, a business partnership has been established. Children visit the sponsor's workplace, and the school is visited by employees of the sponsor. Some of these employees serve as volunteer readers in classrooms, providing adult role models of literate behavior. Parents, too, continue their volunteering activities.

Because so many parents are regular volunteers and visitors at the school, efforts are underway to have social services available on site at the school. The possibilities for having medical and dental services available at the school one day per week are being investigated. While such interagency collaboration is never easy, it simply makes sense to pursue it.

The school added a Title 1–funded four-year-old program this year, though it serves less than half the children interested and eligible to participate. This is a literacy-rich preschool program designed to provide children with the sorts of wonderful experiences with books and print that characterize the lives of more advantaged children. In another attempt to address such problems, the school has hired a home-school coordinator who visits children's homes to provide models and materials for parents to use in reading with their children. A "parent and kids night" has been added to the weekly school schedule. Parents and children come to school to play games, read books, share current events, and snack. These sessions are wonderfully well attended.

Finally, the school has increased the amount of time available for instruction by going to a year-round schedule as a result of a special statewide initiative for rethinking the use of state funds provided for remedial programs. Children attend school for nine weeks and then are off for three weeks. During two of these three off-weeks, however, special literacy support and enrichment activities are offered at the school. All children are welcome to participate in these programs, but children experiencing difficulty learning to read and write are required to attend. The enrichment courses are sponsored by community groups, the YMCA, arts council, and others. This means many kids get an extra eight weeks of schooling each year, and of course, summer reading loss (a substantial and common problem for children from homes with few books) is literally eliminated.

We tell this story of change at one school because it shows how a faculty can alter the outcomes of education by rethinking the process of schooling. This is but a single example of the sorts of change that can be accomplished when a faculty and key administrators/supervisors decide it is time to change. The changes described were begun with no extra funding, but the school faculty soon found that various sorts of funds were available to assist them in their attempts to restructure the school. Such funding did not just fall in their laps. It first required activism and initiative on the part of the school staff.

This school created its own vision of what sort of school it might become. The programs now in place largely resulted from reconsidering how to use the available funds to enhance classroom instruction to better benefit children. The changes made were the result of an honest examination of what was not working. When needed, the staff pursued extra funding sources and found many potential sources available for a school with a better plan. The school still has difficulties to address and to resolve. But it also has a faculty now well experienced in the process of change and determined to continue to improve on their efforts.

REFORMING AMERICAN ELEMENTARY SCHOOLS

Much of the talk about educational reform has focused on high schools with rather less talk about reforming elementary schools. The increased graduation standards, minimum competency testing, emphasis on reducing dropout rates, and so on, all had greater impact on high schools than elementary schools. Nonetheless, a number of efforts across the country focus on restructuring elementary schools. One type of effort aims to make schools more "thoughtful" places with an emphasis on developing curriculum that fosters higher levels of thinking (e.g., Brown, 1991; Tharp & Gallimore, 1988). A second thrust focuses more on restructuring elementary schools so that outcomes for at-risk children are dramatically improved (Allington & Walmsley, 1995; Cunningham & Allington, 1994; Levin, 1987; Slavin, Karweit, Madden, Dolan, & Wasik, 1992). Both efforts have the potential to improve the elementary school experiences of all children.

Several restructuring efforts can be considered "national" efforts with sites in several states and a national headquarters. In this next section we sketch several of these projects and provide information for those interested in more details.

The Accelerated School Effort

The Accelerated Schools model was developed by Henry Levin and colleagues at Stanford University and has been implemented in a variety of schools with high proportions of at-risk children (Levin 1987; Knight & Stallings 1995; Hopfenberg & Levin 1993). The model involves the collaboration of university and school personnel in a restructuring of the entire school. Faculty at individual schools decide what their priorities are and implement day-to-day goals, but all Accelerated Schools have the following common broad goals: (1) the creation of a learning environment characterized by high expectations, (2) the elimination of the achievement gap for at-risk children by the end of elementary school, (3) the daily implementation of a fast-paced curriculum focusing on student engagement, and (4) involvement and empowerment of teachers and parents.

Teachers in Accelerated Schools are involved in in-service training before implementation and then meet regularly to monitor their own progress toward their goals and to decide how their school can progress toward realizing of these goals. Parent education and involvement projects are implemented, and parents are included in decision-making teams. All participants in Accelerated Schools are asked to envision the education they would desire for their own children and then to work toward finding ways to provide that same level of excellence for all the children in their school.

Accelerated Schools move away from tracking and ability grouping and use a variety of cooperative groups and student tutor/partnership arrangements. They see language development as a real goal in every curriculum area and integrate curriculum around themes as much as possible. They optimize discovery learning, hands-on and real-world experiences, and the reading and writing of authentic texts whenever possible. They try to provide opportunities for all children to engage in the arts and to become part of extracurricular activities. All school personnel feel responsible for helping the children develop social and critical thinking skills.

Accelerated Schools do not claim "instant" results. They acknowledge that it takes several years for a school to become the school its staff and community envision. They acknowledge that children who come to school at risk will not all be on grade level the first year. They do, however, have high expectations (supported by their initial data) that given a long-term schoolwide effort toward clearly defined goals, schools with many at-risk children can look like the schools we want for our own children and almost all at-risk children can leave elementary school with solid grade-level reading, writing, and thinking skills. The Accelerated Schools process is designed to be a six-year effort for reforming a traditional school into an Accelerated School. Each year, one grade level, beginning with kindergarten, is reorganized. Since no Accelerated Schools projects have yet been in operation for the six-year period it takes for children to move from kindergarten to through fifth grade, no completed evaluations are available. However, at the initial Accelerated Schools sites, the third-grade student achievement in reading is nearing national average, and math achievement exceeds it. In addition, retentions in grade have dropped substantially.

The Accelerated School process emphasizes a community inquiry to redesign elementary schools so that all children are successful. Over one hundred Accelerated Schools now operate in a number of states. Henry Levin (1987) notes that many economically disadvantaged students begin school with experiential gaps in areas most valued by schools and that in our current schools these children often fall further behind more advantaged peers each year. He argues it is critical that schools set a deadline for closing the achievement gap so that all children will be able to benefit from the regular instructional program by the time they leave for middle school. Without a deadline, some children will remain below level. Setting the end of fifth grade as the deadline gives schools six years (K–5) to accelerate the literacy development of children who started school with few book, story, or print activity experiences.

Accelerated Schools begin by restructuring programs with the funds available. Levin notes that it is more expensive to educate disadvantaged children and children who find learning more difficult. But extra-funding sources are routinely available in allocations for remedial, special, and bilingual education programs. In addition, those involved with the Accelerated Schools projects have generally found other willing donors when a well-conceived plan has been developed.

For information: Accelerated Schools Project, 109 CERAS, Stanford University, Stanford, CA 94305-3084.

The Success for All Effort

The Success for All program was developed by Robert Slavin and colleagues at the Center for Research on Effective Schooling for Disadvantaged Students at Johns Hopkins University (Slavin, Madden, Karweit, Livermon, & Dolan, 1990; Slavin, Madden, Karweit, Dolan, & Wasik, 1992; 1994). Originally implemented in one inner-city school in Baltimore, the model is currently in use in more than 100 schools in 15 states. Success for All (SFA) takes its name very seriously. Every child is expected to be a capable on-grade-level reader by the end of third grade. To accomplish this goal, SFA is a "relentless" multifaceted program.

Based on the belief that "an ounce of prevention is worth a pound of cure," SFA includes both preschool and kindergarten experiences that emphasize the development and use of language. Once children enter first grade, the literacy program is intensive, varied, and closely monitored. Certified teachers are available to tutor children who need such instruction. These tutors are typically teachers with remedial or special education teaching experience. Tutoring occurs in 20 minute periods each day, usually during the hour-long social studies block. Based on a quarterly informal reading inventory and other assessment procedures, children are grouped for reading—across grade levels—into classes that have only one reading level to teach. The reading tutors become teachers for the 90-minute reading block, thus reducing the pupil-teacher ratio for this block to fifteen to one. During the 90-minute reading block, children are engaged in three activities. Each day begins with a listening-comprehension lesson designed to develop language and comprehension skills. Next, primary-grade children participate in a shared story reading in which the teacher reads complex text (written in small type) and the children read simple text (written in large type). The text read by the children contains known words and words they can decode based on the letter-sound relationships learned. Each reading block includes decoding instruction in which children learn the letter-sound correspondences that they then apply to words they read as part of the shared story lesson. (The shared stories were written specifically for SFA by educators at Johns Hopkins University.)

Once children achieve a first-reader instructional level in reading, their reading instruction is carried out using the CIRC (Cooperative Integrated Reading and Composition) model (Stevens, Madden, Slavin, & Farnish, 1987). Children are assigned to five-member heterogeneous learning teams that complete a variety of team activities using the district basal reader series for discussion, composing, comprehension, and decoding activities.

In addition to their 90 minutes of reading instructional time each day, all children are involved in a daily writing/language arts activity. This writing instruction follows a writing process format. Children first write drafts and then take pieces through a three-step revising/editing/publishing process. Children are taught mechanics within the context of revising and editing, and they work with partners and small groups to polish their writing.

The 90-minute reading/language period and a daily process writing period are the heart of the SFA program, but there are other critical components. Children's progress is assessed four times a year, and students who need assistance are provided with daily tutoring. A family support team in each school reaches out to families who need assistance in providing adequate sleep, nutrition, health care, and so on. Each school has a full-time program facilitator, whose sole job is to work with teacher, tutors, and others to ensure that the program is implemented as faithfully as possible.

Initial results for the SFA schools are encouraging. Many more children are achieving grade-level reading and writing skills. Special education referrals and placements have decreased dramatically and retentions in grade have been reduced to nearly zero. Slavin and colleagues sum up their success and hopes for the future:

> The findings of research on Success for All and related prevention and early intervention programs make it impossible to continue to say that the problems of education in the inner city cannot be solved. The Success for All schools, which include some of the most disadvantaged schools in such cities as Baltimore, Philadelphia, Memphis, and Montgomery, Alabama, do not have unusual staffs or principals. If they can achieve success with the great majority of at-risk children, so can most schools serving similar children. It takes money, but increasingly the money is already in place as Chapter 1 funds increase for high-poverty schools, or can be found from other sources. What is most needed is leadership, a commitment at every level of the political process to see that we stop discarding so many students at the start of their school careers (Slavin et al., 1992, p. 90).

The SFA effort is a comprehensive school-improvement program designed to ensure that all children develop reading and writing proficiency in the early grades. A basic premise of SFA is that the best place to work on ensuring children's school success is in the primary grade classroom. A second premise is that we need to be responsive immediately to children's needs for additional instruction. A third premise is that we must be relentless in providing that instruction. A fourth premise is the need to rethink the use of school resources, personnel, and instructional time. The overriding goal of SFA is to have all children reading on grade level by the end of third grade with no retentions in grade or referrals to special education for reading difficulties.

While SFA schools re-group students homogeneously by achievement for part of their reading and language arts instruction, the approach also reduces the size of instructional groups to about 15 students. This somewhat eases the problem of heterogeneity within groups, and regularly assessing performance and frequently regrouping seem to address two other difficulties generally associated with homogeneous achievement groupings. Thus, while such grouping is not our preferred arrangement for instructional groups, in SFA schools, where it is combined with tutorial instruction and cooperative learning approaches, this arrangement does seem to provide children access to increased amounts of appropriate instruction.

Slavin argues that SFA is a money-saving approach in the long run. Current projects are largely funded from existing funds available to the school, but the reduced retention in grade and reduced placement in special education also serve to affect dramatically the real cost of educating at-risk children in SFA schools. However, in too many schools the money saved in such ways is often not made readily available to support new and innovative programs.

> For information: Success for All, Center for Research on Effective Schooling for Disadvantaged Students, Johns Hopkins University, 3505 N. Charles Street, Baltimore, MD 21218.

The Reading Recovery Effort

This is primarily a first-grade intervention developed originally in New Zealand by Marie Clay and imported to this country by faculty at the Ohio State University (Lyons, Pinnell, & DeFord, 1993). The program involves an extensive and intensive year-long training with long-term continuing education required, which makes it unique in many respects. Planned professional development of this intensity is rarely encountered in school improvement efforts. An added feature is the emphasis on developing reflective teachers who are careful and keen observers of young children's learning.

Reading Recovery (RR) is designed to rapidly accelerate the literacy development of at-risk children before failure becomes debilitating. The lowest-achieving children in first-grade classes participate in an intensive daily 30-minute tutorial until they develop self-monitoring strategies and reach the average achievement levels of their classmates. The average RR participant makes sufficient progress in 12 to 14 weeks to be discontinued from the tutorial. The majority of these discontinued children show normal development after release and progress satisfactorily without further help. Studies in both New Zealand and the United

States show the substantial positive effects this intervention has on children's literacy development (Clay, 1990; Lyons et al., 1993). The results of the Columbus City Schools project indicated that more than 80 percent of the children who participated in RR were successfully discontinued after less than a semester of participation. Two years later, as third graders, they continued to achieve reading levels above the statewide average. The results from New Zealand, where the program has a longer implementation record, are more impressive. In other words, RR offers intensive instruction that brings most high-risk first graders up to grade level after a few months of tutorial instruction and, once caught up, most continue to progress with little need for additional support.

RR has provided the impetus for larger changes in a number of school districts where it has been implemented (Lyons & Beaver, 1995). Following the implementation of RR in the Upper Arlington, Ohio, schools, the first question that arose had to do with the nature of the kindergarten program. Basically, the question was whether kindergarten could be redesigned so that fewer children needed RR services. A second issue that arose concerned the reorganization of first-grade classroom programs so that gains made in RR were supported and extended. Finally, the issue of rethinking reading instruction across the elementary grades arose.

In response to these concerns, the fundamental principles of RR were offered in a series of staff development sessions for kindergarten and primary teachers. From this experience, teachers developed a system from evaluating student literacy development that matched the RR philosophy and reshaped the classroom literacy activities so that they more closely adhered to RR principles. In addition, remedial reading teachers incorporated many elements of the RR philosophy into their instruction. This effort resulted in an improved and coherent literacy instructional program that extended from kindergarten onward. The combined efforts of classroom teachers, reading and learning disability teachers, and RR teachers resulted in dramatic increases in the numbers of children who learned to read and write alongside their peers and dramatic reductions in both early grade retentions and referrals for special-education services.

The implementation of RR in the Upper Arlington schools is a good example of reaching beyond a single new effort to address the problems some children face when learning to read and write. RR is most successfully implemented when it has an impact on the quality of classroom instruction as in Upper Arlington. The addition of RR (or any other program) cannot be expected to overcome the problems children experience if the classroom instructional effort fails to achieve high-quality standards. No special program can be as effective as it might be until classroom instruction is exemplary.

While RR does remove children from the classroom for 30 minutes daily, the removal is short term, and in 10 to 14 weeks students are discontinued and return to the classroom and able to read alongside their classmates. Thus, though RR children are pulled out of the classroom for a brief part of the school day, it is only for a short time and the goal is rapid return to the classroom with the original problem successfully resolved.

Some have suggested that RR is an expensive program. However, the effectiveness of the short-term intervention combined with the reported reduction in retentions in grade and referrals to special education seem to make it substantially more cost effective than many other more commonly tried options for addressing the needs of low-achieving students (Dyer, 1992). Given a long-term perspective, a cheap program that has little impact on children's literacy development is the most expensive endeavor. Early, successful educational interventions reduce the costs associated with retention in grade, later remediation, and special education participation.

> For information: Reading Recovery, Ohio Reading Recovery, Ohio State University, 200 Ramseyer Hall, Columbus, OH 54321.

Schools for the 21st Century

The five central elements of the Schools for the 21st Century effort include (1) school-based, year-round, all-day child care for children ages 3 to 5, (2) before- and after-school and vacation care for school-aged children (3) family support through a home visitation strand for new and expectant parents, (4) support and training for family day-care providers in the school attendance area, and (5) a family day-care referral service for the community. Currently operating in schools in a dozen states, this restructuring effort attempts to provide access to high-quality child care through local schools and from this base to establish effective early interventions to foster child health and development (Zigler & Finn-Stevenson, 1989).

The Schools for the 21st Century project serves to redefine fundamentally roles and responsibilities for schools. Much like Martin (1992), who argues that schools are no longer well suited to society's needs, this project works to create schools that operate on a 12-hour daily schedule and provide programs for very young children and family-based interventions. For instance, at the Sycamore Hills Elementary School in Independence, Missouri, the school is open year round from 6 in the morning until 6 in the evening with programs for 3- and 4 year-olds as well as their school-aged siblings (Lawson, 1990). The preschool program seems much like any other well-run day care with opportunities for experience with stories and books as well as lots of free-choice time. For children who would often otherwise be latchkey children, the before- and after-school programs at Sycamore offer homework time and assistance, participation in athletic activities, a variety of craft and hobby opportunities, as well as accelerated learning opportunities for children (both high- and low-achieving students participate).

None of this is without criticism and cost, of course. There are those who believe that schools should concentrate more on improving the educational experiences traditionally offered before taking on new roles and responsibilities. Others worry that early childhood programs will become "too academic" if left primarily to schools to operate. Finally, critics argue that schools are subsuming roles more properly seen as family responsibilities. Proponents, on the other hand, argue that it is time to recognize that schools must change to better meet the needs of a changed society. They also argue that the evidence of the powerful impact of providing high-quality child care and family support is so overwhelming as to demand virtually that schools accept these new roles.

The problem of funding such efforts is also omnipresent, but in Independence, the program began with start-up grants from local foundations and 85 percent of the current budget is supported through parent fees. The school fees for the various child-care efforts are generally lower than the fees levied by private providers with costs at about $60 per week for a full day of child care and $25 per week for the before- and after-school programs.

For information: Schools for the 21st Century, The Bush Center in Child Development and Social Policy, Yale University, 310 Prospect St., New Haven, CT 06511-9944.

School Power

James Comer (1980, 1988) developed and implemented a different sort of school change in the Martin Luther King Elementary School in New Haven, Connecticut. Comer argues that often school-change efforts focus too heavily on curricular and cognitive aspects of the school experience and fail to deal adequately with school-community relationships. Now implemented in a number of schools across the nation, the School Power project encourages student bonding to the school. But developing this bonding involves substantially rethinking and restructuring traditional power relationships.

Comer argues that in many communities a substantial degree of mistrust exists between parents and school staff. Both groups see the other as a primary source for student failure to thrive. This mistrust fosters an alienation of students and their parents from the school and makes it unlikely that any sort of curricular change will resolve student learning difficulties. Thus, Comer and his colleagues set out to address the alienation first, realizing that most school personnel had neither the training in nor past experience of working collaboratively alongside parents to work through school issues.

A governance team of about a dozen members was established for the school. The team was led by the principal and included elected parents and teachers and a member of the non-professional staff. Each team also included a mental-health professional. The team operated by consensus, not by majority rule, to foster cooperation rather than create a situation where someone was a "loser." Teams focused their efforts on solution finding rather than blame placing. Team members acknowledged the legal authority of the principal, but the principal was expected to act in concert with team consensus. Issues from academic programs to discipline to organization of the school day were all in the realm of the team decision making.

Acknowledging that creating such teams and getting them up and running is not accomplished without difficulty, Comer (1988) maintains that the effort's success can be found in improved relations between parents and teachers, improved attendance, and improved academic achievement—the Martin Luther King School achievement test scores rose across five years from the very bottom of the New Haven school performance to third highest.

The School Power projects were among the earliest attempts at implementing some form of shared decision making in school sites, and much can be learned from those efforts. But the focus on school-community relations and especially teacher-parent cooperation is what makes these efforts unique.

For information: James P. Comer, The School Development Program, Yale University, New Haven, CT 06511.

The Coalition of Essential Schools

The Coalition of Essential Schools (CES) has focused efforts primarily on middle school and high school education. Nonetheless, this educational restructuring effort is having an impact on the elementary school curriculum in many sites where CES schools now operate. The assumptions that guide change at CES sites are straightforward:

Intellectual focus. Schools are to be designed to help students learn to use their minds well.

Simple goals. The aphorism "less is more" should dominate curriculum decisions. Teach fewer things better and more deeply.

Personalization. Students learn best when instruction is more personal, involving more student choice and more teacher contact.

Universal goals. "All means all" best summarizes the approach to goal setting. All goals apply to all students.

Student-as-worker. Replacing the teacher-as-knowledge-deliverer with student-as-worker metaphor allows teachers time to personalize instruction.

Diploma by exhibition. The emphasis is what students can do, not on number of pages or units completed nor on time spent in classes.

Attitude. School climate should stress values of unanxious expectation, trust, and decency. Parents must be viewed as active, valued collaborators.

Staff. Generalists first, specialists second. Thus, all staff have multiple roles and responsibilities (teacher, administrator, and counselor/advocate).

Budget. Costs not to exceed those of traditional schools by more than 10 percent, collaborative planning time available, competitive salaries.

The CES effort derives from the work of Ted Sizer (1988) and involves statewide efforts in a dozen states and local efforts across the nation. In addition, the CES projects have initiated collaborative efforts with the Education Commission of the States (Re:Learning), the Comer School Development Program, Harvard Project Zero, and other educational reform efforts. The CES change process involves reorganizing not only the curriculum and the school day and year but reorganizing decision making by "delayering" decisions about what to teach and how to teach. Participatory decision making includes parents and, often, students.

But what makes the CES schools unique is the elimination of subject-matter boundaries and rigid class schedules along with the emphasis on authentic assessment of authentic learning. Integration of mathematics and science, of literature and economics, and of civics and biology are all examples of rethinking the very nature of curriculum and instruction. While this effort began with a focus on adolescent education, more and more frequently the basic principles are being applied to elementary schools. At New York City's Central Park East, for instance, the project began at the high school level but has been incorporated into the middle school and, more recently, the elementary school level. The thoughtful curriculum combined with authentic assessment provides a powerful base for teaching and learning at any age.

For information: The Coalition of Essential Schools, Box 1938, Brown University, Providence, RI 02912.

Change Takes Time as Well as Good Intentions

One can pick up almost any educational journal (or even popular magazine) and find other stories of schools changing for the better. Likewise, a flood of professional and popular books describe school-change efforts (e.g., Allington & Walmsley, 1995; Hiebert & Taylor, 1994). We suggest that it is not for lack of information that change is not more widespread. So what causes some schools to engage in rethinking what they are doing and how they are doing it? What is it that makes the status quo such a popular option? Undoubtedly, the answer is complex, but in the end, we think it is the beliefs we hold about learners and learning that are critical in the design of the schools we have.

Professional Beliefs

Accelerating the learning of at-risk children is an idea whose time has come. With the large-scale evidence provided by the efforts discussed above, it is obviously not necessary to continue to slow down instruction or wait for children to develop. Most children's reading and writing development can be accelerated if schools are reorganized and resources used to create programs that provide children with access to instruction of sufficient quantity and quality (McGill-Franzen & Allington, 1991). However, in too many schools the dominant belief system is that there must necessarily be a bottom group of children who will never catch up with their peers. Adherence to such beliefs may be the most formidable barrier to creating schools where all children learn to read and write. Until teachers, administrators, and supervisors believe that all children can become proficient readers and writers, it is unlikely that efforts to create extraordinary instructional programs will be sustained. Actually, as long as traditional beliefs dominate professional thinking in a school, it is unlikely that faculty will even consider changing instruction to speed the literacy development of at-risk children.

Unfortunately, this belief issue is often a chicken-or-egg dilemma. The nature of many current school programs maintains the popular professional belief system. When schools design and implement instructional programs that alter the status quo, long-standing beliefs are modified. For instance, implementing Reading Recovery in schools has caused a shift in the beliefs of classroom teachers about the literacy learning capacities of at-risk children. As at-risk children are released from the program as successful grade-level readers, classroom teachers question the dominant belief that some children will never learn to read along with their peers. Similarly, reducing the stratification of children into various "ability" groups in Accelerated Schools and CES sites has altered beliefs concerning the potential of many at-risk students. As teacher and administrator beliefs change, shifts in classroom practices become more likely.

However, because current instructional programs often maintain the status quo, it may be difficult to muster any intense interest in changing school programs dramatically without some strong and persuasive evidence. Even then, change proposals will often be greeted less than enthusiastically and with a somewhat skeptical eye. In our experience, reading about schools that work better for at-risk children offers one potential approach for shifting beliefs as does visits to such schools. Small demonstration projects initiated on a school site are also persuasive. In any event, long-standing professional beliefs support most school practices. For professional practice to change, professional beliefs must be addressed.

The difficulty involved in initiating change must be recognized. There is no quick fix. Maintaining the status quo is always easier than involving a school in changes. It is for this reason that changing school programs must be viewed as a long-term effort, not an activity that will miraculously appear after a single workshop or staff-development session. But change is necessary in many schools serving large numbers of at-risk children. In this chapter we have provided examples of efforts that have dramatically enhanced the instructional programs in a number of schools. While each effort was unique, several common themes appear across these attempts to create schools where all children learn to read and write.

Common Features of Successful Efforts

What is it that these school-restructuring efforts have in common? First, the schools reorganized so that classroom teachers were more heavily involved in school decision making. This shared decision making resulted in classroom teachers accepting greater responsibility for instruction. In some schools, parents and community members also joined the school site-based management teams. Each of the restructuring efforts increased teacher and parent input and involvement.

These schools' special instructional programs were reorganized. Extra effort was made to connect special-program teachers with classroom instruction and classroom teachers. Even though some of the schools continue pullout program designs for special instructional support, attempts have been made to ease and facilitate collaboration among the different teachers working with the same children. In some cases, special teachers were redeployed as classroom teachers for all or part of the school day to reduce class size. These schools also offer intensive instructional support when needed, often using a tutorial model for children who most need their literacy development accelerated.

In these schools, staff committed to the idea that all children could learn to read and write, and they worked to make that outcome emerge. But it was not just high expectations and large amounts of reading and writing activity that produced such results. While these seem necessary elements, they also seem insufficient from our reading of the research on school change. What makes these school programs work is a substantial investment in professional development. None of these efforts involved much of an outlay for equipment or for trendy special materials. Each invested in human capital, primarily investments in enhancing teachers' instructional skills.

The schools involved in these efforts allocated larger amounts of classroom instructional time to actual reading and writing activities while using multiple approaches to literacy instruction. These schools emphasize real reading and writing activity during literacy lessons. Each has worked to integrate reading and writing activities. To implement new instructional approaches, these schools also invested in classroom libraries, big books, magazine subscriptions, and student anthologies. Sad to say, but in too many schools, especially those serving large numbers of at-risk children, children often have little to read. Putting books in the classrooms and in the school libraries makes it more likely that children will have books in their hands.

Expanding instructional time by extending the normal school day for some children is another feature of several of these efforts. There were a variety of strategies such as using a before-school period, using part of the lunch period, or scheduling literacy support lessons after school. In some cases, summer programs were developed to extend the school year and to support the gains made during the regular school year, and in the case of the first school we presented, the shift to year-round schooling eliminated the long summer vacation that so often leads to summer reading loss among at-risk children. At this school, special programs were even created to provide literacy support during the three-week quarterly break periods.

The assessments of children's literacy development in these school are tied more heavily to everyday reading and writing than to just end-of-year standardized testing. While such annual testing has continued in most of these school programs, it is the frequent authentic evaluation of reading and writing performances that drives teaching. In some cases, the evaluation system was completely rewritten with a focus on exhibitions and performances by students rather than maintaining an emphasis on daily homework and weekly test scores.

These schools worked to involve families in the schools. They found that parents will come because their children are succeeding and because they see a school community working in new ways to support their children. Parents are not just expected to monitor homework; instead, they are involved in making many of the tough decisions about the use of school resources, about curriculum, and about schedules. Often, family literacy programs were developed with family support services such as establishing a homework hotline or a regular parent-teacher contact program.

Finally, in most of these schools, change started out small, not as a wholesale restructuring of the school. In some cases, change begins in a single classroom. Now one classroom is only a beginning, but it is a beginning. Successful school change efforts take time to accomplish, especially schoolwide change. In these sites it was not unusual to find a multiyear plan for changing current practice. But long-term plans call for a long-term commitment to continuous improvement—commitments from the professional staff and from the district leaders who provide the resources that support the change effort.

■ SUMMARY

Some schools change because the teachers push for change and initiate and carry much of the effort. Other schools change because a school district or building leader pushes change and creates an environment that encourages and supports change. This simplification illustrates the ideas of bottom-up (teachers initiate) and top-down (administrators initiate) approaches to reorganizing schools. Truth be told, we think that few pure examples of either approach exist. In our experience, change has occurred when teachers, administrators, and supervisors somehow come together around a common core of concerns.

Often, educational reformers have failed to understand that schools are collections of classrooms. Rather than attempting to restructure a school as a starting point, it will be more useful to begin by thinking about changing classrooms (or at least one classroom). The change needs to focus on responding more effectively to the needs of at-risk children. The change effort needs to focus on supporting classroom teachers in the process of improving their classroom literacy lessons. In working with schools, we try to begin by starting small while looking at the long term. We begin by asking school staff, "What would you like to see happening more often in the classrooms?" and "What would you like to see happening less frequently?"

After developing some preliminary lists of things that teachers would like to see more and less of, it is time to begin to think about how to foster more of some activities and less of others. For instance, if more time spent reading in classrooms is a goal, then developing classroom libraries of 500 or more paperback titles is a good strategy to pursue. Enhancing access to books increases the amount of reading done in and out of school (Fielding, Wilson, & Anderson, 1986). At the same time, if we can provide classroom teachers with longer blocks of uninterrupted teaching, we can support attempts to expand the time children spend actually reading and writing in the classroom. If the goal is to see children spending less time doing low-level skills sheets, the strategy might be to agree to limit the number of reams of paper available for reproducing these materials (or reassign the aide that runs copies to other tasks).

We might then take the money saved through such reductions and channel it into book purchases for classroom libraries. Time previously spent on seatwork activity can then be shifted to time spent reading, but this works only if children have access to a sufficient supply of comfortable, interesting reading materials. If off-task behavior is a central problem, we might work to ensure that classrooms have large supplies of books that children can read and are interested in reading. The point is that schools can be overwhelmed when they try to change everything at once. Go slow and take the long-term view. Don't forget: There is no quick fix and no one best way.

In the remainder of this book we explore the various aspects of school change in substantially greater depth. We have attempted to offer clearer and more detailed descriptions of such efforts and to offer a clear rationale for why each is critical. In addition, each chapter offers examples from real schools in the process of change.

What Do We Now Know About Reading and Writing?

T he last 25 years have been exciting times for literacy researchers because so much has been learned about the processes of reading and writing. We now have a much clearer understanding of the mental processes that underlie both, and this new knowledge undercuts much conventional wisdom about how we learn to read and write. In addition, we know quite a bit about the kinds of schools and classrooms where all children become readers and writers.

Our goal in writing this book was to bring together all that we know about supporting successful literacy instruction and about accomplishing change in elementary schools. In this chapter we focus on what we know about the reading and writing processes and about how to help children acquire literacy in our schools. We also point to some instances when common practice seems to run contrary to the best evidence on how we might foster reading and writing development in children. We have attempted to provide a summary of important processes and principles but realize that our summaries risk oversimplifying complex issues. Nonetheless, we have undertaken this risk with the hope that interested readers will locate and study the reports we cite as supporting the generalizations, or principles, we offer below.

READING AND WRITING *ARE* THINKING

For much of this century it was assumed that once children learned to decode words, they could read. It was believed that when they could pronounce the words, comprehension would follow, almost automatically. It was also assumed that writing was just writing down words and that writing could not occur until children had mastered the decoding activity (which provided them with the skills to spell the words they were trying to write). Writing instruction was seen as primarily lessons in spelling, punctuation, and the parts of speech. Reading and writing lessons focused more on developing the skills than on developing children's knowledge and thinking.

This focus on low-level skills mastery resulted in an increased number of children who could perform low-level literacy activities. Today, almost all students achieve the "basic" literacy level as set on the National Assessment of Educational Progress (NAEP)—more children achieve this level today than at any point in this nation's history. At the same time, the number of students who achieve the "advanced" literacy level on the NAEP has barely changed. The advanced level asks students to read, write, and think simultaneously. The tasks require students to summarize information read or to contrast two characters or to identify the primary argument in a persuasive essay (an editorial, for instance). Only about 15 percent of students satisfactorily complete such tasks. The focus on low-level skills—locating and remembering specific details, filling in the blanks, circling the answers, pronouncing the words, answering the factual questions, identifying the nouns and verbs, correctly spelling all the words—did not lead to much thoughtfulness by readers and writers. The result was children who could read words accurately but who demonstrated little thinking while reading and little understanding of what they had read. The result was children who could write with few misspellings or punctuation errors but whose compositions showed little thought, persuasiveness, organization, or creativity.

Think for a moment about your own reading and writing. As you read a novel you may find yourself literally transported into the scene. You find yourself liking some characters and despising others. You may notice a resemblance between a character and someone you know in real life. You may "see" the character. As you read a memo from a state education agency official you may find yourself getting annoyed—wondering if the author has any sense of the complexity of the directive issued. You may find yourself comparing the directive to previous directives, mentally noting changes in your responsibilities. In other words, you find yourself thinking. If you compose a memo in response, it matters whether the memo is going to the official who sent the directive or to colleagues who need the information about the new policy. It matters whether you write your memo to summarize the information or to criticize the directive. Both audience and purpose matter when you write. If someone were to walk into your office immediately after you have finished reading the memo, they may find you sitting and thinking. If they come in while you are composing your own memo, they may find you sitting in front of your computer screen just thinking. In fact, if they ask, "What are you doing?" You will likely reply, "I'm thinking [about this silly new policy . . . "]. The point is that whenever adults read and write they think. Reading or writing without thinking would be senseless.

But think back to the reading and writing lessons that epitomized "basic skills" lessons. Many lessons involved no text reading at all, only isolated word and sentence readings. Often, writing involved no composing, just filling in blanks or copying sentences from a book or the board. Recall, locate, list, and copy were words that described the central instructional tasks in many lessons. Thinking was rarely required in the skill and drill lesson.

Children are more likely to learn what they are taught than to learn things not taught. When reading and writing lessons eliminate thinking, children cannot be expected to see reading and writing as thinking processes. When teachers emphasize pronouncing or spelling the words correctly and rarely focus on thoughtful applications of strategies and purposefulness, children not surprisingly become "basic" readers and writers and seldom display much thoughtfulness.

None of this is to argue that children do not need to be taught effective decoding strategies or the conventions of spelling and punctuation. What it does mean is that real readers and writers are constantly thinking while they read and write. It means if we want to create readers and writers, teachers must foster thinking from the beginning lesson. It means that lessons will need to focus on strategies and on selecting the strategy that fits the reading or writing activity. It means that discussion must replace much of the interrogation that now follows reading and writing activities.

Fielding and Pearson (1994) contend "that a successful program of comprehension instruction" should include four components:

1. Large amounts of time for actual text reading,
2. Teacher-directed instruction in comprehension strategies,
3. Opportunities for peer and collaborative learning, and
4. Occasions for students to talk to a teacher and to one another about their responses to reading.

Consider how adults normally converse about materials they have read. Suppose you see a colleague carrying a popular novel into the teacher's lounge. Will you initiate a conversation about the book by interrogating your colleague about the names of characters, the cars they drive, their whereabouts on particular days, and so on (the kinds of questions that dominate classroom exchanges), or will you inquire as to their response to the book? ("How do you like it?") Imagine asking your spouse about a newspaper or magazine story that you both have read. Will you interrogate with questions about specific factual information ("What is the name of the commander of the Coast Guard cutter?"), or is it more likely that your comments will focus on response to the piece? ("Can you believe that?" "Do you think she is guilty?") It might be useful to compare classroom talk after reading with the talk that normally occurs outside of school when folks have read something. Think about conversations about shopping lists or notes written to a friend. Does the talk focus on spelling and punctuation, does it focus on remembering trivial details from the text, or do discussions of purpose, completeness, intention, or meaning usually occur? ("Why did you put cumin on the list?" "What did she think she would accomplish with this note?")

Children need to understand that reading and writing are thinking. They need to understand that neither can be accomplished without thinking. This understanding must be fostered and reinforced continuously in classroom instruction, not just during reading and language arts periods. All teaching needs to emphasize thinking, not just remembering. When classroom instruction fails to emphasize thoughtfulness, it is no surprise that children neither read nor write thoughtfully. But when we look closer at the NAEP data, it becomes clear that it is the lucky children—those with well-educated, advantaged parents—who usually achieve advanced literacy. These children are from homes where parents are more likely to engage them in thoughtful conversations about texts. It also becomes apparent that few at-risk children ever attain the advanced literacy level. These are children who depend primarily on the school to foster thoughtful reading and writing because thoughtful literacy is less often a part of their home life.

Prior Knowledge Plays a Large Role in Reading Comprehension and Writing

The most important factor in determining how much readers will comprehend and how well writers will be able to communicate about a given topic is their level of knowledge about that topic (of course interest in the topic is also important, but often related to prior knowledge). The importance of prior knowledge to comprehension and communication is included in virtually all modern theories of reading (Anderson and Pearson, 1984; Pressley, Wood, & Woloshyn, 1992; Sweet, 1993). According to schema theory, prior knowledge provides a schema—a framework or structure—that helps thinking. Readers familiar with sports, for example, know that a baseball game will have nine players on each side, that the players will field different positions, and what players in each position are supposed to do. These baseball basics are considered by the writer to be "general knowledge" and are thus not explicitly explained in a book or article about baseball. But readers who "know" baseball can listen to or read about a game and have little difficulty comprehending descriptions of games, plays, and so on. This is because these readers literally carry a schema for baseball in their heads. They can envision the field, the baselines, the batter's box, and the dugout. They understand this "technical" vocabulary and much more. When they hear or read about a "double play," a "slider," a "blooping single to right," a "pick-off attempt," or a player "safe, sliding into the bag," these readers create mental images from the frameworks they possess. But readers whose prior knowledge of baseball is limited or nonexistent can read the same words and descriptions and not have the foggiest idea what is going on!

Because comprehension and communication are so prior-knowledge dependent, children whose knowledge of a variety of topics is limited have difficulty comprehending much of what they read and difficulty communicating in writing about many topics. But children who read little have the least opportunity to acquire new knowledge through reading.

Schools must be responsible for helping children learn about the world in which they live. When you think about what we teach children in schools, you can divide almost everything into knowledge and skills. The abilities to read, spell, write, do math, use the computer, sing a song, play the clarinet, throw a ball, and speak a foreign language are all skills—things you can do. The understandings that there are seven continents, each state has two senators, the Civil War was fought in the 1860s, mammals are warm-blooded animals, that Martin Luther King led the civil rights movement are all knowledge—things that you know. For many years, literacy instruction in our elementary schools have focused on skills and largely ignored knowledge, particularly deep knowledge of topics. In many schools with large numbers of at-risk children, teachers are instructed to "teach the basics." The basics usually refer to the three R's—reading, 'riting, and 'rithmetic. The knowledge part of the curriculum, usually found in the subjects of science and social studies, are virtually ignored in the primary grades of many schools that teach a high proportion of at-risk children.

Emphasizing the skill subjects and excluding the knowledge subjects often results in a short-term gain and a long-term deficit. Test scores in schools that emphasize skills in grades K–3 indicate that children do well through the second or third grade, but test scores decline from fourth grade on. After third grade, teachers are supposed to, and do indeed try to, teach the knowledge subjects such as science and social studies. They often find, however, that even their average students can't read the textbooks or "can read them but not understand what they are reading." Children who can read the words but can't understand what they are reading are not really reading. These children who "have the skills" but who lack needed prior knowledge of critical school topics are a legacy of a primary grades curriculum that required teachers to spend all their time "on the basics."

This knowledge deficit, which usually rears its ugly head in third or fourth grade, does not disappear as children move through school. The Scholastic Achievement Test, which claims to predict how well students will do in college, is very dependent on prior knowledge.

Our failure to raise SAT scores in spite of two decades of massive effort may be one of the clearest indicators that schools have focused more on skills development than on expanding children's knowledge of the world.

In a recent demonstration of just how influential prior knowledge can be, Beck and McKeown (1993) produced the passage below.

> In 1367 Marain and the settlements ended a seven-year war with the Langurians and Pitoks. As a result of this war Languria was driven out of East Bacol. Marain would now rule Laman and other lands that once belonged to Languria. This brought peace to the Bacolian settlements. The settlers no longer had to worry about attacks from Laman. The Bacolians were happy to be part of Marain in 1367. Yet a dozen years later, these same people would be fighting the Marish for independence, or freedom from United Marain's rule.

Now, that passage did not make much sense to most of the adults that read it. But read the next passage.

> In 1763 Britain and the settlements ended a seven-year war with the French and Indians. As a result of this war France was driven out of North America. Britain would now rule Canada and other lands that once belonged to France. This brought peace to the American colonies. The settlers no longer had to worry about attacks from Canada. The Americans were happy to be part of Britain in 1763. Yet a dozen years later, these same people would be fighting the British for independence, or freedom from Great Britain's rule.

As you can see in the first passage, a few key words were changed (e.g., Britain, France, Canada). But changing those words was important because most adults were familiar with the original words but were not, of course, familiar with the fictional replacement vocabulary. Most children, however, were familiar with neither. The original passage made no more sense to them than the altered passage. The prior knowledge that we adults have often makes it hard for us to understand the difficulties children encounter in their reading.

CHILDREN BENEFIT FROM DEMONSTRATION AND INSTRUCTION

All children need instruction, but some children need substantial amounts of truly high-quality teaching to learn to read and write alongside their peers. What all children need, and some need more of, is models, explanations, and demonstrations of how reading is accomplished. What most do not need are more assignments without teacher-directed instruction, yet much of the work children do in school is not accompanied by any sort of instructional interaction or demonstration.

Children are routinely asked questions after reading but are infrequently provided with demonstrations of the comprehension strategies needed to answer the questions posed. In short, too often assigning and asking are confused with teaching. When the teacher-directed instructional component is left out of the lesson, it enormously reduces the potential of many activities (e.g., maps, webs, summary writing, response journals) for supporting the acquisition of complex comprehension strategies (Fielding & Pearson, 1994). With no clear instruction, children are left to discover the strategies and processes so important to skillful readers and writers. Some children puzzle through the activities assigned but never discover the thinking patterns that proficient readers use.

The teaching activities of modeling, explaining, and demonstrating are essential elements if all children are to learn to read and write. Teachers *model* the reading and writing processes by engaging in them while children observe. Reading aloud to children, for instance, provides a model of how reading sounds and how stories go. Composing a list of things needed for a project provides a model of one function of writing. Talking about how a newspaper story made us worry provides a model of response to text. Models are essential, but models do not give children much in the way of information about how proficient readers actually accomplish such feats.

Reading aloud to children is one way to model fluent reading and thoughtful talk about books, stories, and responses. While read-alouds have become increasingly popular, recent research indicates that nearly one-third of classroom teachers rarely read children's books aloud to their students (Hoffman, Roser, & Battle, 1993). They also offer guidelines for read-alouds:

- Designate a time each day for reading aloud, not a time-filler slot.
- Select quality literature to read.
- Discuss the books read with children.
- Create groups for children to share responses to books read.
- Reread selected pieces.

We would note that books selected to be read aloud can also be "easy" books. We might select books that at-risk children can read independently, whether we were rereading a favorite book from earlier years or a new, less difficult book that fit a class theme. When teachers read "easy" books aloud it makes it clear that good, easy books are also allowed and honored in that classroom.

Explanation is probably the most common method teachers use to help children understand how one goes about reading and writing. Unfortunately, explanations can get wordy and often require a specialized language. We tell children that a good summary includes "the most important ideas," but some children are left wondering how to tell which ideas are important. Unfortunately, these explanations are often unhelpful—children now can define the main idea, for instance, but they still cannot construct an adequate summary reflecting the important information in a text. Explaining a process is an improvement compared to simply assigning students work, but many children do not acquire useful strategies from explanations alone.

Teacher demonstration and modeling of the writing process can be seen on the video, *The Morning Letter* ($60, A–V Services, Pennsylvania State University, 1-800-826-0132).

Demonstration is teacher talk about the mental activities that occur during the reading and writing processes. Demonstration usually involves modeling and explaining along with demonstrating the thinking that occurs while reading and writing. For instance, a teacher might compose a summary of an informational passage on an overhead projector in front of the class (Cunningham & Allington, 1994). The teacher provides a model of the writing process and, ultimately, a model of a written summary. The teacher might work from a map or a web following an explanation of the essential summary elements. A demonstration would occur as the teacher thinks aloud during the composing, making visible the thinking that assembles the information for the summary, puts it into words, and finally creates a readable summary of the information presented. Similarly, the teacher demonstrates the complex mental processes that readers engage in while reading when she talks children through a strategy for puzzling out an unfamiliar word while reading a story (e.g., "I can try a couple of things: Read to the end of the sentence; look at the word and see if I know any other words that might help me figure it out; ask myself, 'What makes sense here?'; double-check what word makes sense against word structure; read the sentence using the word that makes sense and has the right letters"). Demonstrating such thinking and how thinking shifts from incident to incident ("Here I can look at the picture to get a clue"; "I think the word will rhyme with *name* because it is spelled the same way, and so on), gives children the chance to see that skillful strategy use is flexible and always requires thinking, not rote memory of rules.

Children only infrequently encounter such demonstrations in most classrooms. Children who find learning to read difficult often see the teacher and other children reading and writing, serving as models, but they wonder, "How do they do it?" All children benefit from instruction, but some children need incredible amounts of careful, personal instruction, usually clear and repeated demonstrations of how readers and writers go about reading and writing (Duffy, 1993). Left without adequate demonstrations, at-risk children are likely to continue trying to make sense out of lessons, but will rarely accomplish this feat. Some of these children learn to score better on tests but never really learn to read and write.

If we are to teach all children to read and write, then models, explanations, and demonstrations of how we go about reading and writing will be essential elements of instructional programs. While some children may discover the effective strategies that proficient readers and writers use so easily and flexibly, other children require substantially more careful and personalized teaching to acquire the same strategies.

FLUENCY WITH READING AND SPELLING WORDS IS ESSENTIAL TO READING AND WRITING

Within the last decade, advances in technology have allowed researchers, mainly in the areas of psychology and artificial intelligence, to investigate brain functions, eye movements, and other basic reading processes. The focus of this research was not on how to teach

Writing in front of children while thinking aloud demonstrates composing as a thinking process.

reading or on comparisons of various approaches but rather on what happens internally when we read and how this changes as readers move from beginning stages to more sophisticated reading. We know a great deal more today than we did two decades ago about basic reading processes.

We know, for example, that readers look at virtually all the words and almost all the letters in those words. For many years, it was generally believed that sophisticated readers sampled text. Based on predictions about what words and letters they would see, readers were thought to look at the words and letters just enough to see if their predictions were confirmed. Eye-movement research with computerized tracking has proven that, in reality, readers look at every word and almost every letter of each word (Rayner & Pollatsek, 1989). The amount of time spent processing each letter is incredibly small, only a few hundredths of a second in proficient readers. The astonishingly fast letter recognition for letters within familiar words and patterns is due to our brains expecting certain letters to occur in sequence with each other.

Readers usually recode printed words into sound. Although it is possible to read without any internal speech, we rarely do (Rayner & Pollatsek, 1989). Normally as we read, we think the words in our mind. We then check this phonological information with the visual information we received by analyzing the word for familiar spelling patterns. Saying the words aloud or thinking the words also seems to perform an important function in holding the words in auditory memory until enough words are read to create meaning.

Skilled readers recognize most words immediately and automatically without using context. Good readers use context to see if what they are reading makes sense. Context is also important for disambiguating the meaning of some words (I had a *ball* throwing the *ball* at the *ball*.) Occasionally, readers use context to figure out what the word is. Most of the time, however, words are identified based on their familiar spelling and the association of that spelling with a pronunciation. Context comes into play after, not before, the word is identified, based on the brain's processing of the letter-by-letter information it receives (Stanovich, 1991; Nicholson, 1991). Several studies have found that poor readers rely more on context than good readers, although good readers do use contextual information to verify that what they are reading makes sense.

Skilled readers can accurately and quickly pronounce infrequent, phonetically regular words. When presented with unfamiliar but phonetically regular words—*nit, kirn, miracidium*—good readers immediately and seemingly effortlessly assign them a pronunciation (Daneman, 1991). This happens so quickly that readers are often unaware that they have not seen the word before and that they had to "figure it out." This decoding that good readers do so quickly and effortlessly is usually accomplished by the reader's accessing some known spelling patterns or similar words.

For a long time, the phonics debate centered on whether to teach using a synthetic or analytic approach. A synthetic approach generally teaches children to go letter by letter, assigning a pronunciation to each letter and then blending the individual letters together. An analytic approach teaches rules (the *e* on the end makes the vowel long). Brain research, however, suggests that the brain is a pattern detector, not a rule applier, and that, while we look at single letters, we are looking at them considering all the letter patterns we know. Successfully decoding a word occurs when the brain recognizes a familiar spelling pattern or, if the pattern itself is not familiar, searches through its store of words with similar patterns (Adams, 1990; Goswami & Bryant, 1990).

To decode an unfamiliar word—*knob,* for example—the child who knew many words that began with *kn* would immediately assign to the *kn* the "n" sound. The initial *kn* would be stored in the brain as a spelling pattern. If the child only knew a few other words with *kn* and hadn't read these words very often, that child would probably not have *kn* as a known spelling pattern and thus would have to do a quick search for known words which began with *kn.* If the child found the words *know* and *knew* and then tried this same sound on the unknown word *knob,* that child would have used the analogy strategy. Likewise, the child might know the pronunciation for *ob* because of having correctly read so many words containing the *ob* spelling pattern (Bob, rob, cob, job, sob) or might have had to access some words with *ob* to use them to come up with the pronunciation. The child who had no stored spelling patterns for *kn* or *ob* and no known words to access and compare to would be unlikely to pronounce the unknown word *knob* successfully.

To summarize what the brain does to identify words is to risk oversimplification, but that seems necessary if we want our instructional practices to be compatible with what we know about brain processes. As we read, we look very quickly at almost all letters of each word. For most words, this visual information is recognized as a familiar pattern with which a spoken word is identified and pronounced (aloud or through internal speech). Words we have read before are instantly recognized as we see them. Words we have not read before are almost instantly pronounced based on spelling patterns the brain has seen in other words. Meaning is accessed through visual word recognition but the sound of the word supports the visual information and helps to hold the word in memory.

Reading and writing are meaning constructing activities, but they are dependent on words. All good readers and writers have a store of high-frequency words that they read and spell instantly and automatically. Good readers and writers can also decode and spell most regular words. Decoding and spelling abilities increase in direct proportion to the amount of successful reading and writing children do. Word-fluency activities in classrooms should include lots of writing and easy reading as well as word manipulation and sorting activities designed to help children learn common spelling patterns (Cunningham, 1995; Cunningham & Allington, 1994).

Children Begin to Acquire Reading and Writing Processes Very Early

For most of this century, educators believed that reading instruction should be delayed until children reached a certain level of mental readiness. They believed that for most children, this level of readiness would be achieved when they were about 6 years old. The most influential study (Morphett & Washburne, l93l) actually specified a mental age of 6½ years as the right age to begin reading instruction (but their methodology was enormously flawed). Many educators believed that writing should be delayed until reading abilities were firmly in place and recommended that children begin writing when they were eight or nine years old.

To determine who was ready to read, most children were given readiness tests at the end of kindergarten or after a few weeks of first grade. These readiness tests assessed the skills then believed to be critical for success in beginning reading instruction. Most tests examined the skills of visual discrimination (find the shape that matches the first shape), auditory discrimination (find the two pictures whose names begin with the same sound), letter naming high-frequency word knowledge, and oral language vocabulary.

First graders who scored high on these readiness tests began reading instruction, usually with a basal reader. There were two schools of thought about how to proceed with poor scorers on the readiness tests. Some schools and teachers felt it best to "wait" for the readiness to develop. Other schools and teachers taught the skills—visual discrimination of shapes, auditory discrimination of sounds, letter names, and so on—in an attempt to develop readiness skills tested.

Emergent literacy research began in the homes of young children. The research traces the literacy development of young children from birth until the time they read and write conventionally (Teale & Sulzby, l99l). This observational research showed that children in literate home environments engage in reading and writing long before they begin formal reading instruction. Children born into homes where someone reads and writes with them walk into our schools with an incredible foundation on which instruction can easily build. These children experience an average of over 1,000 hours of quality one-on-one reading and writing activities (Adams, 1990). They use reading and writing in a variety of ways and pass through a series of predictable stages on their journey from pretend reading and scribbling to conventional reading and writing. When parents read to children, interact with them about the print they see in the world—signs, cereal boxes, advertisements—and encourage and support their early writing efforts, reading and writing develop and grow with listening and speaking, concurrently rather than sequentially.

In short, the observational research on young children debunked the readiness/mental age theories on which we had operated for half a century. Rather than needing to learn all the skills—auditory discrimination, letter names and sounds, and so on—before they began reading and writing, children with lots of print experiences learned these skills as they began reading and writing. Readiness to read has more to do with book, story, and print experiences that occur before school entry than with drill on any subset of skills or achieving any particular mental age.

Emergent literacy research has shown us the kinds of literacy activity young children engage in that lead to developing the understandings essential to successful independent reading and writing. A great many important concepts and attitudes develop as children encounter print in various forms. Seven of these stand out and differentiate children who have had many print experiences from those who have not. Children who have had many print experiences (1) know why we read and write, (2) have greater knowledge of the world, (3) understand the conventions and jargon of print (book, page, title, letter, and so on), (4) have higher levels of phonological awareness (e.g., the ability to segment a spoken word, /*hat*/, into individual sounds, /*huh/ah/tuh*/), (5) can read some important-to-them words, (6) know many letter names and sounds, and (7) are eager and confident in their fledgling reading and writing attempts (Pearson, 1993).

In some areas, a rather rancorous debate focused around the term *developmentally appropriate*. Some people use the term to describe preschools and kindergartens without an academic emphasis. These often ardent professionals may assert that books, stories, and print activities in preschool or kindergarten classes are *developmentally inappropriate*. Many argue that, in one way or another, the "gift of time" is what these children need most. We believe that children who arrive at school with few book, story, and print experiences are the very children that need rich literacy environments and activities in their school (or preschool) day. In this we agree with McGill-Franzen (1992) and the National Association for the Education of Young Children (1986). Both offer advice for creating the classrooms we imagine as most appropriate. Likewise, the HighScope curriculum, widely cited as an example of a "developmentally appropriate" approach to preschool education, offers many suggestions for creating a rich preschool literacy environment and wonderful emergent literacy activities.

There has long been a debate over whether kindergartens should be primarily for play and socialization or offer a more academic orientation. Emergent literacy research supports neither kindergartens in which children play and socialize while we wait for literacy development nor kindergartens in which children work on isolated readiness skills. Rather than wait or teach separate skills for children who have not had these early literacy experiences before coming to school, kindergartens and other early school experiences should simulate as closely as possible the "at-home" experiences of children who arrive at school with a familiarity with books and stories and who rather easily acquire fluency with reading and writing. We call these kindergartens "literate home simulation" kindergartens.

CHILDREN NEED ENORMOUS OPPORTUNITIES TO READ AND WRITE REAL THINGS

Peek into the homes of some children and you will see lots of real reading and writing activity. Parents write notes to each other about telephone calls taken and appointments to keep; they write lists and schedules that are posted on the refrigerator; they read newspapers (and sometimes to each other), magazines, bills, letters from grandpa, and books. The parents read to the children and foster their writing (or scribbles and scratches). The parents talk to each other about the things they read and talk to their children about them too. Walk into the child's bedroom, and you will find a bedroom library of personal children's books. When these children go to school, their parents encourage them to make purchases from school book clubs and often sit with them to discuss possible purchases and to hear about the books after they have arrived and have been read. In other words, some children see adults engaging in real reading and writing, talking about what they have read or written, and have adults who read and write with them and talk with them about what they read. These are the children who are likely to find learning to read in school relatively easy.

Imagine now that these already "lucky" children also attend a school where there is lots of real reading and writing activity. These children go to schools where teachers read to them from newspapers and magazines, as well as children's books, every day. Their teachers have bulletin boards and other displays where newspaper clippings, children's book reviews, and stories written by peers are routinely posted and discussed. The children write real things, and the teacher writes on an overhead projector as they watch her compose and listen to her think out loud about what she is doing. She supports their reading by modeling how good readers puzzle through difficult texts. These children write letters that they send, plays that they perform, reviews that they share, lists of questions for an interview they will really conduct, and lists of things they need to buy for the class party. When lucky children attend these classrooms, their literacy is virtually assured.

> "Just plain reading has been shown to improve student's comprehension, even as measured on standardized tests" (Pearson, 1993, p. 507).

But not all children are so lucky. Many children do not come from homes where they have seen adults constantly engaged in reading and writing and sharing and discussing what they have read or written. They arrive at school with no good idea of what reading and writing are for, much less any well-developed sense of even fundamental concepts about print and its relationship to talk.

Imagine that these children who haven't experienced these real reading and writing activities at home come to a school without classroom libraries and where the school library is inadequately stocked with books and other information resources, understaffed (no one is readily available to help children find the perfect book), and largely inaccessible during and after the school day (only weekly class visits are allowed). In some of these schools children are not allowed to take the library books out of the school! A recent study showed that when schools have many children from low-income families enrolled, these schools most likely fit the latter description (McGill-Franzen & Allington, 1993). The children least likely to have books in their homes are the same children least likely to have books in their schools.

Easy access to books, magazines, and other reading materials is an essential factor in schools where children become readers and writers. The classroom library is especially important for classrooms that work to create readers and writers (Fractor, Woodruff, Martinez, & Teale, 1993). Well-designed classroom libraries work to increase the amount of reading that children do (Morrow, 1991). When classroom libraries are well-designed and attractive and offer a wide range of appropriate books and magazines, children are more likely to use the libraries and read more books. This wider reading results in better readers (as measured on standardized tests). But most classroom libraries (90 percent) are not well designed and well stocked (Fractor et al., 1993). Too often, classrom libraries have too few books, too little planning of the display, and little variety in either the difficulty or the types of books in the collections. In fact, by grade five only 25 percent of the classrooms have libraries!

Schools can create wonderful classroom libraries and school libraries, but it takes time and money. But first, schools need a plan. Depending on the school and the community, the plan might be to develop better access to books over a three-, five-, or ten-year period. But until a plan is developed, access rarely improves. Without easy access to books, children are unlikely to become readers and writers.

CHILDREN NEED TO READ LOTS OF EASY STUFF

Before setting out for a week-long vacation, few adults go to the local university bookstore or library and look for a really difficult book to read. Fewer look for a book on a topic they are uninterested in. Though adults know about the joys of learning, many more select an easy book on an interesting topic than select hard books on topics they care little about. Why would this be so? Why would adults ignore the many difficult books available on arcane topics? Why do so many adults read easy, trashy novels? Why do even well-educated adults lean toward such books?

Children who find learning to read difficult are unlikely to find books in their classroom libraries that they can read comfortably. Classroom libraries are more often stocked with books too difficult for these children to handle. The content-area texts (e.g., science, social studies, math) are too difficult for them. Even the basal-reader material is often beyond their reach. Yet, enormous amounts of easy and interesting reading are absolutely essential to developing effective reading strategies, to say nothing of appropriate attitudes and responses. When children struggle with the material they are reading, they cannot apply the strategies that good readers use and do not develop the habits and attitudes that good readers do.

A variety of features influence the difficulty children experience in reading any given text. Most obvious, perhaps, is the complexity of the language and the familiarity (or unfamiliarity) of the topic. Traditionally, structural readability formulas were used to estimate a text's difficulty. These formulas typically used some measure of average sentence length and vocabulary to arrive at a designation of difficulty (usually provided in grade-level terms). But such formulas were never very accurate, even at estimating by grade level, much less predicting whether a text would be easy or difficult for a particular child. While these formulas could provide rough distinctions between texts, most teachers could estimate text difficulty at least as well.

Just before leaving for home, a student selects a book from the book bin.

If these traditional formulas are of little value, what techniques can replace them? How can difficulty best be determined? One obvious technique is to try the book out on a child. In many instances, simply asking the child to read a few pages silently and then asking his/her opinion will suffice. Some teachers use the five-finger rule—where children count the number of unknown words they encounter. If a child cannot read five words on each page, the book is terribly difficult. We would suggest a two- or three-finger rule instead, or a five-fingers for five pages rule. The problem with this approach is that little leeway is provided for texts that have twenty words per page compared to those that have 200 words per page.

Easy reading material develops fluency and provides practice in using good reading strategies. Most reading, in fact, should be easy reading. In developing classroom collections of books for children's self-selected reading, we recommend that about half the books be those that seem easy to read on engaging topics. These easy books should include a variety of genres and formats with our culture's diversity well represented. There is no reason that classroom collections at different grade levels cannot have overlapping titles since not everyone will necessarily read all the titles each year. Besides, rereading a good book should be encouraged. Nevertheless, so many wonderful children's books are now available that collections can be created without overlapping titles.

Finally, it is important to remember that teachers can make books easier or more difficult (McGill-Franzen 1993). Introducing books to children can involve developing specific knowledge that will ease reading demands. Allowing children to discuss with each other the books they are reading is another potential strategy for easing reading demands. Similarly, working to develop background knowledge, perhaps by linking a historical novel to a current

Johnston (1992) provides a detailed listing of reader and book characteristics, which are summarized below, that influence the difficulty of reading activities:

History—familiarity with the text, the topic, the book language, the genre;

Language—complexity of sentences, repetition, rhythm, patterns in language used;

Vocabulary—familiarity, repetition, decodability, and how many new words appear;

Format—complexity of page layout, quality of illustrations; and

Structure—plot complexity.

Readability formula could not address all of these variables, but they are difficult even for teachers to address. Nonetheless, some books are easier than others for all children, and different books will differ in difficulty depending on which children are attempting to read them. A book's difficulty is a quite personal issue. Each of us will struggle with hard books if we are interested in the material. On the other hand, most adults work to avoid even simple books on topics they consider boring.

social studies unit, eases the reading demands made by books and stories. Reading part or all of the book to children eases the demands the book places on readers when they reread the material. Reading books to children often stimulates their interest in reading the book themselves (much like movies and TV miniseries stimulate adults to read the book version).

■ THERE IS NO ONE BEST WAY TO TEACH CHILDREN TO READ AND WRITE

Because reading and writing are complex and children and teachers are different, there can be no one best way to teach reading and writing. The complexity and variability found in every school means there is not, and can never be, one best way to foster and develop reading and writing in all children. The question of how best to teach children to read and write has been argued, debated, and researched for decades, and the question still has no definitive answer. Of course, searching for one best way is likely wrongheaded. However, throughout this nation's history, four approaches to teaching beginning reading have waxed and waned in popularity. Perhaps we should be looking at these approaches for the answer of how best to develop literacy in all children.

Reading instruction began in this country with an alphabetic approach. Children learned the letters and learned to spell and sound out the letters of words. This alphabetic method came to be called a *phonics approach* and has gone in and out of fashion but has always had advocates who insisted it was the only sensible approach to beginning reading instruction. A variety of instructional materials rely heavily on phonics instruction to teach reading, including such programs as *Distar, Spaulding,* and *Sing, Spell, Read & Write.*

A second but common approach has been the *basal reader approach.* All basals include instruction in phonics of some kind. Some basals offer heavy doses of phonics instruction, but most basal programs begin with sight words from predictable stories and place more emphasis on comprehension than on phonics. While basals differ in their emphasis, they all offer stories of gradually increasing difficulty and an emphasis on teacher-guided reading of generally shorter selections. The more recent basals offer original children's literature, both full and excerpted selections, rather than the specially written stories that long dominated those series.

Throughout the years, many reading experts have advocated a *trade-book approach,* for teaching reading. In the 1960s, Jeanette Veatch (1959) popularized what she called an "individualized reading" approach. This approach emphasizes children selecting books they want to read and teachers conferencing with them to provide individual help when needed. In the late eighties, the trade-book approach made a comeback as part of the larger whole language movement.

A fourth approach, which has been more widely used in England, Australia, and other countries, also returned to U.S. classrooms in the late eighties. This *language experience/writing approach* is based on the premise that the easiest material for children to read is their own writing and that of their classmates. In this approach, then, the stories that children themselves compose, orally or in writing, provide the primary reading materials.

Throughout the years, these four major approaches—phonics, basal, trade-book, language experience/writing—have been in and out of favor. Generally, once one approach has dominated long enough for educators to recognize its shortcomings, a different approach with different shortcomings replaces it. The question of which method is best cannot be answered because it is the wrong question. Each method has undeniable strengths.

Phonics instruction is clearly important because one big task of beginning readers is figuring out how our alphabetic language works. Adams (1990) reviewed decades of research and concluded that most children can decipher the letter-sound system on their own, but directly teaching this system speeds literacy acquisition. The need for some explicit decoding strategies instruction is particularly clear for at-risk children who have had limited exposure to reading and writing and have had fewer opportunities to figure out how our alphabetic system works.

Basal instruction gives teachers multiple copies of reading material that they can use to guide children's comprehension and strategy development. The literature selections found in basal readers are organized by estimating their difficulty with increasingly complex selections across the elementary grades. Because basals contain a wide variety of all types of literature, children are exposed to many genres, authors, topics, and cultures they might miss if all their reading was self-selected. In addition, basals outline the major goals for each year and provide an organized curricular plan for accomplishing those goals with ways of evaluating whether students are meeting those goals.

The reading of real books is the ultimate aim of reading instruction, but that aim has often taken a backseat to phonics and basal instruction. Children have been expected to "read when they finished their work" or "read at home." Of course, children who came from homes where books were available and reading was valued were much more likely to engage in real reading than children whose homes lacked these advantages. Better readers were also more likely to complete the assigned work and have time remaining to read self-selected tradebooks. The reemergence of trade-book approach reminds us that the purpose of learning to read is to read real books. Children who read real books understand why they are learning to read and what reading really is.

Writing is an approach to reading that lets children figure out reading "from the inside out." As children write, they spell words they later see and recognize in their reading. Even when they can't spell a word perfectly, they try to "sound spell" it and actually put to use whatever letter-sound knowledge they have learned. Children who write are more avid and sensitive readers. Reading is a source of writing ideas and information. Reading also provides the writer with models of various writing styles. Like reading real books, writing is an authentic activity, and children who write become more fluent in reading (Tierney & Shanahan, 1991).

I Lik MAFNS,

The kindergarten student who wrote this ("I like muffins") demonstrates an emerging understanding of sounds and letters and how speech can be represented by print. The most common labels for this emergent writing is *invented spelling*. However, we do not often use that terminology, preferring instead to label such efforts *sound spelling*. Our reasoning for this is that sound spelling better represents what children do when they first begin to develop an understanding of how talk gets written down— they try to represent the sounds they hear with the letters they know.

In the 1960s, the federal government spent hundreds of thousands of dollars to find out what the best approach to beginning reading really was. Data were collected from first- and second-grade classrooms around the country that used a variety of approaches to beginning reading. The study results were inconclusive. Virtually every approach had some good results and some poor results. How well teachers carried out an approach seemed to be the major determinant of how well an approach worked. Some teachers used what the researchers called "combination approaches," such as language experience and basal or phonics and literature or literature and writing. The study concluded that, in general, combination approaches worked better than any single approach (Bond & Dykstra, 1967). Adams (1990) also concluded that children—especially at-risk children—need a rich variety of reading and writing experiences as well as some direct instruction in letter-sound patterns.

The question to be asked is not, Which approach? but rather, How can we organize classrooms so that we can "have it all"? The great debate still rages because each argument has at least some truth. To learn to read, children must read real books. Children who write become better writers and better readers. English is an alphabetic language, and to read and spell the thousands of words necessary for fluent reading and writing, children must figure out the letter-sound relationships. Finally, basal readers provide multiple copies of varied literature that gradually increases in difficulty and an organized curricular plan that teachers can use to instruct and assess progress.

In addition to support for a multifaceted approach to reading instruction, there is another compelling reason for not limiting our instruction to one approach. Think about your family or a family you know well with two or more children. Have you noticed and heard others remark on "how different the children are"? One child must have a clearly defined routine and set of rules, while the other child does better if allowed more flexibility and self-determination. One child is neat; the other a slob. One child has a restless, creative, problem-solving mind and personality. The other child scores better on standardized tests but is not particularly creative.

Not only do children bring to school huge differences in the amount of reading/writing experiences they have had, but they also come with their own "personalities." The more common term for personalities in educational jargon is "learning styles." Some commercialized programs are based on the idea that you can determine a child's style with a paper-and-pencil test and then teach to that style. Though children clearly do have differences in how they learn best, these differences are not easily categorized into four, or six, or nine styles and such differences have not proved to be measured validly—particularly on paper-and-pencil tests. Educators disagree about learning styles and how the concept is used in schools (Johnston & Allington, 1991). To avoid getting into the "styles debate" but still to acknowledge the unarguable truth that not all children learn in exactly the same way, we have chosen to discuss the different "personalities" of children.

Consider the four reading approaches described earlier and think about the different personalities of the children in your school. Some children appreciate the structure of basal readers. They know exactly what they are going to read and what to do after they read it. Skills and strategies are introduced and reviewed in predictable, logical order. Some children even take pleasure in completing each story and activity page and noting the visible signs of their progress.

This same order and predictability that allows some children to thrive in basal approaches can be a turnoff to children with other personalities. "Reading is always the same," they say. "You talk about what you are going to read, learn some new words, read the story, and do a page in your journal or workbook! Boring!" These adventuresome types like variety—in what they read, when they read it, and what they do before and after reading. Put these children in a literature-based approach with an emphasis on self-selection and varied ways of sharing and they are more apt to become readers.

To some children, their own ideas and imaginations are much more interesting than anything some "faraway" author might have written. These children love to "express themselves." They love to talk and tell stories and be the center of attention. These expressive children also love to write, and as they write, they use and learn words that they then read. The writing personalities will read—but for them, reading is a means, not an end. Reading is one of their sources for ideas about which they can write!

Likewise, some children are better at learning and using letter-sound relationships. They have "an ear" for sounds—much like the ear some have for music. Other children labor over the letters and sounds and aren't able to blend sounds they know into words they know.

One major reason for providing a combination approach to literacy is the different personalities children bring with them into our schools. While it is not possible to determine clearly which children will learn best with which approaches, it is clear that when a teacher provides alternative routes to the goal of literacy, more children will find a route to take them there. Many children are at-risk for failure in our schools because their personalities and the approach taken to instruction do not match. Research, observation, and common sense tell us that no single approach will succeed in teaching all children (Solsken, 1994).

IT TAKES TIME TO TEACH AND LEARN TO READ

It should come as no surprise that children who start school behind their peers often do not catch up in our classrooms today. It should not be surprising, especially if these children attend school for about the same number of hours, for the same number of days, and in the same size classes as the children who began school ahead of them. We can accelerate literacy learning, but teaching and learning take time. Children who come to school with hundreds or thousands of hours of home and preschool experiences with books, stories, and print are way ahead of many less fortunate children. We cannot expect these limited-experience children to catch up to those who arrive with substantially more experience without expanding the amount of instructional time we make available to them.

But most schools offer a standard schedule to all children and often actually organize instruction so that the lowest-achieving children are scheduled for the smallest amounts of reading and writing instruction and opportunity (Allington, 1991). It is important to reorganize schools, classrooms, and special programs in ways that expand children's opportunities to read and write to enhance their achievement. We know that increasing the amount of time children spend actually reading and writing in and out of school affects reading and writing development in positive ways. We know that increasing children's access to good books increases the time they spend reading in and out of school and accelerates reading development. In other words, when teachers have easy access to books, they allocate more time for reading those books. When children have easy access to books in classrooms, they are more likely to spend time reading in school and more likely to take those books home to read.

> Even small amounts of time add up. Finding just 12 additional minutes each day creates an additional hour each week of time for reading and writing activities. That weekly hour results in a day of reading each month and about two weeks' worth of steady reading and writing each year.

When books and magazines are not in ready supply in classrooms, teachers and students receive powerful messages about what is and is not important. When school's have no general guidelines about how much time to allocate to reading and writing instruction, allocations can be expected to vary from classroom to classroom. While time allocated to reading and writing lessons is a very crude benchmark for evaluating any instructional program, it is absolutely essential that teachers have time to teach and children have time to read and write during the school day. Fielding and Pearson (1994) recommend that classroom reading instructional blocks be organized so that children spend more time actually reading than they do learning about reading or talking and writing about completed reading assignments.

We have learned much about the relationship between time and learning, and much of what we have learned has yet to be put into widespread practice. Finding or creating additional time for reading and writing activity is a critical need if all children are to become proficient readers and writers. Finding or creating more time for reading and writing instruction and practice in the earliest grades must become a priority if we are to address adequately the needs of at-risk children. As with most things in life, the old adage that a stitch in time saves nine also holds true for education.

In discussing the potential of early intervention, Slavin (1993) offers a parable about a town with a serious health problem. It seems the water supply was contaminated, causing about one-third of the children to contract typhoid or other diseases. It cost the town millions in medical care for these children. Many required long-term care, and even after treatment, many children still suffered long-term negative health consequences. One day the town engineer proposed installing a water treatment plant that would have prevented virtually all the contamination and associated illnesses. The mayor and town council, however, objected that the proposed plant was too expensive. When the engineer noted the enormous but preventable costs now incurred from the contaminated water, the town officials responded by arguing that most children were not sick, and their current plan precisely targeted the funds to those children who needed them. Besides, if they were to build the plant little money would be left to treat children who had the diseases. Ultimately, the town officials decided not to build the water treatment plant—a foolish decision decided from a short-term economic position.

In many ways, current educational policy reflects the same type of thinking. Enormous amounts of money are allocated and spent to provide remedial services, special education services, drop-out programs, attendance improvement efforts, and so on. Beyond the school, society spends substantial amounts of money to support those adults who were unsuccessful while in school. Hardly any money is allocated to either preschool projects that might expand the time available for learning for at-risk children. Currently, middle-class children are three times as likely to attend preschool than their disadvantaged peers and thus have their advantage enhanced. Fewer than half of all at-risk children have any preschool experience before attending kindergarten (Slavin, Karweit, & Wasik, 1993).

Few at-risk children participate in prevention or early school intervention efforts even though good evidence supports expanding time to learn in these ways. Few schools offer even occasional educational programs for four-year-olds, few have family literacy programs for young parents, and few allow parents of preschool-aged children to borrow books from the school library. This is not because everyone believes that such efforts might fail to prevent at least some of the early school difficulties that some children face. Most people we have talked with about these ideas seem to think they make sense. But such prevention efforts are not available in most schools.

A similar situation exists with summer school as one possible early intervention that would expand instructional time for children who began school with few book, story, or print experiences. It is not that most everyone believes that a well-designed summer school intervention for at-risk kindergarten and first-grade children would have little effect on learning to read. In fact, most teachers, administrators, and supervisors we have talked with feel that summer school would help—and help some children enormously. But like the water treatment facility, summer school as a preventative is usually seen as too expensive.

It takes time to teach and time to learn. Some children will always need more time. But the earlier we intervene with high-quality instruction, the less time is needed to resolve the reading difficulty. The current situation must change if all children are to learn to read and write alongside their peers.

WE CAN HELP EVERY CHILD BECOME A READER AND WRITER

One last finding that will permeate virtually every section of this book must be explored in concluding this chapter—we can teach all children to read and write. For too long our schools have operated from a belief that only some children would become readers and writers. In many cases, this belief system resulted in school programs that delivered just this result. But recent research (Allington, 1991; Cunningham & Allington, 1994; Johnston & Allington, 1991; Slavin et al., 1993) shows quite convincingly that our past does not have to dictate our future. Powerful demonstrations show that by providing access to consistently high-quality instruction, especially in the classroom, we can literally eliminate the traditional "bottom group." Other convincing evidence shows that teachers, administrators, and supervisors find it almost impossible to plan educational programs that contradict their professional beliefs. Thus, the dilemma: As long as we believe that some children will never be readers and writers, we will fail to create schools that fulfill the potential of all children to become readers and writers.

Unfortunately, acceptance of the inevitability of student failure seems typically strongest in schools where many children currently fail. Children are least successful in schools where teachers lack confidence in their own efforts to help children become readers and writers. In these schools, initiating discussion about reorganizing so that all children are successful is often difficult. Of course, society also offers these schools the fewest resources in the face of the most compelling needs (Kozol, 1991).

The key point to be understood is that good evidence shows that schools can organize instruction so that virtually all children can learn to read and write alongside their peers. Children who begin school with few book, story, and print experiences can speed their literacy development and "catch up" with more advantaged peers. But to achieve such outcomes means providing some children with access to larger amounts of higher quality instruction and supplying more actual chances to read and write. Unfortunately, many current instructional programs simply slow the instructional pace for children experiencing difficulty—virtually ensuring they will always be "behind."

SUMMARY

Much has been learned about how children learn to read and write and about how to support successful classroom literacy instruction. Reading and writing are thoughtful, meaningful activities in the real world. Our reading and writing in schools has, historically, not been best described as thoughtful. Instead, the words *trivial, routine,* and even *boring* have more often been used in discussing the reading and writing done in school. (Teachers always banned the one purposeful writing activity, writing notes to friends.) But the goals society has set for our schools have changed, dramatically in some areas, and more thoughtful, or critical, literacy has been called for. Developing basic, or functional, literacy is no longer the charge given schools. Instead, the new literacy standard that has been set for all students is one that focuses on children's thinking before, during, and after reading and writing activities.

It is essential that children have many opportunities to read and write, especially school-day opportunities to read comfortable materials they have chosen and to discuss them with peers. To accomplish this requires greater access to a wider variety of appropriate reading material beyond the basal reader. It also requires time be available every day in every classroom to engage in reading and writing activities. Many classrooms already offer substantially greater reading and writing opportunities than were available just a few years ago, but too often children's actual opportunities to read and write in school are enormously restricted.

Children also need models, explanations, and demonstrations of the powerful thinking strategies that skilled readers and writers use. It is not sufficient that teachers assign, interrogate, and correct students. The potential of teaching routines such as "think-alouds," "public writing/thinking," or personalized conferencing after reading or writing are enormous but generally underused.

For too long the quest has been focused on discovering the one best way to teach reading and writing. We believe that there can be no such approach. Learning to read and write is a complex activity. Children differ, teachers differ, and communities differ, and each work to preclude the discovery of any single best way to develop literacy. Different children, at different stages of development, at different times, in different schools, taught by different teachers, prosper and develop their literacy. Shift any one of these variables and the same children may flounder. What is needed to ensure that all children acquire reading and writing proficiency is a balanced instructional effort that takes advantage of the strengths of the four historically recurring patterns of classroom literacy instruction and the recent knowledge of how children learn to literate.

The literacy goals for our elementary schools have changed, and classrooms must change to meet these new literacy standards. Thoughtful literacy as shown through children's selections of reading materials, discussions of their reading, their writing, and their responses to the reading and writing of their peers is the new literacy goal. If we expect children to achieve this thoughtful literacy, we must change classroom curriculum and instruction in many ways. As schools change to meet the new goal, roles will change and so too will the organization of the school day and the school year.

Who Does What?

A ccording to the National Center for Educational Statistics (NCES), the number of adults working in elementary schools has doubled since 1960! At the same time, class size has not changed dramatically. These contradictory trends can be explained by understanding the substantial growth in the specialists' roles in schools today (Allington, 1994). In 1960, few schools employed reading teachers, learning disabilities teachers, speech and language teachers, art teachers, physical education teachers, bilingual teachers, gifted and talented teachers, and so on. In addition, few schools had librarians (because few had libraries), psychologists, counselors, or social workers on staff. Few schools had assistant principals. As curriculum expanded, elementary schools added more special content-area teachers. As state and federal programs for at-risk children expanded, schools added more special teachers and more paraprofessionals. In special education programs alone, the number of aides has increased from 25,000 to over 200,000 in the past 25 years (Blalock, 1991).

Today, in many elementary schools with high concentrations of low-income children, there are as many special teachers and special staff members as there are classroom teachers. When the paraprofessional staff is considered, there are often more adults who are not classroom teachers than there are classroom teachers! According to recent NCES data, more than half the adults working in the average school today are not classroom teachers. Whenever a school begins to consider reorganizing to better meet the needs of at-risk children, the roles and responsibilities of all professional and paraprofessional staff must be considered.

In this chapter, we explore the roles and responsibilities of the various professional and paraprofessional staff members typically found in elementary schools today. We begin with classroom teachers because we believe that classroom teachers play the critical role in developing the literacy of all children. While parents, special teachers, and paraprofessionals can play important roles, the classroom teacher ultimately has the greatest opportunity to develop readers and writers. In actuality, the roles that other adults play are simply supporting roles to classroom instruction. The traditional roles of the other adults involved with children must also change in many schools. We will discuss some potentially new roles for these adults as we help you reconsider instructional programs.

THE CRITICAL NATURE OF CLASSROOM TEACHERS

Some children come to schools at high risk for failure and succeed. Every teacher knows children who succeeded despite little background knowledge or home support. Some schools and teachers have an astonishingly high number of these "unexpected" successes.

While we must recognize that children's homes and backgrounds influence failure or success, we must also realize that what happens in classrooms minute by minute, day after day, determines how much will be learned by how many children.

As classroom and remedial reading teachers, college professors, and teacher consultants, we have observed, researched, discussed, and worried about children at high risk for reading failure for a combined 50 years. Over those years, we have observed schools where, year after year, children at high risk for failure "beat the odds" and learned to read and write. At first, we thought some strange, mysterious, even "mystical" variable must be at work in these sites. Ultimately, we concluded that schools with success in teaching at-risk children had enormously effective classroom instruction. In these schools, it was not the "super specialist" teacher who was producing the excellent results, nor was it just a new curriculum or a new parent-training component. In these schools, classroom teachers provided large amounts of high-quality literacy instruction. Although special staff members often supported classroom teachers, the high-quality classroom instruction primarily produced the high levels of student achievement. Research supports our observations about schools that achieve success with large numbers of at-risk children. High-quality classroom instruction is the critical variable in literacy development, and there are many common features of that instruction (Bond & Dykstra, 1967; Goodlad, 1983).

While much has been written about "effective schools," attempts to create effective schools from less effective ones have been largely disappointing. Evidence that the "effective schools" movement of the last decade actually created many effective schools (Rowan, 1990) is limited. It seems that the "effective schools" effort may have overlooked a critical and central aspect of schools, especially elementary schools. That is, schools are collections of classrooms—classrooms where, usually, a single teacher and stable group of children meet and interact for about five hours each day. No school can be effective unless the curriculum and instruction offered in the classrooms is effective. In our own work, we have found many more effective classroom teachers than effective schools. Some schools, however, have a larger number of effective classroom teachers than do others. When most classroom teachers are effective, the school appears effective. When many classroom teachers are ineffective, the school appears ineffective.

Though this may seem obvious, we think the implications are important. For too long our efforts in improving school effectiveness have been focused everywhere but on the classroom teacher. Schools have hired specialist teachers; purchased new curriculum materials; added social workers; created discipline, attendance, and homework policies; attempted to entice parental involvement; and mandated more and more testing. In most schools it is difficult to find any major effort or expenditure targeted at improving classroom teachers' instruction.

Classroom teachers have the opportunity to know children better than any other member of a school staff, but often classroom teachers' expertise about the children they teach has not been valued. Much lack of recognition of the importance of classroom teachers' role can be traced to a distinct federal policy of creating an ever-expanding "second system" of specialist teachers and professional staff. Before 1960, and the Great Society programs, including the Elementary and Secondary Education Act of 1965 (ESEA), most elementary schools had few specialist teachers, paraprofessionals, or specialized staff. Beginning with

ESEA and the hiring of remedial reading specialists, through the Education of Handicapped Children Act of 1975 and the hiring of more special education teachers, and to the more recent dropout prevention programs, an era evolved in which most new education dollars went to fund the "second system." Recent studies show the impact most dramatically in urban school systems where today only about one-quarter to one-half of the educational funds go to support classroom instruction—half to three-quarters of the money now supports administration, supervision, and special programs (Fischer, 1990; Harp, 1993).

Recently, Al Shanker, president of the American Federation of Teachers, commented on how General Motors managed to restructure its traditional factory model to produce the award-winning Saturn automobile (*The New York Times,* January 24, 1993, p. 7). GM offered 136 workers from its plants about 400 hours of training within a few months of the opening of the new Saturn manufacturing plant, splitting their hours between classroom and on-the-job training. Every other employee received, and continues to receive, 92 hours of training each year! Over 600 training courses are available, and new courses are developed as the product or the manufacturing process changes. Shanker notes, "Imagine what a training program like this would do for people trying to restructure schools. . . . It is ironic that a bunch of people whose business is building cars understand so well the importance of educating their employees whereas people in education seem to assume that teachers will be able to step right into a new way of doing things with little or no help."

Most educational reform efforts have also been marked by a search for "the one best way" to teach. Curriculum is debated endlessly while what seem to be even more critical elements of schools are largely ignored. The evidence indicates that there is no one best way to teach and that curriculum plans and materials are often overvalued. Not only children differ as learners but so do teachers. In the quest for the "one best way" the obvious has often been ignored—that teachers and children do vary in their preferences, dispositions, values, and efforts. Perhaps it is finally time to think about reducing the risks that children face by recognizing, even celebrating, diversity not only among children but among their teachers also.

Classroom teachers are important, and effective classroom literacy instruction cannot be produced from a single master plan that all teachers are mandated to follow. Classroom teachers need support more often than mandates. Classroom teachers need to be intimately involved in planning school programs and resource allocations. Classroom teachers need the opportunity to work and talk collaboratively about their work with their peers. But powerless teachers do not talk about their work and working conditions if only because such talk is either fruitless, because no one in power is listening, or because it is dangerous since someone in power is eavesdropping. The point that needs to be understood is that many efforts to change schools fail because teachers are important if change is to occur and few teachers actually change simply because change is mandated. Chapter 5 explores in depth the issues of how effective change in classroom instruction can be accomplished.

Catherine Snow and her colleagues have recently provided dramatic evidence of the importance of classroom teachers in developing literacy for at-risk children. In their book, *Unfulfilled Expectations* (Harvard University Press, 1990), they report on a naturalistic study of schools serving children from low-income families. The research team studied the impact of classrooms and home environments on childrens' learning. The table below summarizes the impact of two or more years of consistently high support classroom instruction, a mixed pattern of classroom support, and the effects of placement in low support classrooms for two or more years.

Percentage of Children Who Are Successful with Varying Levels of Home and Classroom Support		
	High Home Support	Low Home Support
Consistent High-Classroom Support	100%	100%
Mixed Classroom Support	100%	25%
Consistent Low-Classroom Support	60%	0%

The findings illustrate the enormous impact of access to consistently high-quality classroom instruction. Anything less than consistently high-quality classroom instruction had dramatically negative impacts on the achievement of children from homes where parents did not provide high levels of home literacy support.

RETHINKING THE "SECOND SYSTEM"

Over the past 25 years, American elementary schools have added and expanded the "second system" of special programs, primarily to try to meet the needs of at-risk children—those children who arrived at school with few experiences with books, stories, or print. However, the development of the second system has used up enormous amounts of money that we could use to fund other efforts or programs. But not just the fiscal costs need examination (Allington, 1994).

Currently, "second system" programs may undermine the critical role classroom teachers play in the futures of at-risk children. For 25 years, classroom teachers have been led to believe that they were ill-equipped to teach at-risk children. Is it any wonder then that many classroom teachers feel a limited sense of professional responsibility for teaching at-risk children in their classroom?

Concerns about the continuing expansion of the "second system," reports of fragmentation, interference, reduced accountability, and limited effects on academic achievement have forced federal education officials to begin to rethink the roles that federal funds might play in addressing the educational needs of handicapped and disadvantaged students (LeTendre, 1991). These two shifts are summed up in the words *collaboration* and *inclusion*. In the federal Title 1 program, this push for collaboration began in the mid-1980s with the call for program coordination with the core curriculum and an emphasis on delivery of Title 1 remediation in the classroom (Johnston, Allington, & Afflerbach, 1985). In special education there has been a more recent emphasis on providing services in the regular classroom environment and a shift to consulting with classroom teachers in an attempt to support modifications to classroom instruction. This "inclusionary" education emphasis is buttressed by increasing evidence that handicapped children's achievement rises with increased integration with no negative effects on other children's achievement (Epps & Tindal, 1987; Gelzheiser, Meyers, & Pruzek, 1992; Sharpe, York, & Knight, 1994). In addition, the Americans with Disabilities Act of 1990 requires that all handicapped individuals, including children, have the right to participate fully in all aspects of American society without discrimination (including, it is argued, instruction in regular classrooms in the neighborhood school).

We expect that federal education programs will actually accelerate these trends over the next few years. In fact, there is every reason to believe that the future will see fewer specialist teachers and staff in schools and greater popularity for alternatives to the traditional models. In the meantime, serious issues need to be addressed about the design and delivery of instruction for children who participate in one or more of these programs (Schrag, 1993).

If classroom teachers are to accept professional responsibility for teaching at-risk readers in their classrooms, school and district policies and practices that support their involvement and their efforts will need to be developed. Schools need to create a general sense that special programs are part of a unified plan of action addressing the needs of at-risk readers. Too often, special teachers and special programs have simply existed in a school but were not really part of the school. Often these special personnel were not supervised by a building administrator. Often, it was neither the administrator nor the classroom teachers who scheduled special teachers' work with children but someone at a district special programs office. In some cases, special program personnel did not attend building staff meetings nor did they participate in staff development activities with classroom teachers. In too many cases, school districts seemed to have engaged in planning classroom and special-program curriculum and instruction as wholly separate entities. In these situations, it is not surprising that classroom teachers felt little involvement with special programs and little responsibility for teaching the students who participated in those programs. Under such circumstances, it is not surprising that administrators and teachers often feel special programs are not doing very well at meeting the needs of children or teachers.

SHARING AND COLLABORATING

To create schools that work for at-risk readers, we need to create a stronger sense of shared responsibility. Shared responsibility is unlikely in schools where classroom and special program teachers share little knowledge of each other's instructional practices. When two teachers working with the same children have little shared knowledge of each other's instruction, it is unlikely that the children are participating in the most coherent and supportive instructional environment.

Developing shared knowledge of instructional practices in classroom and specialist teachers is a good starting point for enhancing a sense of shared responsibility. Collaborative development of shared goals may be the critically important activity, especially in schools with large numbers of special program students (Allington & Broikou, 1988).

Several activities can be used to initiate developing shared knowledge and to foster collaboration between classroom teachers and specialists. First, involve all teachers in staff meetings. Special-program personnel cannot be expected to view themselves as part of a team effort if they are routinely excluded from the meetings of the regular education staff. Second, schedule shared staff development sessions. Too often, special-program teachers attend separate workshops, often in other buildings, during staff development days. While there will be times when special-program staff need to gather for informational and training sessions particularly targeted to their needs, generally staff development must include all professional staff members at the school. It may be useful to schedule special-program staff presentations of their programs during staff meetings or staff-development days. Similarly, special-program staff often benefit from sessions offered by classroom teachers on their instructional programs.

It may be easiest to consider the extent of coordination and collaboration as a continuum. Assess each special instructional program in your school (and perhaps art and music as well) and place each program at the appropriate point on the continuum below.

| ——————— | ——————— | ——————— | ——————— | ——————— |

| No collab- oration, pull-out | A rare example of collaboration | Regular collaboration among some teachers, some in-class teaming | General collaboration much in-class teaming | Everyone works together, in- class teaming most common |

A second set of activities involves getting special-program staff into classrooms more often, even if for brief periods. For instance, when special-program staff come to the classroom to pick up children that participate in their pull-out instruction, two immediate benefits are gained. First, special-program teachers acquire more information about the classroom instruction even from brief visits (30 seconds twice a day). Just coming into the room offers the chance to get a sense of the common kinds of reading and language arts activities. Likewise, these visits provide glimpses of the classroom environment and organization. Second, this strategy of picking children up at their classrooms tends to reduce the amount of transition time spent in the special program classroom. We find children are engaged in academic work more quickly after their walk with the specialist to the classroom, perhaps because some social talk occurs during this time. Thus, picking up children at their classroom provides double benefits.

Another activity that fosters shared knowledge is planning by classroom and special-program teachers. This does not have to be a formal and scheduled activity to be effective. For instance, using a traveling notebook seems to work reasonably well to foster collaboration. The notebook can be just a simple spiral-bound pad with a string run through the spiral binding and looped over a child's neck when leaving for special-program instruction. The classroom teacher simply writes in the notebook the classroom material and pages being used during the lesson that day. In addition, the classroom teacher might jot a comment about the child's performance (e.g., *Tim had difficulty following the story line*) or a particular skill or strategy the teacher feels needs additional attention (e.g., *Tim has difficulty with long words*). The special-program teacher jots notes back to the classroom teacher (*We worked on a Making Big Words activity today*) and returns the notebook with the child after their instructional session. The point is that the notes do not have to be long or complicated, especially if they are written regularly.

A fourth activity is sharing lesson plans. In this case, the classroom teacher shares a copy of his or her lesson plan for reading and language arts with the special program teacher, who uses that as one source of information in planning instruction. Even better than simply sharing the plans is to sit together and create jointly the lessons to be offered in both settings. Of course, this requires time for both teachers to meet, but in most schools such time is available before and after the school day. However, if special-program teachers work with children from many classrooms, the task becomes more complicated.

A fifth strategy to foster collaboration is to create grade-level or grade-cluster teams made up of classroom teachers and specialists. For instance, if the K–2 teachers were a single team that met regularly to share instructional planning and small group discussions of strategies for better addressing the needs of at-risk children, then assigning several special teachers to the team serves a number of purposes. Specialist teachers have the opportunity to listen and learn from classroom teachers and vice versa. As they listen, both groups develop greater shared knowledge and an expanded repertoire of instructional modifications. The specialists assigned to the team would work with children from the classrooms of other team members.

At the Park Terrace Elementary School (New York), teams of classroom teachers meet every morning for about 35 minutes before children arrive. Specialist teachers attend these meetings (as well as other team meetings focused just on targeted children) and work with classroom teachers to address flexibly how best to modify instruction to meet the needs of at-risk children. The design of remedial and special-education services is constantly changing at the school as both classroom and specialist teachers work continually to adapt the intervention to best meet the needs of the students served. But none of this could happen without the collaboration that team membership provides.

A final strategy being used more frequently is having special-program teachers provide their instructional support in the regular classroom rather than in a location down the hall. One goal of "in-class" instructional support is to improve classroom instruction through developing shared knowledge and creating more coherent instructional interventions. In addition, participating students should lose less instructional time in transition from one setting to another.

In-class instructional support, whether remediation or special education, produces achievement gains at least as large as pull-out instruction without having a negative impact on the achievement of other students in the room (Gelzheiser, Meyers, & Pruzek, 1992; Sharpe, York, & Knight, 1994). But proponents argue more often from moral perspective: Segregating at-risk children from their peers is wrong unless large benefits to the children can be demonstrated and such benefits have not usually been reported.

In our view, the critical issue is providing children with access to high-quality instruction rather than the issue of location. But in-class, collaborative instructional models focused on enhancing achievement in the core curriculum of the classroom do, in fact, seem to offer the greatest promise for providing high-quality instruction (and accumulating evidence of their effectiveness). Nonetheless, we see variety in the design of instructional support for at-risk children as a simple necessity. We would have schools offer instructional support that provided flexibility in intensity, location, schedule, emphasis, and so on. No single program design can possibly be expected to meet the needs of all children. That said, we emphasize creating responsive, in-class support, collaboratively planned and offered by classroom and special teachers.

Select a classroom and list below the number of children who participate in some special instructional program. For how many of these programs do the teachers (classroom and special program) exhibit high levels of shared knowledge? What can be done to increase both shared knowledge and collaboration? Can we reduce the number of special programs serving the children at risk in each classroom?

Remedial Reading	Resource Room	Speech
1. _____	1. _____	1. _____
2. _____	2. _____	2. _____
3. _____	3. _____	3. _____

Remedial Math	Counseling/Social Work	Other
1. _____	1. _____	1. _____
2. _____	2. _____	2. _____
3. _____	3. _____	3. _____

How many special teachers work with children from this room?_____
How many children leave the room for part of the day?   _____
How many hours each day are *all* children in the room?   _____

OTHER PROFESSIONAL STAFF IN ELEMENTARY SCHOOLS

Remember the basic premise: The usefulness of other professional staff in an elementary school is best measured by the impact they have on enhancing the quality of classroom instruction. Examining the roles of other staff from this premise provides a substantially different view of their functions and utility.

Bilingual/ESL Teachers

Providing instructional support, especially for literacy learning, is critical when children are acquiring English language proficiency. The fundamental goal of such support is to develop English proficiency as quickly as possible so that the child can prosper in the classroom where English is spoken. Developing native language literacy proficiency (e.g., reading and writing in Spanish) is the initial goal in some programs. Even in these programs, however, developing English language literacy is an ultimate goal (developing bilingual proficiency in English and the native language is the goal).

So how might bilingual/ESL teachers improve the instruction offered in elementary school classrooms? First, they need to be in those classrooms. Similar to the situation of other specialist teachers, bilingual/ESL teachers simply cannot operate solely from separate classrooms. Ideally, they, too, become classroom-based consulting teachers who work with classroom teachers to improve their teaching of second language or bilingual children and work with the children on their classroom tasks.

At the Beall Elementary School in El Paso, Texas, the bilingual teachers operate as classroom teachers and teach in Spanish and English and children learn to read in both languages almost simultaneously. Some classroom teachers at Beall are not proficiently bilingual themselves and offer most instruction in English (to students who exhibit dominant English language proficiency or whose parents wish an English-dominant program). However, the teachers meet as grade-level teams without regard to classroom language. Bilingual teachers have translated English big books into Spanish and translated Spanish big books into English. Both versions of these books are shared in all classes. The bilingual teachers share their expertise concerning problems that appear for Spanish-language speakers in the planned curriculum. They offer advice and support for the monolingual teachers in the grade-level team meetings.

Bailey's Elementary School is a magnet school in Fairfax County, Virginia. A large percentage of their children do not speak English as their first language, with the largest proportion of children speaking Spanish. Instruction at Bailey's is arranged around conceptual units. Units of instruction are organized around large concepts such as change, communication, or habitats. Within each unit, children explore a variety of topics depending on the curriculum demands and the children's interests. In the change unit, for example, second graders pursued the science topic of dinosaurs and fossils along with the social studies topic of families, communities, and family histories.

For half of each day, the classroom teacher teaches the language arts to the whole class together, integrating as much as possible around the unit topic. This instruction is carried out in English. For the other half of the day, the classroom teacher offers instruction in science, health, and math, again integrating as much as possible. During the science, health, and math half of the day, a bilingual teacher takes six to seven children from each of three second-grade classrooms and does the same science, health, and math content with them in Spanish. This Spanish immersion group includes some native Spanish speakers as well as some native English speakers whose parents want them to become bilingual and choose to have them participate in the half-day Spanish instruction.

This arrangement has many advantages. The unit-topic integration is one of the major curriculum adaptations recommended for schools containing large portion of children whose first language is not English (Chamot & O'Malley, 1994). Children appear to develop fluency in English speaking, listening, reading, and writing when their instruction is intensively focused on one topic through which they can learn vocabulary and increase their background knowledge. By focusing on the same topic in both Spanish and English, children from both native languages can transfer whatever prior knowledge they have. Including native English speakers in the Spanish half of the day allows the native Spanish-speaking children to help translate as needed. These native English-speaking friends can return the favor for the native Spanish speakers in the English immersion half of the day. Using science, health, and math as the content of instruction during the Spanish half of the day ensures that children whose native language is Spanish do not fall behind in this content as they acquire English.

We think these schools offer incredibly powerful models for providing high-quality instruction and using the talents of all children regardless of the language they come to school with. In both cases, the bilingual education teachers enhance the the quality of classroom instruction and enhance the learning of many children beyond those targeted for special assistance.

Teachers of the Gifted and Talented

Many schools created gifted and talented programs in the same model as the special education and remedial programs—hiring a special teacher who pulled selected children from their classrooms a few times each week to work on projects wholly unrelated to classroom lessons. The popularity of this model has declined but is still in use in some locales. A more powerful alternative that has become popular involves shifting the focus away from working with a small group of children identified on the basis of some standardized test score to a consultative model with a more invitational approach to participation.

It is becoming more common today to find gifted and talented teachers working with classroom teachers to develop and extend study of a core curriculum topic for interested students. Gardner's (1993) notion of "multiple intelligences" has also been influential in reshaping the nature of such programs. In this case the focus has shifted away from narrowly defined academic skills to a broader view of intelligence that includes artistic, musical, movement, atheletic, verbal, and performance skills as components of intellectual competence. When the gifted and talented teacher works alongside the classroom teacher to tailor curriculum demands and activities to extend the learning of selected students, improved classroom instruction is more likely to occur.

In a recent book, *Playing Favorites: Gifted Education and the Disruption of Community,* Mara Sapon-Shevin (SUNY Press, 1994) argues that gifted education programs disrupt the classroom community, limit classroom teachers' willingness to meet individual needs, and impair the creation of a climate of inclusion and acceptance of differences in humankind. She maps the development of an alternative to the traditional segregationist model of gifted education.

On the other hand, some schools have elected to invest funds in strengthening the classroom instruction so that all students, but especially those identified as gifted, are better served. For instance, in lieu of investing in another specialist teacher salary (and associated fringe benefits), a school might take the roughly $50,000 annual cost and invest in both additional materials and professional development activities. In an elementary school with 20 classroom teachers, that would result in an annual fund of $2,500 per classroom. These funds might go to purchase more and better text resources (e.g., encyclopedias, atlases, magazines, children's books) and improved computer equipment (with telecommunications and CD-ROM capabilities, or simulation games such as Oregon Trail or SimAnt) or to fund a teacher's attendence and participation in a conference on adapting instruction for academically talented children or visit to another school with a classroom-based model already in place. Over five years this design would result in an investment of a quarter-million dollars in enhancing the school capacity for better meeting the needs of academically talented children. Each classroom teacher would have had the opportunity to invest over $10,000 toward the goal of improving the quality of classroom instruction. All the money invested literally stays put and continues to pay dividends to all children.

School Librarians

How does a librarian work to enhance the quality of classroom instruction? Not by checking books in and out of the library. That is a task better assigned to a paraprofessional clerk. Librarians can support and improve classroom instruction when they spend much of their time locating resource materials for topic-centered units or classroom interest areas. Librarians improve classroom instruction when they support students in developing improved problem formation strategies and search strategies for research projects. Librarians improve classroom instruction by keeping the library open for extended hours so that students (and their parents) might use the resources in completing classroom projects and assignments. Librarians can play potentially powerful roles in shaping and supporting classroom instruction.

Social Workers

There has been a recent interest in adding social workers to the school professional staff. Social workers might improve classroom instruction by working with families of at-risk children to improve their capacity to support their children's development of academic and social skills. They might also help children and their families gain access to needed health and social services so that children who need eyeglasses, for instance, are assured of getting them as quickly as possible. Social workers might also work with children outside the regular school day in either individual or small group sessions. However, if children are pulled out of classes to meet with the social worker, the situation is more likely to interfere with classroom learning opportunities than expand them. To avoid this, school social workers could work from early afternoon until mid-evening. This allows contact with teachers at the end of their work day and creates the opportunity for family interventions that are more conducive to most family schedules.

School Psychologists

Currently, many school psychologists have narrowly defined job descriptions consisting primarily of completing individualized assessments of students' achievements and aptitudes as part of the process of completing referrals for identifying students as handicapped. This is unfortunate, and the National Association of School Psychologists is working to end this narrow role definition. The more appropriate role, in the Association's view, would be primarily consultative and classroom-based. In other words, school psychologists would focus more time and effort on assisting classroom teachers in modifying the classroom environment or improving student performance in the classroom.

This recommended role seems to better fit the premise that support staff in a school should be primarily concerned with improving classroom instruction. The shift away from simply testing children and preparing assessment reports is also supported by research on the limited validity of the testing for classifying students and the limited role the testing actually plays in the special education referral and placement process (Mehan, Hartweck, & Meihls, 1986). Reducing the reliance on standardized testing while shifting to more classroom-based evaluations of student performance creates a powerful alternative to the simple labelling of children. The shift to consulting model for working with teachers in adapting their practices and modifying student behavior substantially improves the likelihood that classroom instruction will be enhanced.

Speech and Language Teachers

Mostly primary-grade children receive speech and language services in schools. The most frequently used program design has children leaving the classroom individually or in small groups to work with a speech and language teacher two times a week. This model, however, shows little promise for improving classroom instruction. An improved model places the speech and language teacher in the classroom for most services and targets much heavier reliance on collaborating with the classroom teacher in planning interventions linked to classroom literacy lessons and strategies that support the child's monitoring of appropriate language production.

At the very least, the intervention emphasis must be split between classroom support and individual or small group lessons. When the strategies developed in such lessons are linked to the classroom lessons and supported and extended by the classroom teacher, children can be expected to make better progress. Only small and slow improvements can be expected when language lessons are offered in isolation from the classroom and unsupported during the many hours of classroom instruction.

PARAPROFESSIONALS AND VOLUNTEERS

Most schools make use of paraprofessionals; most have at least a few peer tutors and adult volunteers. Each of these roles can provide useful support for classroom instruction, but each needs to be handled somewhat judiciously to ensure that classroom instruction is improved.

Paraprofessionals

There are a number of good reasons for schools to employ community residents as paraprofessionals including:

- Ensuring community members' active involvement in the school;
- Increasing ethnic and language diversity in the school;
- Freeing teachers to focus on academic, rather than clerical or management, tasks;
- Increasing employment opportunities in low-income neighborhoods;
- Reducing costs compared to hiring more teachers; and
- Providing a potential career ladder for minority teachers.

Little evidence suggests, however, that actually using paraprofessionals to instruct children, even under a teacher's supervision, benefits the children served (Anderson & Pellicier, 1990; Rowan & Guthrie, 1989). Consider that most paraprofessionals are employed in remedial or special education programs. Using the least-well-trained adults to instruct children with the most complex learning difficulties simply does not make sense. Few schools employ paraprofessionals to work with gifted children or to work in advanced-placement classes. Consider that schools with fewer poor children employ fewer paraprofessionals. How is it that paraprofessionals are most likely employed in schools with many poor and special needs children? In schools with patterns of low achievement?

Historically, paraprofessionals are a relatively recent addition to the educational workforce. In the late 1950s, the Fund for the Advancement of Education (Stoddard, 1957) created a blueprint for "the schools of tomorrow." Professionalization of teaching was set as a major goal, and the report decried the substantial time that teachers spent in nonacademic activity. Paraprofessionals were offered as one reasonable solution to altering that situation. Teacher aides would allow, the report declared, the redeployment of teacher time so as to provide more teaching service to each pupil and make it possible for teachers to meet children's individual needs better. Aides would be assigned the duties that occupied roughly one-fourth of teachers' time (e.g., attendance, bathroom, lunch, recess, clean up, preparing to leave, clerical work, and so on). The report noted, "Careful lines are to be drawn between those teaching functions to be performed by the teacher and those chores and other non-professional duties that could be performed by an aide."

However, in an odd turn of events, at least for at-risk children, many schools have come to rely on aides to replace the teacher and to function as tutors, albeit usually with some minimal supervision. Now this seems more often true when aides are funded from special program funds. Title 1 remedial reading aides, for instance, report spending 60 percent of their time working with small groups and 30 percent in a tutorial setting serving an average of 31 students each day. Schools enrolling many poor children are twice as likely to employ aides as other schools (Millsap, Moss, & Gamse, 1993). The situation seems not especially different with special-education aides. The instruction that aides offer is typically focused on low-level tasks and often seems more likely to foster dependence on adults than independent achievement.

Currently, then, paraprofessionals are routinely deployed to work with at-risk children, which is unlikely to enhance the quality of instruction these children receive. If aides were well trained, the situation might be less dismal, but most aides receive little training before or after they begin their job. A few studies have shown that training in specific instructional roles and routines can enhance the quality of the educational intervention offered and improve the outcomes for children working with those aides. But such training seems relatively rare.

Paraprofessionals might enhance the instruction offered in the classroom for some children while not enhancing the instruction offered other children. For instance, one common use of paraprofessionals is to have them work with the lowest-achieving children while the teacher works with higher-achieving children. This design enhances the likelihood that the instruction for the teacher's group will be improved because the teacher does not have to monitor the low-achievement children. However, the design offers little chance of improving the instruction for the low-achieving children.

The "time replacement" model allowed under federal program guidelines is one alternative that can actually improve the instruction for low-achieving children. In this case, the paraprofessional works with the higher-achieving students and frees the classroom teacher to work with low-achieving students. Of course, this results in a reduced likelihood that instruction is improved for the higher-achieving students. Nonetheless, this model seems preferable because it enhances the instruction of the children most in need of more and better teaching.

Paraprofessionals can be employed in ways that improve classroom instruction, but both program design and paraprofessional training need to be focused on that goal if it is to occur. Likewise, classroom teachers need clear understanding of how paraprofessionals might be most profitably used. Too often, neither the paraprofessional staff nor the classroom teachers have received adequate training in the most effective roles that paraprofessionals might play.

We believe that schools should develop career ladders for teacher aides. It is difficult to recommend that aides be allowed in instructional roles without some substantial training (and even then with supervision). Untrained paraprofessional staff might do some of the clerical work and "chores" of teachers and might even be allowed to monitor hallways and playgrounds (although the potential liability problems in such cases seem enormous). The following illustrates a formal delineation of paraprofessional roles that schools might create:

Level 1. Office clerical, classroom chores, AV equipment setup, hallway/entrance monitoring. No specific training in child development, but some in communication with staff and parents, general training in educational lingo and procedures, etc. Aides assist teachers in duplicating materials, binding books, helping with classroom cleanup after project time, locating and setting up audiovisual equipment, and a performing variety of other tasks that do not require direct work with children.

Level 2. General classroom support with some direct instructional contact with children. Initial training in child development, human learning, principles of effective instruction, general classroom procedures, etc., with a one-year supervised internship (paid). At this level, aides would continue with some Level 1 assignments but would also have some direct contact with children. Aides might monitor the classroom, for instance, while the teacher worked with individual or small groups of students. They might read to children or assist in organizing a Reader's Theater project or a book publishing.

Level 3. Instructional responsibilities under direct supervision of certified personnel. Aides earn a two-year postsecondary degree with emphasis on human development and educational processes and satisfactory completion of a two-year internship (paid). They would learn how to observe and record student behavior and strategies for monitoring students while working independently, interviewing students, supporting students during reading and writing and searching for books and information generally. This would require good verbal skills and familiarity with curriculum materials and classroom instructional contexts. Much of the training would be regularly provided. Level 3 aides would become potential candidates for progressing to a bachelor's degree and teacher certification.

This proposal is not unlike some already in existence in several states and those supported generally by the American Federation of Teachers. Ongoing staff development would be provided for aides in all categories (most aides now receive less than nine hours a year of training). Training for classroom teachers is also needed if they are to make most effective use of aides. In many cases, Level 3 aides and teachers might often share the same training sessions.

We would evaluate the use of teacher aides in the same manner as other staff—does their presence positively affect the quality of classroom instruction available to at-risk children? We have no doubt that aides can be trained and employed in ways that routinely leads to an affirmative response, but aides are not teachers and cannot be expected to address the educational needs of at-risk children expertly.

The Ten Best Jobs For Aides

1. Binding children's stories into books.
2. Running the school bookstore.
3. Reshelving library books.
4. Collecting and distributing book club orders.
5. Using a word processor to prepare "galley proofs" of student work.
6. Assisting students publishing a school newspaper.
7. Reading to students.
8. Rehearsing students in Reader's Theater performances.
9. Monitoring students in the classroom to free the teacher to work individually.
10. Setting up and cleaning up after projects.

The Five Worst Jobs For Aides

1. Tutoring poor and/or handicapped children.
2. Drilling and practicing with poor and/or handicapped children.
3. Providing seatwork assistance to poor and/or handicapped children.
4. Guiding oral reading of poor and/or handicapped children.
5. Providing small group lessons for poor and/or handicapped children.

Volunteers

Adult volunteers also work in most schools. The nature of the volunteers' work is wide-ranging, from clerical work in the school library to actual tutorial assistance in some schools. Volunteers work in both before- and after-school programs as well as during the school day. Some work for only short periods, to help construct a new playground or to put on a Christmas pageant, for instance. Others work for longer terms, in some cases for virtually a lifetime.

The guest reader format is one of those short-term, usually single-visit, volunteer opportunities that seems to have the potential for enormous payoffs. The guest reader might be a parent or another community member who simply comes in to the school or a classroom to read from favorite book. Usually the guest reader talks about the book and why it was selected. He or she may also stay and respond to children's questions about the book or the reader's reading habits more generally. In many cases, bringing in adult males as guest readers has been emphasized. For instance, one school has had local firemen, policemen, college atheletes, construction workers, barbers, and others read once a month or so in various classrooms. This was designed as an effort to provide adult male reader role models for the boys in the school, many of whom were from single-parent families and had had few opportunities to see men reading and writing.

At the Louis Armstrong Elementary School in Queens, New York (about a half mile from Manhattan), ten volunteer guest readers from HarperCollins Publishers visit weekly for an hour of reading to first graders. The children are mostly immigrant children, and visitors will hear the lilting accents of the West Indies or the short vowels of the Middle East. The children hear traditional favorites such as Sendak's *Where the Wild Things Are,* Carle's *The Mixed Up Chameleon,* and Bridwell's *Clifford, the Big Red Dog.* They also hear traditional tales such as the Gingerbread Boy, Rudolph the Red-nosed Reindeer, and Three Billy Goats Gruff. This effort, and others like it, serve to introduce children to wonderful books and stories, expose them to rich English language, and allow them to connect personally with adult readers. Such efforts also provide schools with potential advocates for improved resources and increased community support.

In another school, volunteer parents and high school students worked with children to create their own dramatic performances of children's literature. In yet another school, college students majoring in dance worked with children to create interpretations of poetry, song lyrics, and fairy tales they had read. In another case, college athletes tutored low-achieving children, resulting in improved academic achievement for both groups. In many cases, the volunteers worked with children outside regular school hours so as to not interrupt classroom instruction. In the most fruitful efforts, the volunteers also linked their activities to classroom themes.

The use of volunteers should also be evaluated by asking whether their presence improves the quality of classroom instruction for at-risk children. Volunteers can play potentially powerful roles in schools seeking to improve the responsiveness of programs to at-risk children. But volunteers are usually not well-trained or expert teachers and cannot routinely be expected to offer high-quality instruction.

Chris Jennison, a HarperCollins editor, does guest reader duty at Louis Armstrong Elementary School.

HIRING NEW PERSONNEL

A school has a wonderful opportunity to immediately impact the quality of its instruction when new personnel are considered for employment. To ensure that new personnel fit the new roles described, it will be important to design the application and interview process so that experience with and enthusiasm for collaboration, integrated curriculum, inclusion, and authentic assessment, to name a few, are addressed. For instance, the job posting for several positions at South Lake Middle School in Irvine California, listed the following common elements necessary for all positions:

- Knowledge, understanding, and successful exhibition of integrating curriculum and providing connectedness for all learners;
- Knowledge, understanding, and successful exhibition of authentic assessment;
- Successful demonstration of working as a flexible, contributing member of a team of professionals;
- Understanding of the use of technology to support learning; and
- Active pursuit of continual professional growth and commitment to supporting colleagues' growth.

When the opportunity to employ new staff arises, take advantage of that opportunity. Ask about previous collaborative teaching experience, about experiences with inclusionary education, about past work with paraprofessionals and the librarian or art teacher. Involve other instructional staff in the interview and decision-making process. These are the people who will have to work with the new staff member. Most important, do not forget to ask what the candidate has read lately. If we want teachers who develop readers and writers, we need teachers who read and write themselves.

ADMINISTRATORS MATTER

This chapter began with a rationale for refocusing school improvement efforts on classroom teachers. In closing the chapter, a focus on the importance of school administrators seems appropriate. The primary work of the school administrator is the improvement of classroom instruction in the school. Accomplishing this requires substantial familiarity with classrooms in the school and with all those other adults that work there. Working to improve literacy instruction, specifically, requires a fair amount of expertise about fostering literacy development and substantial skills in fostering collaborative relationships. Both areas of expertise have become more central to the role of the administrator as the nature of literacy demands change in American society and as educational policies shift to encourage (or mandate) more teacher involvement in the administration of a school (Beck & Murphy, 1993).

Various terms focus on the changing nature of literacy demands and the changed expectations for school outcomes. Some call it the *new literacy* (Willinsky, 1990), others *thoughtful literacy* (Brown, 1991), and still others use the term *higher-order literacy*. Regardless of the label, the emphasis is away from basic skills mastery and minimum competency achievement and toward fostering thinking through problem solving, application, and discussion. Likewise, whether the term is *teacher empowerment, site-based management, building leadership councils, shared decision making,* or some other, the trend is away from central office decision making and toward local decision making and decision-making teams that involve teachers and parents, not just administrators.

Both trends demand administrators with additional skills, knowledges, and aptitudes for working with people. Both involve negotiating new procedures, processes, and program emphases. We have argued that the classroom teacher and classroom instruction must necessarily be the focus of efforts to reformulate schools. Thus, the primary task of both district and school administrators becomes one of orchestrating resources and collaborative efforts toward improving classroom instruction.

In many schools, change has been the result of much effort, leadership, and support from district or building administrators. In other schools, change has been more difficult because administrators hindered progress more often than fostered it. Administrators have critically important roles in restructuring elementary schools. However, not every school will have an administrator who can or is willing to lead the change process. In such cases, it is most often the teachers who take the lead and who support each other.

But for teachers to take the lead requires supportive administrators at both district and building levels. Ideally, leadership and support are available from school district administrators, especially for building administrators' efforts in supporting teachers. In other words, not only teachers need support—building administrators do also. Sometimes the best support is advice and information. In other cases it is help in accessing needed resources, or it may be providing an "outsider" evaluation documenting progress being made. To experiment, to take risks, building administrators need support from the central office.

It is not the case that elementary school administrators must have all the answers before the change process can begin (Barth, 1990). If that were so, change would never get started. It is also not the case that administrators have to take charge, as it were, and lay out detailed plans for everyone. The ideal administrator is an experienced elementary educator who facilitates collecting information on school programs, who advocates for school resources and for children, and who fosters reflection and collaboration on the part of those involved in the change process.

Administrators also need to foster support for change in the community. Often parents are quite comfortable with the existing arrangements, especially those parents we are most likely to hear from—the parents of the achieving children. Administrators need to foster parent confidence, community confidence, usually by inviting parent and community partici-

Change is hard and change requires taking risks—moving out of comfortable, if ineffectual, routines. Robert Nelson, author of *1,001 Ways to Reward Employees* (Workman Publishing, 1994), notes that too often supervisors engage in only negative reviews of employees' work. "If the only feedback is when they mess up, now that takes a toll over time," he says. The tolls are (1) avoiding risk-taking and (2) isolating oneself as much as possible to avoid criticism. Nelson notes that employees, including teachers, need to hear about the good work they do, and they need to hear about it frequently. If schools are to change, teachers will have to take risks with new ideas, new curriculum, new organizational arrangements, and new collaborative activities. School administrators will have to provide consistent feedback that supports efforts to change.

pation in planning changes. In some cases, simply keeping the community well informed will be sufficient. As schools experiment with various forms of site-based management administrators must develop the skills needed to organize effectively and to support teacher and parent management teams.

Still, it remains essential that administrators have some good sense of what high-quality schools for at-risk children might look like. Administrators must be able to find information needed to weigh the options available. Administrators need to know how to gather, organize, and present information on the effects of decisions about school programs. Administrators need to ask not, "Are we doing something?" but "Are we doing the right things?"

■ SUMMARY

Effective classroom teachers are the only absolutely essential element of an effective school. Everyone else in the school is employed simply to enhance the quality of classroom instruction. One can imagine an effective school without a group of remedial teachers, without a school psychologist, without a gifted and talented teacher, without a social worker, and even without an administrator. Improving schools requires that classroom instruction improve.

However there is little evidence that support staff roles are currently defined as primarily focused on improving classroom instruction. If schools are to become more effective, either those roles require redefinition or the support staff positions should be considered for elimination. The questions that need to be asked are, What could we purchase with the special program funds that will be most likely to enhance the quality of classroom instruction for at-risk children? What sorts of expenditures will benefit these children most? When special programs staff seem to provide little in the way of academic benefit for children they serve and offer little evidence of improving classroom instruction, it is time to consider other ways the funds might be spent.

For too long American educational policy has simply added more and more specialists to the staff of the elementary school, especially those elementary schools serving large concentrations of low-income children. Little attention was paid to the potential interrelationships or conflicts that might arise from this milieu of additional personnel. In some cases these additions have resulted in school days that are so fragmented and classrooms where so many children come and go so often that running an effective classroom instructional program has become almost impossible.

In rethinking how elementary schools might better serve at-risk children it will be essential to begin by clearly examining who does what. A first step in restructuring the elementary school will be to redefine the roles that everyone plays. Classroom teachers will necessarily have to take more responsibility for teaching all children. Specialist staff roles must be reshaped to clearly indicate that their primary purpose is to improve classroom instruction. The administrator's role will also change to supporter of classroom instruction, negotiator of collaborative efforts, and resource seeker.

Books, Basals, and Beyond: The Reading and Writing Curriculum

E
ducators debate curriculum endlessly. Particular curricular emphases come and go in what almost appear to be 30-year cycles (Langer & Allington, 1992). But curriculum materials can play an important role in shaping the nature of classroom instruction. In this chapter, we will describe in some detail many of the most popular models and materials for organizing and engaging children in literacy learning. In our view, the classrooms that work best for at-risk children are classrooms that offer curriculum alternatives in a balanced reading and language arts framework.

CURRICULUM MATERIALS AND FRAMEWORKS

Elementary school reading and language arts materials include a spectrum of different resources, including basal reader series; trade books; skills books; software; student-produced work; and everyday reading matter such as newspapers, magazines, directions, and lists. Curriculum materials can be placed in three broad categories: *materials organized by others, materials organized by the teacher,* and *materials selected by children.*

Most schools rely more heavily on materials organized by someone other than individual classroom teachers or by individual children. These "other organized" curriculum materials include basal reader series, state-mandated grade-level lists of core tradebooks that children are to read, sets of big books, predictable book kits, trade-book sets with accompanying chapter questions and vocabulary lists, software, and skill packages produced and marketed by commercial publishers. Some of these sets of "other organized" materials are comprehensive with the organizational plan spanning K–6 levels, while other sets are far more narrowly targeted—sets of predictable language books, for instance, organized into six levels of difficulty for first-grade classrooms, or computer software promoted as improving reading comprehension skills.

The primary advantage of "other organized" curriculum materials is the savings incurred by not reinventing the wheel in every classroom. The greatest disadvantage of these materials is the lack of control and ownership that teachers experience when these materials form the curriculum. Currently, all instructional areas call for greater teacher involvement in curriculum selection and development. Whether named teacher empowerment, site-based management, process curriculum, child-centered instruction, or any of the other labels that currently abound, a central issue is the control that teachers exert in selecting and developing classroom curriculum. However, local curriculum development and associated staff development can be expensive when compared with purchasing commercial materials (total textbook expenditures in this country equal less than 1 percent of all educational expenditures). In addition, materials created from scratch often fail to meet the standards of quality set by the commercial materials. Nonetheless, we believe that teacher involvement and ownership of the curriculum is an important concern. At the same time we also believe that few school districts or schools either plan such development well enough or fund such development sufficiently. Moving away from "other organized" curriculum needs to be recognized as a potentially powerful educational improvement activity but one that requires substantial time and effort and funding to support.

Common Curriculum Frameworks

In recent studies of elementary school curriculum frameworks for reading and language arts instruction, Allington (1993) found three general patterns of materials:

Basal curriculum. In these schools, the basal readers series provided the core curriculum. In schools using the more recently published series, the curriculum was literature-based with student anthologies containing whole or excerpted literature. Generally, if tradebooks were used they were assigned to a recreational reading time and not integrated into the instructional curriculum.

Basal and books. Two patterns emerged here. First was the use of trade books that came with one of the newer basal programs. The trade books were used to extend thematic reading most often. The second pattern had trade books as an add-on to a basal program. Here the trade books were not linked to the basal lessons in any discernible way. In some cases, a locally developed core books curriculum accompanied the basal. In others, individual teachers used favorite books they had chosen or they allowed students to self-select their books but they insisted on trade-book reading along with basal lessons.

Books. In these schools, trade books were the curriculum. Several organizing frameworks were used including teacher or committee selection of books, individual student selection of books, theme-based approaches, and commercially developed core book plans.

While schools could be described as best fitting one of these approaches, there was often much variation from classroom to classroom. No schools were "pure" examples of any of the three organizational approaches. The amount of variation depended largely on the administrative press on teachers to implement the selected framework. Some schools had rigidly applied basal frameworks and others had the same sort of rigid framework for adhering to a trade-book curriculum. In these schools we found less variation from classroom to classroom (but we still found a fair amount of variation in curricular use). Regardless of which framework was used, teachers seemed more dissatisfied when administrators pressed them to implement a particular framework. In those schools where teachers had been more directly involved in the decision to implement whichever framework was in place, teachers seemed more satisfied with and enthusiastic about the framework and the activities that flowed from it.

Who Selects the Curriculum Framework?

All this points to several tensions that exist in curricular planning. For instance, who is in the best position to decide which framework will be adopted? Historically, such decisions have been made at the district level by school district administrators with or without input from teachers. But school district officials are often far removed from the classroom. It is teachers who have the most information about children in the schools and teachers who ultimately must implement the curriculum framework in their classrooms. But involving teachers in such decisions is messier, more time consuming, and often more expensive than decisions made at the district level. In addition, district administrators have often acquired greater expertise in curriculum frameworks and have more time to develop or review materials. Given the importance, though, attached to teacher ownership of curriculum, it seems foolish to attempt to mandate a plan from a district office. Ideally, the curriculum framework adopted for a school would be the result of substantial teacher involvement.

But involving teachers brings forward another sort of tension. How will the differences in preferences of different teachers be handled in adopting any curriculum framework? Should a simple majority rule? In some schools the faculty is divided as to what type of framework they want put in place. Is there a need for a common curriculum framework across the various classrooms in an elementary school? The arguments for adopting such a plan focus primarily on the potential benefits to children (a coherent framework across the grades is seen as beneficial to children's literacy development). Meanwhile, detractors of such adoptions focus on benefits for teacher selection of classroom curriculum. Although allowing each teacher to choose a framework might benefit students if such choices made teachers more effective.

Another factor is the press from parents for standardizing curriculum experiences. Without a common framework, parents often ask, "Why is the neighbor boy getting such a strong phonics emphasis and my child is just reading books?" or "Why did my son read a number of books last year in fourth grade and this year his sister hasn't read a single one?" Widely divergent classroom experiences, especially between classrooms at the same grade level, often stimulate such parental and community concerns. As one school board member asked, "Why can't we just figure out which books second graders will read each week? What is so hard about that?"

There is no simple answer to these commonly occurring tensions. One can argue for child-centered frameworks where children make more personal choices as obviously important. But one can also argue that individual teachers know their students best and that they should select the framework for their own classrooms to ensure that children are reading and writing a variety of genres. The benefits of some common framework across the several years of an elementary school career is obviously supportable as are the benefits of a common plan across all elementary schools, especially in districts having high student mobility. The press from parents and board members to standardize classroom experiences is also understandable. In these latter cases, one might also argue for selecting a basal reader program to accomplish these goals and avoid the substantial time and cost of developing a local reading and writing curriculum. So what process of curriculum framework development and adoption is a school to use?

We think the key is involving as many different stakeholders as possible in the development process. One reason that so few "pure" examples of the various frameworks actually exist in schools is the negotiations and compromises that took place during the development phase. As discussions continued, persons with different perspectives and preferences came to better understand other points of view. Ultimately, a negotiated understanding, with concessions and shifts from all involved, is usually achieved. Unfortunately, these understandings rarely fit neatly into the various schemes that academics create for discussing curriculum development. But it is the involvement and the opportunity to openly express concerns and feel that the concern has been recognized that allows the organization of curriculum plans to be achieved.

The Monterey Plan. It may be time for a more flexible notion of curriculum frameworks to be considered. The Monterey Peninsula Schools in California developed such a framework. The reading and language arts approaches were similar in many respects to the basal, basal and books, and books frameworks described earlier. They described each approach in a short, simple paragraph that focused on issues such as the role of basals and trade books, the integration of reading and writing, and the selection of readings by teachers and students. Teachers identified themselves as using one of the curriculum frameworks and then met with a supervisor to discuss their classroom program and potential enhancements within the framework selected. Teachers could indicate an interest in shifting to one of the other frameworks and could receive support to develop proficiencies needed to implement it. For instance, a teacher who had implemented a basal instructional plan and wished to shift to a basal and books framework might be given support to attend workshops or courses to become more familiar with children's literature and the teaching strategies used in literature-based instruction.

Each of the frameworks allowed teachers to select from other organized materials and to organize their own curriculum materials. But the three differed in the role that teacher-organized curriculum played. The basal framework, for instance, relied most heavily on other organized materials but still expected teachers to organize the books to be read to children and had child-selected books for the independent reading period. In contrast, the books framework relied most heavily on teacher-organized and child-selected materials but still supported the use of other-organized trade-book packages and excursions into basal materials for particular genres or strategy lessons. This district plan provided clear guidance for teachers along with support for moving from one framework to another. This is one of the few plans we have encountered that legitimized multiple curriculum frameworks and offered incentives to teachers to add to their instructional repertoires.

The broad categories of materials ultimately define children's curriculum experiences. Often, debates about curriculum frameworks are actually debates about materials. It seems important, then, to examine the most commonly used reading and language arts curriculum materials in more depth. Basal readers have been widely used throughout this century; tradebooks have made regular appearances in reading and language arts curriculum across this same period. Likewise, spelling books, skills packages, and language arts basals have routinely appeared in schools. Finally, today we hear more about the potential for technology in developing literacy, especially for helping children become fluent writers.

■ BASAL READERS

The most commonly used reading materials are basal reading series. Most adults grew up in an era when basal reading series were the reading curriculum in elementary schools. The popularity of these programs has waxed and waned over the century, and basal readers have always had numerous critics. The explosion in children's book publishing that began in the 1980s has created a climate in which many schools have reconsidered the role that a basal series play in their reading and language arts curriculum. In addition, basal reading series have changed to meet the new market expectations and so series reflect recent research on literacy learning.

Today, few basal reader series look much like the Dick and Jane series that dominated the market in the 1950s. Award-winning literature abounds, both in excerpted form and, increasingly, in the longer original format. Rarely is this literature edited or its story line altered. One result is that the selections in basals are quite a bit longer than they used to be. At the earliest levels especially, the new readers are also quite a bit more difficult (Hoffman, Roser, & Battle, 1993). Stories in the readers include substantially more vocabulary and more words that will be unfamiliar to most young children. While the predictability of the story lines and the use of patterned language stories have increased, the new series are generally considered more difficult for children in the primary grades.

The quality of the illustrations in basal series has improved as original artwork is now usually included. Other changes include less emphasis on skill and drill worksheets and assessments and more emphasis on the integration of writing and spelling lessons, the response to and discussions of the stories read, and the use of more authentic evaluation strategies. Most series also offer trade-book packages or classroom sets of trade books. These are children's books that have typically been selected to link to the stories in the readers in one way or another (thematically, by genre, by topic, by author, etc.).

Historically, basal reader curriculum were organized around specific skill instruction. More recently, these materials reflect different organizational plans while retaining an instructional strand for developing various skills and strategies associated with developing literacy proficiency. Today thematic organization seems a popular framework for organizing the stories that children read. For instance, one series (Houghton-Mifflin) has themes such as "Problems, Problems!" where anthology selections focus on the problems faced by the characters in the stories to be read, and "Heroic Deeds" featuring stories portraying various sorts of heroic acts.

Another series (Scott Foresman) offers six anthologies at each grade level (as opposed to the traditional five books for first grade, two books for second and third grades, and a single book in each of grades four, five, and six). These "student-sized" anthologies have general themes such as "Caring" or "Growing Up" with genre units and author studies part of the basal organizing framework. The genre units provide several stories from the same genre (such as mysteries, myths, tall tales, biographies) to familiarize the student with each of the selected genres. Author studies present several stories written by the same author and an article about the author or illustrator.

Nonetheless, the primary strength of any basal reader series is the organized instructional focus. Osborn (1989) notes that basal reader series perform a series of functions:

- Organize a large amount of information in one place;
- Provide daily in-service training on up-to-date instructional ideas;

- Provide a general curricular framework for reading and language arts; and
- Offer a breadth and balance of literature and other texts for students.

In addition, one other positive feature of newer basal reader series is the attention paid to representing the diversity of American culture in the stories selected for inclusion. While children's books written by minority authors or featuring authentic depictions of minority cultures or characters are becoming more common, relatively few are published each year. Perhaps because of this, many school and classroom libraries have few books that reflect the diversity of our citizenry and student population. The current situation in elementary schools seems to mirror what Applebee (1991) found in his study of high school literature curricula—basal anthologies provided a much more diverse selection of authors and characters than did the books most frequently selected by teachers for their students to read.

We believe basal reader series have is a potentially important role in the elementary school curriculum. However, the role we see is different from the historical role basals have occupied. The flexible use of a good basal series can play an important role in the balanced reading curriculum. But no basal series can be the whole reading and language arts curriculum. No basal series provides enough reading for anyone to become a good reader. Basal programs severely limit the development of important student book selection strategies. To fulfill their potential, basal reader series must be viewed as nothing more than another useful resource for teachers to draw on while planning and delivering instruction. When basals become *the* curriculum and dominate the instructional decisions of the day (and week), their effectiveness is undermined.

> The number of basal reader programs has shrunk considerably as a result of recent corporate mergers and buyouts. While just a ten years ago one could select from the basal programs of 14 publishers, today the number is half that and continuing to shrink.

Evaluating Basal Series.   So what features of a basal reader series might be important to evaluate? Osborn (1989) describes several "first pass" criteria that reviewers should be aware of when selecting basal reader materials.

1. Examine the instructional activities offered in the teacher edition. Try several of the activities even if in a simulation. Are the instructional activities described in sufficient detail? Do the activities serve the purpose of fostering development of the strategy? Look for coherence and continuity in lesson design. Are the strategy lessons just one-shot affairs with little follow-up or integrated with lessons and activities that follow?

2. Examine the student anthology. Is there a broad representation of differing types of texts? While narrative texts—stories—tend to dominate basal series, there should be balance with informational selections, biographies, and other types of texts, particularly texts more like those found in other subject areas. Examine the length of the selections offered. Do they vary as do selections found in the real

world, or is there some seemingly standard length? Are various ethnic and cultural groups well represented?

3. Examine the ancillary materials (workbooks, journals, software, etc.). Do the activities seem to be ones that will prove profitable (and doable) to the children? Do the activities flow from the strategy instruction? Do the activities require thoughtfulness and understanding on the part of the reader? Do most of the recommended activities foster further reading, writing, or discussion?

To Osborn's list we would add three other criteria:

4. Examine how trade books are integrated into the instructional plan and the purchase agreement. Do the trade books seem to be more of an afterthought than an integral component? Is there a procedure for acquiring suffcent quantities of the trade books? Is there a balance of genres among the trade-book selections?

5. Look at the instructional framework. Does it offer an integrated approach to the language arts? Can this basal series be easily fit into a balanced reading program? Can most units be completed in two or three days so that the teacher has time for other curriculum components? Do reading activities support writing opportunities? Does the series appear to allow flexible usage by different teachers? Does the teachers' edition actually encourage and support such flexibility?

6. Examine the selections offered in the basal series. Can most of your students read them with the amount of support and type of instruction you can provide? Remember that children need lots of opportunities to read easy, interesting materials.

> "For a long time . . . we have been trying to train *stoplight readers*. We ask children to read a bit of a story, stop, and talk about it. But what we should be working for is *flashlight readers*—readers who take a book under the blanket with a flashlight, because they cannot bear to stop reading what may very well be the best book they have ever read. If you want illumination, friends, a flashlight will beat a stoplight every time." From Katherine Peterson, *The Spying Heart* (pp. 137–138).

OTHER LANGUAGE ARTS TEXTBOOKS

In many schools it has been common practice to have a basal reader series, a spelling book, and a language basal series. Some schools have even added a handwriting book and a phonics workbook to this array. Typically, neither schools nor publishers paid attention to integrating the language arts instruction. Thus even when a school purchased these materials from the same publisher, the several daily language arts lessons offered were typically fragmented and incoherent. Now if we want to make learning to read and write as difficult as possible, fragmenting language learning into several unrelated lessons each day would be a good way to do it! On the other hand, integrating the language arts produces the potential for building on the reciprocal processes inherent in learning to read, write, speak, and spell.

As you may have guessed by now, we see little benefit to purchasing some of these commercial materials. The benefits of integration are so obvious that even most of the new basal reader series offer an integrated framework (usually integrating reading, writing, and spelling at the minimum). It only makes sense to design instructional activities that link reading and writing. Well-crafted prose provides a useful model for creating author's craft lessons, for instance, where children study how the story or report is organized, how authors begin, how they close, how they create "pictures in a readers mind," and so on. Learning how stories or persuasive arguments or information is organized is important for comprehension and for composition. As Tierney and Shanahan (1991) point out, integration of reading and writing fosters growth in both areas.

Linking decoding lessons with spelling and with writing and reading also makes sense. Children benefit from reading and writing the same words and from using those words in oral and written language activities. Spelling becomes more than rote memorization when the target words are used in writing activities and also studied in decoding lessons. Phonics strategies become more obviously useful when children actually encounter decodable words in their reading and when the strategies are linked to spelling.

Handwriting series do not seem very useful in our experience. Their heavy emphasis on transcription, letter formation, neatness, punctuation, and spelling, may actually inhibit children's exploration of writing as a learning activity. Children do need to learn about the conventions of written language, but these are far better taught in the course of real writing. Besides, in our experience, no matter what the system, some children (like both of us) know how to write more legibly than one would guess from their writing samples. The time that children might spend attempting to copy neatly will be better spent actually writing and learning that writing is a powerful system for putting your words, your ideas, down on paper.

TRADE BOOKS AS CURRICULUM

A strong, balanced literacy curriculum requires children's access to a large supply of books. Three common frameworks are used for organizing literacy instruction around tradebook reading: self-selected reading, core book curriculum, and thematic approaches. In many schools, these approaches are more or less combined, and in many cases, one of these frameworks sets alongside a basal framework. However, we will discuss each of these frameworks separately and then present a few models of combination approaches.

Self-selected Reading

This approach was popularized by Veatch (1959) and focuses primarily on motivation for reading. Arguing that personal motive is the most powerful force in learning, advocates of the self-selected reading framework represent a very student-centered approach to literacy teaching and learning. Well-stocked classroom and school libraries are central to implementing this framework, and individual book conferences are the primary means of instructional support. Many advocates of the whole language philosophy have resurrected the self-selection framework and argued for a literacy curriculum based on "authentic" reading and writing experiences.

Authentic experiences begin with individual purpose and motivation. When teachers select materials for students to read and topics for students to write about, the reading and writing experiences can be considered inauthentic. Authenticism is based on analyses of real world reading and writing where adults primarily determine what they will read and write and the level of involvement in the activities. As adults we decide which sections of the newspaper to read, which paperbacks to purchase, which manuals we need, and so on. In addition, adults decide whether they will "skim" a text or read it thoroughly. They decide whether to take notes or to write a summary or to discuss the material with peers. Since most reading outside school is driven by personal motives and preferences, proponents of this approach argue that school literacy events should more or less mirror this situation.

Student self-selection provides no traditional curriculum framework for teachers who, instead, respond primarily to children's interests. During book conferences teachers might discuss the book read, respond to journal entries that students elected to create, offer a strategy lesson that seem appropriate to a problem the child encountered while reading, or direct the child to other books. However, at the heart of this approach is the teacher as a source of support when children find support is needed.

While teachers and administrators most often think of children's books as the primary reading materials in literature-based classrooms, we would argue for the need for magazines and and newspapers in classrooms as well. An ever-increasing supply of children's magazines is available (at least 15 with a national circulation), and every classroom would, ideally, have a magazine rack for displaying current issues. If we wish to make school reading more authentic, then we will need to reconsider the role magazines will play in our reading and language arts curriculum plan.

A most useful resource for identifying potential magazines that might be ordered for school or classroom library collections is *Magazines for Kids and Teens* (D. Stoll, ed., International Reading Association, 1994. To order, call 1-800-336 READ.).

Core Books

This organizing framework for elementary school reading and language arts has once again become popular. Turn-of-the-century curriculum guides often listed the core books to be read at different grade levels (Langer & Allington, 1992), and Bill Bennett, as U.S. Secretary of Education, also offered his core reading list for elementary schools. Core lists often represent one of three quite different thrusts. In Bennett's incarnation, for example, core books are selected from "classic" children's books. Thus, many of the texts on these lists represent a Eurocentric view of this nation's history. Such core lists fit reasonably well with the "cultural literacy" notions some have offered. Children's classical literature such as *Treasure Island, Hansel and Gretel, The Adventures of Tom Sawyer, The Swiss Family Robinson, Little Women, Ivanhoe, Alice's Adventures in Wonderland,* and so on would be likely candidates for such a classics—emphasis core book list.

A second approach to core books emphasizes representing the diversity of American culture and selecting books that seem to match children's intellectual and moral development. The 1987 California English Language Arts Framework, for instance, notes that "with a rich and diverse background in literature, students can begin to discover both the remarkable wholeness in the intricately woven tapestry of American society and the unique variety brought by many cultures to that intriguing fabric" (p. 7). In this approach much attention has been placed on representing the diverse experiences of the ethnic, linguistic, cultural, and gender groups that make up our society.

The third approach to organizing core book lists emphasizes popular recent titles and book listings that have substantial appeal to children. As in the self-selected frameworks, student interest and motivation drives the selection process. In many schools, grade level teams develop such core lists to identify which books "belong" to which teachers. For example without such a list the issue of whether to use E. B. White's *Charlotte's Web* in third grade or fourth grade or Scott O'Dell's *Island of the Blue Dolphin* in fifth or sixth grade often arises. In our experience, this is the most common type of core book list in elementary schools— the protective core list.

Any of the core book list approaches seem to violate the fundamental principles of self-selection and authentic approaches to organizing curriculum. Core book lists represent what someone else thinks children should read at different grade levels. Much like secondary school literature curriculum, core book list selections are driven by some larger notion about what children should read and why literature is important. Each of these approaches for developing a core book list framework undermine the principle of personal choice and personal motives in selecting reading materials.

Remain vigilant when considering the purchase of commercially available "literature units" that provide workbook-like materials to accompany popular trade books. Too often these materials offer primarily low-level, ineffectual activities (e.g., chapter vocabulary worksheets that children are to use when looking up words in a dictionary and chapter questions that focus on trivial information). As with any other commercial material, examine the packages closely and ask the following questions?

1. Are the language arts integrated?
2. Do suggested activities engage children in useful work?
3. Do the lesson guides foster reflection and thoughtful literacy?
4. Do teaching suggestions offer actual instructional models?
5. Will these lessons "kill" this good book?

Thematic Plans

Thematic organizing frameworks are rising in popularity as witnessed by the number of new books on the topic (e.g., Downs, 1993; Walmsley, 1994). Always popular as an organizational framework in kindergarten, themes are now increasingly popular in basal reader series and in local curriculum development projects. Thematic organization of literature units is the hallmark of integrated approaches to the elementary school curriculum. Themes with a focus on social studies topics, science content, or health and development are common. So too are more literary themes. Walmsley (1994) offers a taxonomy of theme types:

- **Content-area themes:**
  science (life cycle of the butterfly)
  social studies (westward movement)
  architecture (Native-American homes)
  art (Impressionists and Impressionism)
- **Conceptual themes:**
  growing
  survival
  changing relationships
- **Calendar themes:**
  seasons (winter)
  holidays (Thanksgiving)
  folk events (Groundhog's Day)
- **Biographical themes:**
  George Washington Carver
  Dolley Madison
  Frank Lloyd Wright
- **Current events themes:**
  Somalia
  election
  immigration
- **Form themes:**
  genre (mystery, humor, science fiction, poetry)
  literary (characterization)
  skills (summary writing)

Often, theme units are designed to incorporate more than one of these categories, but the primary organizational purpose can usually be determined. Thematic frameworks may use just children's literature in its various genres (including informational texts for children) or may incorporate other types of written materials. For instance, in a social studies theme unit children might have access to original source materials or might collect artifacts or oral histories (Downs, 1993). In a science theme unit children might gather observational data, conduct experiments, or interview experts. While children's literature is most often central to the thematic approach, many other sources of information might also be included.

In any of the three organizing frameworks for trade-book curriculum, it seems necessary to evaluate the scope of the literature that children will read. In attempting to foster a balance in what children read across six or seven years of elementary school, several questions might be asked about the materials being used.

1. Is there a balance of fiction and informational reading? A balance in the types of writing children do? A balance of genres within the broad categories of reading materials and writing products?
2. Is there adequate representation of the rich ethnic, linguistic, and cultural groups and experiences? Do the repesentations fairly depict the contributions of the various groups?
3. Do children encounter significant works and ideas that broaden their perspectives of themselves and our society?
4. Is there a clear indication of where students will be offered instructional support for developing the strategies all children need to become richly literate? Does the framework provide teachers with evaluation tools to determine children's instructional needs?
5. Does the framework provide teachers with sufficient support for developing the instructional component?
6. Does the organizing framework foster depth of knowing and thoughtfulness?
7. Can the children actually read the recommended books?

Theme-based frameworks can be powerful influences in shaping a more thoughtful curriculum. The development of themes by classroom teachers can serve as an important activity for reshaping literacy instruction in a school. Theme-based planning by teams of teachers can foster involvement and ownership, but developing rich thematic curriculum is time-consuming. In many schools thematic development began small with a single, integrated unit, using historical fiction and biography to develop an understanding of a different historical era in each grade level, for instance. As classroom teachers worked through this theme development and delivery, they grew more comfortable with this framework and often expanded upon the original theme offering.

> For schools interested in using a theme-based approach to integrating the elementary curriculum, *Book Links* (434 W. Downer Place, Aurora, IL 60506), an award-winning magazine published by the American Library Association, provides easy-to-follow bibliographies (e.g., coastal ecosystems, African-American illustrators, Native Americans of the Great Plains) and essays organized by theme. The essays review the texts selected for each theme and usually offer several book-linked activities for students.

No matter which organizational framework is selected for trade-book curriculum the books must come from somewhere. The purchase of book sets for thematic units or core book lists may be handled through a book vendor or a catalog order. Classroom libraries might include a wide range of books selected to meet a variety of criteria. These collections may evolve and expand across time. Books for independent self-selected reading might come from a classroom library, a school library, a public library, a bookstore, or a book club. Each of these book sources fits some situations better than others, but each is important to children's literacy development.

School and Classroom Libraries

In most elementary schools, the school library is a relatively recent addition. Before the passage of the Elementary and Secondary Education Act (ESEA) of 1965, most schools did not have libraries or librarians. After much federal funding (check how many titles in your library now have an ESEA stamp inside), virtually all elementary schools had central library collections and most had at least part-time librarian support. When many of the ESEA programs were merged into a block grant programs in the 1970s and 1980s, federal funds for libraries vanished and the quality and quantity of holdings in many libraries, especially those in schools serving large numbers of children from low-income families, began to deteriorate. For instance, in a recent survey of an urban school library collection we found that almost two-thirds of the books available had been purchased prior to 1975. Two-thirds of the books were more than 20 years old, including most of the informational and references texts. The only atlas available had been published in the 1960s. Even though this school enrolled primarily minority children, fewer than 5 percent of the books were written by minority authors or included minority characters. In addition, this library had fewer than half the recommended number of books, even counting all the outdated ones on the shelves.

The National Library Power Program presents an excellent opportunity for schools and communities to work collaboratively to improve school libraries substantially. Funded by the Dewitt Wallace-Reader's Digest Fund, this program provides both resources and funding opportunities. For further information write The National Library Power Program, American Library Association, 50 East Huron Street, Chicago, IL 60611.

The library collection at this school simply depicted a larger and distressing trend in library facilities in schools with many poor children and schools with few poor children. A recent comparative study (Guice & Allington, 1994) reported that schools enrolling many poor children had 50 percent fewer books than did schools enrolling primarily more advantaged students. Children from poor families not only have fewer books to read in their homes but they have fewer books in their schools and classrooms as well. In 1975, the American Library Association set minimum standards for elementary school library collections (about 20 volumes per child so that a school with 500 students would need a library of 10,000–12,000 books plus media, magazines, and software). These standards were created before literature-based curriculum or thematic units were popular in schools so their adequacy for today's schools, are questionable. Still, very few schools with many poor children even met these standards (although half the schools serving mostly advantaged children did).

Even more alarming is that in California over half of all school libraries have closed in the last ten years (Simon, 1993). Oddly, in this era of an increasing use of literature in elementary schools the national trend is for library funding to be shrinking and, in some cases, vanishing completely. However, it seems the libraries in low-income neighborhood schools are the hardest hit.

Sen. Paul Simon Illinois testified recently (1993) that "the average publication date of a school library book is the late 1960s. Our school library collections are so obsolete that over half of the books on space exploration were written even before *Apollo XI*. An example of this can be found in one of my home state's more affluent school districts where sixty percent of all high school [library's] science books—particularly those about space exploration—are significantly older than the students themselves."

School libraries need to offer children lots of choices, which is why the recommended numbers of volumes seems so high. Libraries need also to have a substantial supply of informational books that would not be necessary in every classroom. Many school libraries have woefully inadequate informational collections. Often the few books available are dated and not accurate or useful.

All schools need wonderful school library collections as well as substantial classroom libraries. Schools serving many at-risk children need especially good collections in both settings simply because these children have less access to books and magazines outside of school. Library collections also need to be easily accessible to children. This means that the traditional "once-a-week" trip cannot be sustained. Libraries need to be available before and after school for children, especially for children with few books in their homes. Libraries need to be available across the school day to children who need access to informational books, atlases, and specialized materials for thematic projects. In other words, most school library collections and services need to expand.

Schools might consider the use of flextime for librarians to extend library access beyond the school day. For instance, librarians might begin their day two hours later than other instructional staff and work two hours later. This is especially important in schools where many children do not have access to books and informational materials (e.g., encyclopedias, atlases, dictionaries) in their homes. Some schools use volunteers from the community or from the student body to support the librarian during the extended hours.

The adequacy of the school library access and collections may also be related to the size and adequacy of classroom libraries in the school, though the two have important but different functions. Classroom libraries put books at the very fingertips of children—a feature that has been shown to be likely to increase the amount of reading children do in and out of school (Fractor, Woodruff, Martinez & Teale, 1993). Determining the appropriate size of a classroom library then is no easy matter. In fact, such libraries need more titles in the primary grades where children might read three or four little books during a single reading block. Nonetheless, we would hazard recommending some minimum-size standards.

Basically, classroom collections of 700–750 books for primary-grade classrooms and 400 books for upper-grade classrooms is the goal to strive for. This might include multiple copies of some books so that children might pair up, or cluster up, and read the same book simultaneously. Regardless of number, the collection should include a broad array of easier and harder books representing a variety of genres and topics.

When creating classroom libraries, remember that every classroom needs a supply of books that readers in trouble can read comfortably. Too often, in our experience, the third-grade classroom collection has no books that children experiencing difficulty with reading can read easily and independently. All children benefit from reading easy material, with an occasional foray into more difficult material, but children experiencing difficulty benefit most of all from a classroom collection that includes a number of less-difficult, interesting books (perhaps a third of the books).

Building Classroom Libraries. Of course the ideal classroom collection cannot always represent an immediate actuality. There are strategies that schools might want to use to significantly expand the choices children have from their classroom libraries without buying all the books at once. For instance, three third-grade teachers could work together to select books for their classroom libraries. If each had $200 allocated for such purchases each year, they could pool their money and with the $600 purchase 200–300 titles each year. Thus they could create three rotating collections of 75–100 titles. Each teacher would then get one of the collections for a three-month period before exchanging that collection for one of the others. Across the school year, the third graders would have the opportunity to select from each of the three collections. In the second year, the collections would be expanded and teachers would rotate three sets of 150–200 books. After the third year teachers may want to hold onto one of the collections permanently and order the popular titles from the other collections for their own personal libraries.

Another strategy for developing the initial classroom library collection is to ask for donations from parents, especially parents of older children. One school managed to collect an average of one hundred titles each year for each classroom using this scheme. Book clubs' bonus books are another strategy for developing or expanding collections. Requesting parent-teacher organization assistance or business support is another possibility. Finally, old basal reading anthologies can be cut apart and some of the selections bound between cardboard covers to create little books. This strategy works especially well in primary-grade classrooms where the largest number of books are needed. Many basal stories are not very different from the books found in the various collections of easy-reading little books.

But every school's budget should contain ample funds for such purchases each year. One way to find the money to buy books for school or classroom libraries is to save the funds from some other category. In a study of the costs of seatwork, Jachym, Allington, & Broikou (1989) found that some schools were spending upwards of $100 per child per year just for seatwork. Most of the costs were for duplicating materials (photocopying, dittoes, etc.). Reducing the average cost (about $50 per student) of seatwork by half would have provided schools with about $25 per child per year! That would provide at least $500 per classroom for the purchase of books—or $250 per classroom and at least $5,000 additional for school library acquisitions.

Involving teachers in decisions concerning curriculum materials takes many forms, but at least one district fostered change toward increased use of children's literature by reallocating workbook funds to individual classrooms and allowing teachers greater control over those expenditures. Below is a message received on a telecommunications bulletin board (Scholastic Network/LitNet on America Online, at 1-800-246-2986) in response to a general query about where teachers found funds for classroom collections.

> Dick, I have been fortunate to teach in a district (Naperville, Illinois) that began reallocating our workbook money about 7 years ago. At the time, we had the choice to continue using workbooks, or receive about $750 each year to purchase literature for our classroom. Our Superintendent of Curriculum required that we write a short rationale on 1) why we were making the change, 2) what literature we would purchase in place of workbooks, and 3) how we planned to use the literature. Now, each of our schools has a rather nice collection of literature that we can use with our students. Along with the choice to change, she offered us outstanding opportunities for staff development. Barb.

Displaying Classroom Collections. Once books have been acquired for classroom collections it is time to think about organizing the classroom reading corner and displaying the books available. Morrow (1991) summarized the research on characteristics of classroom library centers that promoted children's voluntary reading:

- Provided physical accessibility and attractiveness;
- Partitioned off the rest of the classroom on at least two sides to give a feeling of privacy;
- Allowed for an area large enough to hold about five children at a time;
- Offered comfortable seating such as a rocking chair, pillows, and a rug;
- Provided at least eight books of varied reading levels per child;
- Held a wide variety of literature, including picture books, informational books, magazines, newspapers, and so on;
- Circulated new books regularly;
- Displayed featured books on open-faced shelves;
- Displayed attractive posters and a literature-related bulletin board;
- Offered taped stories with headsets; and
- Checked books in and out using a simple procedure.

Her review also notes that children in classrooms with library centers read about 50 percent more books than children in classrooms without such centers. Unattractive shelves of books with their spines displayed were not popular classroom locations with children. Well-designed library areas, on the other hand, were popular and used far more frequently. Adding real-world reading materials, magazines, and newspapers make these centers more attractive and foster reading of a wider variety of texts. Just putting books into classrooms is not enough. Classroom collections need some wonderful "coffee-table" books—those large,

A well-designed and well-stocked classroom library fosters reading in and out of school.

richly illustrated conversation pieces—for children to browse through; in addition, a supply of magazines and a daily newspaper for the upper grades should be added. Classrooms need a set of encyclopedias and other reference books appropriate to the grade level and the topics typically studied.

Now all of this may seem a tall order given current budget situations. But every school needs a vision of what school and classroom libraries need to become. Without such visions, there will be no plan of action. Without some plan of action, nothing will change. If we are to create thoughtful schools where all children become literate, we need school and classroom libraries that provide all children access to the books they will need to accomplish that end.

BOOK CLUBS

Another strategy for putting books into the hands of children is participation in a commercial book club. For almost a half-century book clubs have offered low-cost paperback editions of children's books by mail order. Children's book clubs operate almost exclusively through schools with classroom teachers distributing the flyers listing the monthly offerings. Classroom teachers, paraprofessionals, or parent volunteers typically collect the order forms and the money for children's book orders that are then usually mailed out for the whole school at one time. Several weeks later the shipment of books arrives and each order is distributed to classroom teachers who, in turn, distribute the selections to children. Paraprofessionals or parent volunteers could conduct this activity in most cases, but teacher encouragement and support for book purchases remains an important factor.

Each of the major book club companies (Scholastic, Trumpet, Troll) offer free books or other merchandise credits to teachers based on the number of books children order. Each also offers an array of books that have been selected for particular grade levels representing a variety of children's interests.

> The major book club companies include:
>
> *Scholastic*, 555 Broadway, New York, NY 10012 (212-343-4628)
>
> *Troll*, 100 Corporate Drive, Mahwah, NJ 07430 (201-529-4000)
>
> *Trumpet*, 666 Fifth Ave, New York, NY 10103

In a recent national study of book clubs, Strickland and Walmsley (1993) reported on a number of facets of book club participation. The study, the first of its kind, found participation in book clubs was widespread and that classroom teachers overwhelmingly made the decisions whether to participate and which club, or clubs, to participate in. Almost two-thirds of the teachers using book clubs participated in two or more companies' book clubs. None of the teachers required children to participate, though about half of the teachers reported encouraging participation. In these teachers' classrooms, 60 percent of the children ordered books at least some of the time and 40 percent never, or rarely, ordered books. The teachers felt that parental interest and family incomes were the primary determinants in who ordered books. Participation influenced children's literacy development in a variety of ways, but the most influential factors seem to be:

- Students exercise personal choice in making selections;
- Selecting books requires a personal involvement and investment of time;
- Students experience ownership of books, both physically and intellectually; and
- Shared literacy values are demonstrated among children, parents, and teachers.

Simply put, book clubs offer many children their best chance to have a book of their own.

Book clubs provide children with easy access to quite inexpensive paperbacks (each club offered about 40 titles every month at average costs of $1.50–$2.00 each). Book club selections were substantially discounted from the normal retail price, even for paperback editions. In addition, book clubs provided access to books for children who lived far from a children's bookstore or from a public library. Book club participation seems a wholly appropriate enterprise when we want to increase the number of books children have to read and discuss. However, book club participation does cost money and not all children live in families that have the discretionary funds to purchase children's books, even low-cost books. These teachers were concerned about children from poor families and employed several strategies in an attempt to ensure that all children who wanted to order books were able to. These strategies included:

- Using the credits from other children's orders to purchase books;
- Purchasing books with funds from a parent or community organization; and
- Spending their own funds to purchase the books.

It would seem that schools should be concerned with this issue and develop schoolwide policies for providing all children the opportunity to participate in book clubs. Perhaps all children could be assured of receiving at least one book for each order sent in by the school. Children who receive free- or reduced-price meals might simply be given the forms and told to rank order their book preferences. Using school or community-generated funds, each child would then receive their first choice.

> The Children's Literacy Initiative, based in Philadelphia, has single copies of a wonderful small guide entitled, "Creating a classroom literacy environment" available at no cost. Fax inquires to 215-574-1404 or write them at 320 Walnut St, Philadelphia, PA 19106.

■ BOOK FAIRS

A final strategy for putting trade books into classrooms and children's hands is the book fair. As children's literature has risen in popularity, the use of school book fairs has become increasingly common. Similar in some respects to book club participation, the book fair has one potential advantage—children can handle and preview the books before they purchase them. Another potential advantage is that teachers can usually request that particular titles, authors, genres, or topics be made available at the fair. In most cases, book fairs also earn bonus books for the schools, similar to the procedure initiated by book clubs.

Scheduling the book fair to extend beyond normal school hours and inviting parents to drop in can foster not only more purchases but parent support for reading. Providing some selections for preschool-age children can foster more parent reading before school entry. This seems especially important if few bookstores are available in the area for young parents to shop in. In the same vein, advertising the book fair beyond the school doors can foster community participation. Likewise, scheduling the book fair to extend during parent-teacher conference hours is one way to foster parent participation as is scheduling the book fair during the September open-house period. Posting notices of the book fair in public places and businesses in the neighborhood will attract parents of preschool children.

> Censorship is an issue that schools need to be prepared to deal with, especially when children's literature becomes a focal point of curriculum planning. The two books below offer more than sufficient advice on the legal and practical aspects of objections to books.
>
> Simmons, J. (1994). *Censorship: A Threat to Reading, Learning, Thinking.* Newark, DE: International Reading Association ($16.00, 1-800-336-READ).
>
> Reichman, H. (1990) *Censorship and Selection: Issues and Answers for Schools.* Urbana, IL: National Council of Teachers of English ($12.95, 1-800-369-6283).

READING IS FUNDAMENTAL PROGRAM

The federal government has an inexpensive book distribution program targeted to put books in the hands of disadvantaged children. This is the Reading Is Fundamental (RIF) program. There are almost 4,000 local RIF projects across the country today with the vast majority associated with schools. In most projects, 75 percent of the costs of the books given to disadvantaged children are paid for from federal monies, with 25 percent of the book costs raised from local efforts. Roughly 1,000 RIF projects are wholly funded from local monies, usually funds from corporate partners and local fund-raising efforts. RIF projects are staffed by volunteers since administrative and operating costs are not reimbursable. In 1990, almost 9 million books were distributed to 2.7 million children in all 50 states (Abbott, Yudd-, & Gutman, 1992). Still, only about 5 percent of all school-aged children were served by RIF (or about one of every five poor children).

Unfortunately, obtaining federal funding for new RIF projects is currently very difficult. In 1990 alone, more than 1,000 applications for new projects were declined because of lack of available federal funds. This could change if Congress decides to expand the RIF program, but for now an expansion of federal support is an unlikely bet. Still, schools can develop a locally funded RIF effort and thereby gain access to the inexpensive book list that has been the raison d'être for RIF. In addition, the national RIF office provides guidance and support materials to locally funded projects. The first task is obtaining local funding. While this may seem daunting, we suggest that since most RIF programs are staffed by parent volunteers, the search for one or more local sponsors is best handled by these volunteers. Because RIF requires that at least three free books be distributed to each child, you must determine the approximate number of children to be served. (All children in a school must be served. RIF offers, for instance, Braille books for visually impaired children.) Since RIF limits book costs to a maximum of $5.00, the upper limit is fairly easy to establish. However, few books on the RIF lists cost that much, so you could easily use an average price of $2.50 and set a base estimate of $7.50 per child. You should make sure you have developed a plan for recognizing local sponsors before the search for local support begins. Youth atheletic teams are so successful in gaining local funding from business because they invariably print the sponsor's name on the team jerseys. That sort of visiblity assures that everyone knows who is supporting the effort. RIF projects need to make the same links just as visible.

A related program, Running Start, has recently been funded by Chrysler Corporation and administered by RIF. The program is targeted at disadvantaged first graders and, like the larger RIF effort, provides free books to young children and expects parental involvement in return.

For information about RIF or Running Start, write to RIF, Smithsonian Institution, Room 500, 600 Maryland Ave., SW, Washington, DC 20024.

Similar locally funded efforts have sprung up from time to time as schools develop school-business partnerships. It may be worth exploring whether interest exists in your community for such an effort.

■ SCHOOL BOOKSTORES

Another strategy for increasing children's access to books is organizing a school bookstore. In the same way that many elementary schools run small stores to purchase school supplies (and snacks in some), such stores might add a supply of children's books to their stock. By regularly ordering a few titles, the store can keep books at children's fingertips. If no school store exists, consider setting up a bookstore that also sells some school supplies. Such a store does not have to take up much space—we have seen these stores operating out of a former broom closet and operating from a mobile cart (a sort of kiosk much like those commonly found in malls and airports).

Books can be purchased for the store through a book distributor or local bookstore, in most cases. One school ordered books from book clubs and resold them to children through the bookstore at no profit. The store might only be open one or two days each week and staffed by older children, paraprofessional staff, or community volunteers.

Displays that show off book covers are absolutely necessary when setting up the bookstore. Ordering multiple copies of a few titles, selected to be of interest to a range of children, seems to work better than ordering lots of single copies. Reviews of books ordered might be inserted in the school newspaper or in newsletters sent home to parents (with directions to share with children). Reviews can be written by children (ideally) or by teachers, librarians, or other staff (including administrators).

■ TECHNOLOGY AS A SOURCE OF LITERACY CURRICULUM MATERIALS

Most schools have invested in technology of various sorts, but most classrooms make rather limited use of technology in developing literacy skills because:

1. Many schools provided teachers with little actual training in using the tools purchased;
2. Many provided little time for teachers to develop new lessons or to review new curriculum products; and
3. Many schools relied heavily on one-time grants for purchases, and materials are now dated.

We typically see little technology in use in our visits to classrooms, and even then the most common uses are often limited to very low-level drill and practice activities—the electronic skill worksheet. Some of this has to do with the abundance of older equipment found in most schools, such as older Apple computers with very limited memory capacity. These machines often can support only the simplest software, for example, the electronic worksheet formats. Computerized worksheets and drills are no more useful than the traditional paper-pencil or flashcard activities, and we cannot recommend such materials as solutions to the problems that at-risk children face.

However, powerful technological tools have become recently available, and costs are rapidly dropping. We see an enormous potential for technology in instructional and assessment activities, but to achieve that potential schools must develop far better long-term planning for technology acquisition and implementation than most have today.

A good first step in thinking about technology-based curriculum is to sort through the roles we expect technology could play in some or all of our classrooms. For instance, is technology seen as a potential source of instructional support for literacy? The old electronic worksheets were seen this way (even though they offered little real support for students). Now, early literacy software can place a children's book on the color monitor and provide a variety of supportive activities. The computer will read the story aloud, highlighting each word as it is read. Children can touch objects in the illustrations, and the computer will provide a visual label and a voice reading the label. In some cases, children can type in their own extension of the story, select from the original artwork to illustrate their addition and then ask the computer to read back what they have written. New software products are interactive and instructional. But, of course, such software requires the newer, more powerful computers to operate.

Kathy Pelles, who directs New York City's School of the Future project, argues that technology has the power to develop students' GUMS skills—skills increasingly necessary in our society. The GUMS skills are:

- Gathering information,
- Understanding information gathered,
- Manipulating information gathered, and
- Synthesizing information into useful products.

When students learn to search electronic databases and select and download information, they have acquired an enormous capacity for problem solving. But they still must be able to read that information (though some of it may be auditory or pictorial in nature) and then select and sort through it, synthesize it, and, finally, organize and present it in a comprehensible format to a particular audience. Technology does not reduce the need for thinking or for reading and writing. In fact, technology has the potential to increase and enhance literacy just because it makes much of the tedious work less cumbersome.

A second role that technology might play is to expand opportunities to engage children in reading and writing real things. Using the computer as a word processor or desktop publishing center are two examples. For many kids, the computer solves some difficulties associated with composing, revising, editing, and publishing their work (it also makes the final product wonderfully professional looking with very little computer expertise). Going one step further and linking into a computer network allows children to become electronic pen pals with children around the world. This also allows linking children with similar interests or with a shared problem-solving activity. No matter how you look at it, participating in one of these networks increases the amount of reading and writing that children do. Access to such networks also increases access to an enormous set of informational resources that no single school could ever afford to collect. Thus, potential for improved reports and other assignments is enhanced as children explore these resources.

A number of simulation software packages also expand opportunities for reading and thinking as children learn about geography, biology, life cycles of ants, rain forests, oceans, the Oregon Trail, or city management. Other software programs allow children to compose music for lyrics they have written and to support artistic expression for illustrating their stories.

Finally, a variety of adaptive hardware and software facilitates learning among handicapped children. Examples include word processing software that "learns" an individual's writing style and vocabulary and then finishes words and sentences for the writer. This reduces the number of keystrokes that multiple-handicapped children need to type in a response or to compose a story. Other word processing packages check spelling, grammar, and style for adherence to conventions, a real boon for children identified as learning disabled (and many others also).

In short, the variety of software is enormous and growing every day. We provide but few examples primarily because the technology area is changing so rapidly and new product development has exploded. But the best software available today requires more sophisticated computers than many schools now have, which is why a long-term plan is an absolute necessity. So begin to plan by exploring possibilities and visiting schools and conferences that highlight educational technology. Discuss what sort of technology support teachers envision is a necessity. Involve parents in this process. At the Elsmere Elementary School, three parents provided the primary stimulus for developing network access capabilities and securing donated equipment and a commitment from the district to provide an annual acquisition, training, and maintenance budget for the school's technology effort. These parents provided the expertise and familarized staff with technology and fostered the development of a clearer vision of the roles that technology could play in educating students.

Tech Tips for School People

- People take time to learn new things, even teachers.
- You don't need much to get started, even a garden-variety computer and modem can provide access to telecomunications.
- Offer teachers two types of computer training to suit different preferences—a thirty-hour course that takes them methodically from the start and a one-day intensive course for those who like to experiment first and then ask questions.
- Small groups are better than large ones when you are learning to work with technology.
- Install a few dedicated phone lines precisely where the modems will be located if you are implementing telecommunication. Don't try to use a multiline school phone system.
- To make best use of parents' and community members' expertise, open the school on evenings and weekends to allow these folks to offer classes and individual assistance to staff and students.

Source: Horace: Newsletter of the Essential Schools, vol. 10, Jan. 1994.

It is important to develop a five-year plan and realistic budget expectations that include expenses for training as well as for equipment. Remember that all teachers must eventually become technology literate for the greatest impact—just hiring a computer teacher and stocking a computer lab does not typically enhance classroom instruction. But do not overlook community resources in developing this plan. Local colleges and community colleges often can provide "techies" as resources, at times "on loan" or as part of an internship experience. Parents, retirees, and other community members, and students can often offer useful services and guidance as technology is upgraded and implemented into the school instructional day.

We would close this section by noting that schools might very well consider pursuing donated equipment or purchasing rehabilitated hardware. Often, computers, hard drives, modems, and even software that are being replaced in business and industry are superior to the equipment and programs available now in schools. There have been several examples of such recycling in our communities, but such efforts need to fit into a larger overall plan. Likewise, the purchase of used but rehabilitated computers offers a potential for real savings while still upgrading school technology capacity.

SUMMARY

The basis of any instructional program is the materials and activities that children will work with and on. Textbooks and other commercial curriculum materials can play a vital role in becoming a school where all children are readers and writers. Teaching is a time-consuming occupation, and we simply do not have the time to reinvent the wheel in every classroom in every school. But to achieve our goals both the quality of commercial materials and the quality of their use in classrooms must improve.

American elementary schools present a diversity of frameworks for organizing reading and language arts instruction. While endlessly debated, little good evidence exists that any particular curricular framework reliably produces results that are routinely superior to the others. Instead, in study after study, the classroom teacher is the critical factor. What does seem important about curriculum frameworks is the process involved in selecting any of the various frameworks. Teacher and community involvement in developing curriculum frameworks and selecting curriculum materials seems crucial. Mandated frameworks and curriculum foster resistance and dissatisfaction. It seems important that school staff engage in discussions among themselves concerning the curriculum to be selected.

Most schools do have a framework in place, and the more flexibly that framework works to accommodate the range of teacher preferences and perspectives, the more effective the framework appears to be. All teachers seem to teach better when they are teaching in ways that are compatible with their perspectives on teaching and learning. As was noted earlier, children differ, but so do their teachers. We expect that no curriculum framework will be equally acceptable to all teachers. But at the same time, we agree that children benefit from coherent curricular experiences across their elementary school careers. The tough task is finding the middle ground that offers teachers flexibility and adaptability and offers children some coherence and consistency. But to create schools where all children become readers and writers requires that teachers teach effectively and that children are offered a rich, coherent instructional program with abundant opportunities to select, read, and discuss wonderful books, stories, myths, poems, and biographies (to name but a few).

CHAPTER 6

Time: Minutes, Hours, Days, Weeks, Years

Time matters in teaching and learning. Time is truly important for at-risk children. These children simply have no time to waste. There has been much discussion of the quantity of time American children spend in school, usually in relation to the time children in other nations spend in school. Classroom research has often reported on time allocations in teaching and the use of the time that is available. Teachers are often heard to complain that there is just not enough time to do all that is needed to be done. In this chapter we explore ways in which instructional time might be found or created in elementary schools. We begin with a brief review of the importance of time allocations for teaching.

TIME IS IMPORTANT IN TEACHING AND LEARNING

Across virtually every study of classroom effectiveness in elementary schools one finding stands out. That is, teachers who allocate more time to reading and language arts instruction are the teachers whose children show the greatest gains in literacy development. Another finding of those studies is that the amount of time allocated to teaching reading and writing varies substantially between schools. Often, much variation can be found within schools as different teachers schedule more or less reading and writing time. (Denham & Lieberman, 1980)

Surprisingly, though, schools with many at-risk children routinely seem to schedule less classroom reading and language arts instructional time than do schools with few at-risk children (Birman, 1988). In this national study, classroom reading time was inversely related to the number of children from low-income families. Classroom teachers in schools with the fewest low-income children routinely allocated substantially longer periods of time for teaching reading and writing than did those schools with many poor children—about 25 percent more time each day. Another way of looking at those findings is that schools with lower reading achievement routinely allocated less time for reading instruction than schools with higher achievement—an odd plan for accelerating literacy development. Actually, one might have expected just the opposite finding—schools with many at-risk children allocating larger portions of the day to reading instruction—but that simply was not the case.

Of course, not all schools that serve primarily children from low-income families offer reduced amounts of reading and language arts instruction. In fact, one characteristic of low-income schools that exceed expected achievement levels is that substantial blocks of time are allocated for literacy teaching and learning (Knapp, 1991). One possible explanation for the more common pattern—less time for literacy lessons in schools with high concentrations of poor children—may be linked to the beliefs of the professional staff in the school. If poor children are seen as slow, unmotivated, or unlikely to ever achieve grade-level proficiency, then teachers and administrators would have to act contrary to their beliefs to design programs that attempted to accelerate literacy learning.

Several years ago, we were asked to work with an urban elementary school where reading achievement was substantially below both national and district averages. The reading achievement in the school ranked near the bottom of all city schools. After just one day in the building, a fundamental issue concerning instructional time surfaced. In this school, all classroom teachers offered forty-five minutes of reading instruction daily as per an administrative directive. Contrast that with the nearly two hours allocated in the suburban elementary schools our children attended! It is a long story of how this situation came to be and how it was ultimately altered (with substantially improved achievement as one result), but the terrible fact remains that many children in the urban school were not acquiring literacy simply because they were not being taught very much. Since most teachers in the building had taught there for some time, they were largely unaware of just how limited their time allocations for instruction were.

We believe that it is important for teachers to share information on classroom schedules in the hope that greater schoolwide consistency in allocations of time for literacy lessons might be achieved. Our general principle in establishing basic allocations is to ask: How much time is needed to teach all children to become readers and writers?

Site-based leadership teams, administrators, or teacher teams might take an "inventory" of the time currently being allocated for literacy learning in the school. Because not every activity or lesson is necessarily offered every day, such inventories (or status checks) are usually best done for a week of instruction. Presenting the findings (without teacher identification) leads to useful and interesting discussions about why differences exist.

Time is important in elementary schools. Teachers who view developing children's literacy as among the most important tasks they face typically allocate larger amounts of time to literacy instruction than teachers who rank literacy development third or fourth on their list of importance. Teachers who believe that all children can learn to read and write allocate more time than teachers who believe that some children are unlikely to become literate. But many of the teachers we talk with have no good idea of how much time they should be allocating to reading and writing instruction and few have any good information on time other teachers allocate. This lack of information may account for the fact that in most schools we find some teachers allocate twice as much time to reading instruction as other teachers.

■ SOME KIDS NEED MORE INSTRUCTION AND THAT TAKES MORE TIME

One way to think of the differences children bring with them as literacy learners is to view these differences as primarily differences in how much instruction and how much practice they will need to develop reading and writing proficiencies comparable to their peers. Children exhibit real differences in the ease with which they acquire almost any skill, strategy, or understanding. Children also differ in the ease with which they acquire literacy. But understanding that some children will need more instruction or more opportunities to see a strategy modeled for them is quite different from viewing those children as unlikely literacy learners. Understanding the importance of providing more instruction and more reading and writing opportunities to children who find learning to read difficult forces us to consider how time to accomplish these increases might be captured or created.

The differences children exhibit in their proclivity for literacy learning may stem from several sources. Some of these differences may be explained by the experiences children have in their homes and communities. When children see adults reading and writing, they usually are interested in learning to read and write themselves. Of course, children who have many experiences with reading and writing before they come to school often arrive at school with a head start on literacy learning compared to some other children. Often their literacy has already "emerged," and they can recognize some words and many letters. They may arrive doing a fair approximation of writing. Children with far fewer of these experiences start school behind their more advantaged peers. These children have invested less time in literacy activities and usually their development lags behind those peers who have invested more time. Spending more time in school developing their literacy will undoubtedly be necessary, at least initially, until these children have caught up with their peers.

Expanded preschool experiences rich in literacy learning might provide this extra time. The time might come by enrolling such children in summer-school programs before entering kindergarten and between kindergarten and first grade. Parent training might be another avenue if started early enough and parents are supported adequately. But if children with few home experiences with print and stories, with little in the way of preschool experiences with print and stories, are just plunked down in kindergarten with more advantaged peers, most will never catch up. Children who have spent little time with books and print before they begin school will necessarily need more instructional time allocated to them when they arrive at school.

Imagine this eager learner, Willie. Now, Willie was read to since he was able to focus on a book (about six months of age). Willie had his own magnetic letters and scribble pad with colored markers. But Willie never played much with those things; he preferred his Legos. Willie may be an engineer in the making because he was playing with the "eight-year-old-and-up" Lego kits before he started school. When Willie arrived at school, he did not compare well to his peers on letter naming and letter formation, or coloring in lines, or tracing dot-to-dot figures. Willie preferred to play in the block area (the classroom had no Lego area). Willie was attentive during story-reading sessions—he loved a good story—but Willie liked building, stacking, and imaginative play with the small toy cars in his desk.

As the year wore on, Willie's teacher was worried. During a parent conference, she mentioned her concerns to his parents. She also suggested that Willie seemed "developmentally unready" for promotion to first grade. These comments spurred Willie's parents into action. They began to spend some time each evening working with Willie on letters and words. They reviewed schoolwork with Willie. They worked on proper letter formation by having Willie copy notes they had written to his grandmother. They played, making word games using the magnetic letters on the refrigerator. Willie got a strong dose of individual attention, especially from his mother who had been a primary teacher before she went into educational sales. Willie was promoted, but his parents hired a wonderful tutor to work with him during the summer and sent him to a summer day-care program with an academic component. Willie went on into first grade and never looked back. Willie's parents continued their involvement (as do most middle-class parents) throughout elementary school and Willie thrived. He still liked Legos best of all, but he loved reading informational books (usually cars, trucks, trains, and planes) and mystery books (he ultimately owned and read the complete *Encyclopedia Brown* series).

Willie's story is a middle-class kid story that recurs hundreds of thousands of times each year. Wille's parents did what most middle-class parents do—they gave Willie substantial amounts of high-quality literacy lessons to catch him up. But had Willie not had such well-educated and financially successful parents, his story might have turned out quite differently. We tell Willie's tale because it represents the effects of extraordinary instructional time and attention. Willie needed extra instructional time, and luckily for Willie, his parents had the time, the educational backgrounds, and the financial resources to provide that additional instruction. But when children are not as lucky as Willie, where will the extraordinary time and instruction come from?

Children differ in how much instructional support they will need to become readers and writers. Some children, like Willie, are lucky to have parents with substantial educational, financial, and attitudinal resources available. Other children need extraordinary instruction but must rely on the school to provide it. Whenever such support is needed, extra time must be found to schedule the extraordinary instruction. Both teaching and learning take time. Whenever children need more teaching, schools must find or create more time. Unfortunately, few schools organize instructional programs in ways that offer additional time for teaching children needing extraordinary support. Perhaps this is because the differences in childrens' literacy learning have not been viewed primarily as differences in the amount of instruction they will need to develop into readers and writers alongside their peers.

CREATING TIME TO TEACH AND LEARN

Most American elementary schools are open for instruction for 180 to 190 days each year. Most children spend between five and six hours a day in these schools. However, in many schools, one-third to one-half of the school day is scheduled for nonacademic activities. Routine activities such as arriving in the building and hanging up coats in cubbies or closets, taking attendance, making announcements, gathering lunch money, and the like often take 15 to 30 minutes at the beginning of each school day. Recess and lunch periods combine to occupy another 45 to 60 minutes. Snack time, bathroom, safety patrol, birthday celebrations, holiday festivities, testing and a host of other nonacademic activities may eat away another 30 to 50 minutes. Packing-up activities at the end of the day as children prepare to leave on different buses or as walkers and bus riders prepare to leave at spaced intervals take 15 to 20 minutes. Suddenly, the six-hour school day offers only four hours of academic instructional time!

Over the past 30 years, most elementary schools have hired special subject teachers to offer weekly art, music, and physical education classes for children. As libraries were developed in elementary schools, children were scheduled for weekly library visits. Thus, another 45 to 60 minutes each day are now typically scheduled for participation in these beneficial but non-core-curriculum activities. At the same time, in most states, additional topics have been added to the elementary school curriculum. Is it any wonder, then, that so many elementary school teachers report that the lack of time needed to get everything done that has to be done is one of the most pressing problems they face?

Consider that, to this point, we have not even addressed the issue of special-program participation during the elementary school day. When children participate in Title 1 or resource-room special education classes or in speech-therapy or gifted classes, they are usually scheduled out of their classrooms during those three or so hours that remain after the routine activities and the special subject classes are completed. Some classroom teachers have no academic period when all students are present! At-risk students often have no long blocks of uninterrupted literacy instruction as they, instead, move from room to room, program to program, teacher to teacher, for their instruction.

This "planned fragmentation" of the elementary school instructional day creates difficulties for classroom teachers as well as for at-risk children. Often only relatively short blocks of time are now available for classroom teachers in many elementary schools. But coherent, high-quality classroom literacy instruction—essential for at-risk children—is most easily achieved when classroom teachers have large blocks of uninterrupted time.

Creating "Safe" Blocks of Classroom Instructional Time

As a first step in enhancing the time available for classroom teaching and learning, create "safe" periods or "safe" days in all classrooms. For instance, primary-grade classrooms might be offered the entire morning time block as a "safe" block when no special subjects would intrude nor would any children be scheduled for special-program participation. Primary-grade classes would have art, music, physical education, and library only in the afternoons. Children in those classes who receive speech and language therapy would only be scheduled for those services in the afternoon. Likewise for children who participate in Title 1, bilingual, or special education programs away from the classroom. Thus, primary-grade teachers could plan to have the whole morning for instructing all children. Upper-grade classes would have the afternoons protected from intrusions. The special subject classes and the special instructional programs would serve children in the upper grade rooms only during the morning time block.

Other schemes accomplish the goal of providing longer blocks of uninterrupted classroom teaching and learning time. For instance, you might schedule special subjects and special instructional programs on different days for different grade levels. Perhaps primary grade classrooms would have all special subjects and special-program participation scheduled for Tuesdays and Thursdays only. This would leave the classroom teacher with three whole uninterrupted days each week to teach! It is true that on Tuesdays and Thursdays, little time would be left perhaps, for classroom instruction—at least for instruction when all children were in the classroom. Nonetheless, there is little evidence to suggest that such a scheduling plan would result in less learning on the part of any children. As you have probably figured out, under this plan the upper-grade classes would have Tuesdays and Thursdays as "safe" days. More time, however, should be available for classroom instruction on the remaining days in these upper-grade classrooms since the specials are spread over three days instead of two.

Providing extended "safe" periods of time for classroom academic instruction requires little real restructuring of teachers' roles and responsibilities. In many cases it does require,

however, that special-subject teachers' schedules and special-program teachers' schedules (and those of special-program paraprofessionals) are developed at the building level. This will require a shift in many school districts where these teachers have had their schedules set at the district level rather than the building level. Such shifts may also require a revision in special program applications to state and federal agencies. Nonetheless, creating "safe" time periods is a good idea that seems quite easily achieved in most schools. What is required, though, is a commitment to focus attention on the availability of classroom instructional time as a first priority in schedule making.

Extended Time Plans

Another restructuring of school schedules can complement providing "safe" instructional periods in the classroom. The basic notion involves extending the school day by a little or a lot for some or all of the children. We will begin by detailing a plan that extends the day a little for some of the children.

Students who participate in special instructional programs during the school day receive no increased instructional time. In fact, good evidence suggests that these students actually see a reduction in instructional time (Allington & McGill-Franzen, 1993). This happens because it takes time to leave the classroom, travel to a special program room, and settle in for instruction (and to depart that room, return to the classroom, and settle in). This lost time is called transition time, and it eats minutes away every day. Even if transition time loss is only 10 minutes a day (and most studies indicate a 20- to 25-minute daily transition time loss), nearly an hour each week is lost for children who participate daily. A loss of 10 minutes' time from a 30-minute special-program period means the special teacher has to be at least 50 percent more effective than the classroom teacher just to keep the participating children even with the progress they would make if they did not participate.

> Why should Ronald lose 20 to 25 minutes of instruction each day (1½ to 2 hours every week) just to go down the hall to complete vocabulary workbooks with an untrained teacher aide? By the time Ronald packs up and leaves his classroom, travels down the hall, greets the aide, waits for other children to arrive, and finally gets his workbook from the aide, 10–12 minutes have passed since he put away his classroom work. The vocabulary workbook is the least effective way to develop vocabulary, and the aide offers no instruction; she is not allowed to "teach." So Ronald works on some words that are not in his reader or his library book or even his science book. When his pull-out remediation session ends, it will take him another 10 to 12 minutes to pack up, say good-by, and get back into his seat in his classroom. Ronald is scheduled for a half-hour of remediation, but he is actually "unavailable" for classroom instruction for 40 to 45 minutes each day, and he typically works about 20 of the 30 minutes for which he is scheduled. Given these time realities, the aide needs to be a lot more effective than his classroom teacher just to keep him from falling further behind. It won't be, and Ronald won't get better at reading this year.

In addition, children who leave the classroom during the school day miss the instruction offered while they are absent. Currently, children who are finding learning to read difficult are most often scheduled for special instructional programs during some part of the classroom reading and language arts time. Thus, participation does not typically provide them with more instruction but with different instruction. Without real increases in instructional time or intensity, special programs cannot be expected to accelerate children's literacy learning. Without a collaboratively planned, coherent curriculum focus, we can expect more often to confuse children than to assist them.

The problems of interrupted classroom instruction and decreased instructional time for at-risk children can be addressed in several ways. First, special instructional program teachers might be shifted onto flextime schedules. Remedial, special education, bilingual, migrant, and gifted and talented teachers would not work the same hours as classroom teachers. Depending on the school and the community, these teachers might come to school an hour earlier than classroom teachers, or they might arrive an hour or more later. Some of the children who participate in the special instructional programs would then work with these teachers either before or after school.

In virtually all schools, for instance, some children walk to school and thus pose no transportation problems should their school day be extended. Even in schools where many children ride buses, bus transportation is often available after the regular school day as buses make several runs to transport children from different schools in the system. Even if special transportation must be arranged, the idea of working outside the regular school day has much to recommend it. Of course, flextime scheduling of special program teachers will not allow all participating children to be served in an extended day program, but moving even some of that instructional support into an extended day program expands the potential opportunity to learn for those children served.

One elementary school's faculty is scheduled in the building from 8:00 until 4:30 each day while children attend from 9:00 until 3:00. Each teacher and administrator (and librarian, nurse, secretary, and janitor) work with at least one child for a half-hour each day before or after school. Classroom teachers usually work with a child from their classroom while others work with whichever children seem particularly well matched to their strengths and interests. In addition, a few other adults, usually parents of children who attend the school, also work before or after school with children. These adults typically work with kindergarten and first-grade children and simply sit with them while they read and reread simple predictable books. The children read or reread four or five of these little books each day.

These before and after school efforts are so successful that only a few children participate in any remedial or special-education program beyond second grade (although a few upper-grade children do come to the extended day program when they need extra assistance). The children who participate vary as their need for extraordinary instructional support varies. Some children come regularly, while others are scheduled only after an illness or when a brief review or reteaching is necessary.

Saturday School

Another option to consider is developing a Saturday School instructional program for at-risk children. This effort might be staffed by special instructional program personnel who work a Tuesday through Saturday schedule instead of the normal Monday through Friday week. Alternatively, Saturday School could be a half-day program, and these teachers might work only a half-day on Friday, working instead the half-day on Saturday. Otherwise, Saturday School could be staffed with a combination of special teachers and classroom teachers, all earning extra pay for the extra service.

As long as the Saturday School instructional program offers a strong focus on teaching, this design expands children's opportunity to learn. A blend of tutorial, small-group, and large-group instructional activities could be organized to fill either a half-day or a full-day program. Children and their parents value Saturday School when real assistance is available.

Summer School

The availability of summer school instruction has decreased substantially from the late 1960s. This is unfortunate since summer programs offer the potential to expand children's opportunity to learn. Access to summer school seems especially important for at-risk children. Research suggests that disadvantaged children acquire literacy at approximately the same rate as their more advantaged peers during the school year. But advantaged children continue to develop literacy abilities during the summer (though not as rapidly as during the school year), while disadvantaged children actually lose literacy abilities during the summer months (Hayes & Grether, 1983). This "summer reading loss" is critical since these children begin school with fewer literacy experiences than their more advantaged peers and thus are "behind" them in literacy development from the start of school. While school experiences develop literacy in all children, it is the disadvantaged children who most often lose ground over the summer. Thus, even when the school is doing a good job, disadvantaged children often cannot match the rate of literacy development year after year because the lack of summer literacy experiences leads to an overall loss of some of the gains made in school.

Summer school could take several forms. In some Philadelphia elementary schools that serve many economically disadvantaged children, the faculty decided to use federal Title 1 program funds to extend the school year for a month. In this case, remedial services during the regular school year were substantially reduced to fund the summer school effort. However, these teachers were interested in shifting to this extended time model for another reason. Very simply, the number of children participating in one or more special instructional programs during the school year had grown so large that classroom teachers felt they had been rendered largely ineffective. So many children were coming from and going to special programs all day long that it was difficult to carry out effective classroom instruction. Moving to the summer school design not only worked to reduce the children's summer reading losses; it also resulted in enhanced classroom instructional efforts (Winfield, 1991).

Another school's summer program was redesigned so that all children participated in a daily half-hour tutorial focused on reading and writing strategy development, spent another hour and a half in independent and small-group literacy learning and practice, and spent a final hour in art, music, or creative dramatics linked to the children's books they were reading. In addition, the school opened its library for the summer, and funds were allocated to give each child a paperback book each week for their bedroom libraries.

A third school selected the Foxfire model for their summer school effort. Children engaged in authentic literacy activities that included collecting and illustrating (with artwork and Polaroid photos) oral histories of buildings, companies, and people in the neighborhood. The summer school took the shape of collaborative work teams and looked more like a newsroom, we suppose, than an elementary school. But children were almost constantly reading, writing, editing, summarizing, transcribing, discussing, and illustrating real stories of real places and people. Using desktop publishing software, the students created reports of their work that were then bound into books by paraprofessional staff in the fall and added to the school library collection.

A fourth option is the summer drop-in center. In this case, fewer staff are needed and most activities are group oriented, often as cooperative learning groups. Most activities are scheduled in a single large-group area or outdoors but the school library remains open. In some cases, bookstores, book fairs, and sleepy-time read-ins (where everyone sleeps over in the gym) are also scheduled. Story-hour sessions are a regular feature with older children also available to read selected books to small groups of preschoolers or primary students. Either morning hours or an evening schedule seem most popular, with parents more often available in the evening for joint children and parent activities. This model emphasizes increasing the access children have to books with a much smaller focus on instructional intervention. Thus, enhanced achievement results from additional independent reading more than from additional instruction. But the need for only one or two staff members along with several volunteers (perhaps high school students or folks who are school-year volunteers) make this an inexpensive option.

A final option is quite different from traditional notions about summer schools but deserves consideration. The idea is to offer community-based access to books, stories, and print activities during the summer months. Many towns and cities offer a variety of summer recreational activities for children, many quite educational though rarely book oriented. We think schools need to become much better partners with other community agencies, especially for the summer months. The basic notion is to work with these agencies to develop ways to enhance children's opportunities to read and write during the summer. For instance, in one town an honor library of children's books, mostly paperbacks, was set up at the town recreational park where children came to swim, play in Little League and soccer games, and participate in assorted other forms of recreation. Children simply took home books they wanted to read, and everyone hoped they remembered to bring them back. The book collections were a bit ragtag to begin with and more so at the end of the summer, but hundreds of books were taken home each week and only a few were lost forever. Some of the recreation staff found that story-time activities were a wonderful way to occupy children during rest periods and waiting-for-parent periods at the end of the day. Such activities increased parental awareness of the honor library and increased the use of books by children.

This strategy is inexpensive because it involves no summer professional staff time. At the same time, we must note that often children making the greatest use of the library were children who were not usually considered to be at-risk. Nonetheless, we offer this as our final model because of its simplicity and potential for increasing the time children spend reading. Such a plan could be easily expanded to other summer venues such as the YMCA/YWCA camps and centers or even to neighborhood commercial establishments such as grocery stores or ice cream shops. The basic goal is to put books into the community and stimulate community interest in reading to and with children.

The Arbor Hill Elementary School in Albany, New York, represents one example of the development of extended time programs. Using a combination of local, state, and federal funding, Arbor Hill Elementary literally operates from 7:30 in the morning until well into the evening and offers Saturday School and summer school programs. An Early Bird Story Hour is staffed by paraprofessionals each morning before the school day begins. Then a breakfast program feeds most of the students before classes begin at 8:45. After 3:00, at a time when many urban elementary schools are emptying of children for the day, Arbor Hill Elementary begins a schedule of homework support sessions, piano lessons, drama club activities, karate, ballet, gymnastics, science projects, craft projects, and a Police Atheletic League sports program. Nearly three-quarters of the 750 students participate in one or more of the scheduled activities. After 5:00, other activities are offered for students and their parents, including aerobics classes, adult and parent education sessions, computer classes, and so on.

Summer schools work when they expand children's opportunities to actually read and write and to receive instructional assistance and support. Nonetheless, it is possible to design summer school in the programs that do not work very well. In one program we studied, children attended summer school in the mornings for five weeks. But the only reading or writing instruction they received was during a daily half-hour instructional block. Even though instructional groups were small (two to four children), the daily half-hour resulted in only an additional 10 to 12 hours of reading instruction (or roughly equivalent to the reading time available during one and one-half weeks during the school year). No one should expect large gains from 10 to 12 hours of small-group instruction. In an attempt to make this summer program "fun," the planners included much playground time, much arts and craft time, and much breakfast, snack, and lunch time. Of course, not much time was left for teaching children to read and, predictably, participation generally fostered little reading or writing development.

Support for summer school and year-round programs is growing among parents as the number of work-outside-home mothers increases. America is no longer an agricultural society where children are needed to work in the fields during the summer months. It may be that all schools need to consider expanding the school year, not so much to catch up with our international competitors, but to catch up with the rest of American society.

MAKING SENSE OF TIME

Having lobbied hard, to this point, to convince you that time is a critical facet of planning and organizing literacy learning programs, we need to try to sort out a few of the bugaboos that enmesh issues of time in school. We would first note that spending twice as much time engaging in ineffective instructional practices will hardly produce any desired result. While time matters, how time is used matters more. Setting aside large blocks of uninterrupted time or extending the school day or year are good beginnings, but only beginning steps.

Planned Time. Much of what has been discussed concerning time so far falls into the category of *planned time allocations*. In fact, much of what policy makers and educational planners usually discuss (and sometimes regulate) falls into planned time allocations. For instance, most state education agencies mandate the length of both the school day and the school year. While these vary from state to state, the differences tend to be fairly small. School districts also regulate time usually by electing to follow the minimum length school day and year. Across a state, then, most kids go to school the same number of hours each day and the same number of days each year. This is so even though it is obvious to virtually everyone that some districts have substantial numbers of at-risk children and other districts have but few.

This situation may be changing, however. Recently, one state legislature considered revising the traditional compulsory attendance laws. Rather than setting a single standard (say, 180 days) of attendance for all students, the proposed law sets attendance standards based, in large part, on student achievement. Schools would be required to offer literally year-round classes for children who were lagging behind peers academically (and candidates, say, for retention in grade or special education placement). Again, the fundamental rationale for redefining compulsory attendance lies in the notion of expanding instructional opportunity for some children. While some additional state funds would be available to support this change, the pressure would be increased on schools to focus on academic progress during the school year or face increased costs of operating the mandated summer program.

Sometimes well-intentioned principals create interruptions during instructional blocks. During a recent morning observation in an elementary classroom we listened to nine intercom interruptions. None of the announcements was particularly important with reminders of a school roller-skating party, a Cub Scout den meeting, a special soccer-club program, a cafeteria menu change, an upcoming bake sale, and so on. Each announcement was made separately, and though each took less than one minute, each announcement effectively stopped all classroom work while everyone stared up at the box on the wall. If schools use public address systems, use should be sharply limited to one or two brief periods at the very beginning or end of each day and in the case of true emergencies.

Perhaps it would be reasonable to have the length of the school day and school year differentiated by the characteristics of children who attend each school. Schools that enroll large numbers of children who have had few book and print experiences or children whose parents lack most of the educational and financial resources to provide extraordinary instruction for their children might be open year round and routinely offer extended day and Saturday School sessions. But that would only address the issue of planned time allocations. While that is a good first step, how that time is used by teachers and children is even more important.

Allocated Time. While virtually all elementary schools in any state operate for the same number of hours each day, these schools will differ in *allocated academic learning time.* Even though the school bell rings to start the school day, that bell does not signal the beginning of time actually allocated to academic learning. Wander into almost any elementary school classroom and look at the schedule on the chalkboard or glance at the teacher's plan book. If the school bell rings at 9:00 to signal the official start of the day, in most classrooms academic learning time begins between 9:15 and 9:30, after the morning setting-up routines (attendance, lunch counts, announcements, flag, etc.) are completed. The length of setting-up time varies by school and by classroom within schools. For instance, in some schools, the Pledge of Allegiance is a communal activity led from the principal's office via the intercom system, and classroom teachers must wait for the signal to begin this activity. Likewise, in some schools, attendance and lunch counts are taken over the intercom and teachers and students wait until their room is called before beginning the day. In some schools, morning announcements via the intercom delay beginning the academic time for several minutes, and so on. Within classrooms, routines vary with some teachers using less than half the time to accomplish the daily setting-up activities. In any event, the start of the school day rarely signals the start of academic learning time.

In addition to setting-up activities, other scheduled activities eat away at the availability of academic learning time. For instance, when lunch is scheduled for the period from 11:30 to 12:15, the actual loss of academic learning time is closer to 11:20 to 12:30. This occurs as children and their teachers end an academic activity early to pass in papers, clean off desktops, and begin to line up to make an orderly exit to lunch. Similar losses of academic time occur when children go to and return from recess periods and special classes or library visits. Whole-class bathroom breaks, snack periods, and unscheduled interruptions such as announcements over the intercom or visitors at the door just increase the academic learning time loss.

The amount of time allocated to reading instruction in the early grades seems to have declined over the years while the amount of time spent on other things has increased across the elementary school grades. The table below (derived from Borg, 1980) presents the average number of minutes allocated to reading instruction and to management, transition, and wait periods in second and fifth grade classrooms for three eras.

	Grade 2		Grade 5	
	Reading	Nonacademic	Reading	Nonacademic
1904	157	7	119	7
1926	137	11	108	10
1980	88	44	110	47

In addition, the amount of time spent in art, music, and physical education has increased, nearly doubling for both fifth graders from 35 minutes to 65 minutes each day.

Available Time.   Planned academic learning time always exceeds the *available academic learning time.* Not all the time actually available for academic learning is necessarily used for academic activities by each classroom teacher. Even if it were, there would likely be substantial differences in how different teachers elected to use that time. Consider, for instance, that in one study of 100 classrooms (Fisher & Berliner, 1985) second-grade teachers varied from 60 to 140 minutes of daily reading instructional time; or that over a school year, one fifth-grade class had less than 1,000 minutes of comprehension instruction (less than 10 minutes daily), while other classes offered more than 5,000 minutes; or that one second grade class spent 9 minutes of instructional time on money concepts, while other classes averaged 315 minutes. Such differences can sometimes be explained by noting that different teachers emphasize different subjects and different content within a subject area. In other cases, the differences are explained by noting substantially different uses of available academic learning time; some teachers simply get to teaching more quickly and more often than do others.

We have found that teachers often do not have a clear sense of how much of the available academic learning time should be allocated to reading and language arts instruction. In many schools, teachers seemed to have worked out a consensus on this issue, but in others, no one seems very much aware of what others are doing or how much time they allocate for different subjects. At times, teachers are surprised to find out that they allocate only half as much time to reading and language arts activities as other teachers at the same grade level in their building. We are not suggesting that such issues be mandated but rather that time allocations be discussed and considered.

Engaged Time.   Even when similar amounts of time are allocated to reading and language arts activities in classrooms, major differences in literacy learning outcomes can occur. This is because attention to learning is normally a prerequisite to actual learning. Again, classrooms differ in student engagement in the learning activities. The amount of *time engaged in learning* is the most potent predictor of literacy learning (and virtually all other sorts of learning). In the study of 100 teachers mentioned above it was noted that in some classrooms about half the children were actually engaged in the learning activities in front of them, while in other classrooms about 90 percent were engaged. Children who are engaged in academic work learn more than those children who are simply sitting at their desks daydreaming.

Engagement in learning is important, and two factors, task difficulty and task interest, are related to the likelihood that students are engaged in the learning activity. The activity's difficulty is important because most of us work assiduously to avoid tasks that are impossible for us to do. Most of us even work to avoid tasks that are very hard, unless we have a tremendous interest in actually doing the task. Adults, for instance, usually avoid difficult books (we even hire accountants to avoid reading the tax manuals) unless the book covers a topic we are enormously interested in (and even then we more often search for easy books on the topic). Most adults try to avoid uninteresting books. The worst-case scenario is being required to read a difficult book on something we have no interest in (perhaps a scholarly text presenting economic analyses of educational productivity). Children are not very much different from adults in all of this. Too often we point to the "distractability" of the child who is off-task during a lesson or activity rather than consider alternative explanations. In such situations it is important to first evaluate the "holding power" of the activity by assessing the difficulty of the task and the interest it generates.

Much has been written about students' on-task and off-task behavior. We know that off-task behavior is associated with lower-achieving students (though hardly exclusive to them), but often the reason children are off-task is not understood. During reading and language arts activities, on-task behavior is associated with access to comfortable reading materials. Gambrell, Wilson, & Gantt (1981) observed differences in on-task behavior when good and poor readers were reading materials of varying degrees of difficulty. Poor readers were generally off-task more often but they were also more often confronted with reading materials that were quite difficult for them. When poor readers had access to reading materials they could read comfortably, their off-task behavior became comparable to the good readers. But in classrooms, poor readers are far more likely to be given materials to read that are difficult for them. Schemes using a single material for all students often creates difficulties for lower-achieving readers. In these cases one might expect increased off-task behavior from children who find the reading quite difficult.

Tasks Are Important. This brings us to a final point. The *type of literacy activity* that children are engaged in during the available academic learning time is important. It does matter what kinds of work children spend their time doing. In fact, the nature of the academic work that children do is probably the best predictor of what it is that they will learn. For instance, word-search puzzles seem to have a fairly substantial holding power for most children. Unfortunately, children can do word searches without being able to even read the words! So while we might enter a classroom and see all children hard at work, or engaged, in completing a word-search activity, it would be hard to say what, if anything, was actually being learned.

On the other hand, we might enter a classroom where many children are quietly chatting to each other and assume they are not engaged in learning—just talking. But a closer look would find them discussing what they have just read with one another. This type of activity builds the authentic conversations that all literate people have with one another about books. Enter another classroom and we might see children lolling about all over the room engaged in silent reading of self-selected children's books. Now this view does not look very much like the traditional classroom nor very much like the traditional reading lesson. But it is the time that children actually spend reading and writing and engaged in conversations about that activity that is the most powerful factor in developing children's reading and writing.

Classrooms differ enormously in the amount of time children spend engaged in actual reading and writing activities. One federal study of schools in three states that served many low-income children (Knapp, 1991) noted that in some classrooms children actually read only 5 minutes daily while in other classrooms children averaged 48 minutes of actual reading each day. In some classrooms, children spent only about 15 percent of the time allocated for reading instruction actually reading. In other classrooms, children spent over 75 percent of that time reading. A similar pattern of variation existed in writing activity. In some classrooms, children averaged only 8 minutes a day of writing, and in others they averaged 48 minutes. In some classrooms, children did less than 1 extended writing activity each week, and in other classrooms children averaged eight. Schools with higher achievement levels had more teachers offering longer blocks of time for both reading and writing. Still, the extent of variation was surprising and found to be related to teachers' training and beliefs about the children they taught, school and district curricular policies, and school and district provisions for staff development. These variations were not just random occurrences but were largely predictable from teacher, school, and district factors.

Given that most children are in school about six hours each day and have about five and one-half hours of that time allocated to instruction, it is surprising that so many children spend so little time actually reading or writing in school. Teachers (and often their administrators) in many schools seem uncomfortable when children are *just* reading! These teachers seem to view engagement in reading as more a leisure activity than real educational work. Similarly, they seem uncomfortable when children are *just* writing or sharing their stories with other children. Often, traditional seatwork activity assignments make these teachers more comfortable. Some teachers and principals see seatwork as the real work of the school literacy program and assign only small amounts of reading and writing. Unfortunately, such a view is sadly out of date given what we have learned about how children might best spend their time to become readers and writers.

The time children spend in traditional seatwork activities is relatively useless as far as developing reading and writing proficiency (Leinhardt, Zigmond, & Cooley, 1981). It is not that all seatwork tasks are themselves largely irrelevant to effective strategy development, but rather that often the seatwork simply does not focus on strategy use. Instead, much seatwork has only required that children be able locate information and copy it onto a worksheet. Most seatwork has presented low-level tasks and occupied time that might better have been used to expand the opportunity to read and write. Far more powerful are occasions when children spend large blocks of time reading and writing and interacting with their teachers about the books they are reading and the stories they are writing. At-risk children, especially, benefit from both increased opportunities to read and write and increased instructional guidance teachers can provide. Of course, for reading to replace seatwork we will need to make access to interesting, comfortable reading material as easy as access to worksheets. Too many schools make workbooks, worksheets, and dittoes far more accessible than books, magazines, and newspapers. Many schools spend far more on seatwork supplies than on books and magazines for the classrooms. The basic question that needs to be asked is, Do teachers find it easier to access 25 workbooks than 25 tradebooks or 25 copies of a magazine?

Is Time a Problem in Your School?

Should providing more time for children to read and write and more time for teachers to teach reading and writing become an immediate priority? To answer this question, information about what is *really* happening is needed. Here are some possible ways to gather that information.

1. *Ask people.* This is the direct route and so obvious it is often ignored. Ask classroom teachers to keep track of the time they spend in all activities for one week and then have them figure out how many minutes were spent in teaching reading and writing and how long children were actually reading and writing. Ask special teachers to keep track of their time, too. You can also ask children to log

their activities for a day and then figure out how many minutes they spent reading and writing.

2. *Observe in classrooms* with the question, "How much reading and writing instruction and actual reading and writing are occurring?" After visiting classrooms, note what is actually happening during the time allocated for reading and language arts. After a few weeks, estimate how much of the allocated time children are actually engaged in literacy promoting activities.

3. *Shadow some children* whose literacy development is of concern. Focus in on three or four children who are struggling with their literacy development and see how much time they are engaged in literacy-promoting activities. If the child goes to a special class, determine how much time that child loses traveling to and from and getting started. Determine what the child missed while out of the classroom. When the child is engaged in classroom activities, observe carefully with the "What is this child really doing?" question in mind. If the class in engaged in self-selected reading, does this child spend most of his or her time traveling back and forth to the bookshelf? If the class is writing, how many words does this child actually write? If the teacher is working with the class or a group that includes this child, does this child appear to be attending to and able to profit from the instruction?

Prisoners of Time was the title of the report of the National Education Commission on Time and Learning (1994), a legislatively established independent commission charged with providing a comprehensive review of the relationship between time and learning in U.S. schools. After reviewing the limitations of schooling defined by the same minimum time requirements for all students the commission noted:

> Learning in America is a prisoner of time. For the past 150 years, American schools have held time constant and let learning vary. . . . It should surprise no one that some bright, hard-working students do reasonably well. Everyone else—from the typical student to the dropout—runs into trouble. . . . In the school of the future, learning—in the form of high measurable standards of student performance—must become the fixed goal. Time must become an adjustable resource.

SUMMARY

Time matters in teaching and learning literacy. Time matters because it takes time to teach and it takes time to learn to read. Some children require greater opportunities to engage in reading and writing and need greater access to their teacher and to instructional guidance and support. Both take time. Schools can organize the instructional day in ways that increase or decrease the amount of instructional time allocated to classroom instruction. Too often, current school policies work against teachers having large blocks of instructional time available. So do special instructional programs that pull children out of the classroom or send special teachers into classrooms to work with children. We have proposed creating "safe periods" for each classroom—periods in which all children are available to participate in classroom instruction. Extended time programs, before and after school, Saturday School, and summer school all offer real opportunities to expand the instructional time available to both teachers and children.

Classroom organization and management affects the instructional time children have each day. In the schools we have studied we have invariably found two classrooms, at the same grade level, where opportunity to read and write differed enormously. Some of this difference is attributable to differences in the value the teachers assign teaching reading or differences in teacher understandings about what time allocations are considered appropriate. Often these differences in beliefs and understandings are linked to differences in professional-development opportunities offered in different schools. But these differences can also reflect differences in the structure of the school day and the efficiency with which teachers accomplish routine tasks such as opening and closing activities and transitions from one activity to another.

However, while time allocations are critical, the way children spend allocated time is just as important. Simply increasing the time that children spend on tasks that offer little potential for fostering literacy development is not, obviously, a sensible plan. Thus, when addressing the issue of time, schools must necessarily consider how children spend the time now allocated. In some cases, a best first step would be to improve the quality of the tasks that children do during the time currently available.

Time is important, and at-risk children have no time to spare during the school day. Even small amounts of time lost daily can accumulate to large amounts across a year or across an elementary school career. Creating schools where all children become readers and writers requires careful consideration of how the available time is used and how additional instructional time for children who find learning to read difficult might be found or created.

Tests, Authentic Assessments, Portfolios, Report Cards, and the Evaluation Process

P robably no other educational topic generates as much conversation as does testing. Some folks argue that tests play an essential role in advancing educational reform, while others argue that tests inhibit the most needed reforms. As with many other educational issues the talk about testing often represents the situation as dichotomous—supporting either more and better testing or rejecting all traditional testing in favor of alternative assessment procedures. We believe that there is a middle ground that offers a more balanced alternative. Obviously, current testing programs have limitations and unintended effects, but the alternatives proposed to replace current practices also have limitations. Traditional large-group testing can play a useful role in creating schools where all children become readers and writers, but many common testing practices will need to be reconsidered to achieve that potential. Likewise, many alternative evaluation procedures have the potential for improving instructional efforts, but public confidence in these procedures and professional expertise in their use will need to be fostered before that potential can be fulfilled.

In this chapter, we briefly review the limitations of traditional assessment before offering a plan for improved use of standardized achievement tests. We also describe a number of alternative strategies that have been advanced for evaluating both individual literacy development and the effectiveness of instructional programs.

TRADITIONAL TESTING PROGRAMS

A recent national study (Barton & Coley, 1994) reports that the most common testing programs in elementary schools involve the use of group-administered paper-pencil tests with primarily multiple-choice reponse formats (although this is not typically true of writing assessments). Two types of these tests have long dominated school testing programs for reading achievement: nationally normed standardized group achievement tests and the tests accompanying basal reading series. The former have usually been administered annually, most often near the end of the school year. Basal testing has usually occurred three or four times each year. While the tests share common design formats, some significant differences can be found in the tests' construction and most common uses.

Standardized Reading Achievement Tests

The use of standardized achievement tests has grown substantially in the last 30 years. Some of this growth was fueled by the accountability movement as states imposed annual testing programs on schools. Before 1975, only a few states mandated testing, but by 1990, 47 states required schools to test students. In 39 states, student performance was compared with state performance standards (Coley & Goertz, 1990). Even in the three states not mandating testing, most schools tested children on standardized achievement tests. Most schools in the 47 states where testing was mandated did substantially more standardized testing than was required.

Barton and Coley (1994) report that most statewide assessments use multiple-choice formats for evaluating reading proficiency, but 38 states collect writing samples for evaluating writing proficiency and 6 states now collect information from student writing portfolios. The report also notes that much current activity is found in states focused on developing alternative assessment formats, but only 5 states currently have such assessment options in place. Current assessment programs will change and the traditional standardized achievement test results will become less important as alternative forms of assessment are developed, validated, and implemented. But for now, most schools continue to use traditional assessments.

Standardized achievement test data have two basic uses. Test scores are often used to rank-order school performance and, inappropriately, to rank-order individual children's performance. Administrators can find out how their school's performance compares with other schools and, in most cases, how performance compares with other schools with similar students. Thus, in an ideal world, standardized achievement tests might provide a reasonably efficient and cheap means of estimating how well instructional programs are doing. But it is not an ideal world. There are the now-routine reports of widespread use of unethical and ethically questionable practices regarding the administration, scoring, and reporting of standardized achievement test results.

Probably the most important change schools could make would be to end the use of standardized achievement test performances to rank students and to place them in groups or programs. Very simply, standardized achievement test performances are not very reliable estimates of individual children's reading development. A look in the technical manual of most tests will quickly confirm the inappropriateness of using such scores as measures of who reads best (or worst). Standardized achievement tests work reasonably well when comparing performances of groups of children (e.g., classes, grade levels, schools, or district aggregate performances), but they are just not good measures of individual achievement and should not be used to promote or retain children or to assign children to reading groups, to special programs, or to particular levels of basal readers.

Haladyna, Nolan, and Haas (1991) offer a listing of current test preparation practices with a judgment of such practices' ethics. Their basic criteria for the ethical judgments were derived from the question; *Will the practice artificially raise test scores without actually enhancing children's reading development?* In other words, will the practices simply make the school look like it is doing a better job than it is? Below is their listing of practices with their rating of the ethical value (E = ethical, U = unethical, HU = highly unethical).

- **E**   Training general testwiseness.
- **E**   Increasing motivation through appeals to parents and students
- **U**   Developing curriculum based on test
- **U**   Presenting children with items similar to those on test
- **U**   Using *Scoring High* or other score-boosting workbooks or software
- **U**   Altering test administration procedures (e.g., adding time)
- **HU**   Dismissing low-achieving students (including handicapped) from test
- **HU**   Presenting students with items verbatim from tests prior to administration
- **HU**   Altering answer sheets or discarding some tests

While some items seem patently obvious as to the ethics involved, others, such as use of special workbook practice, were widely practiced even though deemed unethical (because while scores rise, the children do not actually read any better). Virtually every practice listed was in use in some locations. The question that remains is whether the problem is the tests themselves or the practices of educators involved with the testing programs.

Standardized tests are built on probability theory (remember the coin-flip analogy from your tests and measurements class?). The basic premise is that no test performance is ever a reliable measure of individual reading development but that the tests scores achieved by some children overestimate their actual reading development and the scores achieved by other children underestimate their actual development. Theoretically, all this error is supposed to be balanced when performances of a number of children are aggregated. Test publishers have actually worked hard to illustrate the lack of reliability in individual performances. Figure 7.1 is an illustration of a test publisher's report of the scores of one child on a standardized achievement test. Notice how the test scores are represented as bands in the display to the right of the reported national percentile ranking (PR) and national stanine (S) columns. These bands indicate the range of scores that best represent this child's academic development. The bands in the illustration better communicate the meaning of the test results by graphically illustrating the lack of precision inherent in the specific test scores reported (the "word reading" percentile ranking of 52 actually is better represented as a score falling into a range of scores somewhere between the percentile ranks 39 and 65). In a footnote on this report, the test publisher indicates that overlapping test bands denotes no "meaningful difference" in the scores reported. Notice that only the "listening comprehension" measure does not overlap other scores—even though the percentile rankings between 52 to 70 are reported on the other five measures. The key point is that standardized achievement tests, although offering an illusion of precision, are not reliable estimates of individual reading development.

Figure 7.1
A sample pupil profile from a popular standardized achievement test.

TESTS	NATIONAL PR	S	NATIONAL PERCENTILE BANDS
Work Study Skills	65	6	
Word Reading	52	5	
Reading Comprehension	68	6	
Vocabulary	70	6	
Listening Comprehension	95	8	
Spelling	52	5	

National Percentile Bands axis: Below Average — Average — Above Average
Scale: 1 5 10 20 30 40 50 60 70 80 90 95 99

It is also important to note that even if standardized achievement tests were much more reliable estimates of individual reading development, they would still suffer some problems of validity. Such tests do not measure everything that children might know or be able to achieve. In fact, standardized achievement tests assess only a narrow range of the reading processes that children are expected to develop. Such tests do not measure, for instance, whether children read widely across a variety of genres, authors, and topics. They do not tell us whether children can discuss what they have read or synthesize across texts or compare one author with another. The tests do not really tell us much about reading habits or strategies that children might use. They do not provide much information about comprehension processes, since the tests measure primarily the lowest level cognitive processes operating on short pieces of text. They do not tell us whether children have refined strategies for selecting books or for locating materials to pursue developing expertise on a topic. In short, current tests measure only a few aspects of reading development.

For an assessment to be valid it needs to measure not only what is taught but also what is important. Today most standardized reading tests measure neither very well, although test developers have made some important improvements in recent years. But standardized tests can provide snapshots of the reading development of groups of children and can play a useful role as part of a broader and more comprehensive program evaluation effort.

Standardized Language Tests

While there are standardized tests of language achievement, these suffer the same problems as noted for reading tests, with one additional difficulty: Children do not actually write at all on the most commonly used standardized language tests. We can see virtually no role for the group-administered language achievement tests.

One potentially useful standardized language test is the *Test Of Written Language* (TOWL), published by Pro-Ed Publications of Austin, Texas. This standardized test offers a number of subscales and provides for grade-level comparisons for the writing samples children produce. We mention this test simply because it was designed largely for use in individual diagnostic assessments of children in remedial or special education programs. The test is a useful addition to a school psychologist's repertoire of assessment tools, especially if the psychologist has rarely evaluated children's writing development. We feel that assessing writing on the TOWL makes it more likely that children participating in remedial or special education programs will actually be offered writing instruction and have composition goals included on individual educational plans. In the best of cases, the TOWL actually serves an instructional role by fostering the development of more appropriate assessment strategies in those who learn to use it.

A Role for Standardized Reading Achievement Tests

As a first principle, we suggest that schools need to be clear about how they will use standardized reading achievement test results for. Keep in mind that such results cannot be used to sort individual children accurately or to rank-order children on literacy development. Neither can they be used to inform instructional practices specifically, although they might play a general role in this realm. We think that standardized achievement tests are best used to monitor basic reading achievement patterns in a school. Every child does not need to be tested every year to accomplish this, however. For instance, standardized achievement test performances of second- and fifth-grade students might be collected annually, and each year the results would be compared with the achievement of previous second- and fifth-grade

Having second- and fifth-grade achievement data available (even anonymous data) across a three-to-five-year period allows school personnel to broadly examine the effects of changes made in various aspects of the program. For instance, a school staff might collect (or recover from older school records) the achievement test scores for a three-year period when the instructional programs were relatively stable before implementing a new program design (shifting to whole-day kindergarten, adding Reading Recovery as an intervention for at-risk first-grade students, shifting to a multilevel, nonability grouped primary-grade reading program, or increasing the number of trade books available and the time spent in school actually reading). Continuing to collect the second- and fifth-grade test scores over the next three years would allow school staff to examine the effects of such changes. There are two questions to be asked of the data:

- Has the average reading achievement level of second graders increased since the intervention? (Fifth-grade scores would not be expected to have yet improved.)
- Are fewer second graders exhibiting substantially delayed reading development?

The two questions focus on longer term effects of interventions, but it is the longer-term effects that are important. Short-term improvement, which is the usual focus of evaluations, are fine, but if those effects are not maintained across the elementary years, the intervention's usefulness is questionable (or the intervention needs more long-term supportive efforts). Continuing to collect annual achievement data at second and fifth grade will allow school staff to examine continuing effects of two sorts. What intervention effects appear some five years later at fifth grade? Is the original effect sustained or enhanced as the intervention ages?

students. This would provide a faculty with one sort of information for monitoring the general reading development in the school. Second grade is a reasonable point to begin because test performances of younger children are even less reliable than the results achieved by older children. Also, by the end of second grade the school has had three years (grades K, 1, 2) to develop children's literacy, and one would hope that many children who began school with few book, story, and print experiences would, by then, have accelerated their development and caught up with their peers. Fifth grade is a good point to again assess achievement, before children are off to middle school, as a way of monitoring development across the next three years of schooling (grades 3, 4, 5).

It might be best if schools gave standardized tests anonymously to students—that is, with no names recorded on the tests. This would ensure that schools did not use test scores inappropriately to make decisions about individual students while still providing information on how well school programs were fostering basic literacy achievement. Remember, though, that standardized tests measure only some of the many things children need to learn. Nonetheless, a second- and fifth-grade anonymous achievement-testing program allows school personnel to monitor the effectiveness of instruction and provides one basis for making decisions about program effects. The standardized reading-achievement-test results would become part of an annual school report presented to the board and the public.

Basal Testing Programs

Historically, the testing packages that accompanied basal-reader series focused on short-term assessments of skills mastery. Some basals offered an end-of-week mastery test for monitoring student development. Unit tests, quarterly tests, and end-of-book tests were also part of virtually every basal package. The problem was that these testing programs were rarely adequately field-tested and virtually never underwent any state or national norming process. The tests were more often criterion-referenced than norm-referenced—it was far less expensive and less time-consuming simply to set some performance criterion than to actually administer the tests to large samples of children (as is the case with the nationally normed standardized achievement tests). The basal tests, though, were often designed to mirror the most common standardized test formats (e.g., multiple-choice) so as to provide children practice with those test items and to ease scoring of the tests for teachers. Traditional basal tests, though, suffer enormous problems with reliability of the scores. Standardized test developers spend much time and money field testing and norming tests on large samples of children to enhance the performance of their tests and still are largely unable to develop tests that provide reliable and accurate information on individual children's reading development. Basal publishers skipped the field-testing and norming processes altogether, and their testing programs simply produced even less reliable information than that offered by standardized reading-tests.

Current basal programs still offer these traditional testing programs, but most have reduced the number of such tests and expanded the testing formats to include open-ended responses and some measures of higher-order thinking. In addition, basal publishers now offer a variety of alternative assessment options including some sort of portfolio procedure. The new basal assessments can provide a framework for shifting away from isolated skills assessment and toward ongoing evaluation of children's acquisition of higher-order strategies and processes. This is especially helpful for teachers with little background in alternative assessment practices.

ALTERNATIVE ASSESSMENTS

Over the last few years, much has been written about the potential of alternative forms of assessment for improving educational practices. Much of the impetus for change has come from implementing more naturalistic assessments of students' writing since the new writing assessments seemed to foster an increased emphasis on students' actually writing during the school day (Koretz, Stecher, Klein, & McCaffrey, 1994). Proponents of replacing traditional achievement tests with alternative assessments argue that the new assessments will foster changes in instruction—primarily with a shift toward more thoughtful teaching and learning.

Some proponents use the term *authentic assessment* to describe the nonstandardized assessment processes that schools might implement. But, actually, assessment possibilities range broadly along several continuum. For instance, assessment practices can range from wholly personal to externally imposed. Assessments can be done in the context of daily work or isolated from daily activities. Assessments can be individual or group focused. Assessment results can be diagnostic or simply summative with little feedback on performance or how performance might be improved. In other words, assessment is not simply standardized tests *or* portfolios.

Educators are interested in alternatives because they recognize the several common limitations of standardized testing practices:

- The tests are based on models of literacy that separate reading and writing.
- The tests assess components of reading in isolation from the curriculum.
- The tests assess only narrow aspects of reading and writing processes.
- The tests reduce a complex array of learnings to a single number or grade.
- The information from tests is too general to be useful for teaching.
- The test results are often misinterpreted by parents, teachers, and administrators.
- The tests developed by outside experts lead few teachers to ownership of results.

The idea behind developing more authentic assessments is that the most common limitations of traditional assessment practices can be overcome by more personal and more integrated evaluations drawn from the daily work that children do in the classroom. So what sorts of authentic assessment alternatives have been offered to improve upon the current situation?

Observational Records

Teachers continually observe children in their classrooms, but many teachers are hard-pressed to discuss the development that is occuring right in front of them. For instance, when asked to describe children as writers, teachers often focused on neatness, punctuation, and spelling and had little to say about the genres of writing that the child use. Many teachers had difficulty discussing critical features of writing like cohesion, plot or character development, organization of information, or argument. Many did not seem to observe how children gathered information, developed stories, or revised and edited their works. A similar situation existed for reading development, with many teachers unable to describe children's reading development much beyond noting their rank in the classroom (in the low group) or their "reading level" (in the 3/1 reader, still reading easy books) or offering some comment about skills development ("has difficulty with short voweis"). Impoverished observations such as these usually stem from (1) limited skills for observing children's literacy processes and (2) limited expertise about how reading and writing competence develops in children.

The $64 question is; do teachers develop expertise that results in better observation or do they enhance expertise by learning observational strategies? The answer, we believe, is yes! Acquiring more complex understandings of how children learn to read and write improves observational skills. But acquiring observational strategies also helps develop greater teacher understanding of children's literacy learning. So what observational strategies might teachers need to better understand learning to read and write?

Learning to Observe Children's Reading. A first step in learning to observe is learning to record what one observes. The human brain can hold only limited amounts of information in an active bin, and the constantly active classroom environment provides millions of bits of information every day. At the end of the average school day, children and activities blur together without some sort of record keeping. Stopping by after school to ask a teacher about the specific performances of a single child during the morning reading lesson usually results in broad generalities rather than insights as to specific strategy use. For instance, teachers may talk generally about a child's engagement or lack of it but will usually be unable to link engagement and disengagement to specific activities, tasks, or student interest in or facility with assignments given. Only by more closely observing children and recording what has been observed can teachers begin to provide more specific information about children's learning.

The time-tested observational stalwart is recording oral reading errors and behaviors. There are several forms for such recording, but all generally provide the teacher with a record of how accurately different children read the material. Even if the record provides only an accuracy rating (92 percent of words accurately identified), the record is more useful than the very general information available from teachers who do not make oral reading records. Children need much exposure to materials that they can read nearly error-free (97–98 percent accuracy). When children receive a steady diet of reading material that they read with lower accuracy, reading development is inhibited. Hence, the need for classroom teachers to observe and record reading accuracy regularly.

However, if the oral reading record is a bit more detailed, indicating, for instance, which words the child had difficulty with, the record provides better information for instructional planning. A child who has consistent difficulty with words of three or more syllables provides evidence of the need for better strategies for dealing with longer words (often the strategies that work on shorter words do not work on big words). Similarly, if the oral reading record contains information about a child's phrasing and fluency when reading aloud, it provides yet more information on the sorts of instructional interventions we might consider (opportunities to reread, taped read-alongs modeling fluent reading). A reading teacher or special education teacher might use the records from that day's classroom reading lesson to offer a personalized strategy lesson immediately, thereby making it more likely that such support lessons actually address current instructional needs.

The particular form of the oral reading record is less important than the existence of some record. Whenever children read aloud in classrooms, teachers should be evaluating that performance in some manner. Our favorite recording technique is the "running record" scheme devised by Marie Clay (1993) in her *Observation Survey of Early Literacy Achievement*. That technique requires only lined paper and a pencil for recording the reading performance. As children read, the teacher makes a check for every word pronounced correctly. Each line on the recording sheet corresponds to a line in the text being read. When a child mispronounces a word, the teacher writes down the mispronunciation instead of recording a check. Noting page numbers on the recording sheets makes it easy to later compare the child's reading to the text. Establishing reading accuracy is quite easy because teachers only have to count the checks for each correctly pronounced word and count the mispronunciations recorded. We would strongly recommend Clay's little book to schools interested in developing good records of children's oral performance (as well as observing writing progress and evaluating children's developing concepts about print and books).

Even more basic is simply recording oral reading fluency as good, fair, and poor. As simple as this might seem, fluency or the lack of it provides good evidence of the ease or difficulty the child is having with any given text. Teachers literally just listen, usually with the book closed, as the child reads aloud. Regularly recording the fluency level of children's reading provides good information for planning instruction and for evaluating its effects. If oral reading remains a struggle, the difficulty of the materials, the procedures for introducing the materials, and the child's strategies for predicting and self-monitoring need to be evaluated.

But oral reading is only a small part of the reading activity in any classroom. So how do teachers observe silent reading? One good source is to consider how we observe other adults when they read. For instance, by sitting in an airport, it is easy to observe the different materials being read (newspapers, magazines, popular novels, technical materials, memos, children's books, etc.). Formally collecting information on these different materials could be considered research. If we were interested in what reading went on at airports, we could routinely collect this observational data. Depending on the fundamental purpose of our observation, we might collect more detailed records on title and authors or on types of materials or on the readers' genders. We might even chat briefly with readers to gather information on motivation, response, habits, and plans. Teachers (and adminstrators) could collect similar information from observing silent reading activity in classrooms.

We might also want to note general reading speed or observe and note the discussions that follow a reader's completion of a book. We could collect information on partner roles during paired-reading activities. By conferencing with or interviewing children, we can add information on response to books, reasons for selecting certain books, and so on. Outside of school we rarely interrogate people to find out if they are really reading that newspaper in front of them! We rarely quiz friends or loved ones to ensure they understand the novel they are reading. Instead, we watch, we discuss, we share. Such activities are also useful and powerful in school and can provide wonderfully rich assessment opportunities if we simply record what we see and hear.

Learning to Observe Children's Writing. But reading is only a small part of the literacy work that goes on in classrooms and only a small part of any good observational scheme. Schools need records of children's writing development. Evaluating a student's essay by assigning a grade provides little information for instructional planning. Grades provide little information to writers on how the piece might be improved. Grades offer little information for support teachers about which aspects of writing need attention. Grades offer little information to parents about how a child's writing is developing.

On the other hand, written observations about what development was noticed in each child's work provide enormously useful information that can be communicated to children, to support teachers, to parents. Even observations of spelling development or attention to writing conventions (capitalization, punctuation) provide useful information about lessons needed and which students should be included. While samples of children's writing can be saved in a portfolio system, the interpretation of a child's writing development on a particular assignment is needed for the next day's lesson. So saving writing is not sufficient. Teachers also need to record their observations of children's writing development regularly.

Writing Samples and Scales.   Because writing results in a visible, external product, assessing and evaluating children's writing development seems easier than monitoring their reading development. Children's writing development can be looked at in a variety of ways. Many teachers and parents keep samples of writing, including first-draft writing and published pieces. Looking at first drafts written several months apart should provide information about whether the writing is becoming better organized and clearer and whether the child is moving toward proficiency with expected punctuation and other editing considerations including more conventional spelling of words. It is also helpful to look at the first and final drafts of the same piece. This snapshot of the writing process will tell you if children are becoming better able to revise, edit, and polish their writing.

Figure 7.2 shows a portion of the K–2 writing fluency scale developed by one school to help teachers focus on the writing development from kindergarten through second grade. In this school, teachers collected five writing samples from each child—end of kindergarten, middle of first grade, end of first grade, middle of second grade, and end of second grade. These writing samples were all focused on the same topic, a topic such as "Things I Like to Do" or "A Day in Our Classroom," which most children knew a lot about. These writing samples were then scored by two persons using the *K–2 Writing Fluency Scale* and placed in the child's cumulative portfolio. The growth and development of writing fluency was clearly documented by comparing the five writing samples focused on the same topic across two and a half years of school.

Many states have mandated end-of-grade-level writing tests for children from third grade on. Certain types of writing—descriptive, narrative, clarification, and so on—are expected at certain grade levels, and on a designated day, all children at a particular grade level write to the same writing prompt(s). These writing samples are then scored. In most cases, they are scored "holistically" by teachers trained to use a writing scale. Children's writing is evaluated against some common standard sample.

Of course there are always problems with any kind of one-shot, one-day assessment. Certain children do not perform well on any kind of tests. Everyone has "bad days." Certain prompts are more relevant to some children than to others. Although the scorers are trained to achieve reliability, there is sometimes a very fine line between a sample scored 2 and another scored 3. Despite these problems, we believe that such mandated writing tests provide more useful information than most other standardized testing. Children cannot "guess" their way through the test, and the test closely matches the terminal writing behavior expected from an educated person. For evaluating an individual child's development, we get more information by looking at a portfolio containing many samples written across time and some first to final draft companion pieces. But for deciding how well a school is meeting the challenge of producing clear, fluent writers, most state writing assessments provide useful information.

One effect of the increased mandated testing of writing is that children now spend more school time writing. For years, various groups tried to convince teachers of the clear research finding (Hillocks, 1986) that time spent on worksheet activities emphasizing written language mechanics—punctuation, capitalization, grammar, usage—were largely wasted time

Figure 7.2
A Sample of a Primary Writing Fluency Scale

PRIMARY WRITING FLUENCY SCALE

1. Emerging

__ Expresses ideas mainly through
  pictures or letter strings.
__ Uses some sound spelling
  according to beginning sounds
  heard.
__ Focuses on topic.
__ Writes one or two bare ideas.

2. Developing

__ Relates sentences to topic.
__ Writes sentences that may be short or repetitive.
__ Uses some detail that may be presented
  in list-like form.
__ Uses sound spelling that can generally
  be read by others.
__ Uses some punctuation and capitalization
  but may be inconsistent.

3. Early Fluent

__ Focuses on topic.
__ Uses sentences in logical order.
__ Uses varied sentence patterns.
__ Uses some evidence of detail
  or elaboration.
__ Uses sound spelling, if needed,
  to express ideas.
__ Uses clear or vivid language.
__ Shows growing ability to handle
  mechanics.

4. Fluent

__ Shows organization or sense of story.
__ Has clear beginning, middle, end.
__ Connects related ideas smoothly.
__ Expresses several ideas with detail or
  elaboration.
__ Show originality in word choice.
__ Spells most words correctly.
__ Shows excitement, humor, suspense, or
  some creative element.
__ Shows growing control of writing through
  generally correct mechanics.

because children did not transfer these skills to their own writing. As long as the mandated tests tested these skills in a multiple-choice format, teachers continued to teach them in an isolated-from writing-worksheet way. Now that the assessments focus more on how clearly children communicate ideas in writing, composing has finally replaced worksheets in many elementary classrooms.

Writing assessments usually include evaluative criteria for spelling accuracy, punctuation, and grammar, but the evaluation of children's writing goes well beyond these features. Teachers do need to monitor children's adherence to such conventions, especially in pieces that are being revised and, perhaps, published. Children do need instruction on these conventions, but these lessons need to draw from children's own writing, not some arbitrary skills hierarchy. Teaching the conventions of writing is most powerfully done in the context of children's writing activities—their attempts to communicate their ideas in print. Proficiency in writing is fostered when teachers write in front of students and demonstrate how they think as they compose, revise, and edit.

Teachers can gain enormously high-quality information about the acquisition of literacy by observing children's writing. Composing is really a window to the thinking processes children use. Whether observations focus on the development of control over print and composition conventions such as spelling, punctuation, and grammar or focus more on issues such as topic selection, argumentation, clarity, or fluency of writing, children's compositions provide a rich record of literacy development.

Many of the state writing assessments use a form of wholistic scoring that draws heavily on the original work of Richard Lloyd-Jones (1977). He called the procedure "primary trait" scoring and offered "rubrics" for evaluating persuasive essays on a 0–4 scale as follows

0. No response, fragment

1. Does not take a clear position or offers no reasons for position taken

2. Takes a position and offers one unelaborated reason

3. Takes a position and gives one elaborated reason, one elaborated and one unelaborated reason, or two or three unelaborated reasons

4. Takes a position and offers two or more elaborated reasons, one elaborated and two or more unelaborated reasons, or four or more unelaborated reasons.

This scoring, with its focus on meaning making, has become known as (w)holistic assessment.

Book Selection.   Teachers may observe how capable children are at selecting books for independent reading. Some children, usually at-risk children, seem to spend much of the time allocated for independent classroom reading "wandering" around the book display area and spend more time considering selections than actually reading (Michelson, 1993). Some of this wandering seems to have to do with (1) the limited supply of books available in most classrooms that at-risk children can actually read and (2) a lack of motivation stemming from unsuccessful experiences with books and reading in the past. However, many at-risk children find selecting a comfortable book difficult because they have not yet developed any good sense of what books they might like best nor strategies for determining what books are manageable for them. Failing to observe and record during book-selection periods and failing to observe and record the appropriateness of books children select, all lead to a sort of "blindness" by teachers. Without good records, the teacher has little information to interpret and little basis for instructional intervention. Without such records, support teachers have little information to guide the instruction they offer.

Records of which books children have read are also useful. Too often, schools lack adequate information on students' reading habits and so find it difficult to plan programs to increase the amount or breadth of reading. Several possibilities might be considered. The first is to have children keep a reading log, which is filed at the end of each year in the student cumulative file. The student log can be easily photocopied so that both the school and the child have copies. Such reading logs usually contain books read as part of a planned curriculum and books read independently. When books are part of the planned curriculum, it may be easier to consider simply reproducing the book lists for each grade level and indicate which titles individual children actually completed. If the planned curriculum contains book options from which children (or their teachers) can choose, this is often an ideal procedure. But these procedures do not allow for easy information gathering about reading habits of individual classes or grade levels. For reading logs or lists to be useful a school needs some method to organize the information. Information on individual reading habits is most useful when the records of individual children are pulled together and summarized at least annually.

Such summaries might be largely quantitative in nature and simply indicate the number of titles read. Schools with access to even this information can judge the adequacy of in- and out-of-school reading. Such information also provides at least a crude basis for judging whether targeted interventions (e.g., adding books to classroom libraries, adding a Reading Is Fundamental project, or expanding book club participation) have an impact on children's reading behaviors. However, gathering better information on what books children read and whether they read them in or out of school provides a stronger basis for planning instructional, curricular, or organizational changes. We think it is quite useful, for instance, to know whether most fifth graders have read one or more biographies (or read historical fiction, mystery, and so on). Some of this information could be gathered from interviews, surveys, checklists, analyses of library records, and so on. But routinely gathering and summarizing such information produces better and more accessible information.

Checklists. The use of checklists has become increasingly popular, but we are not quite sure why. Often, the checklists reduce reading and writing to very simple lists of attributes. While such checklists offer a shorthand for recording observations, the checks do not offer nearly as clear a picture as do "quickwrites" or "sticky-label notations" as discussed below. Of course, the checklist's value depends heavily on the nature of the items to be checked off. We see a potential role for checklists in organizing observational information, but the use of checklists would follow the gathering of richer observational data. For instance, checklists could offer a quick way to record the range of book genres a child has read. A form with a comprehensive listing of the texts children would be expected to read (or be able to write) could provide, at a glance, useful information for planning future lessons.

Managing Observational Records. How can teachers manage all these written records of classroom observations? How can such observations be organized so that they serve useful functions for planning instruction or evaluating reading and writing development? We suggest a two-pronged approach to observational records. First, we would have each teacher carry a clipboard at all times during the school day. On the clipboard we would have two sorts of record-keeping devices: blank sheets of lined paper and a sheet of large self-adhesive address labels (the sort you peel off and stick on large envelopes). The teacher would pay particular attention to gathering observational records about one focal child each day. A blank sheet of paper would have the child's name on it and might be used to record oral reading performance or to summarize responses to a brief interview or a structured observation of on-task behavior. The mailing labels would be used for recording information bits on the focal child and on other children across the day. The labels would be attached to individual children's record folders for later use. The teacher might place the full-page records in a child's folder or discard them after the observations have been interpreted and summarized.

At the end of the school day, the classroom teacher will create a *quickwrite* based on the observational records of the day's focal child. This quickwrite should take no more than six to ten minutes and can be organized around the following topics:

- work the child was successful at
- work the child had difficulty with
- strategies the child needs to be taught
- actions to take
- actions other teachers can take

The teacher can compose this quickwrite summary and insert it in a child's folder or jot it in a class notebook kept readily available for review when planning lessons. When this procedure is used, a quickwrite summary of each child is produced eight to ten times each year as are an array of sticky-label observational records. This information is particularly useful for planning with support staff, collaborating with other teachers, and conferring with parents.

Observational records are incredibly useful sources of information for evaluating children's development across time. Such records are far more useful than traditional gradebook entries for planning instruction or evaluating children's growth. A key, though, is the permanence of such records. Too often teachers have jotted notes on students' papers only to lose those notes for planning when the papers are returned to the students. The information collected during observations is not wholly unfamiliar to most teachers nor is the process of interpreting that information largely unfamiliar. What is unfamiliar is the process of gathering and storing observations and then using those records to plan lessons or to evaluate children's development. If in evaluating children's work the goal is to make sense of their development or lack of it, teachers need to look beyond the surface of an individual's performance and they need to track performances across time. Proponents argue that engaging in this sort of "kid-watching" develops teachers' expertise and understandings of how children acquire reading and writing skills. This, in turn, results in higher quality instruction and increased ownership of the outcomes of instruction. As teachers work to develop better classroom-based observation procedures that are incorporated into the assessment program, they accept more responsibility for what children learn from the lessons they teach. But it is also useful to encourage children to accept more personal responsibility for their learning.

Student Self-Evaluations. One unique aspect of the argument for authentic assessment is the inclusion of students in the evaluation process. Developing students that are more personally reflective about their work is a potentially powerful goal of authentic evaluation activities. As children develop their understanding of reading and writing they can become actively engaged in improving those processes. For instance, teachers can ask children to evaluate a story or a book rather than simply ask children questions about what they read. This is the same thinking about books that adults do—adults rarely interrogate each other about a book's content or character names. Children might write or talk about their book selection and whether they are happy with it. Having children audiotape or videotape an oral reading segment of a book or a story to take home to parents, to give to grandma, or to keep at school to be added to over the years is a powerful demonstration, especially if the child prefaces the rendition with a short introductory comment on why he or she selected this segment for taping.

When children compose explanatory notes about a piece of writing, notes that describe how satisfied they are with the piece, how it came to be written, and so on (these can be attached to their writing), it often offers wonderful insights into how the composing process was displayed in this work. The use of self-evaluation is not just asking children to grade their own work—that is a remnant of the traditional assessment practices—but asking children to think and talk about their reading and writing in ways that have generally been absent from our schools.

Interviews.   There are two broad categories of interviews: structured and spontaneous. Structured interviews provide a framework for asking each child for the same information. Spontaneous interviews are tailored to the moment and provide teachers with insights into the thinking processes that children are then engaged in. As with other information, teachers need some system for recording at least the essence of the children's responses to the interview queries.

Johnston (1992) discusses asking children to describe themselves as readers and writers. In some classrooms children could only offer brief and rank-ordering comments such as, "I'm pretty good. I'm in the Robins group." In other classrooms, children provided different responses, such as, "I like mysteries right now but I've been sort of stuck on them all year. I mean I have only read mystery books all year! I probably need to read some other stuff, too."

Similarly, some children seem unable to talk about their writing processes, or as one boy said, "We had to write about our summer so I just made something up." In another school, a different boy described his current writing project this way: "Well, I'm really interested in Native Americans. So I decided to write about the Navajo people. But when I started finding books and stuff, I thought, 'I can't write all this,' so I decided to write on Navajo homes. After I read a bunch of stuff, I found out that it was really the Hopis that built some of the best cliff dwellings so I decided to write about them instead. Actually, I ended up writing about one village called Walpi that was built on the top of a mesa." While these boys were in the same upper elementary grade, the interviews elicited quite different responses about the writing they had just completed.

Interviews can be useful because children often repeat what they hear from their teachers. If reading evaluation focuses on rank-ordering or number of books read or test scores, that is often the criteria children use when they report. On the other hand, if classroom evaluation of reading has focused more on selecting good books, summarizing and responding to those books, and sharing the books with others, the talk elicited is quite different. Likewise, if classroom evaluation of writing has focused on clearly communicating information when writing, on the uses of writing, and on the processes of planning, revising, editing and so on, that is the sort of talk children also engage in. But if length, penmanship, spelling, and so on are the classroom evaluation currencies, children's talk focuses on those features of writing instead.

One way to get a sense of how students understand a school's literacy lessons is to interview children. For instance, while walking through your school you might want to ask children the following sorts of questions:

Have you read any good books lately?

Tell me about the reading you are doing right now.

Who is your favorite author?

What sorts of books have you been reading lately?

Tell me how you chose this topic to write about.

Do you have any other pieces of your writing that I could read?

What do you like best about this piece of writing?

Interviewing children can provide us with extraordinarily useful information. But to be most useful for planning, modifying instruction, or evaluating programs, that information must be recorded, interpreted, and summarized. The children's responses do not have to be recorded verbatim, but notes taken should reflect or summarize the responses given. As with other information in the classroom, interview summaries can be attached to school records or placed in portfolios for later use.

PORTFOLIOS

We purposely saved portfolios for later discussion because everyone seems to focus on them as the basis for "authentic assessment" while ignoring the larger question of what information might be collected in the portfolios. First, there is only general agreement about this. Different people have offered different suggestions for portfolios (and in some schools, portfolios are little more than a place to store completed dittoes for awhile). So we will sketch four types of portfolios (though in our experience few pure examples of any of these types exist).

Best works portfolios (also called showcase portfolios) are collections of children's best work. Most often the children themselves select these pieces and usually explain why they included the piece. In some schools these best works portfolios reflect children's work over several years (or even a school career).

Process portfolios include several versions of work as it has developed over time. For instance, such a portfolio might contain drafts of early versions of a paper or poem to show how the piece developed over time. Again, these are usually organized by the children.

Progress portfolios are often managed by teachers rather than children. These include collections of work intended to illustrate children's development over time. Often teachers include their observational records, notes, and checklists in such portfolios and use the collection in instructional planning and end-of-year evaluations.

Accountability portfolios are relative newcomers to this arena, and many are not sure they are good company for other types of portfolios. The impetus for accountability portfolios seems to have been fueled by the actions of several states (e.g., Vermont, Kentucky) that are attempting to shift statewide assessments to more authentic procedures. These portfolios usually contain items of student work mandated by a state education agency. The mandated items usually include some sample of best works as well as samples of required work. The purpose of these portfolios is to evaluate the quality of schooling.

Much of the interest in portfolio approaches to assessment is because of the strong evidence that assessment practices drive instruction. As long as tests primarily measure student progress in meeting low-level literacy demands, classroom programs will focus more on that teaching than on developing higher-order literacy. Thus, persistent efforts have been made to shift assessment away from traditional practices. There is little doubt that the statewide high-stakes testing that became so popular during the 1980s had an impact on instruction— today viewed as a largely negative impact.

Likewise, good evidence shows that use of portfolio assessment practices can have a dramatic effect on instruction. Vermont's adoption of portfolio assessment for literacy and math has had a substantial intended impact on the instructional practices and activities that routinely occur in classrooms (Koretz, Stecher, Klein, & McCaffrey, 1994). In fact, establishing a portfolio evaluation process may be the best method for stimulating professional conversation about a school's goals and needed curriculum shifts. When teachers have to decide what items will go into portfolios, when they must decide on the criteria for evaluating those items, and when they share student's work in an attempt to establish consistent scoring of work, it is enormously unlikely that teachers can avoid engaging in professional talk about goals, curriculum, and outcomes.

Developing a Portfolios Plan.   In most cases, a school portfolio plan will include more than one type of portfolio collection. But what might a school portfolio plan look like? The answer depends on the intended use of the portfolios. Just as with the development of a plan for standardized testing, the first step in developing a portfolio plan is to consider how student portfolios will be used. If portfolio collections are to be used as one part of a program evaluation process, the school plan will likely include some "mandated" components. Likewise, if the portfolio is partly to demonstrate competence necessary for promotion to the next grade level, some components will undoubtedly be standardized or included in all student portfolios. In the case of such accountability portfolios, schools often minimize student involvement in selecting the works in an attempt to ensure greater comparability of all portfolios (standardizing the contents of portfolios makes comparative judging easier).

However, if a school faculty is primarily interested in increasing student ownership and involvement in their work, the decision to allow students more individual leeway in creating their portfolios would become more important than standardizing components. Thus, in developing best works, process, or progress portfolios it could be expected that work included would be more individual and less standardized.

After several years of development and experimentation, the public elementary schools in South Brunswick Township in New Jersey have created a portfolio process that seems manageable in terms of time and paperwork and provides a rich compendium of information on each child's literacy development (Educational Testing Service, 1991). Each portfolio includes the following:

- Self-portraits that children create at the beginning and end of each year.
- An interview protocol, completed each September, that includes questions on favorite pastimes, reading at home, and responses to school.

- A parent questionnaire that asks for assistance and information on their child and attempts to foster collaboration.
- Concepts About Print (CAP), Marie Clay's assessment of understanding of conventions of print and books. The CAP is given at the beginning and end of kindergarten (and at later points to children experiencing difficulty).
- The Word Awareness Writing Activity at the end of kindergarten and in first grade.
- Unedited writing samples. These may include teacher translation if sound spelling, handwriting, or other problems make them difficult for others to understand.
- Running records of three reading samples collected near the beginning, middle, and end of year. Each sample includes a comment on which strategies children used.
- Three records of a child's retelling of a story.

The teachers also use a single numerical scale for rating all the work in the portfolio (ratings are from 1 to 4 indicating more- or less-developed literacy). The scale focuses on the development of strategies for making sense of print and characterizes children's level of development at the beginning and end of each year. This scoring allows quick comparison of development of groups and subgroups of children in the district (e.g., contrast development in different schools, contrast development of boys and girls). The schools are developing a best works portfolio process. While the current portfolio process functions primarily as an accountability tool for literacy learning, adding a student organized portfolio brings another dimension to this evaluation effort.

DeFina (1992) presents very practical information about implementing process portfolios in schools. He suggests several steps that need to be planned:

1. *Explain and educate.* Portfolios are not often well understood by anyone except those professionals who have long used them (e.g., artists, journalists, photographers, architects). Before jumping on a portfolio bandwagon, take time to help everyone develop a richer understanding of what portfolios can be and how they might improve the educational process.
2. *Decide how to and when.* Phase in portfolio evaluation over a period of time. Start small. Move slowly. Begin by implementing portfolio evaluation where it best fits into the current system (often, writing portfolios are a good first bet).
3. *Demonstrate and decide.* Students, as well as teachers (and parents), need demonstrations of how portfolios might be put together. It might be good to begin with diversity and work for more commonality of included works. Display portfolios at the school entrance and at faculty meetings and parent nights.
4. *Establish the role of portfolios in grading.* Because portfolios are designed to show development and aimed at showcasing individuals' work, whether portfolios will be used in assigning grades needs to be determined.
5. *Rethink the classroom environment.* Classrooms must have some place to store portfolios—a location where children can access them easily. Likewise, an area for reviewing portfolios is very useful since the contents usually take more space than a single student desktop provides. Do classrooms have portfolio display tables?

6. *Organize.* For portfolios to work, they need to be integrated into the classroom schedule. Children will need time to conference with the teacher on the portfolio's contents. They also need time to select, review, and comment on the contents. Teachers also need time to jot notes and summaries to be included.

Involving parents in the portfolio process is important. For instance, while waiting their turn at parent-teacher conference nights, parents might review their child's portfolio and write responses to be included in the portfolio file. Likewise, interviews with parents or checklists parents complete can also be added to portfolios. Simply using the portfolio as a discussion starter with parents is often powerful (and a good basis for a parent-teacher conference).

Managing Portfolio Collections Over the Long Haul. In many cases, schools are interested in maintaining portfolios across the elementary school years or even longer (K–12). This idea can be recommended for many reasons, but such long-term collections create storage, security, and management problems. The amount of work samples from each year that should be kept in the long-term portfolio must be addressed. In the case of a K–12 time span, saving even three to four pieces of work each year produces a fairly thick file by graduation time. Should the school keep the original works or copies of the originals? How does one store nonstandard sized works (e.g., drawings, journals), or should everything be stored in standard sizes only? We opt for storing copies of original works, ideally photocopies that have been reduced or enlarged to the standard 8½ × 11 page size. But this requires both equipment and personnel.

Other solutions involve the creative use of technology. For instance, schools are storing portfolio collections on multimedia and retrievable on computer. The Grady Profile Portfolio Assessment (St. Louis: Auerbach Associates. 1-800-77-GRADY) software allows teachers to retrieve and review multiple samples of students' written work as well as samples of oral presentations. This access to a whole chronology of work is possible without the storage problems common to paper portfolio systems. The technology for scanning children's work onto computer drives is easily available, and the storage of photos, audio, and video records is available but not yet widely used. Still, the idea of being rid of piles of student paper, of scanning the composition into the computer rather than photocopying for a traditional hanging file, is appealing to us. The funds schools have traditionally invested in purchasing standardized tests and test scoring services (plus the costs of filing those test sheets or entering scores on computerized student records) seem sufficient to cover the costs associated with these high-tech storage and retrieval solutions.

At the Key School in Indianapolis, children are videotaped each year as they share a book, read aloud from it, read a self-selected piece of their writing, and discuss it. The power of video to track children's development across time is enormous. Imagine a child study committee being able to call up both a video record of a third grader who had been referred for their consideration and a computerized collection of reading and writing performances across a three-year period. Imagine being able to share that information with parents during conferences or with board of education members. Portfolios hold potential for improving education because involvement in the portfolio process stimulates thinking about teaching and learning by children, teachers, parents, and others.

GRADES AND REPORT CARDS

Every day, in every classroom, children engage in reading and writing activities that provide teachers with abundant opportunities to evaluate development. Current classroom evaluations are often not very informative or educational. Ideally, a teacher's evaluation of student work would assist students in understanding what additional learning or demonstrations of learning were needed to improve on the performance being evaluated. Likewise, evaluations would inform parents and other teachers of what strategies had been acquired and indicate those that were yet undeveloped. What sense can a student, a parent, or another teacher make of some of the traditional evaluation messages? What does 88 mean on a comprehension assessment done after a second-grade student has been involved in a guided reading of basal story? What does a grade of B– mean on an assignment to compose a persuasive essay in fifth grade? What sense can anyone make of a smiley face or a "Good Job!!!" written on top an assignment?

The research on grading is clear on at least one issue. There is little evidence that grading practices provide reliable estimates of student learning (Stiggins, Frisbie, & Griswold, 1989). The lack of any clear and consistent school policy on grading practices may be the most important reason for this. Consequently, teachers develop their own policies, and these vary widely from teacher to teacher. Even when teachers do not give letter or number grades and use another scale (e.g., needs improvement, satisfactory, mastery of objective), there is little evidence that teachers teaching similar material at the same grade level evaluate the same things in the same way. Teacher grading policies vary by the weight they give to:

- effort
- timeliness
- test scores
- extra-credit efforts
- creativeness
- compliance
- neatness
- homework
- makeup work
- participation
- attentiveness

Not every teacher, for instance, records the grades given homework assignments. Some give allowances for estimates of effort while others do not. Some offer students opportunities to retake tests or to redo assignments, but not all do. Perhaps more important, all teachers at the same grade level do not create the same assignments or even teach the same content. Thus, a grade for an individual assignment means whatever the teacher wants it to mean, and a report card grade means the same. Because grades are rarely tied to any common content or standard, grades rarely indicate what students know about a subject or what strategies they have developed. Prominent evaluation specialist Gene Glass argues that grades are "essentially arbitrary" and points out that there is no good way to make meaningful distinctions between a C plus and a B minus (Willis, 1993).

Current grading practices seem to assume that grades have a motivational characteristic—that students will work harder to achieve better grades. But since effort is not often a particularly salient feature of grading practices, it does not often work out that way. Too often classroom evaluations only rank-order children—much like standardized test reports. That is, some children receive good grades or positive comments and others receive lower grades and few positive comments. This situation is most troubling for at-risk children—those most likely to receive a steady stream of lower grades and less positive comments. Even when these children are developing improved reading and writing strategies, their performances will usually be ranked behind their peers who have not found learning to read and write difficult. Motivation research (Brophy, 1987) suggests that success precedes motivation, not the other way around. Thus, traditional assessment practices are rarely motivating to the very students who need the most motivation because they will have to work harder and longer than other children to catch up.

Imagine, for instance, the child who takes a traditional spelling test each week. Because the spelling curriculum is usually graded, the words on the list are simply harder for children who read less well. So even with equivalent time and effort in studying, these children can be expected to spell fewer words correctly than those peers who have had no difficulty learning to read. A child who improves from 10 of 20 weekly words spelled correctly to 12 of 20 correct will rarely feel better than the child who shows no improvement in maintaining a steady stream of 18 or 19 of 20 correct without studying. The child who learns to spell 5 new words but still gets only 12 correct is hardly motivated by his grade, especially when the child who previously knew how to spell all of the words achieved 20 correct with no studying.

How to determine grades in a literature-based program, especially a program moving toward the wider use of more authentic assessment processes, is often discussed. Some argue that grades and portfolios mix like oil and water—that the ranks that grading entails are counterproductive and the antithesis of student-centered authentic assessment. Peterson and Eeds (1990, p.73) offer a form developed by one teacher required to assign grades even though she would have preferred not to. The grading process is clear and focuses more on quite objective responsibilities in that literature-based classroom.

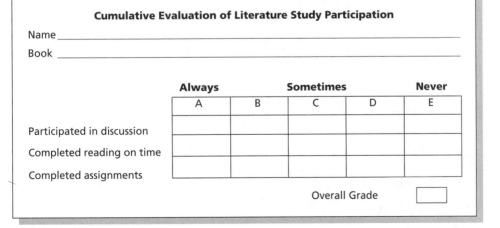

Cumulative Evaluation of Literature Study Participation

Name _____

Book _____

	Always		Sometimes		Never
	A	B	C	D	E
Participated in discussion					
Completed reading on time					
Completed assignments					

Overall Grade ☐

This should not be construed so much as an argument to include effort in grading as it is a question of what grading practices are attempting to achieve. Are grades supposed to inform students as to what strategies they need to acquire; or are grades just to let children know where they stand, academically, among their peers, or an estimate of who might have put forth the greater effort completing the assigned work? If the former is one intended purpose, then it might be useful to interview students and ask them to explain what an assignment grade means or what a report card grade means. It may also be useful to interview parents and find out what they think grades mean and how they interpret low grades. Do grades clearly inform other teachers what children have learned or what they need to be taught? Do grades help teachers make sense of children as learners? A very basic question, then, is, Why are grades given?

The difficulty with grades is that in giving grades we try to reduce a variety of complex cognitive activities to a single letter, number, or rating. Some children do not put forth much effort to receive high grades and other children put forth much effort only to receive lower grades. Some children develop many new skills, strategies, and knowledges and still receive low grades while others learn few new skills but obtain better grades. How does one adequately communicate progress toward learning goals across a six- or eight-week period to a single mark or grade? If we want assessment practices to foster learning and enhance student motivation, grading and report cards must be substantially rethought.

Report Cards.   Some teachers have already told us of the difficulty they have when, after adopting more authentic assessment practices in their classrooms, they are still forced to give a grade on the report card. If they grade on effort primarily, there are howls from predictable corners—from students and parents who have always gotten good grades with little effort. If they grade on growth, the same is true. But if they grade using an estimated rank-ordering, children who have worked hard and even those who have exhibited substantial development may receive low grades that undermine the mentoring relationship that has been developed and continued effort toward further improvement. But who says that either grades or report cards are necessary?

The general public is usually reluctant to give up report cards and the grades students carry home. Report cards are familiar and traditional. Often, the reluctance to give up report cards stems more from a lack of familiarity with alternatives than from any real satisfaction with report cards as we typically know them. A proposal simply to toss out report cards and grade entries in students' cumulative files will not likely be met with wholehearted approval by the public. Even given their limitations, the average citizen feels comfortable and familiar with traditional grades and report cards. Thus, changing the current situation will require some work. So what can be done?

Afflerbach (1993) outlines a procedure for rethinking report cards (and that also seems to apply equally as well to grading). He provides four assumptions about effective reporting of student progress to parents and poses several questions for discussion and resolution. The assumptions are:

- Representatives from all groups who read, write, or rely upon report cards should be involved in changing current practices.
- Reports should provide useful information about reading and writing development for other teachers, parents, and students.

- A flexibility must be designed into reporting procedures that allows different teachers to communicate their knowledge of children's development.
- Reports must be manageable for teachers and for parents or students who read them.

Improved communication of children's literacy development is an enormously worthwhile goal but one that cannot always be achieved without much discussion. Creating a team to study, discuss, and, ultimately, propose changes in current procedures is the first step in a long process. The team will need teachers from different grade levels, parents, administrators, and, possibly, a representative from the school board (some schools might also add students to the team). Afflerbach proposes four questions that need to be addressed:

- What is the purpose of the reading report card (and who is the audience)?
- What role does the report card play in communicating reading assessment?
- What are the responsibilities associated with the new report card?
- How can the school ensure that new report cards will be understood?

If the purpose of report cards (and grades) is simply to provide a rank-ordering of students, most schools will not have to revise much current practice. However, if the intended purpose of report cards is to inform parents about children's literacy development and to provide students with a larger sense of ownership of their development, then most current report cards will need drastic revisions. Johnston (1992) asks whether all teachers need to use a uniform procedure for reporting to parents. We know, for instance, of schools where all teachers do not use the same reporting system but can elect one of several formats for reporting progress to parents (traditional report card, individual narratives about each student, or parent conference). The uniformity of teacher reports to parents is a not a given the school starts with but rather a condition it needs to consider.

Schools need to consider whether or not the report card should be the primary method of communicating information to parents. Most schools organize parent-teacher conferences, and information on literacy development might be better communicated in this face-to-face format. In some schools, students not only attend these conferences but also present their work, along with a discussion of it, to their parents and their teacher. Schools opting for these teacher-parent or student-run conferences might rely far less on traditional report cards to provide parents with information.

The tradition of report cards being sent home simultaneously for all students is yet another area that needs to be considered. If teachers are to compose narrative-style report cards for each student, it is almost essential that such report cards be released on a staggered basis. For instance, after perhaps four weeks of school the teacher might begin using the quickwrite procedures to create a narrative report that would be sent home with the student the following day. In some cases, the student might stay after school and work with the teacher as he or she writes the narrative. In such cases, a "best piece" work might be attached and become the focus of the evaluation sent home. If teachers wrote one narrative each day (Monday through Thursday), each child would have a narrative report written roughly every six to seven weeks—or at least as frequently as most schools now release report cards.

Acceptance for such radically revised procedures may not come easily, at least initially. But parents report that the written comments on current report cards are the component they find most valuable. Teachers, on the other hand, currently find the spaces for comments too small. When they must create every report card over a single weekend, teachers report not having adequate time to develop the written comments fully even if space is not an issue. In addition, not all teachers accept the premise that rank-ordering children is potentially damaging and not particularly motivating for any group of students. Very honestly, such changes in assessment and reporting to parents requires teachers to know their students better and to know more about how children learn to read and write, and not all teachers are readily motivated themselves to take on these tasks. It is not that shifting reporting practices in this way takes enormous amounts of additional time—once learned the procedures become part of the daily routine—but that incorporating these practices into the daily routine requires some substantial shifts in traditional teaching as well as testing. But to create schools where all children are successful will require substantial new learning by teachers and substantial shifts in instructional practices. If instruction is to shift, assessment must also. In fact, shifts in assessment may well be the best way to foster shifts in instruction.

NATIONAL STANDARDS

There is currently a flurry of debate and development in the area of national standards for all school subjects, including reading and language arts. Proponents argue that such standards are critical if American education is to be substantially improved. They argue that national educational goals will provide a common blueprint for teaching and learning, for assessing students, and for evaluating schools. Most other developed nations, they argue, have such standards. But critics note that American schools are already more alike than different. They point to the potential of these high national standards to disadvantage further at-risk children. Critics point to the long tradition of local control of education and suggest a wariness of any federal, or national, scheme to mandate standards and standardization. Nonetheless, national standards have already been developed in several subject areas and standards for reading and language arts are under development. In addition, several pieces of federal legislation now link the evaluation of federal education programs to national standards.

At this point, we remain somewhat pessimistic about the potential for national standards to effect education substantively. Perhaps the current interest in creating "delivery standards" to accompany the content standards will prove useful in reducing the enormous disparity that currently exists in the funding of American schools. Perhaps national standards will be a powerful lever for changing both curriculum and instruction. But, in our view, the primary problem facing American education is less one of deciding what needs to be taught and more one of determining how schools can become institutions that better foster, support, and extend high-quality teaching.

SUMMARY

As Farr (1992) noted, "The assessment puzzle can be solved. The solution, however, is not as simple as identifying a nonexistent test that will do the whole job nor as arbitrary as eliminating most reading assessment" (p. 36). The standardized achievement testing that has long dominated elementary reading assessment must be supplemented or replaced by more authentic assessments of literacy development. Different assessment practices better fit one purpose than another but few of the traditional practices well-fit the purposes of improving instruction, educating teachers, motivating students, or informing parents or policy makers about how well literacy is being fostered. While both commercial standardized tests and state-mandated competency tests are being revised, such testing currently has limited potential for anything but inhibiting change. Still, until alternatives are more fully developed and better known, standardized achievement tests will remain at the forefront of educational change efforts. Thus our call to begin to administer such tests anonymously. This would work to ensure that children were not mistakenly harmed by unreliable assessment reports and would also limit the current abuses of tests in many schools.

Most school communities will not easily implement a full-scale shift to the nearly exclusive use of authentic assessment. But authentic assessment practices do hold enormous potential for changing what and how we teach and how children come to be readers and writers. Because of this enormous potential for reshaping the ways teachers, parents, and children think about teaching and learning, we encourage schools to foster and support a steady shift to rely more on authentic assessments in evaluating the work done in schools.

Professional Development: Key to the Change Process

R ecently, the local newspaper carried a story on a Board of Education meeting in a nearby school district. The board had added $5,000 to the existing $22,500 annual budget for professional development. A board member commented that such a sum would create "a truly outstanding in-service program." This budget item represented 0.0008 percent of the school district's $35.8 million total budget! Unfortunately, many school districts—in fact, most—allocate similarly minuscule funding for professional-development activities and then puzzle over why change in schools is so slow. Imagine, for instance, that school districts routinely followed the advice offered by the U.S. Secretary of Labor to American businesses and invested 1 to 1.5 percent of the annual operating budget to "worker retraining." Such an investment was critical, he argued, for industry to keep American workers competitive in the global marketplace. Is it any less likely that similar levels of investments might keep our schools competitive? Imagine if that local school district invested even 1 percent, or roughly $330,000, additional funds in professional-development support! Instead of allocating a miserly $4,500 per building, each school would have had approximately $60,000 annually to fund curriculum improvement and teacher development.

In most school districts, roughly 80 percent of the annual operating budget is invested in salaries. Education *is* a people business. Schools do not improve unless a faculty improves. Elementary schools will change only when new strategies and new knowledge become incorporated into everyday practice. But one is hard-pressed to locate school districts that invest 1 to 1½ percent of the annual budget in supporting the professional development of district employees. We are not sure exactly why this is so, but we do have a few hypotheses.

The first is the rather dismal track record of much of the "in-service training" that has been offered in schools. Suffice it to say that little evidence supports continuing the traditional "one-shot" in-service training workshop. Given the very limited effects of this popular format for teacher retraining, we are not surprised that few school district administrators see a need to invest more money in expanding these opportunities.

A second reason for the woeful inadequacy of professional development is that most schools lack experience with activities that have a demonstrated record of fostering positive change. While research on professional development is still in its infancy, a number of basic findings can be used to enhance professional development efforts. Not surprisingly, much of this information has not yet found its way into many schools because of its only relatively recent availability. One goal for this chapter is to introduce some of key findings that have been reported in more detail by others (e.g., Fullan, 1991; Little, 1993; Richardson, 1990).

A third reason may be that many believe that professional development is more an individual responsibility than a school responsibilty. Linked to this is often the notion that if teachers want to improve their professional practice, they will seek out appropriate activities themselves. Of course, it is true that teachers have a personal responsibility to engage in professional development across their careers. But, at the same time, school districts have a responsibility to support the professional development of their teachers. Professional development is a two-way street. Schools need to offer a variety of supportive frameworks to ensure that teachers have appropriate opportunities to engage in professional development activities. Teachers have the responsibility, at least, to take full advantage of the opportunities offered.

Finally, in most schools, no one carries much responsibility for fostering professional development among teachers and administrators. For instance, principals often have some responsibilities for professional-development activities focused on classroom teachers, but someone else is responsible for reading teachers, special-education teachers, paraprofessionals, food-service workers, librarians, and so on. Professional-development activities are fragmented with no overall plan of action or schoolwide focus. When a school's professional-development opportunities are best characterized as a series of separate, unconnected activities, there is little reason to expect that the efforts will produce any substantial change in educational practices or produce any great benefit to teachers or to the children they teach.

Creating schools where all children learn to read and write will require a broad, long, and well-planned effort. Before more money is sought to support the necessary professional-development activities and opportunities for teachers and administrators, most schools would do well to rethink wholly the nature and purpose of professional development in relation to the needed changes. A good first step is to examine the current school structure and organization with an eye toward identifying where professional-development concerns might most profitably focus.

◼ LOOKING AT YOUR SCHOOL

Research on schools suggest starting with a school inventory. No two schools are ever identical in staff quality, curriculum organization, teacher involvement, and so on. Rosenholtz (1989) identified three broad types of schools. The first were *moving* schools. In these schools, roughly 80 percent of the teachers viewed professional improvement as a lifelong endeavor. They felt they faced new challenges each year and noted various ways they had adapted and continued polishing their teaching repertoires. Teachers in these schools tended to be more collaborative and more likely to seek out ideas from colleagues. They were more likely to have a shared consensus about important goals and to seek out professional-development opportunities. In interviews, they talked about how much they had yet to learn and noted questions that challenged them. In particular, they sought to improve their efforts to teach all children, especially children who found learning difficult. In many senses, moving schools were "self-improving systems."

At the other end of the continuum was the *stuck* school. Here, few teachers saw professional development as an ongoing challenge. Instead, most felt they had "mastered" the necessary techniques by the end of their third year of teaching. In these schools, teachers saw little need to improve or to engage in any sort of extended professional-development activities. School learning difficulties were felt to be primarily the fault of parents, not of ineffective instruction. While these teachers might want a workshop on a new reading series, they were generally not interested in engaging in study of literacy learning so they might better understand their own teaching processes and their students' learning. In stuck schools, a vicious cycle ensued. Teachers felt they had little need for improved instructional repertoires, and they rarely were receptive to suggested professional-development activities. Those offered rarely had any impact, which led teachers to view the activities as increasingly useless. This, in turn, resulted in fewer professional-development activities being offered and, therefore, an instructional environment that steadily declined in quality. Stuck schools often became more dysfunctional and, over time, offered fewer opportunities for growth to either teachers or children. (Rosenholtz labeled schools that were not moving enough to rank moving nor stuck enough to rank stuck *in-between,* the third type of school.)

But even the "worst-case-scenario" stuck schools have some faculty who would have fit quite nicely with the faculty of the moving schools. The trick, of course, is to build on that group of teachers, no matter how small, who are eager to engage in professional development and continued growth.

> Most schools already have at least one *conversational community* or group of teachers who meet regularly but informally to talk with each other about instructional practice (Guice & Allington, 1994). Such groups are found even in schools that seem to fit the stuck criteria, although the communities there often go to great lengths to mask their conversations from other peers. It is unlikely that any school can improve without large numbers of the staff involved in a conversational group. The key issue is developing, fostering, maintaining, and making the conversations more beneficial.

McLaughlin and Yee (1988) described key features of schools that seemed to parallel the "moving" schools. They focused on teachers who thought of teaching as a career rather than as a job. But such teachers were found far more often in schools that shared five characteristics. These schools were best described as:

- *Resource-adequate* instead of resource-deprived. Teachers had at least the minimum curriculum materials and classroom resources needed to accomplish their goals.
- *Integrated* rather than segmented. Integrated schools had a unity of purpose, shared goals, and a shared sense of responsibility. Segmented schools, in contrast, had clear divisions within the faculty, an us versus them attitude about school administration, and little commitment to any common vision of what the school should or could be doing.
- *Collegiality* versus isolation from peers. Multiple collegial interactions created a school where colleagues were seen as a constant source of support and ideas for improving teaching. When teachers felt isolated in their own classrooms, they often failed to go beyond complaining about students and parents.

- *Problem-solving* orientation instead of problem hiding. In a problem-solving environment, teachers assumed a need for continued learning about teaching. They developed a stronger sense of group and were likely to reflect routinely upon their own teaching. In problem-hiding schools, on the other hand, teachers kept to themselves and rarely shared concerns or difficulties with their peers.
- *Investment centered* rather than payoff focused. When schools were investment centered, teachers were seen as resources rather than as problems. Through a variety of methods, investments were made in improving teaching, not just by rewarding the few who were deemed superior teachers. In investment-centered approaches, teachers were encouraged to take risks and to seek out resources for improvement.

Few schools were well described by all of these features. Unfortunately, some teachers work in isolation in segmented schools more likely to engage in problem hiding than problem solving and to focus more on ferreting out "incompetent" teachers than investing in teacher development. Most teachers do seem to have minimally adequate resources, thankfully, but teachers in schools serving the largest numbers of at-risk children are those most likely to also work in resource-deprived settings (Kozol, 1991).

It might be useful at this point to assess your school on the five characteristics sketched above. To do this, simply place a mark on the continuum to indicate qualities of your school.

Resource adequate	|————————————|	Resource deprived
Integrated	|————————————|	Segmented
Collegial	|————————————|	Isolated
Problem solving	|————————————|	Problem hiding
Investment centered	|————————————|	Payoff focused

All but the first items are largely characteristics that can neither be developed by mandate nor ensured by regulation and monitoring. What steps can be taken to improve the situation in your school?

Creating schools where all children learn to read and write will only occur with movement away from teacher isolation and problem hiding. Throughout this book, we have attempted to portray the resource-adequate classroom in an integrated environment focused on collegial problem solving. In this chapter, we attempt to build on these features and portray an investment-centered approach to creating schools that work better for all children. It is the classroom teachers working in any elementary school who will bear the brunt of the work ahead and also the brunt of responsibility for creating classroom environments that foster literacy in every child. Only by investing in classroom teachers can any school hope to become a school where all children learn to read and write. Remember the principle that opened this book: *A good school is but a collection of good classrooms.*

THE FUTURE DOES NOT HAVE TO LOOK LIKE THE PAST

Investing time, energy, and money to support the professional development of teachers simply makes good sense. Continuing professional development is essential as schools restructure to meet society's increased expectations. Becoming a school where all children acquire thoughtful literacy will go a long way in meeting the new goals set for schools, but becoming a school where all children read and write thoughtfully will require teachers and administrators to develop new skills and strategies. To begin, consider professional-development opportunities in your school. It will be useful to reconstruct what topics have been the focus of any recent traditional staff-development efforts. To complete the chart below, you will need to locate information on the topics that have been the primary focus of sessions that teachers have participated in. Simply place a check in a box to indicate the topics of sessions offered this year, in the past two years, and three or more years ago. At this point, the inventory only indicates the breadth of topics covered (feel free to add additional boxes for other topics).

Once you have portrayed the breadth of topics, you need to highlight any topics that have received a sustained focus across a two-to-three year period (highlight those rows with checks in all three columns). Now tally any topics where the professional-development opportunities involved actual classroom collaborations between teacher-participants (in each others' classrooms) or presenter-teacher collaborations in the teachers' classrooms (e.g., demonstration teaching, coaching). Finally, identify where the professional-development opportunity was formally evaluated for changes in classroom practices or changes in student achievement (i.e., someone observed in classrooms to document changes, collected and analyzed achievement data from students of participating teachers).

Focus	This Year	Last Year	2–3 Years Ago
Reading			
Writing			
Math			
Science			
Social studies			
Art/Drama			
Special education			
At-risk students			
Technology			
Drugs, alcohol, etc.			
Multiculturalism			
Instructional (e.g., activity-based)			
Organizational (e.g., ungraded)			

Completing such an inventory is important to identify long-term professional-development projects, activities that actually involved going into classrooms, and those that were evaluated for success in changing teaching practices or enhancing student achievement. Support will be easier to gain for future professional efforts if a historical perspective is presented with a longer term plan for supporting professional development and an evaluation component. The inventory is also a potential problem-solving activity. Gathering information on past efforts should provide a better understanding of which past efforts seemed most and least effective.

Personal Professional-Development Activity

To this point the inventory taking has focused primarily on "official" school-sponsored professional-development activities—those rather more formal opportunities sanctioned and supported by the school, school district, or state education agency. But other sorts of professional development need to be considered, particularly personal ventures.

These opportunities are not school derived or funded even though a school might view such activities as beneficial and encourage participation. It is time to recognize that teachers engage in a wide variety of activities that can foster professional development (e.g., undertaking personal professional reading, attending noncredit computer workshops at the local community college, guest lecturing in a college class, and so on). The checklist provided earlier focused attention on the more traditional school-sponsored opportunities, but now you might simply list the various personal ventures that teachers engage in to enhance their professional competence. We find that in most cases school administrators are not aware of all the personal ventures of teachers. Administrators usually create only a short list—a list that enormously underestimates the personal ventures of teachers—especially teachers in learning-enriched schools.

We mention this because our experience in schools suggests that another characteristic of the "moving" school is institutional knowledge and recognition for the personal professional-development ventures of teachers. For instance, if personal professional reading were considered one useful strategy for continued professional growth, one might expect to find a large supply of current professional publications within easy reach of teachers in a school. Within easy reach does not mean in the library or in the principal's office. Instead, it means on the bookshelf in the faculty room and in magazine racks located there. Back issues of magazines might be stored somewhere else, but recent issues would be right at hand. We would go a step further and suggest that when personal professional reading is valued we will see professional articles being routed to teachers, see notes about new professional books in the daily announcements, and find that some time at each faculty meetings is spent discussing professional reading. In fact, a regular "teachers as reading professionals" group might meet to discuss recent books or articles.

Ideally, schools should have a collection of classroom-focused videotapes that teachers might draw on. Recently, a number of such collections have been developed by several universities, publishing houses, and professional associations. In addition, schools should provide encouragement and information about local professional groups such as affiliates of the International Reading Association, the National Council of Teachers of English, Phi Delta Kappa, and Teachers Advocating Whole Language. Schools interested in fostering continuing professional development should make that interest visible throughout the school.

We believe that every elementary school should have a current professional library that includes recent books and professional magazines. As a starting point we suggest the following books and magazines concerned primarily with children's literacy development.

Books	Magazines
Cunningham & Allington, *Classrooms That Work: They Can All Read and Write* (HarperCollins)	*The Reading Teacher*
	Learning
Hansen, *When Writers Read* (Heinemann)	*Booklinks*
Gardner, *Multiple Intelligences* (Basic)	*Elementary School Journals*
Marshall & Tucker, *Thinking for a Living* (Basic)	*Language Arts*
Perkins, *Smart Schools* (Macmillan)	*Teaching Exceptional Children*
Routman, *Transitions* (Heinemann)	*New Advocate*
Stires, *With Promise* (Heinemann)	*Education Leadership*

Inventory Answer-Giving and Problem-Solving Opportunities

Another question about recent professional-development opportunities to pursue is the extent to which the current activities might be classified as problem solving in their overall focus. This criteria is important because the most powerful evidence is that which teachers develop themselves. It is common to have a presenter simply intone, "Research indicates. . ." and, perhaps, even distribute a summary of relevant research. But many teachers and administrators are hardly impressed by such efforts unless the "research" supports their personal beliefs and personal experiences (Richardson, 1990). Examine school responses to just three research-based principles:

- Retention provides no benefit to children.
- Heterogeneous groups benefit all learners.
- Children need enormous amounts of easy reading to become proficient readers.

It is not difficult to find schools that are "aware" of these research findings but where students are still retained and still grouped homogeneously for instruction, where classroom schedules and curriculum materials are organized so that most children spend little time actually reading, and many children rarely read anything that is easy for them. Often explanations of these practices invoke "practical knowledge" derived from experience. ("Don't tell me retention doesn't work, just look at Jalen Jones!").

The best possible avenue for altering teacher beliefs is to engage teachers in problem solving through gathering local data on the question. Retention effects, for instance, can be examined by gathering information on 10 to 20 children who have been retained and comparing their school progress with other low-achievers that were not retained (or just by studying their performance later in school). Alternatively, examining records of children who drop out of the local high school will often highlight the substantial overrepresentation of children who were retained.

Likewise, collecting information on the relative difficulty of texts read by higher- and lower-achieving readers will often highlight that some children have few easy-reading opportunities. Examining the time allocated for actual reading and writing during the school day may suggest that less time is spent this way than expected. Local data-gathering is a useful activity if only as a status check—gathering descriptive information provides all teachers with a better understanding of the variation in local practice and provides some information to complement the research summarized in professional journals.

Problem-solving activity is useful because teachers have an opportunity to reflect upon both intended and unintended effects of educational practice. Gathering even descriptive information on teaching practice and student outcomes also provides a basis for discussion and reflection. Teachers do not make decisions mindlessly, but teachers do justify decisions based on past and prevailing practice—the practical knowledge gained from experience and from their own sense of what works for them in their classrooms. Unfortunately, what works for teachers does not always work for kids. Likewise, long-standing practices, or traditions, are not always the most effective practices. But if teachers are to consider changing current practice, more than an "expert" asserting, "Research says . . . " will be required.

Who Participated in What?

As a final step in completing an inventory of current professional development opportunities and activities, return to the checklist we presented earlier. How many of the school-sponsored activities involved virtually all classroom teachers, regardless of their grade-level teaching assignment? How often were first-grade and fifth-grade teachers offered the same sessions? Did this occur in many cases, even though the professional concerns of teachers of 6-year-olds and 11-year-olds are generally quite different?

Now note the number of workshops that were offered for only relatively inexperienced teachers (one to three years' experience). What about workshops for only teachers with more than 20 years' experience, or for teachers with no previous professional-development activity in process approaches to writing, or for teachers with a broad background in children's literature? Again, most professional development programs fail to distinguish among even the broadest differences in teachers. It is the "one-size-fits-all" approach that undermines the potential that many professional-development activities offer.

How much professional-development activity was scheduled during the regular workday or work year? Conversely, how many of the activities were "voluntary" and scheduled after a long school day, on weekends, or during summer vacation periods? While many sorts of professional development need to occur during the normal workday, teachers also need longer blocks of time to puzzle through new ideas together and they need time to accomplish this when they are fresh and relaxed.

So WHERE TO GO FROM HERE?

Completing a fairly comprehensive inventory of recent professional-development support in a school is a useful starting point for rethinking the nature of future professional-development efforts. Well-designed professional-development support will be the key for helping stuck and "in-between" schools become moving schools. But an array of activities are available, and deciding on just what professional-development support to provide is an important next phase.

What Is the Role of Outside "Experts"?

If the one-shot workshop approach has little effect on teacher change, is there any useful role that outside experts, or consultants, can profitably play in professional development? We think there is (but then we both do consulting work with schools). But outside consultants play only a small role in any effective professional-development plan targeted to change substantially the educational practices of school. Nonetheless, outside consultants may be useful in any of the following roles:

- *Conversation starter.* Often an outside consultant can be very effective in initiating needed discussion. For instance, a consultant's strong presentation on why inclusionary and collaborative educational models are essential if all children are to learn to read and write can serve as the initiating event for discussions about restructuring the traditional segregated pull-out models for addressing the needs of at-risk children. Many teachers, both classroom and pull-out teachers, are quite satisfied with the traditional segregated model. Most have no extended experiences with any other instructional plan. Just hearing a rationale for change, learning about the evidence indicating that traditional models do not serve most children well, and having alternatives sketched may prod some teachers into conversations about changing local practice. In some cases, the consultant at the initiating event functions a bit like a lightning rod—attracting the heat that the issue may initially generate.

- *Surveyor of the larger landscape.* External consultants often have a broader familiarity with educational practices. Consultants visit a number of schools each year and observe and discuss local practices in each site. Thus, consultants usually have a broader view of prevailing practice than those who have worked for many years in the same school. One sad fact is that most educators have rather provincial knowledge, usually limited largely to knowledge of their own school or school system. Consultants draw on an array of school experiences that provide a richer vision of the possibilities for improving school practice. Consultants are not usually more creative than school personnel but their breadth of experiences simply provides many more examples of educational practices to draw from.

- *Content expert.* None of us can be an expert on all things. Often, consultants offer an odd combination of a breadth of experience on a narrow range of topics. In our cases, we think of ourselves primarily, as "reading experts" and most often when we work with schools, we focus on the reading and language arts curriculum and instruction. Neither of us has much to offer as far as improving the math program in a school, nor much to offer concerning art, drama, theater, or music (except that we think they can and should be better integrated into the reading and language arts curriculum). Likewise, other consultants view themselves as cooperative learning experts or classroom management experts and may or may not have much expertise in teaching reading and language arts.

    If improving the reading and language arts instruction in a school is an important priority, obtaining the services of a consultant with expertise in that area could make sense. But most consultants will know very little about any school they visit, though they know much about their specialty and have had broader school experiences. Thus, what consultants can accomplish is limited unless they work long enough with a school to become familiar with the current program, the professional staff, and the current classroom environments.

- *Evaluator.* Often, the notion of evaluation is narrowly conceived in education. Many consultants who do not consider themselves evaluation experts can, nevertheless, be very useful as independent evaluators for change projects. We have found that having a set of naive eyes and ears around can be useful (naive here means not expert on local practice). A consultant can often simply ask the right questions quite naively. For instance, one school had moved to trade books as the sole curriculum material for reading instruction, and the teachers and administrators were quite proud about having "thrown out the basal!" Yet after visiting classrooms at the site the consultant asked a number of questions that teachers found difficult to answer about observed local practices (e.g., questions about the mindless use-response journal activities observed, about the limited range of genres found on the core book list, about the preponderance of story map worksheets that occupied children, about the limited representation of minorities on the core books lists, and about hundreds of chapter question dittoes that had been included in the locally developed curriculum packets). The consultant not only raised questions about these issues but also pointed to several articles and books that would address these concerns. Ultimately, the consultant was able to assist in enhancing the breadth of the core books lists and expand the time available for children to actually read and write each day.

  The consultant never completed a traditional evaluation report (although a two-page site report summary was developed), but the role she played was that of an outside, expert evaluator, nonetheless. Consultants can provide useful feedback, or evaluation, but that role seems currently underdeveloped and underused. Asking consultants to complete a single-page site report, even consultants providing only a single session, offers the potential for gathering an outsider's perspective on the school and the school staff.

- *Partner in change.* Consultants can become partners in promoting change, but most usually do not. This is because of the substantial time it takes to foster real change. To become a partner in change will almost always require at least a one-year commitment to work in the school and with the teachers, and often, an even longer horizon can be expected (although intensity of involvement should lessen across time).

Regardless of the role an external consultant is selected to fill, schools can enhance the usefulness of a consultant by providing that person with better information than is usually provided. Consultants can only act on information they have about a school. With little information there will be little tailoring of the sessions to the school's needs. Conversely, when schools provide information about the curriculum's special program organization, previous initiatives in staff development, and the primary issue needing to be addressed, consultants can usually produce far more useful workshops. As consultants, we find having dinner (or breakfast) with school staff members useful before beginning the workday at the school. We also find that having time, while at the school, to visit classrooms and talk with teachers and administrators enormously useful. More schools need to try to arrange consultant schedules to include such activities.

Remember that old saw about an expert being someone from out of town? There is some truth to this, at least in our experience. That is, most school districts we visit already have staff who would offer advice, information, and proposals virtually identical to ours. But no one wants to hear those ideas (at least not from those people). One very real function of a consultant is to express the ideas developed locally by those not considered experts in their own communities.

Alternative Professional-Development Opportunities

Little (1993) describes a number of alternatives to the traditional workshop-by-an-expert approach to professional-development opportunities. Each of these deserves full consideration as potential paths for sustained teacher development.

- *Teacher collaboratives/networks.* Typically such efforts are subject-matter specific. The Philadelphia Alliance for Teaching the Humanities in Schools (PATHS) is one example. In this case, teachers work with the various humanities collections and their curators and archivists in Philadelphia. PATHS involves teachers in original research, in "pure" intellectual activities divorced from the everyday classroom practicalities, and in summer institutes held at the sites where the collections are stored.
- *Subject-matter associations.* Active involvement in professional organizations, such as the International Reading Association, the National Council of Teachers of English, or the Association for Supervision and Curriculum Development, can have substantive effects on professional development. Teachers become part of a larger professional community that extends far beyond their classrooms and, because of this, broaden perspectives on teaching and learning. Even when teachers do not take on leadership roles in these organizations but read the newsletters and journals and attend state, regional, or national conferences of these groups, there seems to be a benefit in professional development.
- *School/university partnerships.* A number of larger-scale partnerships have emerged over the past few years, but still, this alternative is very limited in scope. However, many classroom teachers have become involved on a lesser scale through the student-teaching function. As colleges and universities attempt to

For information on membership:

International Reading Association, P.O. Box 8139, Newark, DE 19712-8139 (302-731-1600)

National Council of Teachers of English, 1111 W. Kenyon Rd., Urbana, IL 61801-1096 (217-328-3870)

Association for Supervision and Curriculum Development, 1250 N. Pitt St., Alexandria, VA 22314-1453 (703-549-9110) restructure preservice teacher education, larger roles, including in many cases adjunct faculty status, are developing for classroom teachers who provide the field-based experiences.

- *Special institutes and centers.* Most often these opportunities are linked to colleges and universities, but the teachers who participate, such as teacher-researchers, at the National Research Center for Literature Teaching and Learning at the University at Albany, State University of New York, report appreciating being involved in the "real work" of the projects as opposed to simply being talked at. Likewise, when teachers are involved in nonresearch-focused initiatives such as the Bay Area Writing Project or the Children's Choice Awards for children's literature, they report substantial professional-development.

To these alternatives we would add several more:

- *Teachers as Readers groups.* This national project was initiated by the Association of American Publishers and is supported by several professional organizations. More recently, an Administrators as Readers group has been added. The primary activity involves teachers or administrators agreeing to read children's books and professional books and meet monthly to discuss their reading. The Teachers as Readers effort typically involves a segment of the faculty at individual schools and was developed as a strategy for enhancing classroom teachers' expertise in children's literature. Administrators as Readers usually involve administrators from several schools and, perhaps, several districts who meet regularly to discuss books they have read.

  In some schools a variation on this theme is the Summer Readers projects. In one school, this project offered teachers the opportunity to earn extra salary during the summer months while reading and discussing children's books. The primary goal was to develop substantially greater teacher expertise in children's literature as the school moved to a literature-based reading and language arts curriculum. Teachers would read literally hundreds of children's books over a period of a few weeks and discuss many of these books with colleagues.

For information: Teachers as Readers, Association of American Publishers, 220 East 23rd St., New York, NY 10010.

- *Telecommunication/computer bulletin boards.* Virtually every commercial on-line service (e.g., America Online, GEnie, CompuServe, Prodigy) offers educational bulletin boards and on-line conferences that link teachers and administrators across the nation. On the day this chapter was written one could participate in hundreds of bulletin board events including (1) discussing how to stop violence in schools (including experiences with and resources for peer mediation, (2) conversing on-line with children's author Patricia MacKissack, (3) discussing how inclusionary education is working, (4) discussing construction of portfolios for reading and writing, (5) receiving technical support for solving a problem with a

CD-ROM curriculum package, and (6) discussing Lois Lowrey's recent book, *The Giver,* with an on-line Teachers as Readers group. In addition, each of the services provides access to enormous databases with information about teaching, learning, curriculum, and so on. Not only can information be located, but articles and reports can be read on the screen or printed for distribution (all provide access, for instance, to ERIC database). Virtually every elementary school already has everything but the modem and the on-line account number needed to hook an office or classroom computer to other sites around the nation and the world. Beyond that, the monthly school access fee is low (e.g., currently $25–$40) if use remains reasonable but rises as more time is logged on the networks. It is not the expense that is keeping schools off the information highway.

For information:	
America Online	1-800-827-6364
CompuServe	1-800-368-3343
GEnie	1-800-638-9636
Prodigy	1-800-776-3552

- *Data-gathering groups.* One example of such a group is the "cadres" established in Accelerated Schools (Levin, 1987). These cadres are groups of teachers (and parents or other community members) that set a particular question as their group focus. For instance, the issue of flunking low-achieving students might be selected for study. The cadre would search out external evidence and gather data about the effects of local practice (Allington & McGill-Franzen, 1995). Once the data are gathered, cadre members discuss the evidence and prepare a brief summary statement of findings to share with the larger faculty group. In some respects these data-gathering groups function a bit like the traditional teacher committee structure. The important shift, however, is reflected in the name. The shift is to the collection of data, both external and local, on the question under study.
- *Personal professional-growth plans.* This process is becoming more popular in schools, but we still see relatively few formal arrangements for personalized professional growth in most schools we visit. Nonetheless, the potential of such plans seems substantial, especially when viewed from a career-cycle perspective. The Gloversville, New York, schools have created one such process. In this case, the professional growth plan largely replaces the traditional teacher-evaluation process for tenured teachers. Instead, teachers and their building administrator jointly construct professional-growth contracts focused on mutually agreed professional goals. Once the goals are set (perhaps enhanced understanding of theme-based, literature-based reading instruction or organizing multi-age classrooms), teachers research at least two articles or books on the topic and locate a conference or institute on the topic that they might attend. They then meet with other teachers on their instructional teams (grade-level teams at the elementary school

level) to discuss their professional-improvement plan and how it relates to team planning responsibilities. Finally, teachers prepare a professional-growth portfolio that contains a minimum of ten items (personally written professional article, lesson plans, photos, student work, video of a lesson, etc.). This portfolio is shared with the team and the school administrator at the end of each school year.

- *Annual reports.* Another strategy is adapted from the "annual report" format that many colleges and universities use as an end of year faculty report. A simple outline that requests information on professional-development activities during the past school year provides not only a forum for reporting personal professional-development activity (noncredit workshops, association memberships, Teachers as Readers participation, personal professional reading, etc.) but reinforces the focus on the expectation of continued professional development.

- *Professional portfolio.* Similar in some respects to the annual report alternative, teacher-developed professional portfolios foster reflection on professional practice. A teacher's professional portfolio might include such personal evidence of professional growth as a journal of responses to books and articles read, videotaped records of lessons, samples of personally developed curriculum plans or documents, student portfolios with annotations explaining the significance of each included piece of student work and so on. The question to be asked of a professional portfolio is, How do the included documents demonstrate professional development and personal reflection on professional practice?

- *Videotapes.* Over the past five years, there has been an explosive growth in the availability of potentially useful educational videos. Since most teachers, like eveyone else, own videotape players, creating a library of videotaped recordings (VTR) focused on professional-development topics only makes sense. Today, some VTRs allow teachers to see an innovation in use in other classrooms, to observe an important educational summit, to view a television special on an educational topic, or to evaluate a presentation by an educational authority. Some VTRs will be best viewed at home, alone. Others will be good conversation starters for faculty meetings.

Among a number of VTR distributors are two good sources to begin establishing an educational video library. The Association for Supervision and Curriculum Development (703-549-9110) offers an array of titles including "Involving Parents in Education," "Shared Decision Making," and "Schools of Quality" and also offers an audiocassette subscription to its primary professional magazine, *Educational Leadership.* A commercial firm, The Video Journal, also offers VTRs on a variety of topics (1-800-572-1153).

- *Fifth-year sabbatical option.* Barth (1990) suggests offering teachers the option of receiving four-fifths of their pay for five years, with the fifth year free from teaching responsibilities. During the fifth year teachers might return to higher education to earn additional credentials. Alternatively, teachers might use that year to

Photos of the classroom instructional environment might be included in a professional portfolio or annual report. This shared writing chart, for instance, represents part of one teacher's work on a water theme in her primary class.

In (science) we are studying (water)

Why do we need water?
We drink water. (Tyler)
We take a bath in water (Jessica K)
We play in a swimming pool (AnneCole)
Animals need water. (Brandon)
We use water to brush our teeth (Andrew)
We wash dishes in water (Darcel)
You take a shower in water (Jamel)
Water helps our planet, Earth (Justin)
You need water in wells to keep fish alive (Zed)
Water helps plants grow. (Nicki)
You need water in cars. (Kamran)
You need water to wash your car. (Whitney)
You need water to help grass grow (Casey)
Flowers need water. (Ronald)
We need water to wash our hands (Jennifer)
We need water for coffee. (Randy)
We need water to play in a sprinkler (Kristin)
We need water to go on a slip and slide (Zack)
We need water to put out a fire! (Tyler)
We need water to grow trees. (Raheem)
We need water to wash our hair. (Charlotte)
We need water to wash our clothes.
We need water to fish, ride in boats, and to water ski. (Miss Williams)
We need water to flush toilets.

H_2O = water.

We must not waste water.

We must (conserve) H_2O!

read professionally, to visit other schools, or to brush up on a hobby. Since the teacher is working for reduced salary, schools would exert little control over the nature of activities the teacher might select during the sabbatical year. But this no-cost option would provide time for professional renewal and development.

- *Automatic leave policy.* Barth also recommends that schools automatically accept any teacher's request for an unpaid leave of absence, noting that teachers only request such leaves when personal or professional demands or opportunities create the necessary conditions. Whether the request comes from stressful conditions, unexpected opportunities, or simply a desire to reflect on one's career choice makes little difference. It does not make sense to force teachers back to work when leave has been requested.

PROFESSIONAL DEVELOPMENT ACROSS THE CAREER CYCLE

When teaching is viewed as a career, as opposed to a job, teachers are more likely to be viewed as developing professionals than as employees. Each teacher selected for employment is more likely than not to spend his or her professional career in the same school district. Currently in many schools, the average age of classroom teachers is between 35 and 50 years. This represents, typically, between 12 and 25 years of experience. The key question that needs to be asked is whether most teachers have dramatically improved their practice across those time periods. As we noted earlier, in some schools this seems generally to be the case.

The common situation found in many schools today—teachers stuck in terms of professional growth—is often cited as a reason for undoing current tenure protections. We would argue that it is better evidence that schools need to rethink radically the support provided for fostering professional development. In most cases, the inventory suggested earlier will illustrate that many schools have done little that might be expected to alter the current situation. In rethinking professional-development opportunities, we suggest that teaching must be viewed as a career and that professional development must be designed to meet the differing needs of teachers across their careers. Leithwood (1990) sketches the development of teachers' instructional expertise using the following stages:

- **Developing survival skills.** Beginning teachers arrive with less than fully developed knowledge of classroom management, limited knowledge and skill in using a variety of instructional models, poorly developed self-reflection on teaching, and limited knowledge for evaluating student performance. Most beginning teachers, for instance, know little about the actual teaching of reading or writing and many tend to be familiar with but a single instructional model for such lessons.
- **Becoming competent in the basic skills of teaching.** Over the first few years of teaching, teachers either develop basic teaching skills or they leave teaching. This development includes learning more effective classroom management, using several teaching models, habitually using certain teaching models with certain subjects, and begining to link evaluation to student learning, but many of the known assessment strategies are not well suited for this purpose. Teachers become more

comfortable with a single model for teaching reading and, often, another for teaching writing, usually the prevailing instructional model found in the school. But teaching follows certain routines, and evaluation is still focused on learning problems, not teaching adaptations.

- **Expanding instructional flexibility.** After a few years of teaching, perhaps three to five years, classroom management is largely automatic. Teachers have figured out what strategies work best for them and now employ them automatically. Often, teachers now become aware of alternative instructional models for teaching reading and writing and begin to consider expanding their repertoire of instructional skills through experimentation. Evaluation options also expand, and assessment strategies move closer to intended purposes. We have seen many experienced teachers begin adding trade books and process writing to their instructional repertoires in the past few years. Similarly, many teachers are developing thematic approaches and attempting to integrate reading and writing activities and to experiment with alternative assessment forms (e.g., portfolios).
- **Acquiring instructional expertise.** As teachers continue to develop professionally, classroom management literally disappears as a concern. Developing teachers create a fairly broad repertoire of instructional strategies that they feel comfortable with and can deploy depending on the instructional setting and situation. They elect certain teaching models depending on the students and the goals of the intended lesson. Teachers evaluate students using an array of techniques and use the evaluations to modify instruction.
- **Contributing to colleagues' instructional expertise.** At this stage, teachers display a breadth of competence. They are reflective concerning their own practice and able to assist other teachers in developing instructional expertise. At this stage teachers have the potential to be powerful mentors. They have developed their instructional expertise and have also developed a reflective stance about their teaching. Thus, rather than simply having less-experienced teachers mimic their teaching, reflective teachers understand how their practice has changed (and continues to change) and are better able to work alongside others as they work through the development of their instructional repertoire. As mentors, they understand that less-experienced teachers cannot develop new strategies without much support and extended opportunities to try out new ideas while receiving supportive assistance.
- **Participating in a broad array of decisions at all levels of the educational system.** At this final stage the teacher exercises positive leadership for school improvement. The teacher has a breadth of experiences and broad understandings of how educational institutions work and how the current educational program in their school came to be.

Of course, there can be no single process of development that all teachers move through and no fixed timeline for general professional development. Still, it seems unlikely that most teachers could move through the stages without spending two or three years in each stage. Thus, we might expect most teachers would be fairly well established in their classroom routines after five or six years but, at this point, to have developed only a few instructional strategies. There is evidence that at this point some teacher's development stagnates. In these cases, teachers seem to get stuck after becoming basically competent at instructional delivery. Their classrooms do not change much from year to year. We see the same posters, same themes, same projects and so on.

It might be useful to think of the faculty of your school and estimate where in the development stages sketched above each teacher falls. What distribution results? Ideally, schools would have faculty that ran across the spectrum (assuming the faculty included some newer teachers). Are many faculty stuck at a stage that represents less than their potential for development?

| —————— | ————— | ———— | ———— | ———— |

survival   competence   flexibility   expertise   contribution   leader

Actually, even stuck teachers change, but they do so in very modest ways and usually very slowly. Often, the changes are surface-level changes—a little more writing but still a formulaic writing that is graded and corrected in red pen—not a transformed writing activity that shifts the focus from simple neatness and spelling to one of constructing effective messages. One might see children's literature used in these classrooms, but often the literature is "high-schoolized," or taught a chapter per week with isolated vocabulary activities, chapter questions, and so on (others have dubbed this "basalizing" literature, but to us it looks more like traditional high school literature lessons). In other words, a new material is simply adapted to fit practiced routines. What we do not see in such classrooms is child-centered, thoughtful use of children's books as the basis for learning literacy. Instead, the materials have changed but the instruction has actually changed little.

PROFESSIONAL DEVELOPMENT: AN ACTION PLAN

If we want to create schools where all children acquire reading and writing proficiency, most schools will have to change. But schools do not change. Instead, it is the teachers and administrators who change the instructional practices that occur in the school. Unfortunately, most people find change upsetting and difficult—two reasons few schools (or companies) change much or fast. However, if American education is to maintain public confidence, change must come to our educational system and that change will have to begin in elementary schools.

Throughout this book we have proposed a number of changes we feel are necessary. Many readers are overwhelmed by the sheer size and complexity of the changes needed at their schools. But change can be managed (somewhat). Change processes can be made more or less comfortable. Change can inspire people or it can simply wear them out. We would like to suggest several principles for attempting to change the instructional practices in any school.

1. **Involve teachers in planning and gathering local data.** Teachers must be involved in planning change, and gathering local data is a good beginning. Much

of the useful data are already available but usually have not been organized in useful ways. Given the sheer quantity of testing, for instance, we might expect that all teachers in a building could quickly answer the question: What proportion of fifth graders (or fourth or sixth) have developed reading and writing abilities sufficient for success at the middle school? But in many districts, virtually no one at an elementary school can answer that question. Part of the problem is that hardly anyone at the elementary school knows anything about the reading and writing demands at the middle school—an odd situation in an educational "system." Often hardly anyone can answer any of the following questions:

- What proportion of children are identified as handicapped? Is that number comparable to the national average? How many children have been declassified each year for the past three years? Is that number comparable to other schools?
- How many children are retained in this school each year? Are there certain grades or teachers more likely to retain children than others? What is the long-term effect of retaining children in this school?
- How many books does the average child attending this school read during any calendar year? How many are read as part of the school curriculum plan? How many read for pleasure? How do the numbers compare to other schools? To community expectations?
- What is the most common sort of homework assignment students are given? Do all teachers assign homework? Do teachers here assign more or less than teachers in most other schools? What is the purpose of homework?
- How much time do our children spend actually reading and writing in school each day? Are we satisfied with that amount? If parents were aware of the amount would they be satisfied? Are there any substantial variations from one classroom to another?
- Does the pool of at-risk children get larger or smaller with each ensuing year of schooling? (In effective schools, the pool is reduced.)
- What genres (e.g., mystery, historical fiction, fantasy, biography) of reading and writing will all students be familiar with by the end of fifth grade?

In our minds none of these are trivial questions, but in most schools no one has anything but a "best guess." We strongly believe in beginning with a good look at local data because it is familiar information in so few schools today. Such a procedure also establishes an "inquiring mind" mind-set necessary for a problem-solving course of change. But local data collection can go on interminably and raise more questions and issues than can possibly be addressed right off. We mention this because in some sites the sheer magnitude of the problems identified through the local data gathering has undermined the motivation to initiate change. So, after initial local data collection, we suggest that some priorities need to be established.

2. **Decide what you need more of and less of.** We have found the *more/less* strategy useful for beginning to think about change in instructional practice. Its basic

premise is to identify some instructional practices that should be increased and some that should be minimized. For example:

- More opportunity to read during the school day, which can be accomplished if children spend less time on worksheets.
- More reading outside school and less low-level homework.
- More integration of writing with reading activities and less isolated writing that is separate from reading.
- More collaboration among special teachers and classroom teachers and less planning in isolation.
- More reading of "comfortable" books and stories and less reading in quite difficult texts.
- Longer blocks of uninterrupted classroom instructional time and less fragmentation of the school day.
- Larger numbers of books in classrooms and fewer skill and drill materials.
- More decoding lessons drawn from reading and writing activities and fewer decoding skills in isolation.

These more/less statements represent only a few of the themes in this book and yet are applicable to many schools. The idea behind this strategy is to make changes fairly concrete and easily measured. Too often in schools where children's literacy achievement is less than optimal, the focus is too broadly conceived as "increasing reading achievement." This gives teachers almost no direction for needed changes. By focusing on changes that have a demonstrated relationship to achievement, the change process becomes easier to manage. In the examples provided above, individual classroom teachers can gather data on their own instructional practices as evidence that change is occurring.

3. **Identify teachers who want to improve.** Roland Barth (1990) identified three types of teachers usually found in schools. The first was the resisting teachers who largely rejected scrutiny and counsel from others and seem to resist reflecting on their own practice. The second group, and largest overall, was comprised of teachers who rethought their own practice but did not generally welcome outside scrutiny or others visiting in their classroom. The third group actively pursued self-examination and fit most conceptualizations of the reflective teacher. These teachers literally threw open their classroom doors to all comers. They sought peer feedback and were eager to engage in professional discussion of classroom practice.

   In an ideal world, we would arrange schools so that teachers in the first group were encouraged and supported in their shift to membership in the second group and, ultimately, the third group of teachers. Unfortunately, Barth notes that in most schools the competitive and evaluative pressures force shifts in the opposite direction. The prevailing climate moves teachers toward increasing isolation. What works to change this climate? Barth reports that he found that just listening, really listening, to teachers complaints, concerns, and suggestions made an enormous difference. He writes of how small encouragements to teachers to pursue the initiatives they raised seemed to kindle the sparks that had begun to die out.

Building on Barth's recommendations, we suggest finding those teachers who are doing more of the things you like to see in the school and encourage and support those teachers. Find those teachers who would like to change but have been at least temporarily defeated by a system of mandates and negative reinforcements. Encourage them to take the risk. Help teachers find others to talk with and problem-solve with. Sympathize more often than you criticize. Get into classrooms and help. Administer reading inventories alongside teachers who feel they have few appropriate books for many of their students. Then find appropriate books for their classrooms. Even a few books will help.

Publicize the more/less items widely and be quick to praise any evidence of progress. Put the items in the weekly parent newsletter and feature classrooms that have made shifts in the desired direction. Target single more/less items for a single-week focus for the whole school. Step in and try to make it more likely to happen. If increasing the amount of reading is on the list, consider, for instance, a whole day "read-in" where children read self-selected books and magazines all day. Open the library, bring out every classroom set of books you can find, invite teachers, children, and parents to donate old beanbag chairs and other soft, squishy places for reading. Set up discussion areas and book commercials where kids can go to find new books to read. One possible result is that kids will actually read all day. When this happens, many teachers experience dramatic shifts in beliefs about students' reading interest and abilities and about the power of self-selected reading. The point to be made is not that every day should be like this but that some days should.

4. **Look long.** Too often the search is for some mythical "quick fix" to all problems schools encounter. Changes to "dramatically improve reading scores this year" will more likely result in some manipulation of the assessment process than beneficial changes in instructional practices. Changing instructional practice is a slow business. Teaching is a complex activity, and changing well-established instructional routines takes time and energy. Change is not amenable to simple mandates. Change follows after teachers acquire new knowledge and experiment with using that knowledge in their own classrooms.

For instance, using a literature-based curriculum, especially one that emphasizes the need for children's self-selected reading and writing, requires teachers substantially more expert about children's literature than most teachers are today. But simply providing professional-development opportunities to expand expertise with children's literature is insufficient to implement literature-based instruction. Teachers need to acquire a repertoire of instructional practices that were less necessary in basal reader curriculum because the teacher manuals provided many suggestions for the general structure of the lessons.

As another example, consider learning to collaborate effectively with other teachers. Mandating collaboration simply does not work very well because collaboration is a complex activity. Specialist teachers often have to acquire greater expertise about classroom instruction and the core curriculum before they can begin to plan collaboratively. Special-education teachers, for instance, often have little working knowledge of classroom instruction and little familiarity with classroom core curriculum materials. Even when teachers develop such knowledge, the problem of planning an instructional intervention for a learning-disabled student collaboratively with the classroom teacher remains. The complexity of change is increased if the change is not only to collaborative planning but also to inclusive education and the two teachers are expected literally to coteach the special-needs child.

The basic point is that change is hard and takes time. Fullan (1991) suggests that expecting schools to change in any substantial ways will take ten years of change activity. Unfortunately, few schools plan change at all and those that do rarely extend planning beyond a single year. Our experiences have been more comparable to Fullan's than different. We have seen dramatic changes in segments of schools in shorter time periods, but for change across an elementary school his ten-year estimate seems appropriate (see also Walp & Walmsley, 1995, or Levin, 1987, for other examples).

We suggest that combining the more/less and the look long strategies produces what many teachers see as a workable overall plan for educational change. But continuing local data gathering is also important because it provides real evidence that changes in teaching practices are taking place.

5. **Focus on one classroom at a time.** Remember that schools are collections of individual classrooms and change comes one classroom at a time. Much has been written about the need for "systemic" change, and we could not agree more that such change is critical. But systemic change is not systemwide change, at least in the sense that everyone in the system has to change simultaneously. Systemic change involves the changes that teachers have little control over and that are needed to free teachers to engage in local problem solving. Needed systemic changes include restructuring of how fiscal, curricular, and organizational issues are addressed.

But any school improvement needs to start in only one classroom. Improvement in that one classroom, like all other classrooms, takes time and is the result of the teacher changing and improving on prior practice. That improvement is professional development at its finest. A focus on individual classrooms is a matter of scale and perspective. If we consider all that needs to be changed and all the people who will need to change to restructure a school wholly, the task seems enormous (because it often is). Enormous tasks, regrettably, often undermine initiative—the task seems just too large in scale. But, individual classrooms, especially when we begin by working with teachers interested in change, seem a much more manageable project.

6. **Think commitment, not control.** Today education is undergoing an enormous upheaval as legislatures and other policy makers rethink how to support the educational process. Central to this upheaval is a recognition that the centralized control strategies that have been so popular in the last half century simply have not achieved the desired ends. Increasingly stringent state and federal regulation has not resulted in higher achievement and may have, unintendedly, worked to limit educational opportunities for at-risk children. Similarly, school district

administrators have realized that increasing the number of central office mandates has not improved the quality of instruction nor has it resulted in reliable improvement in student achievement. Very simply, everyone is coming to realize that neither excellence nor equity can be mandated from afar.

Replacing these control strategies are policies intended to enhance teacher commitment to education, to their teaching, and to their students (Rowan, 1990). Thus, site-based management and shared decision making have been introduced in schools across the nation. Turning more control over to teachers, it is argued, will result in greater investment in teaching and in improving instructional practice. But many teachers remain quite skeptical about these shifts. They remain skeptical for good reason. In too many sites, shared decision making and site-based management have been implemented in name only. In these cases, teachers still have little or no authority over budget issues, curriculum issues, or scheduling, all central to effective classroom instruction. Instead, they are charged with making only trivial decisions and even these have been, at times, countermanded by district officials.

For instance, in one school we worked with, teachers were quite unhappy with the standard report card process. After a year of meetings and research and compromise, they produced a proposal for a different procedure for reporting to parents. After several months, the proposal was rejected as not fitting the district's computerized record-keeping system. No alternative was offered. No compromise. No suggestion was offered for altering the computerized record system. Such responses from district officials kill teacher consideration of further involving themselves in the change process.

The potential of shared decision making and site-based management has been well documented in settings other than schools. These strategies are designed to foster increased commitment to improving education on the part of the very people who are most central to instructional practice—classroom teachers. These strategies are not simply means to absolve school and district administrators of responsibility but to shift their role from plant foreman to team facilitator. Principals and district officials remain important players but they become more service-oriented personnel under site-based and team decision models. The responsibilities shift from enforcing compliance with mandates, rules, and regulations established by others to facilitating efforts toward improved local practice.

Time for Professional Development

We conclude this chapter with a focus on one of the true dilemmas of school reform—finding time for professional development. Some have suggested that schools should resist scheduling professional time at the end of the school day because teachers are tired after a long day of work. In addition, after-school efforts provide only short blocks of time for professional-development activities. A better idea, say these professional-development proponents, is freeing teachers for half or whole school days to pursue professional development. Others respond that such a plan disadvantages students who lose their regular teacher to professional-development days. Better to schedule development for the summer months in their view. But summer efforts do not immediately allow teachers to experiment with new ideas in their classrooms. Summer efforts are also often more expensive and more difficult to schedule, say proponents of school-day professional-development activities. So when should professional development occur?

Professional development should occur before school, after school, during the school day, during summers, and during professional leaves. Professional-development activity should be virtually continuous across the school day and school year and across teachers' careers. Perhaps one primary difficulty of past professional- development efforts has been an emphasis on trying to select the one best model, the one best schedule, the one best topic, and so on. This thinking leads to compartmentalized notions of what constitutes a professional-development activity. Consider the array of activities that have been sketched in this chapter. Some, such as a Teachers as Readers group, seem to lend themselves to after-school time slots than other suggested activities. On the other hand, observing in another teacher's classroom obviously better fits into the regular school-day schedule. But summer might be the most appropriate time to schedule an intensive session for teachers to familiarize themselves with an array of new children's books and integrate these books into existing thematic units.

Finding time for professional development will always be problematic, given other demands upon educators. Still, most teachers are in front of students for only about four to four and a half hours each day. This leaves three to four hours of time available for other activities each day. When professional conversation is viewed as important, schools seem to find or create time for teachers to converse with another. Some schools use morning team meetings, others a block-scheduled team time during the day, and others an after-school collaboration period. The point is that many schools have found time for professional conversations and other staff-development activity—but to find the time requires that someone goes looking for it.

Other schools create time for professional development. At the Bellevue Elementary School in the St. Louis, Missouri, area, the staff has extended each school day by ten minutes to gain a half-day each month for extra professional-development activity. In other schools we have visited, similar plans have created early release times for students on Fridays and late arrival time at 11:30 for students on Wednesdays so that teachers could work together. In another school, an hour-early release of students each Friday created a monthly Saturday professional half-day for teachers.

SUMMARY

The last ten years have been exciting times in American education, and the next ten promise to extend the excitement. Classroom teachers have been asked to (1) use children's literature for reading instruction, (2) implement process-based approaches to writing, (3) teach math as problem solving, (4) reduce reliance on homogeneous groupings, (5) include handicapped children in the classroom social and instructional milieu, (6) increase the use of technology in instruction and help children develop technological proficiency, (7) integrate the curriculum, (8) use more authentic assessment strategies, (9) work more collaboratively with special teachers, and (10) become involved in shared decision-making processes as part of site-based management. These ten items only partially represent the new expertise and the new roles classroom teachers have been expected to acquire. Yet, often, support for developing the needed expertise and for practicing the new roles has been in short supply. To achieve the necessary changes teachers need support—both collegial and administrative.

In schools with at least minimally adequate resources, instructional improvement is largely a people-improvement undertaking. Schools improve only as fast as the instructional practice of teachers improve. Teaching well is a lifelong learning process that requires career professionals willingly engaging in a variety of self-improving development activities. Many schools currently do too little to either foster or support such lifelong learning. Teachers need to be viewed as substantial resources, and providing professional-growth opportunities for the teaching staff must be recognized as a long-term investment in maintaining high-quality instruction.

Hyde (1992) notes that merely exposing teachers to new ideas will not change practice unless the teachers enact the new ideas in their classrooms. However, movement can best be accomplished by stimulating an interest to entertain involvement. He suggests that good evidence has been accumulated, and to stimulate a willingness to change in veteran teachers, it is necessary that schools:

- Provide experience with teaching approaches that hold promise,
- Allow teachers to choose areas of experimentation,
- Provide time and autonomy to experiment, and
- Work to nurture peer encouragement.

To create schools where all children learn to read and write, schools must become sites where teachers more often work collegially in a problem-solving framework focused on improving instructional practice. For too long educational policy and reform initiatives have largely ignored supporting classroom teachers. For too long schools have failed to foster collegiality and professional conversation. It is time to alter the situation and begin to reconsider how to create schools where all teachers learn and all acquire new instructional strategies continuously across their careers. Creating such support for teacher professional development is the first step toward creating that school where all children become readers and writers.

Family Involvement

T he roles families might play in educating their children has once again been thrust into the spotlight by national policy statements and the media. With the much ballyhooed America 2000 came the first national education goal: By the year 2000 all American children will start school ready to learn. This goal, and the particular wording of it, created much discussion. What child was not "ready to learn"? What did "ready to learn" mean? Some asked whether it might not be more appropriate to set as the goal: "By the year 2000 American schools will be ready for all learners." The net effect of placing school readiness as the first national education goal was to lift concern about families and children during the preschool years high on the national agenda.

Several surveys of educators identified the lack of school readiness as a primary problem confronting schools. Thus, calls for more and better publicly funded preschools were common (though funding was not) as were calls for expanding parent-family training efforts. In addition to the attention families attracted in discussions of the first national educational goal were other shifts in policy and practice that brought discussions of family roles and responsibilities to the forefront. One shift was an increasing amount of homework that elementary school children were assigned as a result of a call for more time spent on homework in *A Nation at Risk* (National Commission on Excellence in Education, 1983). Elementary schools implemented homework policies, in some cases even for kindergarten, and with homework came increased expectations of families in supporting and monitoring homework completion. There was, and is yet today, little evidence that increasing homework in the elementary grades has any positive effect on student achievement (at the high school level there is some such evidence). Nonetheless, while homework was uncommon for elementary students 20 years ago, today it is a common, if often unfortunate, experience for children.

Thus, two shifts in national education policy increased the attention paid to the role families might play. But what is the responsibility of families? Only a short time ago that responsibility was basically seen as providing a healthy, happy, and well-behaved child for the school to educate. If families met these responsibilities and ensured regular school attendance, most teachers felt lucky. When did it become the family's responsibility to supervise daily worksheet completion sent home as first-grade homework? When did it become the family's responsibility to take a fourth-grade child to the public library to locate information on Chile for a written report assigned as an out-of-school activity? When did it become common to assign families the responsibility for developing initial literacy so that a child would meet a school's kindergarten entrance standard?

The point that needs to be made is that American schools have recently been raising minimum acceptable levels of family responsibility for educating their children. This is true even though some schools had little success in getting families to meet the previously lower levels of responsibility. It is undeniable that families are important in the education of children. But families send their children to school to be taught, and many families have historically viewed that as the end of their responsibility. In fact, Lareau (1989) found that many working-class families simply viewed schooling as the school's job—not theirs. These families resented homework. They saw it as an attempt by the school to shift the workload to families. Many felt that if the child did not get the work done in school, either the teacher had not done a very good job of teaching or the child should be kept after school to complete the work under a teacher's supervision.

Many working-class families saw schoolwork as fitting only into the school day. Work not done in school today could be done there tomorrow. This view revealed an interesting parallel to the parents' work lives. These blue-collar parents did not bring work home. They left the job at the time clock. Their view of schooling was similar. This represented an enormous gap between the views of teachers and the views of families in the working-class communities. In middle-class, white-collar professional communities, families more often took a different view. These families often asked for more homework for their children. This seemed to parallel their work lives. The adults in these families often brought work home to do in the evenings or on weekends. They viewed homework as normal. Complaints about homework focused on the low quality of much of the work assigned and the lack of careful evaluation of homework by teachers.

In the 1993 *American Teacher Survey* (Metropolitan Life), 69 percent of the teachers rated federal support for developing programs to help disadvantaged families work with their children to prepare them better for school as needing the highest priority for funding. Three-quarters of all elementary teachers and 82 percent of inner city teachers rated it as a highest priority item.

American educators are expecting more family involvement with their children's schooling today than they did only a few years ago. At the same time, larger numbers of children from families living in poverty are filling our schools, more children are living with a single parent, and more children are living with two parents, each working at full-time jobs. Very simply, educators are raising the demands on families as parental resources are shrinking. Simultaneously, families are raising their expectations of schools with calls for more early education programs, more after-school programs, and higher levels of performances from students.

All of this is, of course, what makes an educator's life today so exciting. But solutions must be developed because schools cannot be effective without the confidence and support of the families of the children they teach. This chapter develops plans for reaching out to families, involving families, and supporting families. Families are the ultimate consumer of schooling because they choose to have the children stay or leave. However, families differ considerably on their knowledge of schools and the liberty they have to choose alternatives for their children. But borrowing the premise of customer satisfaction from the Total Quality Movement of Edward Deming puts family satisfaction at the forefront of evaluations of elementary school quality.

■ REACHING OUT TO FAMILIES

Too often educators wait for families to contact them. They send home notices for parent-teacher conferences and, perhaps, PTA meetings, but too often they make no personal contact with families until some real problem exists. It seems better to think about ways to ensure that every family hears from the child's teacher personally before problems arise. For instance, Palestis (1993) describes the family outreach program in the Mine Hill, New Jersey, schools as part of the school district's obligation to the community. All Mine Hill school teachers are trained in family involvement using the *Parents on Your Side: A Comprehensive Family Involvement Program for Teachers* (Canter & Canter, 1990). In addition, teachers send NCR two-way communication forms home. The form has spaces for a teacher message and a reply (or question) from home, while providing both parties with a copy to keep. Each child has a Friday Folder that contains all graded assignments, homework, tests scheduled for the next week, and a family-teacher two-way communication form that either party can use to initiate a conversation. When families enter an elementary school in the Mine Hill district they find a family center in the lobby with family education materials, including pamphlets, magazine articles, videotapes, and so on, that they can borrow. Finally, teachers are given time to contact families with Happy Calls during two periods each week. These calls are simply to comment on progress and good deeds of children. This effort reflects the strong commitment the school district has made to keeping families informed—the first step in reaching out to families.

Many schools produce a monthly or even weekly newsletter for families. Researchers at the Center for Disadvantaged Students at Johns Hopkins University studied what information in school newsletters families actually read. Not surprisingly, families liked articles by and about children the best. They liked articles on classroom activities, social events, school programs, and recipes, too. Families reported that their children also read the newsletter, particularly articles about and by children. When student names appeared in the articles, families were more likely to read those aloud to their children (Herrick & Epstein, 1991).

Print is not the only media for reaching to families. Radio and television offer other possibilities for brief public-service messages. Creating one such ad each month, especially for radio, does not involve enormous effort. In large metropolitan areas, the messages to families might be addressed to all families in the district but still feature a single school, or even classroom, project. The message needs to communicate: "We are your schools. These are your children." The ads can offer sources for more information or invitations to visit schools generally or a particular school.

In larger metropolitan areas, cable television service is now common. Each cable television system is required to provide public access channels. These channels can also provide a vehicle for reaching out to families. Schools need to worry less about producing slick-looking programs and more about putting children and schools on the screen in activities such as school plays, concerts, performances, guest readers, visiting authors, science fairs, and art exhibits. Families will tune in when the channel features children and their performances, products, displays, and productions.

Much of this outreach can be integrated into the reading and language arts curriculum. Newsletter production, not just the writing of articles, provides real-world experiences for children in composing, editing, and publishing. In addition to building oral language, the radio and television productions might involve scripting, editing, and captioning activities.

Involving Families

Reaching out to families is a necessary first step, but it is only the first step. The ultimate goal is increasing the quality and amount of family involvement with their children's education. Before working to improve family involvement, schools must clarify precisely what they want families more involved in. The importance of clarifying the meaning of family involvement became clear during the implementation of a requirement to "involve" families in schools to garner additional funding through the Arizona At-Risk Pilot Project (Vandegrift & Greene, 1992). While family involvement was mandated, it was never defined. A variety of strategies were developed by participating schools, including workshops, parenting classes, newsletters, home visits, advisory committees, social events, and so on. But teacher surveys after the first year of implementation suggested that family involvement had not increased. The common complaint was that the school offered a variety of new activities but families largely stayed home anyway.

In analyzing the activities and the teacher evaluations, the program evaluators were able to describe two dimensions of family involvement that seemed part of the definition. First was the notion of *supportiveness*. Families support their children and are understanding and reassuring. These families care immensely about their children, their well-being, and their education. Second was the notion of *active participation* in that families are making visible attempts to show their supportiveness. Visible, in this case, meant visible to teachers and, most commonly, involved volunteering at school, attending school functions, and initiating communication with teachers. Unfortunately, this definition of family involvement requires high levels of commitment and participation. It also requires that families have:

- Free time from work,
- Child care for other children,
- Transportation to the school,
- Clothing they felt comfortable appearing in school wearing, and
- Money to pay for all of the above.

While some families are lucky enough to have such resources, many poor and working-class families do not. Consider that the majority of the working poor are single women with children. These parents work the longest hours for the smallest paycheck. These are the parents with the smallest discretionary incomes, often lacking small amounts of money for bus fares or baby-sitters. They are also the parents least likely to have child care readily available and affordable. They are the parents most likely to be working between 3:00 in the afternoon and 9:00 in the evening, the time schools schedule most family activities. These parents are often supportive parents but not parents who are actively participating in school events.

In developing a broader framework for considering family involvement, Vandegrift and Greene (1992) suggest that there are four basic types of families, as illustrated in Figure 9.1

Figure 9.1
Family-involvement categories.

++ Family *supports* child and is *actively involved* in schools	+ − Family *supports* child but is *not active* in schools
− + Family is *unsupportive* of child but *active* in schools	− − Family is *unsupportive* and *not active* in schools

below. The families everyone wants to see are those that are both supportive of their children and actively participating in school activities. These families not only support their children but reach out to the school by visiting, calling, and volunteering.

A second type of family is supportive of children but does not actively participate in school events. Adults in these families may have bad memories about their own schooling, they may be embarrassed by their lack of education or their children's difficulties at school, or they may simply feel inadequate in school settings. These families may also lack transportation or child care. They might have work schedules that conflict with school events.

Some of these families will be limited by *all* of these factors. However, absence from school events does not indicate a lack of family support for the children. These families may help with homework and provide the safe, nurturing home that is essential. These families may actively discuss school work and read newsletters or watch cable television productions of school events. They may be more than happy to use a school voice-mail system for communicating with teachers (even when they are unlikely to respond in writing). These families might welcome videos on parenting that can be viewed in the home. Thus, these families can be involved and their involvement enhanced even without attending school functions.

A third group of families—we hope a small group—participate in school activities but are not supportive of their children. These families show up for everything, but observing their behavior with their child makes one shudder. These families ignore or abuse their children but still put on the appropriate front at school. These are the families that complain to teachers about their "stupid kid" and who harangue and belittle the child in front of peers and teachers.

The last group of families, we hope small as well, are neither supportive of their children nor do they participate in school activities. Sometimes it is simply that the families' own problems have taken precedence over children's education and development. The stress that low-income families feel, the inadequacy that eats away at them, may undermine many of the supportive feelings parents typically feel about their children. An alcohol or drug addiction may also create such dependencies that normal human functioning is virtually impossible.

The last two groups of families present schools with the most difficult problems. In most cases, schools will need to work with other agencies to address the difficulties faced by children in these homes. However, when parent support and involvement are unlikely, schools must redouble their efforts to support the children. This may mean developing peer tutoring or pairing children with a adult volunteers. It may mean involving children in an after-school or Saturday School homework support class. It may mean providing breakfast and snacks. Some children may need another adult in the school assigned as their advocate. Schools cannot penalize children for the families they have. Instead, schools must develop ways to support children if family support and involvement is in short supply.

When the broader view of family involvement is considered, it is easier to develop different strategies to reach different families. Family involvement begins with reaching out to families, not waiting for families to come. Unlike the cornfield baseball diamond in the movie *Field of Dreams,* simply creating family nights and parent events at school does not ensure that they will come. Reaching out to families is the first step in building family involvement because informed families view the school and its staff as caring immensely about their children. A second step is actually listening to families. Too often, schools create family-involvement efforts with no input from families.

If increased family involvement is needed in your school, a good starting point is asking what the school offers that makes it an attractive place for families to visit. Some schools have coffee and a parent lounge. Families are made to feel welcome, and schools encourage family members to stay around once they enter the building. Some schools create parent-advisory breakfast groups that meet weekly on an open-invitation basis. These before-school or early school-day affairs offer child care, conversations rather than lectures, and an opportunity for families to be heard. Other schools have created community advisory boards with church leaders, business persons, families, and civic leaders. These boards also meet regularly to discuss the school, the programs, the children, and the community.

The Arizona At-Risk Pilot project concluded that the most successful family-involvement projects began when families had personal contact with someone from the school community (even other families) and high levels of active parent participation were not required, at least initially. Something as simple as receiving a Happy Call from the principal or teacher can provide much of the needed impetus to increase involvement.

TAKING INVENTORY OF FAMILY INVOLVEMENT

As with most other areas, a school might begin by inventorying current school resources, attitudes, and policies concerning family involvement. Are families, for instance, really welcome at the school or do current policies work to restrict family presence and involvement in the building? In one school we visited, family members had to complete an application at least one week in advance of any classroom visit or activity involvement and then wait for written school approval to be granted. In contrast, a nearby school encouraged family members to drop in at any time, and the school administrator offered a brief but continuing orientation session to provide community visitors with basic operating procedures and ideas for different types of educational involvement. Near a coffeepot by the school's entrance a small gaggle of parents can be found at almost any time of day, usually talking quietly about their children and school programs. Some schools do even more to welcome families and community members into schools, but all schools need to ask whether families and community members are actually welcomed in the building.

> In Chapter 4 we discussed the power of high-quality classrooms in overcoming home effects on learning, summarizing the work of Catherine Snow and her colleagues. But Snow and friends also noted a difference between teachers in high-quality classrooms and those in other classrooms. The difference was found in family involvement. Families were far more likely to participate in school events and communicate with the teachers in the high-quality classrooms. Snow et al. noted that the teachers in the high-quality classroom made many more personal parent contacts than did other teachers. The teachers in the high-quality classrooms routinely called families, wrote notes, and met with families before and after school. Perhaps families were more involved because these teachers were more successful with their children than other teachers. It is clear that teachers can involve low-income families, but the contacts must be initiated by the teacher, the contacts must be positive and personal, and the teacher must be persistent.

Next, you might evaluate the number of positive personal school-family contacts that have occurred over the last month—especially the number of such contacts with the least-involved families. Ask whether the school-family contacts have been largely negative messages about children and whether even these have been bureaucratized messages sent on form letters. If the overwhelming majority of contacts between school staff and families in the past month have not been of the positive, personal variety, you have found the obvious starting point for increasing family involvement.

Next, look at the events offered for families. Has there been an array of levels of possible involvement offered over the past few months? Have school-based activities and events been scheduled at the families' convenience? Have families been offered clear, consistent, and achievable ideas for involvement in their children's education?

As a final information-gathering step, you may want to ask family members to evaluate school and teacher efforts in communicating with them and involving them in the educational process. The evaluation might be in survey form, which asks for ratings on features such as whether the school:

- is a good place to send children,
- treats all children fairly,
- frequently contacts families with good news,
- makes families feel welcome,
- makes it is easy for families to get information.

In addition to a survey, schools might also conduct a series of focus-group sessions with adults from the community, parents, and, perhaps, older adolescents who attended the elementary school. Usually, focus groups respond to series of topics, and a record of the discussion that represents the various points of view expressed is kept. Focus groups often work best if they are organized and run by someone other than those being evaluated, in this case school staff members. Schools might have community members run the sessions and keep a record of the discussion flow, but the groups set the general topics to be discussed. Well-organized focus groups can provide a rich source of evaluative information to schools.

Finally, you might routinely request family evaluations of school programs—much the way most colleges collect student evaluations of courses and faculty each semester. It has always struck us as odd that so few schools have developed such procedures. While evaluations from families will not always provide sufficient information to make decisions about programs and policies, annually gathering such information offers the opportunity to receive feedback from a school's most important constituency—students' parents and family members.

If schools are to foster family involvement, it will be important to gather information on existing efforts and on parent, family, and community satisfaction with those efforts. As new efforts are implemented, it is important to monitor the effects. As with most other areas of school operation, routinely gathering information on program outcomes, including evaluations from participants, provides a better basis for decisions about continuing the effort or changes that might be necessary.

SUPPORTING FAMILIES

Schools must complement families in educating children. Some families need more support than others to become more involved in their children's education. When children come from families, for instance, where intergenerational illiteracy is evident, it seems obvious that schools cannot expect those families to provide much home support for children's literacy development. Even when adult family members are functionally literate, but undereducated, little home support can be expected. The scope and seriousness of intergenerational poverty and illiteracy has resulted in the recent focus on family literacy efforts by social and educational agencies. The National Center for Family Literacy (Darling, 1993) defines comprehensive family literacy programs as comprised of four components:

1. Basic literacy instruction for families,
2. Preschool and literacy education for young children,
3. Family education and support activities, and
4. Regular parent and child activities.

Such family literacy programs take many shapes. Services are delivered at school sites, community sites, or in homes. Some are characterized by intensive short-term intervention efforts and others by less intensive long-term programs. Usually though, the planning of these programs has to assume the need for long-term support if for no other reason than it took generations to create the family that exists today and it will take time to alter the current situation.

Family literacy programs are potentially powerful support programs. However, these programs, like most family support efforts, cost money to develop and maintain. But Head

Start, Even Start, Title 1, special education, and other state and federal funding support are available for such efforts. In addition, funds through foundations, social service and employment agencies of state and local governments can often be located to support such efforts.

Virtually any comprehensive family support program that one might design will require some substantial interagency collaboration. Comprehensive family support usually involves working with the social services community, the health community, and, often, agencies involved with employment and training. In most communities, these agencies and their services are neither well coordinated nor available at a single site. One focus of the Success for All schools has been achieving greater communication and collaboration with various agencies (Dolan, 1992). Is it possible to move health and social services into the school site? If not, can they be located near the school? Failing all else, can families find out at the school, for instance, exactly where they need to go and who they need to see to get eyeglasses for their child? Can they find out about GED classes with free child care at the school? Can they participate in adult basic literacy training at the school?

Interagency coordination of services and collaborative efforts present many bureaucratic obstacles to overcome, but the first obstacle is lack of school awareness of support services available to families and precisely how families access those services. In some schools, no one even knows where the Head Start program is offered much less how to enroll children. In other schools, the Head Start program and the kindergarten and primary teachers use a common curriculum framework and common method of reporting children's development to families. In some schools, no one has ever considered applying for an Even Start family education project because the focus is on preschool-age children and their parents. In other schools, an Even Start effort links preschool and adult-education programs to family involvement in school programs. No one is aware in some schools that Title 1 programs must have a family-involvement component and that Title 1 funds can be spent supporting most of the activities described in this chapter. In other schools, Title 1 Parent Advisory Council members work actively on shared-decision-making teams and regularly sponsor family educational support activities. Virtually no effort goes into complying with the parent involvement mandated by the Individuals with Disabilities Education Act (IDEA) in some schools, but in others parents are actively involved in developing the IEP and the school can draw upon this pool of child advocates to work with families to discern what educational options might most benefit their handicapped children.

It is never easy to establish comprehensive family support programs, but an increasing interest in interagency collaboration in federal and state agencies may offer new opportunities for developing and funding such efforts.

SCHOOL-LINKED SERVICES: AN INTEGRATED APPROACH TO CHILDREN AND FAMILIES

Imagine that the mother of a first-grade student walks her son to school and brings his baby sister along. While she delivers her son for another day of classes at the school, the young mother stops in to see the school nurse to have her daughter's temperature checked and a throat culture taken. Then she moves to the satellite Women, Infants, and Children (WIC) office to be recertified for continued participation before dropping her daughter off at the on-site day-care room. Next, she spends two and one-half hours in an adult education program where she works on her high school GED. The focus of her literacy-development activities, however, is children's books and family stories rather than the more traditional skills workbook. That afternoon, after having lunch in the day-care room with her daughter, she works in her son's classroom as a paid assistant, practicing her reading skills by introducing little books to small groups of children. This paid internship is part of a planned educational program that will lead to a Child Development Associate (CDA) certificate jointly planned and funded by the state Department of Social Services, the Department of Labor, Head Start, and Title 1.

Such a scenario could occur today but usually does not. Instead, the young mother would have to schedule and visit three, four, or five different agencies at just as many sites to accomplish the same activities. The scenario described above is one example of what might be accomplished with school-linked services. School-linked service models are analogous to the modern supermarket in that they attempt to offer "one-stop shopping" sites for a wide array of children's services. School-linked services is a radical idea in an era when 170 federal categorical programs provide educational and other services to school children. But the current fragmentation, duplication, and lack of communication hardly serves children well. The basic idea behind school-based services is to restructure the delivery of most social, educational, and health programs targeted for children and their families so that a coherent, continuous, and supportive effort with an emphasis on preventive intervention can be offered.

So what might school-linked services programs look like? Two models, provide a glimpse of just what the future might hold. The New Beginnings effort at Hamilton Elementary School, located in one of the poorest and most ethnically diverse neighborhoods in San Diego, targets broad services to all families who live in the school attendance area (Payzant, 1994). The collaborative effort involves the city, the city schools, the county, the community college, the housing commission, the medical school, and the health center. A space crunch, common in most elementary schools, resulted in locating the New Beginnings School-Linked Services (SLS) effort in a modular building that was transported to the school site. All new entrants to the school report to the SLS site where they are enrolled in school and scheduled for any social or health services they are eligible for. Through a shared resourcing agreement, a nurse practitioner is available on-site and a pediatrician is available part-time. A case-management approach, where one professional manages all interactions and services provided to a family (as opposed to a series of such staff from each agency working with the family), is viewed as a primary key to preventing children from falling through the cracks in the health, educational, and social services networks. A common eligibility form has been designed to simplify applications to several educational, health, and social service programs. Teachers at Hamilton have been involved in planning and implementing the project and now are working with the New Beginnings staff members rather than just referring children to various agencies. Families are more involved in school and are more frequently attending parenting education classes. While the New Beginnings project has occasionally stumbled while breaking new ground, the effort serves as a model that other schools might emulate.

School-linked services efforts in Baltimore have been fostered by the Success for All (SFA) program and its "relentless" approach to addressing the needs of at-risk children (Dolan, 1992). While SFA sites vary considerably in the nature and scope of collaborative efforts, each site offers more such services than is usual in city schools. In some SFA schools, health services are provided on the school site by public-health nurse and physicians. In other schools, the state Office of Mental Health provides on-site family counseling, adult education with child care is available (both family literacy and vocational training), food banks distribute federal surplus foodstuffs as well as donated items, Boys' and Girls' Clubs activities are offered after school and on weekends, and social workers funded from shared educational and social services resources work with families in a case-management model, thereby reducing overlapping responsibilities.

Some state and federal agencies have encouraged developing more comprehensive school-linked services, and several demonstration programs exist around the country. Several lessons have already been learned from these efforts (General Accounting Office, 1993):

- Leadership from the top is necessary. Commitment from a school superintendent and the Board of Education with commitments from state agency heads work to ensure success. When a principal, program director, or department head attempts to create the collaborative links without top-level support, much more effort seems necessary and success is less likely.
- Leaders selected to head the effort must have a talent for coalition building. Even after initial stages of planning are complete, successful efforts need on-going nurturing of the original coalition members and efforts at expanding membership of that coalition.
- Model programs vary as a result of different constituencies with differing needs. No single model can ever work. All models do not have to incorporate all possible other services and agencies. Create a program based on local needs and resources and local commitments.
- School staff need to be involved from the get-go. Teachers, especially, are central to the success of school-linked services since they are the members of the coalition who have the most regular and sustained contact with the children. Thus, teachers are, literally, the eyes and ears (and noses) of any school-linked services effort. Do not delay teacher involvement—have teachers active on the initiation team. School-linked services does not mean teachers have more to do. In fact, now teachers often have less to do but more children often receive desperately needed services and support.
- Plans must be made for offering school-linked services during periods when the school is not operating. Most other state and federal agencies for children and families work on twelve-month schedules and many work seven days a week (health and law enforcement, for example).
- School-linked services should not interrupt further children's academic work during the school day. Before-school and after-school services, Saturday service provision, and vacation services are all needed to achieve this. However, these efforts are also often more convenient for families. Do not fall into the trap of designing school-linked services to operate only, or even primarily, during normal school hours.

School-linked services are neither simple to create nor a panacea that will solve all the problems educators face in working with children from families in trouble. Nonetheless, it seems that virtually everyone agrees that it is time to rework the archaic and convoluted system of services that now exist in most communities. Schools seem a logical location for services targeted to serving the needs of children. School-linked services is an idea whose time has come.

> Collaboration is a process to reach goals that cannot be achieved acting singly. . . . As a process, collaboration is a means to an end, not an end in itself. . . . Because collaboration involves sharing responsibility, it requires consensus building and may not be imposed hierarchically. It is likely to be time-consuming, as collaborators must learn about each other's roles and responsibilities. . . . Collaborators must also acquire expertise in the process of group goal setting (Bruner, 1991, p. 6.)

■ PLANNING FOR FAMILY INVOLVEMENT

At this point, it may be useful to begin developing a three-year plan for increasing family involvement. The initial step is planning to improve a school's outreach efforts. Just what is currently being done and what else is needed? A second step is to evaluate the current parental involvement using some scheme similar to the four parent group schemes presented earlier. What is the current nature of family involvement? What areas should be targeted for immediate attention? What resources seem needed? Perhaps most important, school staff must be asked whether they are committed to increasing real family involvement in the school. Are you ready and willing to involve families in activities that have the potential for giving families a voice in how the school works?

> It may be useful to examine the *Family Involvement Seminar: Why Family Involvement?* produced by the Appalachia Educational Laboratory ($10 from AEL, P.O. Box 1348, Charleston, WV 25325). The package includes activities, handouts, transparencies, and sample agendas. Traditional and nontraditional family involvement roles are presented in a seminar format that encourages teachers and parents to puzzle through defining desired family involvement together.

A variety of initial small steps might be taken to enhance family involvement in schools. A first step would be to enhance school-to-home communications. Ames and her colleagues (1993) studied how school-home communications influence parental involvement. They found substantial variation among teachers in the frequency of communication from school to home. Some teachers rarely contacted families, while others were characterized as high-communication teachers because home-school communications were, literally, a daily event. They found high-communication teachers felt they were better able to meet the needs of difficult children and had more strategies for motivating and involving children in their schoolwork. Families of children in high-communication classrooms evaluated teachers as more effective, held stronger beliefs in their children's potential, and reported higher levels of involvement with their children's schoolwork. Children in the high-communication classrooms reported high levels of academic competence. School-home communications took the form of classroom newsletters, personal notes and telephone calls, review activities, and work folders that children regularly took home.

The focus of the most effective school-home communication was developing better understandings of classroom activities, curriculum, and plans; providing information on children's progress, accomplishments and improvement; and offering information and direction on ways to help at home. Many low-communication teachers, in contrast, contacted families only when a child was in serious trouble (either academically or behaviorally). Ames and her colleagues commented that:

> Teachers often contact parents to tell them that their child is having trouble and is not motivated, and then expect this information will stimulate the parents' assistance. Our initial findings suggest that such communications may not have the intended effect and may only discourage parents and make them feel less comfortable with the school and with their role as a helper.

A rich array of school-home communications fosters family involvement. But the most important communications must come from classroom teachers. When classroom teachers reach out and communicate regularly with families, especially about positive aspects of children's school experiences, families respond positively and increase their efforts to support their children.

A good beginning then is to establish improved communications from classrooms to homes. Perhaps like the Mine Hill schools a time should be set aside each week for each teacher to call families. Establishing a voice-mail system to facilitate telephone communications between teachers and families offers promising prospects. Assisting teachers in developing weekly classroom newsletters, perhaps attached to the weekly school newsletter, would enhance families' awareness of classroom activities. Developing clear guidelines on homework and creating homework help packets or weekly work folders for families might also be considered.

In the Success for All schools, teachers met and prepared monthly at-home-work packets for students at each grade level (Herrick & Epstein, 1991). These activities were developed by brainstorming current curricular topics that were to be covered during the month ahead. After selecting a single topic, the teachers developed games and activities that worked to develop the skills or strategies and that families could do with their children. These were packaged in resealable sandwich bags and sent home with a simple set of directions for families. In some cases, teachers introduced the activity in classes so that children were familiar with the routines.

An evaluation of this procedure found that about two-thirds of the urban families used these packages with their children on at least several occasions and that the children from these homes had higher achievement at the end of the year. A key to the success of the packages was developing activities that were easy to do (e.g., nursery rhymes in kindergarten) and that families found useful. Rather than attempting to move families into hour-long nightly tutoring sessions, these teachers took a more modest approach.

The Parents as Reading Partners (PARP) program operates in several states and encourages a fifteen-minute daily parent-child reading time. Of course, children and their families need access to books to participate in this activity and that presents a potential difficulty in many low-income families. Schools need to make appropriate books available if the PARP program is to be initiated. Some schools using this activity send small books home each night in those same resealable sandwich bags. Some rely more heavily on Reading Is Fundamental (RIF, 600 Maryland Ave., SW, Washington, DC 20024-2520) to provide children with books for their homes. However, in most cases RIF cannot supply enough books for daily home reading.

A final caution about using PARP is in order. In some communities it has become competitive with classes striving for a banner or a pizza award and with some children being cast as pariahs because their families do not participate. In addition, when competitive pressure rises high enough, families cheat and indicate they read with children when they did not. Honestly, it seems impossible to actually read for 15 minutes each and every night all year long. Guidelines for PARP need to suggest but not require reading every night (maybe five of seven nights), and competitions should be avoided.

When encouraging families to read to their children at home, it is wise to be aware of Pat Edwards' cautions—many undereducated families do not know the routines of reading to children even if they read reasonably well themselves. Adults who grew up in homes where parent-child reading was not common have no background of life experiences to draw on when schools suggest they read to their children at home. Edwards (1989) found enormous gaps between the read-aloud practices teachers expected and what the family members actually did. Because of this she developed a series of videotaped lessons for families (available from Children's Press, 1-800-621-1115). These tapes form the core of a family-training workshop series. The tapes present real adults learning to read to their children and learning all of those many and varied subtle moves, prompts, and gestures that make reading to children a valuable activity.

Christine Sylvester, who teaches at LaFollette Elementary School in Milwaukee, uses classroom videotapes of lessons, field trips, guest readers, book sharing, and so on as a take-home activity. The tapes emphasize focusing on just one or two children's involvement in a classroom lesson or activity. By setting the camera on a tripod and placing the microphone near the targeted children she can capture voices and images while still teaching. She may have a child introduce or summarize the recorded event but often uses only the classroom video clip. Families can view the lesson with their child and discuss what is going on. The tape is sometimes used as a classroom learning activity as she replays it having the children comment on what they are doing and what else they might have done before sending it home. The tapes are an enormous hit with parents and children as well. The tapes seem to reduce the formality of the first teacher conferences and also open up opportunities for teacher and family communications.

Terri Austin uses student-run parent conferences in her classroom at the Ft. Wainwright Elementary School in Fairbanks. The basic idea is that students create portfolios of their work across the marking period and develop written rationales for the inclusion of each piece. The work is organized and stored in colorful three-ring binders. Students come to the parent conference and present the work and explain why it was selected. Other work they did across the period is photocopied for family members to take home with them. Family members, teacher, and student discuss the portfolio work, the other work samples, the effort, and the goals for improvement during the conference. Again, the strategy of involving students seems to increase the interest and involvement of families.

Are You Ready for Authentic Family Involvement?

The nature of family involvement is changing as states mandate new relationships between communities and their school, between families, parents, community members, and educators. Many of the new roles are strikingly different from baking for a school bake sale or other traditional volunteer roles. Kuykendall (1992) notes that while family members still play such traditional roles as tutors, volunteers, and neighborhood coordinators, they might also be involved as members of:

- staff selection committees
- local school leadership teams
- school disciplinary teams
- school interior-design improvement teams
- school publicity teams
- volunteer coordination teams
- merit pay committees

Her listing includes assignments with real potential influence on school operations. These might be thought of as authentic family involvement because the roles concern the business of running schools. She argues that many families, especially minority and low-income families, respond far more positively to involvement that has real potential for changing schools. Historically, schools have often tried to keep families in "safe" involvement activities—where families did what they were told, not where they offered advice on what schools should do. Too often the communications to low-income families have had a condescending tone. Too rarely have teachers and administrators actually spent much time listening to low-income families and even more rarely have these families felt their comments, ideas, and criticisms were taken seriously. School-home communications must become two-way communications with schools honoring the family members' voices.

Kuykendall notes that just getting information about schools, policies, practices, and procedures has often been difficult for low-income families. Too often these families have heard replies such as these:

"We aren't allowed to give that information out."

"That would take too much time."

"It will cost you three dollars for each page."

"We aren't required by law to do that."

"We have a policy against that."

"You will have to talk to someone downtown."

"That's just the way we do it here."

Families are often refused outright any explanation of procedures, stonewalled, or discouraged from pursuing the matter. For instance, consider what happens when a parent

Here are some of the books published in one classroom. Parent volunteers assemble the blank books with a dedication page at the beginning and an about-the-author page at the end. Children copy their revised/edited pieces into these books and then illustrate them. These child-authored books are popular reading choices during self-selected reading.

requests his or her child be placed in or transferred out of a particular classroom or program. Now, granted, it is less complicated to stonewall or to simply refuse to discuss the request than it is to listen and present the rationale for the existing placement. Perhaps attempts to shrug families off are so common because decisions in schools are, at times, rather quite arbitrary. But not attending to real parent concerns about issues and not addressing needed changes in policies and procedures work against families developing confidence in the school and work against building family involvement.

Putting families in positions where they might have a real voice in school affairs will make schooling more complicated. Perhaps that is why schools have long sought more innocuous roles for families to play. But real involvement also requires real investment and investment requires a confidence that the efforts expended will result in changes for the better. Real family involvement will reduce the autonomy of school staff. Initially, increased involvement may result in increased criticisms of the school as it becomes clearer to families how the school works (or does not work).

At this point, if increasing family involvement is still on the agenda (and it really has to be) it is probably time to bring in some parents to assist in the planning. Remember that families of preschool children should probably be included—those children are your future students. Remember that families of older and younger children need to be involved because the needs of these families are often different. Include families that are representative of the cultural, ethnic, language, and social class diversity of your school. For instance, if many families have not graduated from high school, several members of that group should be represented. If many families speak Spanish or any language other than English as their native language (or only language), they too need representation (even if this means finding a bilingual teacher or parent to translate). Families with handicapped children need to be heard as well. Initially, give families chances to talk while the school staff listens and takes notes. Do not begin by outlining what can and cannot be done. Do not begin by responding to every idea with, "We tried that once," or "We couldn't afford that." Just listen and list. Think of the time as the opportunity to brainstorm and to gather information.

Select specific topics or work with family and community participants to select topics that will focus discussions. Topics such as homework, discipline, attendance, report cards, parent-teacher conferencing, working in classrooms, and so on are all good starting points.

In the Accelerated Schools model, the school community creates cadres around issues. Membership includes teachers, parents, and community members. For instance, one group might examine scheduling in the school, perhaps looking at expanding the school's use or extending the school day. Another group might look at discipline procedures; another at testing, grading, and homework practices. No single group is expected to take on the job of addressing all issues. This model seems particularly useful since it prevents groups from becoming paralyzed by having too many issues to achieve any focus or real work toward resolution. After a brainstorming session or two (or three or four), it will be useful to consider forming smaller study groups to examine a smaller range of issues and develop some sense of options and opportunities to report back to the larger group.

In the school governance model developed by James Comer (1988) and used as the general model for the Chicago school reform effort, committees of equal numbers of parents and teachers make most decisions about school policies and practices. The general rule is that decisions are made by consensus not by majority vote. This seems similar to the way a jury functions except that the committee can explore and refine the options until a consensus is achieved.

For information on family involvement in schools, you may want to write the following sources for newsletters, pamphlets, and other information (often free):

Center on Families, Communities, Schools, and Children's Learning, Johns Hopkins University, 3505 N. Charles St., Baltimore, MD 21218

National Center for Family Literacy, 401 South 4th Ave., Suite 610, Louisville, KY 40202

Office of Educational Research and Improvement, Department EIB, 555 New Jersey Ave., NW, Washington, DC 20208

SUMMARY

No school can be truly effective without parent support and involvement. As American society changes, schools must also change and so too the relationship between families and schools. The American family has changed enormously in the past 25 years with more single-parent households, more mothers in the workforce full-time, and more working poor families. In many respects American families today may have fewer resources for school involvement than was previously the case. Teachers notice these changes. But there is no reason to set expectations for involvement that many families cannot meet. Schools cannot penalize children for their families' limitations.

Nonetheless, many schools could make substantial improvements in the parent outreach, involvement, and support programs they offer (or should be offering). The first step is simply improving communication between the school and families. That involves enhancing efforts to let families know what is going on at the school through telephone calls, newsletters, videos, and television and radio productions. Because classroom teachers are the most important members of the school staff, they must be involved in any attempt to improve communication. Some schools are using technology, voice-mail systems, or classroom videos, for instance, to create new methods for teachers and families to communicate with each other. Other schools are simply improving on old methods of newsletters and moving school fairs to Saturdays or Sundays.

At the same time, there is a definite shift to new forms of family involvement as state and federal agencies mandate family participation on advisory boards, councils, and governing bodies. This form of participation was often not what schools had in mind when they sought to increase family involvement, but family and parental involvement in governance is increasingly common. Authentic involvement in running a school can create more complicated administrative situations and require new roles and skills for principals and teachers. But it is this sort of involvement that seems to have the potential for revitalizing the relationship between schools and families. Central to shared decision making is the quality of information gathered about program outcomes, including satisfaction of families with the efforts of the school.

Finally, the idea of creating interagency family support services and family literacy programs especially is generating much activity. The goal is to create an intensive and long-term effort to break the cycle of intergenerational illiteracy and poverty that entraps too many families in America today. In these situations, schools operate within a consortium of social, health, and employment training agencies to foster parent-support efforts.

Most schools can substantially improve their efforts at involving families in the education of their children. But as American society changes, schools must also change. School programs must complement family efforts and must extend support to children whose families are simply unable or unwilling to provide the support needed to become readers and writers.

Schools That Work for All Our Children

T he preceding chapters have offered a general framework for reconsidering the schools we have. We believe the ideas and issues presented in this chapter fit within that framework but are more often "site-specific." That some schools have 5 percent of their children identified as handicapped and other schools have 30 percent identified suggests substantial differences in these schools. Some schools routinely educate 85 to 95 percent of handicapped students wholly in the regular classroom, and other schools educate none in this setting. Likewise, some schools enroll many immigrant children and others few. Some schools have a linguistically and ethnically diverse student population, and others are much more homogeneous in this regard. Some schools have many children from families served by one or more public health or social service agencies, while other schools have few children whose families receive any such services.

This diversity in schools requires approaching potential restructuring quite flexibly. It means that different schools will be presented with different challenges and have access to different resources in their efforts to restructure schooling. We must make it clear, however, that we firmly believe the framework we have provided earlier will improve schools for *all* children. Our focus in this chapter on only some groups of children is meant to point to specific ideas and issues that may need to be incorporated into our general framework.

WHAT IS SPECIAL EDUCATION? WHY IS IT?

Two landmark civil rights acts have forever altered the educational experiences of handicapped individuals in this country. The first, the Education of All Handicapped Children Act of 1975 (PL 94-142), now known as the Individuals with Disabilities Education Act (IDEA), entitles handicapped children to a "free appropriate" public school education in the "least restrictive environment." The second, the Americans with Disabilities Act of 1990 (ADA), an even stronger civil rights statement, assures handicapped citizens full participation in virtually all segments of our society. These two legislative acts create a strong legal entitlement for educating handicapped children in their neighborhood schools with placement in regular classrooms that provide special services and necessary adaptations in furniture, equipment, and curriculum.

While the U.S. Department of Education has taken a strong stance supporting the Regular Education Initiative and inclusive education (Will, 1986), the courts and the U.S. Office of Civil Rights have, perhaps, been even more forceful in asserting the rights of handicapped children to an inclusive education in a neighborhood school. Currently, the way schools include or exclude handicapped children from the mainstream education process widely varies. In some states, few handicapped children (10 percent) are educated outside their neighborhood schools and regular education classrooms. In other states, most handicapped children are educated away from neighborhood schools and in separate classrooms for all or part of the day. If there is any single predictable trend in the education of at-risk and handicapped children it is the continuing press to adapt our classrooms to better serve all children (Goodlad & Lovitt, 1993).

Inclusion and Collaboration

The Regular Education Initiative was launched a decade ago when Madeline Will (1986), then undersecretary of education, wrote that the burgeoning enrollments in special education were alarming and, perhaps, indicated that regular education programs were reneging on their responsibility to educate all children. Others noted the extensive fragmentation of school experiences that many low-achieving students, including handicapped students, encountered as they moved from the classroom program to a special program and back. Will called for closer collaboration between regular education and special education staff and for renewed efforts to adapt regular education programs to the needs of children who varied, often minimally, from normal achievement or behavior.

Rising special education enrollments seem linked, however, to increasing accountability pressures placed on schools rather than any real increase in the numbers of children who were, indeed, handicapped in the traditional sense. For instance, in New York state, the numbers of young children identified as handicapped significantly increased as the stakes attached to statewide testing rose. Once school performance became public record and was published annually in local papers, more and more children were identified as handicapped before the administration of the first statewide assessment in third grade. The reason seemed clear. The scores of children identified as handicapped were excluded from these reports. In fact, in six schools reporting substantially improved achievement on the statewide assessments, the rise in scores was almost wholly attributable to increased numbers of low-achieving children identified as handicapped and excluded from testing. Some school administrators admitted using the classification process to improve reported achievement. (McGill-Franzen & Allington, 1993). Convincing anyone to accept responsibility for children who find learning difficult is a problem in high-stakes educational environments. As suggested earlier, most state high-stakes testing programs need to be changed to include all students and, thereby, eliminate incentives to classify children to remove them from accountability rolls.

Nonetheless, the evidence available suggests that not only does inclusive and collaborative education work to produce improved academic performances of handicapped children (with no negative effects on nonhandicapped peers), but better social relations between handicapped and nonhandicapped children also result (Allington & McGill-Franzen, 1994: Gelzheiser, Meyer, & Pruzek, 1992; Epps & Tindal, 1987). But creating a school where all children are educated together is not necessarily an easy task. This seems especially true when accountability standards offer little recognition of the extraordinary efforts needed to educate some children. When public displays of a school's student performance are posted or published in the local paper, it is not surprising that teachers become less willing to voluntarily accept low-achieving, at-risk children as their responsibility.

Achieving inclusion may be easier than achieving collaborative teaching. For a long time both classroom and special-education teachers have simply "done their own thing." It was a rare school district that set the regular education curriculum as the standard for special education students. The most common curriculum was a watered-down version of the regular curriculum, emphasizing isolated skills development and, often, nonacademic skills and self-esteem. Special education teachers were often unfamiliar with the regular curriculum and rarely used regular curriculum materials. Few special education programs set goals for "declassifying" students. Few special education teachers expected accelerated learning and a return to the regular classroom with no need for additional assistance. As one administrator put it, "Special education is for a lifetime."

This scenario may soon change, however, as a result of a recent U.S. Supreme Court ruling in *Shannon Carter* v. *Florence County* (McGill-Franzen, 1994). Shannon had been diagnosed as having a learning disability with an attention deficit disorder, resulting in substantial underachievement. At issue in this case was whether Shannon's parents could be reimbursed for enrolling her in a private, non-special-education school when dissatisfied with the Individualized Educational Plan (IEP) developed by the public school district. That IEP called for Shannon to achieve only four months' academic growth each school year in reading and math. The Court held in favor of the Carters, noting that Congress intended handicapped students to benefit academically from the special-education services to be provided, and the IEP was "inappropriate" since it held no benefit for Shannon, who would only continue to fall further behind her peers given the IEP goals established. Justice O'Connor, writing for the majority, noted that "public educational authorities who want to avoid reimbursing parents for private education of a disabled child can do one of two things: give the child a free appropriate education in a public setting, or place the child in an appropriate private setting. . . . This is the Individuals with Disabilities Education Act's mandate, and school officials who conform to it need not worry." While the legal issue of focus was whether parents could unilaterally reject an IEP, enroll the child in a private school of their choice, and then be reimbursed for the costs of a non-special-education private school, the opinion of the Court seems to redefine an "appropriate" education for handicapped students. Special education services are to accelerate learning so that handicapped children will have their achievement normalized as Shannon did while at the private school. In fact, the Court decision emphasized the academic benefits Shannon received from the private school placement in weighing the decision.

The Shannon Carter case may have also stimulated recent efforts to return all handicapped children to public accountability rolls. The National Association of State Boards of Education recently released "Winners All," a call for holding all students to the high standards proposed for America 2000 goals. Likewise, several influential research and advocacy groups have also called for bringing academic accountability to special-education programs. The general direction of movement is for reporting annually all handicapped children's academic gains as well as including handicapped children on all statewide and district achievement assessments. In fact, recently passed federal educational legislation, the Goals 2000, Educate America Act (PL 103-227), provides funds for studies to gauge progress being made toward including and accommodating handicapped children on national assessments such as the

National Assessment of Educational Process (NAEP) and on proposed assessments of student attainment of national standards. In addition, policy shifts are underway in several states to accomplish much the same—including handicapped students on statewide assessments. Thus, the "appropriateness" of educational programs provided for handicapped children is likely to be evaluated soon against evidence of accelerated achievement. In one version, the expectation that achievement gaps will be closed is quite explicit along with targeting a date when achievement will be normalized and special education services no longer needed.

But special education programs cannot achieve such results alone. The only strategy for developing programs that accelerate handicapped children's learning is one in which classroom teachers play a central role. This shift, judging the adequacy of efforts to educate handicapped students from analyzing inputs (e.g., smaller classes, individualized lessons, specially certified teachers, and so on) to evaluating outcomes (e.g., academic gains, social growth), is similar to the shift that has occurred in the federal Title 1 remedial program. So where does a school begin to address this shift in focus?

The CSE

As a first step, schools will have to examine the current function of the Committee of Special Education (CSE)—the federally mandated interdisciplinary group that renders decisions about identification, placement, and IEP appropriateness. The intention behind the interdisciplinarity in the CSE was to assure that a variety of views were heard. The mandated regular-education staff member was intended to offer a balanced view of how children with special needs might be educated in the regular classroom. The special-education member was to offer expertise on how the curriculum and classroom instruction might be adapted to meet the needs of such children better. The school psychologist was to provide expertise in the areas of psychological needs and interventions and psychometric assessment. Other members were to provide specialized expertise that created a balanced team for considering how to best adapt regular education to meet the needs of children experiencing learning difficulty.

However, in too many cases, the CSE serves primarily to certify that a child is handicapped after referral by a teacher and to verify that placement in the special class with the lowest enrollments is appropriate. Virtually every study of how the CSE functions points to a series of routines very much like that cited above (e.g., Mehan, Hartweck, & Meihls, 1986). Too often the CSE simply "rubber stamps" the recommendations of the teacher, the psychologist, or the CSE chair (often an administrator). There is little evidence that most CSE deliberations thoughtfully analyze the current classroom placement and recommends substantive adaptations of the existing program, though this seems obviously intended in the regulations' language. How can it be demonstrated that a child cannot benefit from adaptations to the current classroom program if no adaptations are recommended, implemented, and evaluated? Yet, the language of the law indicates that only after adaptations have been implemented and shown to not benefit the child can more restrictive educational settings be considered (e.g., 45 minutes of daily resource-room instruction). In many schools, the child's classroom teacher does not attend the CSE meeting and does not participate in discussions of how the classroom instruction might be modified. This lack of participation, undoubtedly, undermines the likelihood of adaptations occurring and the full collaborative involvement of the classroom teacher in implementing any special educational interventions. When schools leave classroom teachers largely outside the CSE process, it should come as no surprise that teachers develop a sense that meeting the needs of handicapped children is the responsibility of someone else.

The IEP

Once a child is identified as handicapped, an IEP be must developed. Again, in most schools, classroom teachers have little involvement in this phase of the process of designing an appropriate educational intervention. It was intended that the IEP development would also be a collaborative effort among the classroom teacher, the special education teacher, and the parents (that is why all these persons must sign off on an IEP). Not surprisingly, when schools routinely leave developing the IEP to special education personnel, classroom teachers feel a reduced sense of professional responsibility for educating even the mainstreamed handicapped child. When CSE meetings are not scheduled at the convenience of parents, it is not surprising that parent involvement is less than satisfactory.

An IEP does not have to be a narrowly focused skills-driven document with a multitude of small behavioral goals. Over a decade ago, Hasselriis (1982) noted that nothing in the regulations suggested breaking learning into detailed lists of skills to be mastered. He offered the following IEP goals developed for a child identified as learning disabled.

Annual Goals:

She will branch into at least two additional areas of interest in her reading.

Her retellings will contain personal associations appropriate to the text.

The student will perceive herself as a reader and will voluntarily read a variety of books.

Short-term objectives:

She will participate in daily sustained silent reading.

Retelling will be incorporated into content class reading assignments.

She will start a journal for personal writing and add to it daily for ten minutes.

She will be asked to produce written retellings of readings and class discussions in content classes.

Each of these goals and objectives is measurable and each is holistic and curriculum focused. But such goals are rarely found on an IEP even today.

Perhaps classroom teachers should develop the IEP in most cases since (1) they are the people most familiar with the child's educational development, (2) they are the people most familiar with the core curriculum, and (3) the handicapped child usually spends more time with regular education teachers than with special education teachers even after classification.

If schools had the classroom teacher draft the IEP and then revise it with special education personnel and parents, the nature of IEPs might change dramatically. So, too, might the level of professional responsibility held by the classroom teacher.

Improving Educational Programs for Handicapped Children

To improve educational programs for handicapped children several things must occur:

- Regular education personnel must become collaboratively involved in identification, instructional adaptation, IEP development, and the monitoring of the learning progress.
- Special education personnel must become collaboratively involved with regular education personnel and develop a close familiarity with regular education curriculum goals and materials.
- The educational focus for handicapped children must become success in the regular classroom.
- Special education has to be viewed as a short-term intervention in most cases with some near-term end point identified when children are no longer expected to need special education support.
- Special education programs cannot be administered from afar. Each school must have the flexibility to design appropriate interventions without much regard for past practices or some standard program.
- Accountability for academic acceleration of handicapped students must be implemented.

CHILDREN AND SPECIAL EDUCATION SERVICES

Three categories of special education classifications account for about two of every three children identified as handicapped: learning disability, attention deficit disorder with or without hyperactivity, and behavior disordered/emotionally impaired. Because these classifications are so prevalent and because so little evidence exists to support current educational interventions as providing any substantial academic benefit, each of these classifications is discussed in some detail below.

Learning Disability

It has been 20 years since learning disabilities (LD) became a recognized (and reimbursable) handicapping condition. But in that short period of time, LD identification has exploded from a noncategory to over half of all children now identified as handicapped. Coles (1987) provides a readable and comprehensive treatment of the development of the LD field and the issues to be confronted. Suffice it to say that even today there exists little evidence that children identified as LD differ cognitively from other low-achieving students. Children identified as LD are usually children experiencing difficulty in learning, especially in learning to read and write. They are usually children from low-income families. They often exhibit some difficulties in social skills or aggressive behaviors. They often exhibit difficulties in language learning areas. But LD is a socially constructed belief system, not a demonstrated cognitive/neurological disorder or deficit. Identification as LD depends on the beliefs of the school personnel, not on a particular array of behaviors or test results. The LD child in one school is the attention deficit disorder child in another, the slow learner in another, the emotionally disturbed child in another, the remedial reader in another, and the language-impaired child in yet another school (Allington & McGill-Franzen, 1994).

This is not meant to deny that some children experience substantial difficulties with literacy learning. Instead, it is meant to point out simply that identification as LD does little to address the instructional problems some children present. There is good evidence that children identified as LD benefit most from larger amounts of higher quality literacy instruction than is normally needed for other children to succeed. There is no good evidence that LD children benefit from specific curricular approaches often touted as the solution to their problems. Some children simply need more and better instruction, and LD children are among those children. The current fragmented curriculum many LD children receive often produces disastrous results, which seems to stem from the fact that these children benefit most from a consistent and coherent curricular approach to teaching them to read and write. Very simply, LD might be thought of as "cognitive confusion" about literacy learning. Programs that present LD children with multiple curriculum emphases and changing curriculum demands cannot be expected to result in "cognitive clarity" and successful literacy acquisition.

The best hope for LD children is a strong classroom literacy program taught by an expert classroom teacher who is provided adequate support in adapting instruction in a highly personalized fashion. Currently, LD children are among those students most likely to drop out of school and most likely to enter adulthood with low levels of literacy and limited employment skills. Obviously, the programs now in place too often fail to provide substantial academic benefit to LD students.

ADD and ADHD

More recently, the number of children (most often boys) identified as exhibiting attention deficit disorders (ADD) or attention deficits with hyperactivity disorders (ADHD) has dramatically increased. Often, the ADD or ADHD classification is linked to identifying a child as learning disabled, although this is not necessary. The most common treatments for ADD and ADHD, unfortunately, seem to rely heavily on the use of stimulant medications (e.g., Ritalin), with at least one-half million children prescribed the Ritalin and with some estimates nearer one million children (Coles, 1987). One is tempted to recall a similar period in the 1970s when hyperactivity was a common diagnosis. However, the landmark report by Schrag and Divoky (1975) seemed to quell the surge in administering pharmaceutical stimulant drugs common at that time. Today, children are again being identified as "immature," "antsy," "inattentive," "hyper," and so on, and many are again being administered stimulant drugs as a primary treatment. Thus, it would seem important to summarize what is currently known about ADD and ADHD and the effectiveness of the drug treatments.

Swanson et al. (1993) summarize the research on the effects of stimulant medication on children identified as exhibiting an attention deficit. This research shows that such drugs are more effective in influencing behavior than enhancing learning. One can reasonably expect a temporary improvement in behavior, especially in impulsivity and overactivity, with a decrease in aggressive behavior and negative social interactions. At the same time, the researchers note that no significant improvements in reading skills, athletic skills, or positive social skills should be expected nor should long-term improvement in academic achievement be expected.

It seems obvious that ADD/ADHD is a "transactional disorder," a difficulty some children exhibit interacting with their social world. While exhibiting no intellectual deficiencies, these children are more active, more socially abusive, and more often disliked by peers and hard for adults to love. Many of these children do not "outgrow" the behavioral style that sets them apart—as adults they are more likely to change jobs frequently, have legal difficulties, especially concerning substance abuse, and experience problems with long-term relationships. But this is not true for all such children. About half the children identified as ADD/ADHD seem to function quite well as adults (Henker & Whalen, 1989).

Unfortunately, diagnosising ADD/ADHD is still "in the eye of the beholder." The criteria include items that describe virtually any child at some time:

- fidgets with hands or squirms in seat, has difficulty waiting turns
- blurts out answers
- has difficulty playing quietly
- has difficulty sustaining attention to tasks
- interrupts or intrudes on others
- loses things necessary for tasks at school
- fails to finish chores
- does not seem to listen, etc.

In school, such behaviors often follow from difficulty with the demands of the work presented or from less than a keen interest in the more passive activities common to classroom learning.

Obviously, children vary in their level of physical activity and social skills, they differ in literacy development, and they differ in terms of an independent interest in school-related learning. Some parents worry about children on the passive end of the scale, though few teachers seem to show much concern about the "bookworms" who would rather stay inside and read than go out and engage in physically active play. In school, it is the child at the other end of the activity spectrum that draws attention. Children who are very active, are often inattentive, and have difficulty with peer relationships because of aggressiveness are a cause for concern. But before labeling and introducing drug therapies to such children, a judgment must be honestly made as to who will primarily benefit from such a course of action. The research offers little promise of academic or social benefits to the child who is labeled and medicated.

Some evidence shows that nondrug therapies, such as cognitive-behavioral approaches, work to reduce inappropriate behaviors and enhance academic performance (Reid & Borkowski, 1987). In some cases, such methods have been used with medications with good results. Similarly, drug therapies combined with parent training has demonstrated positive effects on social and academic performances (Anastopoulos, DuPaul, & Barkley, 1992). This ten-step parent program focuses on developing a more supportive home environment that emphasizes a consistent approach to behavior management and social development.

As with most other issues of importance, school communities should examine the long-term effects of current policies concerning children identified as ADD/ADHD. Where do most referrals for ADD/ADHD come from? Do most children receiving medication prosper academically? For those children with normal intellectual capacities, academic success would seem a reasonable expectation if drug therapies are intended to address academic learning. Do these children graduate from high school and become productive citizens in the community?

"Given the potency of these drugs, they should not be given before more benign methods are attempted. But, given their effectiveness and relative safety, in combination with the intractability of ADHD, stimulants should not be rejected out of hand. To detect side effects and to demonstrate continued efficacy, comprehensive monitoring must be done throughout the course of the treatment, not only during the initial dosage adjustment phase, and drug holidays are often advisable. And, finally, given their limitations, stimulants should rarely, if ever, be used exclusively. Pills cannot teach the skills most hyperactive children lack" (Whalen & Henker, 1992, p. 341).

There will always be children who are more active, distractible, and bothersome than others. The central question is, What sort of responses to such children might schools consider? For instance, would regular opportunities to engage in large-muscle movement activities stem some of the activity problems (as recess periods have been reduced or eliminated, have more children been identified as ADD)? Can classroom teachers develop more effective routines for engaging all children in their work (do classrooms have sufficient collections of books that low-achievers can read and want to read)? Can cognitive control strategies be developed in children having difficulty staying on task or interacting with peers (making rules and routines explicit seems to assist some children, allowing greater flexibility in rules and routines assists others)? Decisions to employ stimulant medications with difficult children cannot become routine. Using such medications on active children seem to benefit adults (parents and teachers) more than they benefit children.

Behavioral Disorders/Emotional Handicaps

Probably no other category produces such problems with so few workable solutions as the seriously misbehaving child. Most schools have but a single strategy for dealing with children who are aggressively misbehaving—send the child away. In some cases, the child goes to another school or to a self-contained classroom with other misbehaving children. Few schools have an effective intervention plan for altering the child's behavior and returning the child to the classroom with substantial improvement in ability to control emotions and behavior. This is not to condone the aggressive, belligerent, and potentially dangerous behavioral displays that some children exhibit. But it is necessary to ask how current programs benefit the child exhibiting the misbehavior. We see the need for developing a school strategy for working more effectively with such children and their families in an attempt to improve behavior and socialization. Removing such children from the regular classroom or the school solves the school's problem but rarely addresses the child's problems in any useful way.

> *Video Workshop,* sponsored by the National Association of Elementary School Principals, produces *Episodes in Discipline: Strategies That Work* (video), 3 Regent St., Suite 306, Livingston, NJ 07039 (201-992-9081).

We would suggest that school personnel first take stock of current resources for addressing the issue of the seriously disruptive student. Who has the responsibility for evaluating the situation and implementing any sort of intervention? In our work in schools, we have found that in too many cases no one is charged with such responsibilities. Instead, many different staff members are seen as potentially responsible. For instance, classroom teachers are told to "bear with it" or to attempt to implement a reward/punishment scheme—to develop clear rules about behavioral expectations. Rarely, however, have teachers had much training with designing and implementing such classroom approaches. Principals often find unruly students sitting in the outer office, waiting for some form of punishment or using the area as a cooling-off site. But for seriously disruptive students, the wait in the outer office can turn that location into a maelstrom. In some schools, the special education teacher is asked to serve as a resource, either in the classroom or by working with the child outside the regular classroom. In other schools, a guidance counselor or a social worker or a school psychologist is asked to intervene, but these staff members do not necessarily have the time, skills, or training to implement any sort of effective intervention. For instance, simply scheduling the seriously disruptive student into a small group-support session for 30 minutes a week is unlikely to provide an effective resolution. The more recent addition, an in-school suspension room, also removes the child from the classroom and often offers little in the way of an effective plan for resolving behavioral difficulties.

Generally, the seriously disruptive child is no stranger to punishment. These children often come from homes where they have been punished quite severely though inconsistently for misbehavior. They are also likely to receive many more commands from parents than other children, often with no explanation. Employing control-oriented approaches to behavioral problems, approaches that emphasize imposing external standards, have not worked nearly as well as approaches emphasizing internally derived standards (Becker, 1992). These children do not respond positively to escalating penalties and harsher behavioral standards and punishments. Instead, they simply grow angrier and more disruptive.

Schools might consider a variety of approaches in better addressing the problems that seriously disruptive students create. For instance, at Boy's Town, where many such children are enrolled, a long-term staff development project has focused on helping teachers develop more effective routines and responses to such students. One strategy is to help staff learn to break the cycle of aggression-counter aggression by developing responses such as lowering the voice (instead of raising it), shifting to less confrontive postures, and using third-party observers in the classroom to identify teacher responses that generally create increased negative reactions by students. (Such students are likely to perceive sarcasm, criticism, shouting, and posturing as aggressive attacks and respond with increased aggression.) Other strategies include helping teachers learn to provide four positive comments for each corrective they issue, role playing and rehearsing specific incidents and appropriate responses, providing meaningful rationales for behavioral routines (rather than dictums), and developing effective consequences for maintaining appropriate behavior (Dowd & Tierney, 1992).

Schools that work well for all children make a concerted effort to help children develop a personal responsibility for their own actions. Children need to accept responsibility for their learning as well as for their behavior (and often the two are related). At the same time, schools must accept the responsibility to help all children learn more effective self-monitoring strategies. We are of the opinion that simply ordering children around is not the preferred model for schooling. Thus, in addressing the issue of behavior problems, we offer summaries of three interventions that focus on developing students' competence.

Glasser's Control Theory. The work of William Glasser (1986; 1990) provides one of the most sensible and comprehensive treatments of behavior problems (including lesser problems such as motivation). He argues that all human behavior is an attempt to satisfy one of five basic needs: survival, love, power, fun, and freedom. He attempts to show that all of us control our own behavior and how coercive school power creates many of the difficulties often attributed to children. His characterizations of schools as, unfortunately, holding fast to the "Boss-Teacher" model in an era of shared decision making is quite compelling.

Glasser's work is provocative in other respects as well. For instance, he counsels that calling parents into the school is an admission that the school cannot handle its own problems. He suggests that students often benefit from being transferred out of classrooms where they have built up a negative reputation because even after they have learned control strategies they find themselves in an "old" environment where they may be "discriminated" against because of past incidents. He emphasizes ignoring who was at fault and focusing on looking for solutions generated by the child. His approach involves students—in whole class groups, cooperative teams, and individually—in social problem solving, curriculum problem solving, and outcomes assessment. His work in schools has earned him accolades from a wide range of educators, and his work has the best supporting documentation available.

Dreikurs' Logical Consequences. Less well known, and older, but still with substantial credentials, is the Logical Consequences model of Rudolf Dreikurs (1982). In this approach all behavior is again seen as purposeful. People behave in certain ways to gain attention, exercise power, exact revenge, or display an inadequacy. Dreikurs identified several subtypes of attention-getting behaviors and argued that, generally, children worked in a hierarchical sequence from gaining attention to displaying inadequacy. The approach rests on a democratic teaching style that provides reasonable guidance but emphasizes developing understanding that decisions are linked to responsibility. Children are involved in setting portions of the academic agenda as well as general routines and rules for classroom deportment. Like Glasser's Control Theory, Logical Consequences focuses on trying to understand why children behave the way they do and how to help children learn the consequences of their behavior. Evidence from schools adopting this approach indicates a reduced incidence of minor and major behavioral problems.

A final effort that schools might consider is adopting one of several new approaches to conflict resolution. Since many behavioral displays result from personal conflicts between students, these approaches can stem much of the aggressive behavior found in many schools. Approaches to conflict resolution usually involve two sets of activities: training professional staff in conflict resolution strategies and training students to resolve conflicts through peer mediation. Both activities work to develop shared norms and strategies for dealing with conflicts (Johnson & Johnson, 1993).

Two groups have developed and implemented conflict resolution programs in schools nationwide and continue to provide resources and training for other schools interested in adopting the process:

- National Association for Mediation Education, 205 Hampshire House, Box 33635, Amherst, MA 01003-3635 (413-545-2462)
- Educators for Social Responsibility, *School Conflict Resolution Program,* 23 Garden Street, Cambridge, MA 02138 (617-492-1764)

The central question that must be asked is, How can this school more effectively solve the problems of students who exhibit serious and continued misbehavior? Segregating these children into special classes or special schools offers few benefits to anyone. For schools, segregation is incredibly expensive while being largely ineffective both behaviorally and academically. For segregated children this approach leads to neither improved self-control nor improved academic achievement. The child simply grows up to be an angry, illiterate adult who can now do real damage (or we can support him in prison for the rest of his or her life, another expensive outcome).

Almost directly in contrast to Control Theory and Logical Consequences one finds Canter's (1989) Assertive Discipline. Widely used, Assertive Discipline takes a stern and generally inflexible approach to discipline and behavior. His four steps—establishing rules, tracking misbehavior, using punishment, and implementing positive consequences—seem logical for an adult-centered setting. The approach is also easy to use because it simplifies and standardizes traditional school rules. However, some evidence shows that discipline and behavior problems actually increase after the system is implemented. The rigidity of the system allows for little latitude in dealing with infractions and works against developing internal self-control strategies in children. In short, Assertive Discipline does little, if anything, to address the underlying cause of behavioral problems. The approach seems to benefit educators more than children since continued misbehavior leads to suspension, solving the problem the school is having, but suspension is unlikely to enhance either the behavioral controls or achievement of the suspended child.

There are no easy answers here, but it does seem that schools need better programs than what now usually exist. Perhaps it is time to think about short-term segregation with intensive intervention and a scheduled return to a regular classroom (though we believe Glasser is correct in suggesting a return to a different classroom). All children benefit from learning to take greater control over their actions. But as with most other areas of learning, some children need more and better support than others to achieve these goals.

MISSING SCHOOL AND MOVING AROUND

At-risk children miss more school and move from school to school far more frequently than do other children. In either situation, it is more difficult to provide a high-quality education. But schools that work well for at-risk children have processes and procedures for more effectively dealing with both problems.

Missing School

Teachers cannot teach children who are not in school. In some elementary schools, nearly one-third of the students are absent on any given day. Many schools have some children who have routinely been absent at least 20 days each year. Nationally, between 5 and 10 percent of Title 1 participants miss 20 or more days of schools. Twenty days is a whole month of schooling. Across an elementary school career, 20 days absent each year equals missing one full year of schooling. One-third of the children participating in any compensatory education program miss between 5 and 10 days of school each year (one to two weeks), or about twice as many absences as other children.

So how can schools increase attendance rates? At the Westmere Elementary School in Guilderland, New York, the principal had developed what might be termed the "relentless" approach. First, when children did not show up for school, the school called the home to talk with a parent about the absence. The call might have come during the day, at dinnertime, or the following morning, but parents came to expect a call. The legal framework holds parents responsible for school attendance of children. Thus, the school had every right to expect children to be in attendance, and this was communicated to parents.

Still, some children were absent because they failed to get up on time and missed the bus. In this case, the principal got in his car and drove to pick them up, if necessary. If getting up on time was a routine problem (perhaps the single mother worked late hours), the school purchased an alarm clock for the oldest child. Bus drivers were told to wait at least two minutes for some children, sounding the horn every 15 seconds. If that failed to increase attendance, then the family went on an early morning telephone list and they could expect a call approximately 30 minutes before the bus was scheduled to arrive. If no one answered, the principal reported, he went to the home and banged on the door until someone got up, dressed the children, and put them in his car to go to school.

This "relentless" strategy worked to solve virtually all of the attendance problems the school experienced. The principal reported that implementing this approach beginning on the first day of school paid big dividends. After the first month, hardly any child missed a day of school for any reason other than illness. The principal remarked, "We can't teach children that aren't here. It shouldn't be our job to make sure kids come to school, but if we don't do it, who will?"

We have encountered other school administrators with almost identical attitudes and similar strategies. In one urban school, the principal organized neighborhood walkers into teams that got each other up and off to school. If one child was not ready when the team came by, then one team member (or a parent) stayed and waited for that child to get ready. In this case, team members called those children where rising on time for school was a problem. Team members knocked on doors to hurry tardy children up. In this school, the team approach worked well even though many families had no telephone.

Finally, in another urban school district, school and town officials collaborated to refer parents of children exhibiting attendance problems to the family court system under a child neglect provision. Since state law required school attendance, the courts held assuring attendance was a parental responsibility. After only a few months (and after a number of parents appeared in family court) attendance improved dramatically. However, such a strategy needs to have support in other segments of the community because taking parents to court does not often heighten those parents' satisfaction with the school. We do not recommend this strategy but mention it to illustrate the seriousness some schools exhibit concerning attendance.

Each school needs to take a hard look at current attendance patterns. If attendance is generally high (97+ percent), a few children may still present attendance problems (often they are low-achievers) and the school needs a strategy for dealing with them. However, if attendance drops much below 95 percent, the school needs to evaluate attendance issues more thoroughly and redesign efforts more broadly to ensure high daily attendance.

High Mobility Families

"The United States has one of the highest mobility rates of all developed countries," according to the U.S. General Accounting Office (1994). The GAO report notes that low-income families move more often than higher-income families and that children who frequently move experience substantially higher rates of grade retention, low-achievement, behavioral difficulties, and dropping out than similar children whose families do not move. One in six third graders have attended at least three elementary schools since the beginning of first grade. If these children were evenly distributed across all elementary schools, the average third-grade classroom would enroll four of these highly mobile children. But, of course, these children are not evenly distributed across schools.

Schools with many poor children, inner-urban schools, schools with substantial numbers of students from immigrant families, schools serving military installations, and schools enrolling children of migrant worker families are the schools where highly mobile children are concentrated. But all schools have some children who have attended many different schools and all schools have children who depart before the year is completed and others who enroll some time after school commences. In fact, only 25 percent of all third graders have attended only one school, according to the GAO study. While highly mobile children are most at risk, any child who has changed elementary schools seems to be placed at more risk than a child who has never changed schools.

Most schools have no special programs or procedures for addressing the needs of students transferring in or out, according to the GAO study. Classroom teachers reported that, often, children simply appeared at the classroom door with a note indicating they were to be added to the class listing! Thus, with little, if any, forewarning, teachers were expected to integrate children into classroom routines and provide appropriate instruction. Records from previous schools often arrived days or weeks after children and in too many cases never arrived. Even when schools received the records, teachers were not necessarily told of their arrival. When teachers did examine the folders they often found outdated or sparse information about the academic performance and curricular placements.

Homeless children present special problems for schools, but these problems are no greater than those faced by the children themselves. While the total number of homeless children is not easily estimated, over 300,000 children spent some time in a state-certified shelter in New York last year. The number of children who spent time in a noncertified shelter or with relatives or on the street or in an auto might double that number. The federal McKinney Homeless Assistance Act of 1987 provides guidelines for educational rights of homeless children (and substantial amounts of money to states to assist in meeting those guidelines). Perhaps the most important aspect of the federal act is the guarantee that homeless children can choose to attend school at either their last address or the address of their temporary home. While not requiring transportation for students to the school of their choice, several legal rights organizations have set out to establish that right legally, arguing that denial of transportation for homeless children effectively eliminates the choice guaranteed under the federal act.

Several steps might be taken to improve on the current situation. The first step would be to prepare a child-transfer card system that parents would present the new school when enrolling their child. This transfer card would contain particularly relevant data on student curriculum placement and special program participation. For instance, the card might include grade placement, reading level and curriculum materials currently used, writing levels and curriculum, math level and curriculum, and whether the child qualifies for free- or reduced-price lunch, participates in Title 1 remediation or an ESL program, has been identified as learning disabled, or is involved in a behavioral improvement program.

In an ideal world, transfer cards could be standardized so that teachers had an efficient method of locating information about curricular placements and special program participation. Developing a simple system for communicating important academic information to other educators is a first step. Ideally, the classroom teacher from the departing school would also write a short essay on the child that would accompany the transfer card and provide a telephone number so that the receiving teacher would be able to call and talk about the transferring child.

A second step is to develop a procedure for supporting the classroom teacher attempting to get to know the entering child better. Often a single half-hour of released time to work individually with the transferring child is sufficient to establish current reading and math levels and to gain insight into the child as a learner. But few schools seem to have any such procedure in place. So teachers try to find out about transferring children in a "catch as catch can" fashion. When implementing a released-time procedure, it will also be useful to consider providing classroom teachers with information on strategies for brief, informal evaluations of learners' achievement and attitudes.

A third step is to consider how to support children who have transferred in. Again, most schools had no standard procedures, but classroom teachers have developed a number of supportive processes. For instance, appointing several children as "tour guides" to help the new student learn the geography and routines of the school. Several students are initially appointed to optimize the likelihood that a good social fit will be found. Other teachers have the student and several peers develop a brief "autobiography" that can be presented to the class and may feature family pictures and information about the child's previous school and region.

ETHNIC, LINGUISTIC, AND CULTURAL DIVERSITY

In 1990, the U.S. Census Bureau indicated that one-third of all school children were members of an ethnic minority group (African-American, Asian, Latino, Native American, or Pacific Islander). By 2000, more than 40 percent of school children are predicted to be minority groups members. Today, in thirty-three of the largest school districts in the nation, students from ethnic minority families already represent a majority (Lara, 1994). It is difficult to find an elementary school that does not enroll children from a range of ethnic groups and children who come from homes where English is not the dominant language. The Census data show that almost half the Spanish-speaking and Asian respondents indicated that English was not the primary language of the home. Schools have proportionally fewer teachers from ethnic minority groups than they have minority students. There is a dramatic shortage of teachers who are bilingual and almost no teachers who speak East Asian, Eastern European, or African languages (e.g., Hmong, Malay, Polish, Croat, Swahili, Arabic). The curriculum focus in most schools remains largely Eurocentric with little literature, history, or geography representative of the larger global community or even the rich diversity of American society.

Schools must change to better meet the needs of increasingly diverse students. Schools need to become model communities that value the richness of different cultural traditions, achieve bilingualism, and integrate truly all members of society into a just community. In this section we offer a preliminary exploration of some fundamental concerns and some opportunities that schools might elect to recreate themselves to achieve a fuller participation of children from diverse families.

Children from Afar—Immigrants

America is today, literally, a nation of immigrants. All but a very few citizens are products of immigration from somewhere else at some distant or near point in time. Immigration to America has always been quite high compared to immigration into other countries, and that remains the case today.

Immigrant children often provide many challenges for schools, usually problems associated with designing effective classroom instruction for children whose first language is not English and who may not, in fact, speak or understand anything but the most basic English words. As refugees from nations torn with conflict arrive here, schools are facing other problems as well. Often these conflicts have wholly disrupted schooling in those countries, in some cases for a long while. In other cases, the immigrant children are members of a persecuted class and have been denied schooling even when available. Thus, schools are serving more children who have limited literacy development in their first language. These low-literacy children may arrive here at age 10 or 11 having no previous school experience and no previous literacy instruction. In addition, many have experienced horrific traumatizing situations that few of us can, or care to, imagine. Combine this with little proficiency in English and the problems presented to schools become quite substantial. Unfortunately, some of these children are placed in special-education classes rather than provided appropriate instructional support.

Immigrant children and their families benefit from programs that develop understandings of American schools and the schooling process. For instance, some parents may not understand the difference between textbooks assigned to a child for the school year and a library book that must be returned in two weeks. Likewise, everything from grading practices to volunteerism to grade levels to compulsory attendance may seem foreign. Of course, organizing sessions for parents (and older students) often means locating someone who can serve as a translator for the session (and for other school contacts as well). A good first step, then, is to think about providing introductory workshop sessions with a translator.

One very useful resource for information on effective programs for immigrant students is CHIME, a clearinghouse for information on immigrant children linked to the National Coalition of Advocates for Students. CHIME publishes a newsletter (*New Voices*), provides annotated bibliographies of selected works focused on educational interventions for immigrant children, and publishes *Meeting the Challenge: How Communities and Schools Can Improve Education for Immigrant Students* ($10). You can call them at 1-800-441-7192 for a variety of free materials or write to CHIME, 100 Boylston St., Suite 737, Boston MA 02116.

Barth (1990) describes an even more proactive initiative. An elementary school that enrolled mostly white, English-speaking students was informed in the spring that a number of Cambodian refugee children would be attending the school the following fall. The teachers, principal, and parents decided that it would be important for everyone in the school community to be familiar generally with Cambodian culture, language, and geography. Thus, that spring, "getting ready for the Cambodian children" became a broad-based theme of education at the school—in reading and language arts, social studies, art, music, and science. Everyone learned to say something in Cambodian. Classroom lessons focused on prejudice as well as on Cambodian culture and geography. In the end, when those Cambodian children and their families arrived to begin school in the fall, they found teachers and others (including custodians, teacher aides, cooks, bus drivers) who could greet them in their first language and classroom displays of Cambodian life, art, and history. They found an interpreter on site to answer questions and explain general school policies. Few immigrant children have ever felt so welcomed to their new school.

Children Whose First Language Is Not English

Some children, many of them immigrants, enroll in school with little knowledge of English—these students are firmly monolingual. Others arrive with a firm control over their first language, which is not English, and some familiarity with English. Others arrive and seem to be almost bilingual even if just beginning school. Finally, many children arrive at school speaking only English. We include this final group because they are the largest and because we often forget that they are one of two groups of monolingual children in the school. In a changing world economy where bilingualism is increasingly useful and important (which is why so many states have added study of foreign language to high school graduation criteria), it would seem that fostering bilingualism for all children might easily be set as an educational goal.

Schools might think of children whose first language is not English as resources (since most American schools are better equipped to teach these children English than to teach the English monolingual children to speak Cambodian or Spanish). But such thinking seems generally uncommon (Piper, 1993). We suppose that schools should be passionately fostering bilingualism and obviously not attempting to undermine first language acquisition nor ignoring literacy development in the first language. But how can that be done in an era when fewer than half of our non-native English-speaking children participate in any sort of school-based native language instructional support?

Several federal educational programs of course, might be used to provide services. Title 1, for instance must enroll second-language learners with low reading scores. Funds provided under the Bilingual Education Act (Title VII), the Emergency Immigrant Education Program, and the Transitional Program for Refugee Children are also available. But federal funding notwithstanding, many schools could create an improved instructional environment for children whose first language is not English. Not every program enhancement is expensive. In fact, some of the most powerful and promising activities, such as the earlier-noted school response to Cambodian immigrant children, are low-cost or no-cost efforts.

Schoolwide Efforts. In one school, several bilingual dictionaries were developed cooperatively by English-speaking and non-English-speaking children (even monolingual, English-only children worked on the project). This activity, of course, is useful only when children with limited English proficiency (or their parents) are literate in their first language. But the development of these dictionaries targeted vocabulary drawn from the core curriculum rather than simply using someone else's idea of a core vocabulary word list. The dictionaries had sections for social studies, science, and math vocabulary, as well as a general vocabulary section where words common to the language arts curriculum were located. As one literate Asian mother commented, "This is such a good idea because now we can be so much more helpful at home." Copies of the dictionaries were kept on an office computer file so that they could be updated each year and even personalized for particular teachers. This effort cost virtually nothing because most of the work was done by children (and a few bilingual parents who proofed the final copies).

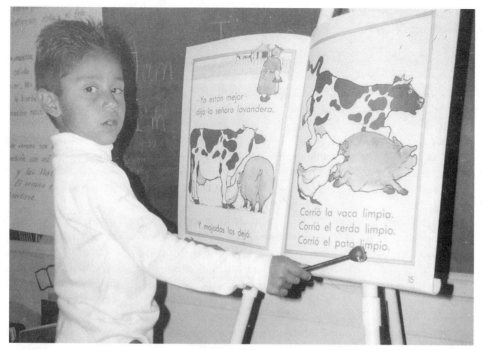

Many favorite big books are available in both English and Spanish. Here, a young man leads the class in a rereading of the Spanish-language edition of *Mrs. Wishy Washy* (Wright Group).

This school also used a "language buddies" system to support non-native English speakers. Each non-native English-speaking child was paired with at least one language buddy, often an older student with more developed English language proficiency. The school opened the school library and media center after school to provide a quiet but comfortable work space for the language buddies' activities. The older children often helped the younger children with homework or with reading and writing assignments, especially if no one in the younger child's family had yet developed those skills. Whenever possible, children with the same first language were placed in the same classroom (easier in this school with a mostly multi-age classroom organization) so that the children could support each other's learning.

Finally, children with a non-English language proficiency served as tutors for English-only children who were interested in learning a second language themselves. In other words, a voluntary after-school program was developed where children might learn the rudiments of Lao, Swahili, Polish, American sign language, or Spanish. The "staff" were the students with proficiency in those languages being taught and, sometimes, parents, community members, or staff members who spoke those languages.

Another important issue is the supply of foreign-language children's books available in classroom or school libraries (and foreign-language software as well). Children literate in their native language need to continue their reading in that language, too. In fact, developing and refining literacy skills in any language provides substantial benefits for English language literacy acquisition. Native language literature also gives children culturally relevant material, enhancing both interest and comprehension processes. Similarly, providing a supply of English-language children's literature that focuses on the countries and cultures of the non-native English-speaking children holds promise for fostering English literacy development of those children and helping other students develop a better understanding of their classmates' cultures. Professional magazines such as *BookLinks* serve as terrific resources for locating books on ethnic groups, nations, or regions of the world (e.g., Caribbean literature).

Another source for such books and volunteer readers is the parents of the second-language learners. Walters and Gunderson (1985) describe a program that recruited parents to serve as volunteers to read books to children in their native languages. These parents are often more aware of second-language children's books than the school librarian. But it is not just parents who can serve as resources. Schools can tap others in the communities, for their expertise and to serve as guest readers. We can think of no reason to not include such adults in a guest reader program, reading books in their native language. What better way to show respect for other cultures than this? Because fairy tales are often universal, guest readers might present another culture's version, in the native language, to English-speaking children and then "translate" or summarize the tale afterward.

Vasquez (1993) discusses a telecommunications-based option. The intervention is an after-school program for Latino children called *La Clase Magica*. The Spanish-speaking children in this project are involved in a computer-based role-playing activity where they report their progress to the Wizard and attempt to gain information about solutions to problems encountered during the computer adventure. Students write letters and progress reports to students in other school sites also involved in the activity through a telecommunications network.

Other schools might consider using telecommunications networks (such as the Scholastic Place Network on America Online) to link second-language children to other speakers (readers/writers) of their native language. This seems especially useful for children who have limited access to other children who share their native language. Such a system might replace the language buddy intervention when no appropriate language buddy is available. Locating an on-line partner would require posting a query to other users on the network, but the potential seems promising.

Classroom Links. Such activities are wonderful, natural extensions of well-designed classroom interventions offered under the auspices of English as a Second Language (ESL) or bilingual education programs. They are almost essential in today's schools where children of multiple foreign-language backgrounds are enrolled. In the most common situations, schools simply cannot provide native-language instruction for children from, say, 13 different language backgrounds. Many schools find providing support for even the most common native language—Spanish—difficult because of the limited supply of certified Spanish bilingual teachers. The problems of locating qualified teachers with proficiency in Lao, or Portuguese or any of the other less common languages is enormous. Nonetheless, children who arrive at school speaking these languages and with little proficiency in English and with little possibility of home support for English acquisition need instructional support.

Yet this support must be linked to classroom instruction. There is just too little evidence that providing a traditional "skill and drill" standard ESL curriculum is sufficient. Just as with remedial and special education, efforts supporting children acquiring English as a second language must be focused on children's progress through the core curriculum. Segregated interventions are less powerful than efforts linked to and offered in the regular classroom.

The most promising approach, in our view, is the Cognitive Academic Language Learning Approach (CALLA), a strategy-based intervention that targets high-priority content from the core grade-level curriculum in supporting learners acquiring English in the classroom (Chamot & O'Malley, 1994). CALLA develops from the premise that second language learners are, like all language learners, most successful when the language learning activity is meaningful and authentic. Unlike the most traditional approaches (e.g., audiolingual), natural language use involving central curriculum topics is emphasized rather than drill and practice on isolated sentences selected to emphasize certain grammatical structures. When ESL and bilingual-education teachers use the CALLA intervention design, the focus is on supporting learning in the classroom while developing language proficiency.

> If ESL students are to catch up academically with their native English-speaking peers, their cognitive growth and mastery of academic content must continue while English is being learned. Thus, the teaching of English as a second language should be integrated with the teaching of other academic content. . . . All content teachers must recognize themselves also as teachers of language (Cummins, 1994, p. 56).

Of course, classroom teachers are important to the success of children acquiring English language proficiency. Implementing the CALLA design requires closer collaboration between classroom teachers and specialist teachers (when these specialists are available). But classroom teachers might routinely make other adaptations for children acquiring English as a second (or third) language, although many of the practices that benefit any child who finds learning to read difficult also produce real benefits (e.g., increased opportunities to read and write, expanded access to personalized instruction, enhanced family involvement support).

Reading to children fosters vocabulary growth. This seems doubly true for children learning English. The language of books is simply different from the language of talk and the language of television (two other primary sources of language exposure). Thus, the classroom framework offered throughout this book, with an emphasis on reading several texts daily, provides more support than many traditional classroom environments. Similarly, the useful role of big books, language experience stories, predictable texts, careful strategy instruction, and repeated readings of little books are all important aspects of providing enhanced classroom support for children acquiring English as a second language (Rigg, 1989).

Finally, traditional educational assessments have not served second-language learners well. Traditional assessments of learners acquiring English proficiency typically underestimate potential for learning—Cummins (1994) calculated an average three-year underestimation. The suggestions offered earlier for valuing more authentic measures of literacy development hold true here also.

Adapting classroom lessons is made easier when teachers have better knowledge of children's literacy development in their first language, when they have a variety of appropriate materials, and when they have considerate support from specialist teachers. In too many schools, classroom teachers have too little support. Virtually all schools can enhance the existing educational support for learners acquiring English proficiency. As greater numbers of these children enter schools, it is imperative that adaptations be made. As illustrated here, many useful efforts can be implemented with little added costs and modest effort.

> Oral proficiency in a second language and literacy development should not be confused. Some children seem to develop an oral facility while still having difficulties with written language. Others develop literacy ahead of oral language proficiencies. It is important that teachers do not overemphasize, for instance, oral reading and pronunciation accuracy while undervaluing comprehension and understanding. Similarly, the traditional notion that children cannot read and write a second language until they can speak that language with facility has been thoroughly discredited. In fact, all children, including second-language learners, acquire more control over language through their experiences with reading and writing (Weber, 1991).

Children from Ethnic, Cultural, and Religious Minority Groups

The children attending our schools represent the diversity of our society, but too often our curriculum fails to mirror that diversity. Much diversity can be found among native-born children whose first language is English. Asian-Americans, African-Americans, Native Americans, Pacific Islanders, and many children of Latino descent are from families with a longer history in this country than, say, many Irish-American families. We would have schools celebrate the diversity that marks this unique nation by examining community histories and family histories. It is in these local histories that diversity can be treated most naturally.

Family stories, oral histories of community members, local history projects, and collaborations with state and local history societies all offer enormous potential for helping all children understand the unique contributions of the diverse community membership. Much interest in such projects can be stimulated by well-stocked collections of children's books that represent diverse authorship, characters, settings, and eras as well as genres. In fact, for many children, literature may offer the only opportunity to acquire understandings of other cultures and the experiences of members of ethnic minority groups.

Imagine including stories of Mormon, Muslims, and Mennonites with the usual inclusion of stories about Methodists (or other mainstream religions). Imagine stories developing the experiences of Korean-American, Russian Jewish immigrants, and Navajo children in our society today. Imagine planning social studies curriculum focused on the experiences of children during different historical eras emphasizing the diversity of childhoods in America across the past three centuries. Imagine fifth graders who could construct a reasonably accurate diary entry for children from different geographical regions with membership in various ethnic or religious groups at various points in American history (a diary entry describing a day in the life of an African-American slave child in Virginia in 1800, a midwestern Methodist farmer boy in that same era, a New England blueblood daughter in 1900, or a Chinese-American daughter in San Francisco in 1900).

Shirley Brice Heath has written a powerful book recounting cultural differences in three communities and how schools responded in ways that fostered learning. Her book, *Ways with Words* (Cambridge University Press, 1983), is a classic text on language use in classroom and communities.

Roland Tharp and Ron Gallimore include a detailed accounting of restructuring of curriculum and classrooms in the Kamehameha Elementary School that resulted in dramatic improvements in the achievement of the Hawaiian children that attend the school. Their book, *Rousing Minds to Life* (Cambridge University Press, 1988), offers a vision for a school that develops thoughtful literacy in all students.

We emphasize the importance of stocking schools (and curriculum) with books representing the diversity in our culture because the best evidence available suggests that few schools have even minimally adequate collections in this regard. Without a planned approach, school collections develop into collections of books that represent only a narrow slice of the American experience. In fact, one strength of basal reader anthologies is their inclusion of a much broader array of peoples and their stories than is commonly found in school-developed core book literature curriculum. Basal anthologies better represent the diversity in our society than do most school book collections.

Providing children with access to stories representing the diversity of American society is seen as one way to foster tolerance through increased awareness of the contributions and experiences of diverse members of our society, to reduce prejudice, and to improve achievement of minority students. Providing access, however, may be the easiest part of creating schools that celebrate diversity and actually achieve the goals noted above. More difficult is achieving balanced portrayals of different groups. For instance, many are wary of creating a "victims" curriculum where the focus is primarily on the trials and tribulations of various ethnic minorities rather than their contributions to our society. Likewise, many are wary of "heroes" approaches that primarily focus on the outstanding achievements of selected successful minorities without developing an understanding of the struggle many minority groups have faced.

Religious tolerance is another potentially heated issue. How can schools foster an understanding of the Hindu or Muslim religions without fostering concern from both Muslims and Christians, for instance, about the accuracy and worthiness of the information? Yet, it is difficult to understand cultures without developing some sense of the role that religion plays and some sense of beliefs central to the dominant religion.

Finally, how do schools foster the sense of diversity without developing stereotypical views in students? For instance, the nature of Navajo and Iroquois cultures were quite different. The experiences of Northern black freemen were different from those of Southern black slaves of the same era (and different from those of Northern white Americans). The members of the various Asian and Indo-Asian cultures that have immigrated to this country in the last century also represent enormous diversity themselves. Similarly, the variety in the experiences of Cuban immigrants contrasted with Mexican immigrants or Latinos moving stateside from the U.S. territory of Puerto Rico are quite diverse. Thus, exploring diversity must foster an appreciation of diversity within ethnic, cultural, or religious groups. One recommended strategy is to plan to use several works for each cultural group—works that collectively indicate this group diversity and works that represent both the positive and negative aspects of minority experiences.

James Banks, director of the Center for Multicultural Education at the University of Washington, argues that emphasizing broad conceptual themes such as "immigration," "racism," "intercultural interaction," "folktales," and so on is one useful strategy for incorporating the experiences of diverse groups of people into a school's curriculum. These themes can be studied for a full year, and across that period the experiences of various groups contrasted and compared.

> In her new book, *Other People's Children: Cultural conflict in the classroom*, (The Free Press, 1995), Lisa Delpit notes, "I have found that if I want to learn how best to teach children who may be different from me, then I must seek the advice of adults—teachers and parents—who are from the same culture as my students."

There seem to be several broad principles for framing education that fosters an understanding of and a respect for the diversity in our society (Education Research Service, 1991). First is to develop a pro-student philosophy. Do teachers see minority students as potential lawyers, teachers, and brokers or as children who are likely to never succeed? Are cultural differences viewed as limitations or as useful resources (e.g., is fluency in Spanish seen as a limiting factor or as an added bonus? Is familiarity with Hopi customs and religious rituals seen as interfering with learning or as a rich background to foster learning?)?

A second principle is that no one method is best for teaching any students or group of students. Children are individuals—all children. We worry that stereotypical notions about how best to teach X kind of students will undermine learning generally. We are wary of the various "learning-styles" authorities who argue for particular instruction patterns for different ethnic groups. We are wary because each child is unique. We will admit that traditional classroom organization and interactional patterns often did not provide a good fit between some children's experiences before school and after enrolling. We encourage modifying classroom organization in ways that produce a better match between cultural patterns and teaching activities (e.g., cooperative learning is seen as a better fit with many minority cultures than traditional competitive organization structures). But much of this book has argued for a shift away from traditional organizational patterns to better meet the needs of all students.

The "principle of least change" is the third key to instruction that celebrates diversity. This principle suggests that schools attempt only the minimum changes necessary to produce more desirable learning outcomes. The idea is to implement a minimum set of changes selected for the greatest impact. By limiting the scope of proposed changes, this principle responds to education's practical realities. Rarely do teachers, students, or parents respond well to massive changes in the normal course of events.

Finally, keep everyone's attention on the goals of educating for diversity. Return regularly to the three goals set earlier: (1) foster tolerance through increased awareness of the contributions and experiences of diverse members of our society, (2) reduce prejudice, and (3) enhance minority-student achievement. No matter what changes are implemented, unless one can point to progress toward each of these goals, the changes seem fruitless.

SUMMARY

Let us reiterate a critical point we made to begin this chapter. This book was designed to offer school administrators, supervisors, and teachers useful information on creating schools that better benefit at-risk children. In this chapter, we have attempted to focus on specific groups of children often placed at risk in the schools we have. These children present special problems for educators who are concerned about the academic progress of all children. Nonetheless, we will argue that the information and ideas offered in the first nine chapters of this book provide a broad framework for rethinking the nature of schools with an eye on enhancing the learning of all students but especially those students at risk of school failure. Enhancing school and family relations works to benefit students acquiring English as a second language just as much as others. Creating a high-quality professional development plan can work to benefit immigrant students as well as LD or ADD students.

Increasing children's access to books and to opportunities to read and write benefits minority students, poor students, learners acquiring English, LD students, and so on.

Nonetheless, some students do present special difficulties. Schools simply cannot keep adding new programs and new staff in an attempt to deal with every student presenting a special problem. In short, schools must work to foster change in classrooms, and change in classrooms is more likely when schools (1) have created a plan, (2) support teacher change efforts, and (3) remain focused on the key outcomes desired.

In this chapter, we have attempted to address a range of concerns. The issues underlying these concerns have begun to attract the interest of state and federal policy makers, and, we expect, this increased interest will likely result in changes in the rules and regulations governing the programs designed to fund efforts to meet the needs of all children. Thus, schools will have the opportunity to experiment (at least initially) with different ways of doing the things they now try to do, to serve children with special needs better. Ultimately, we expect that enormous rethinking will be needed as federal and state programs are restructured to become more effective and more efficient.

11

A Tour Through a School: What to Look For

I n this chapter, we want to take you on a school visit. The school we are visiting is a school in which many children arrive at school at risk for school failure, but all become readers and writers. In this school we put together many of the separate components described in the previous chapters, so it may sound "too good to be true." While we admit that we have not seen a school with all these components in place, we have seen different combinations of the components in many schools. We intend for this school to be "ideal," to help you develop your vision of what a school might look like after many years of hard work when commitment, caring, and determination are present. (The school tour is based on examples from Cunningham and Allington's *Classrooms That Work: They Can All Read and Write* (1994) in which you can find more detail about the classroom instruction.)

BEFORE SCHOOL STARTS

We arrive at Becoming School, Anywhere, U.S.A., around 7:15 in the morning. Although school doesn't officially start until 8:30, some children are already being dropped off and other children are walking toward the school. The school administrator greets the children as they walk through the door, calling each by name and sharing a quick conversation with some of them. Teachers are arriving on site to begin their day with grade team meetings. The school office staff is on the telephone reminding several families that children should be up, dressed, and about ready to leave for school. As the year wears on, fewer of these calls are needed.

Most children head directly to the cafeteria where a nutritious breakfast awaits them. Once fed, the children go in a variety of directions. Some head for the gym or playground where they shoot baskets or play on the swings and slides. Some of the younger children head for the kindergarten room where they take part in a story circle as community paraprofessionals read to small groups of children and have them sing songs and repeat common nursery rhymes. Other children head to the media center where they look at books and magazines, work on projects, or do their homework. Several children are at work on the computers. Other children are watching a video about pyramids. Some children are met by the reading teacher, the learning disabilities teacher, or the English as a Second Language teacher. These teachers work on a flextime schedule and provide services before school to almost one-quarter of their caseload. Several children head for the music room where they put in their practice time on their musical instruments. A few children who aren't feeling well go to the school clinic, which is staffed each morning by a community health nurse practitioner. Still other children head for the guidance room where a community-school counselor helps them develop conflict resolution skills to resolve some problems they are having.

As eight o'clock approaches, activity at the school picks up. Buses are scheduled to arrive by 8:10 so that children who need breakfast can eat and be in their classrooms by 8:30. Teachers are in their classrooms greeting children by 8:15. As children enter the classrooms, they take their cards from the attendance board and place them in the appropriate lunch option slot so that instructional time is not wasted taking attendance and figuring out lunch. Shortly after 8:30 a paraprofessional makes his rounds to record attendance and lunch counts. By noting the cards remaining on the attendance board and the number of cards at each lunch option, this assistant can do the attendance and lunch counts for the entire school with little or no interruption for teachers. Latecomers know they must track down this assistant and report their presence and lunch choices.

How time is spent is a critical factor in how well children learn to read and write. If each teacher spends 10 of the instructional minutes each day getting attendance and lunch figured out, that is 1,800 minutes annually—30 hours, one entire week—of lost instructional time. Multiply that times six years of elementary school and you have gained 30 days or one-sixth of a school year! Administrators can work to have routine duties handled efficiently by someone other than the teacher.

At 8:15, some other important people—surrogate lap readers—head to classrooms. Becoming Elementary School has an intensive parent education program, including the importance of reading and how to read to your young child. Each Friday, prekindergartners, kindergartners, and first graders take home a numbered packet containing six books that parents/caretakers are requested to read to their child. Children return the packet on Thursday and are given a different packet the next day. On Thursday, the lunch/attendance assistant returns to the prekindergarten, kindergarten, and first-grade classrooms and picks up the tray of returned packets. He then assigns each child a different numbered packet for the following week and returns the tray with the new packets and reminder notes to be clipped to children who forget to return the packet on Thursday. On Friday morning, as he makes his attendance/lunch rounds, he collects the late-returned packets and returns with their new packets, which they take home that afternoon.

With these book-distribution procedures in place and the how-to-read-to-your-child video training, most parents do read most of the books to their children most weeks. But, most is not all. Some parents did not come for the training. Others just can't (or won't) find the time. Still others can't read—or they can read in their first language but not in English. Convinced that regular lap-reading is the most critical component in children's early reading success, Becoming School has a Plan B for children whose parents do not read the books to them. (With little children, it isn't hard to find out which parents did and which didn't. Just ask them. They'll tell you.)

Each child whose parents/caretakers do not read the books to them is assigned a surrogate lap reader. Many of the surrogate lap readers are parents who drop their own children off at school and then are willing to donate 10 minutes of their time to lap-read with another child. Each morning at 8:15, they head to their surrogate child's classroom (or to the cafeteria if their child is a latecomer, breakfast eater), gather him or her up and read from the packet of books (which for these children stays in the classroom rather than going home with the child). In addition to the volunteer "drop-in-while-you-drop-off" parents, other school personnel read to certain children.

Becoming School has a child advocate program. Children whose parents do not come for parent conferences, IEP meetings, and so on, are assigned a school employee—another classroom teacher, specialist teacher, paraprofessional, custodian, or secretary—who will be that child's advocate. This person fills in for the parent at conferences, and so on, and touches base with the child regularly. When the child in need of an advocate is also a child in need of a surrogate lap reader, the advocate fills this role, too, if possible. (Classroom teacher, administrator, and secretary advocates can usually not be surrogate lap readers at 8:15 because they are needed at their posts, but others—paraprofessionals, specialist teachers, and so on usually can.)

At 8:30, the instructional day begins, and as we peek into classrooms on our way to the prekindergarten and kindergarten classes where we will start our tour, we notice that in almost all classrooms, instruction has actually begun.

> These before-school options indicate that the school is committed to providing children with nutritional and health services they need along with opportunities to do homework, work on projects, practice musical instruments, etc., if they don't have these opportunities at home. The nurse practitioner, the counselor, and several of the specialist teachers begin and end their day earlier than other staff members (some specialists begin later and depart later to work with other children in after-school programs). The other activities are supervised by volunteers or paraprofessionals.

◼ VISITING IN THE 4- AND 5-YEAR-OLD CLASSROOMS

We begin our classroom visits in the 4-year-old classes (prekindergartens). As we enter, the children are gathered at various centers engaged in the exploratory activity that is the work of 4-year-olds. Children work with sand and water, build with blocks and Legos, work with a variety of art materials, put puzzles together, and engage in activities in the dramatic play center, which this month is set up as a grocery store. (The area has numerous cereal boxes and other packages found in grocery stores. Signs telling what is on sale and how much items cost and shopping lists are provided for children to follow.) They also write messages and notes to each other (most of which only the writer can read) in the writing center and read (or have a grandparent volunteer read to them) a variety of things—big books, little books, magazines, signs—in the reading center.

Many children have had 1,000 or more hours of "informal" literacy encounters before coming to school. From these encounters, they develop critical understandings about reading and writing and "I can" attitudes toward their inevitable inclusion into the literate community.

1. They know that when you read or write there is some story or information that you are trying to understand or communicate.
2. They know that reading and writing are two important things that everyone who is bigger than them can do and that since they want to be big, too, they must learn to do.
3. They know from the overwhelming adult approval and pleasure at their fledgling attempts at pretend reading, reading some signs and labels, and writing that they are succeeding at mastering this mysterious code.

Our major literacy goal in classrooms for 4- and 5-year-olds should be to simulate the reading and writing encounters many children have had, which lead them to develop these critical understandings and attitudes. It is important to think of at-risk kindergartners primarily as children who have had few print, story, and book experiences. Thinking of these children as "inexperienced" creates a different view of instructional needs than thinking of them as "developmentally delayed," "language impaired," "slow," "unready," or any of the other labels commonly given to children who enter school inexperienced in literacy activities. The critical nature of providing these children with a print-rich, story-rich, book-rich classroom becomes clear when we take this view.

During center time, the teacher circulates, greeting children and helping them to get the day off to a good start. As always, she has her file-folder labels on a clipboard and, when she notices accomplishments, problems, or other things she wants to remember, she records this by putting the child's initials, the date, and her comment on one of the labels. At the end of the day, she will stick them to each child's anecdotal record folder. Today, she jots notes about a child "reading" a little book in the library corner to a stuffed animal, noting that his voice sounds like a reading voice and that he is doing a good job of telling a story that matches the pictures. She notes that another child is drawing at the writing table and "reads" her drawing to the teacher. Another child has created strings of letters and "reads" her "writing." These notes describe the different levels of conceptual development each child exhibits about writing.

The teacher tries to talk with each child during the morning center time and spends a few extra minutes with the children she has identified as being most "at risk." She engages children whose English acquisition has lagged behind peers (because English is not their first language or because they have had few real conversations with adults) in some conversation about what they are doing at the center. She points to things in the pictures they have painted or to their block construction and fosters their talk with her about what they are doing. She asks about the little books they are "reading" and the writing they produce. Because these conversations are one-on-one and related to something they are actually doing, the children are more willing to talk than they are in a small-group or whole-class setting. She also notices that children talk with each other more during center time. In fact, knowing that listening and speaking are major language goals, she encourages this child-child talk as she visits the centers and engages the children in conversations. She gets them to talk to her and to one another about what they are doing. Later, during both story circle times she will read and reread favorite big books and encourage children to chime in and read along with her as she points to the words.

> Reading and writing are language. They are integrally connected with listening and speaking. Classrooms in which many at-risk children become fluent readers and writers are classrooms in which listening and talking are important, encouraged activities. "Silence is not golden!"

While we could stay in the 4-year-old classes all day, we must move on if we are to visit classrooms at all grade levels. As we enter the kindergartens, children there are also in center-based activities that look very much like the centers we saw in the 4-year-old classes. In addition to the reading and writing you would expect to find in the reading corner and at the writing table, literacy activities are apparent in other centers. This month, the dramatic play center has become a restaurant. The children ordering food are "reading" the menus and the waiters/waitresses are "writing down" their orders. In another area, road signs are an important part of the play as children construct a village with blocks.

The teacher circulates through the centers, talking, observing, and making notes on her clipboard file-folder labels. As she stops in the writing center, she is once more reminded that all children can write if you accept whatever writing they do. She picks up a paper that is clearly a list in "scribble writing." "Read to me what you wrote," she asks. The child proceeds to point to each scribble and tell her that these are foods he likes to eat and reads the foods. The teacher notes on the child's label that he can read his scribbles and seems to have top-bottom and left-right orientation but no specific letters yet. Another child has made a drawing of himself and his pet and has labeled the drawing with his name and his pet's name. One child is writing sentences that have many correctly spelled words in them and other words clearly readable from his sound spelling. Yet another child is listing animals, copying the words from the newspaper animal board, the animals listed down the side of the data chart, and a book on animals he picked up from the bookshelf next to the writing center.

When the teacher goes to the rocking chair and sits down, the children realize that center time is over. They quickly clean up what they have been working on and come to sit on the floor. As the teacher waits for everyone to come, she leads the children in some of their favorite songs, chants, and fingerplays. When the whole group assembles, she picks up her newspaper and says, "I found something last night to add to our animal board."

She then shows them a picture of a baby tiger born at the zoo and reads them the beginning part of the accompanying article. After a brief discussion, she cuts the picture and article from the newspaper and adds it to a board already full of information/pictures/words about animals. Several other children have brought animal pictures/articles they have found and as they tell about each one—where they found it, who read it to them, and so on—it, too, is added to the collage. She then takes some index cards and writes labels on them—*pit bull, zoo, python, Siamese cat*—reads each aloud, exaggerating and segmenting the sounds, and attaches these labels next to the pictures/articles. This animal board bears little resemblance to the neat, bordered bulletin boards sometimes found in classrooms. It is cluttered with a motley collection of animal-related articles, pictures, and words that the teacher and children have been on the lookout for since they began their animal unit. It is clear from the responses of the children, however, that they are proud of "their" animal board and that they are learning that magazines and newspapers are a real-world source of information to which they have access.

The two classrooms we have visited are print rich. In addition to lots of different kinds and sizes of books are boards such as the animal board that tie into the unit being studied and that have words as well as pictures. There are signs and cereal boxes and labels and lists. A variety of writing surfaces and implements are readily available for children to write with. (Worksheets are not part of print-rich preschool and kindergarten classrooms.) Successful classrooms for at-risk readers immerse children in language and in the variety of print we encounter in our everyday world.

Next, the teacher takes out a big book of *Brown Bear* by Bill Martin. It is clear from the responses of the children that they have read this book several times before. The teacher points to each word as the children read in chorus with her:

"Brown bear, brown bear, What do you see?"

Before turning the page, she asks the children if they remember what the next animal is going to be. Most children know that the red bird is next. She turns the page and the children are delighted to see that they are correct. Led by the teacher, who continues to point to the words, they all read:

"I see a red bird looking at me.
"Red bird, red bird, what do you see?"

Once the book has been read and enjoyed again, the teacher passes out two or three words to each child. The words have been written on sentence strips and then cut so that the size of the strip each child is given matches the size of the word written on it. Being the Words is a favorite activity in this classroom. They have been the words before to make the sentences in other predictable books and in chants and poems but this is the first time they have gotten to be the words for *Brown Bear.* The children eagerly look at the word they are given and then up at the still-displayed *Brown Bear* book. Some children recognize some words—particularly the concrete ones. The child holding the word *bear* says, "Oh, boy! I get to be the bear!" Other children recognize the color words—*red, yellow,* and so on. Children who get commas, periods, and question marks clearly recognize these as punctuation marks used in sentences.

The teacher then opens the book back to the first page and the children eagerly read,

"Brown bear, brown bear, what do you see?"

As they read, they look at the words/punctuation marks they are holding to see if they are any of the words in this sentence. Some children immediately recognize their words. Others need help from the teacher or a child sitting near them. The children then come up next to the book and get themselves in order to make the sentences. Once the words are all in place, the children who aren't words for this sentence read the sentence as the teacher moves behind each child holding a card.

These children sit down and the teacher displays the next page. The teacher points to the words as the children read,

"I see a red bird looking at me."

As they read, they look at their words to see if they are any of these words. Again, the children who are the words in this sentence get themselves in correct left-right sequence (with a little help from their friends), and the other children read the sentence.

The children continue to be the words for a few more pages. The next several pages are matched and sequenced much more quickly as the children begin to realize where their words come in the pattern. After making seven pages in the book, the teacher collects the word cards, assuring the children who are complaining about not getting to be the word yet that they will be the words for the other pages later in the week.

The teacher then leads the children in a quick "get the wiggles out" movement activity in which she has them move like the animals in the *Brown Bear* book. After this brief but essential break, the children settle down and the teacher picks up a marker and gets ready to write. She "thinks aloud" about what she might write, and the children watch eagerly, encouraging her to "draw something!" The teacher tries to model different levels of writing on different days. Some days, she writes a whole paragraph. Other days, she writes a sentence and then illustrates it. On some days, she draws a picture and labels it. On still other days, she writes a list. As she writes, she sound spells some words, saying the words aloud very slowly and putting down some letters to represent the sounds. In this way, she demonstrates for the children the different levels of writing and shows them that all these ways of writing are accepted. On this day, she writes two sentences:

Mr. Hinkle will vzt us aftr lunch.

He will brng his pet trtl.

She doesn't read the words aloud as the writes them, except for saying the words very slowly when she is using sound spelling to model this for the children. The children all watch very closely and try to read what she is writing. Many of them recognize the words *Mr.*, *lunch,* and *pet.* She then draws a simple picture to illustrate this sentence and labels Mr. Hinkle and the turtle. The children are amazed to hear that Mr. Hinkle—who teaches fourth grade—has a pet turtle.

Snack time is next and the teacher passes out peanuts. The children look up at the "food board" and notice that the teacher has attached a picture from the peanut jar to the space under the letter *p.* As they munch on their peanuts and whatever else they might have brought for snack time, they review the other foods they have so far on their food board. So far, five letters have food pictures attached to them:

b—bananas; d—donuts; m—milk; j—juice; p—peanuts

After snack time, some children go to their tables, others go to a corner of the room that contains all the predictable big books they have read this year, and others go to the reading corner, which has puppets and stuffed animals in addition to books. The observer would have trouble knowing which children were supposed to go where, but the children know exactly where to go. Each child has one day when they can read in the reading corner, another day when they can read the big books and on the other three days they read at their seats. This procedure has been in place for two weeks now and is working quite well. Having all the children spread out in the room created problems because there just weren't enough good "spreading out places." This new arrangement seems to have just the right balance of freedom and structure so that the children spend most of their time actually reading (or pretend reading—if that is where they are!).

Reasonable and Observable Literacy Outcomes for Kindergartners

1. They "pretend read" favorite books and poems/songs/chants.
2. They write and can read what they wrote even if no one else can.
3. They "track print," that is, show you what to read and point to the words using left-right/top-bottom conventions.
4. They know "word" jargon, can point to just one word, the first word in the sentence, just one letter, the first letter in the word, the longest word, etc.
5. They recognize and can write some concrete words—their names and names of other children, favorite words from books, poems, and chants.
6. They recognize if words rhyme and can make up rhymes.
7. They can name many letters and tell words that begin with the common initial sounds.
8. They are learning more about the world and are more able to talk about what they know.
9. They can listen to stories and informational books and retell the important information.
10. They see themselves as readers and writers and new members of the "literacy club."

The children reading at their tables find trays of books there. The trays contain a variety of books and are rotated so that each table gets a different tray each day. One tray is filled with animal books—the topic they are studying in combined science/social studies units. Included in the tray are the two books children listened to at the listening center this morning. Many of these books are too hard for most of the children to read, but they love looking at the pictures and do find some animal names they recognize.

A second tray contains books gathered up for the last topic studied—weather. The children enjoy looking at these books, most of which have been read to them, and many can read the predictable books.

Another tray of books contains "oldies but goodies," which the children want to read again and again. All children can make attempts at reading such favorites as *Go Dog Go* and *The Three Little Pigs.*

Another tray contains class books. These books, written during shared writing and illustrated by the children, are perennial favorites of the children. The first class book contains a photo and a few sentences about each child in the class. This is still one of the most popular books and is reread almost every day by someone. Currently they are writing and illustrating a class book about animals, which will be added to this tray when it is finished.

There are also two trays of library books—one tray contains those checked out from the public library and the other those checked out from the school library. The teacher has arranged with both libraries to check out 20 to 30 books to keep in the classroom for a month. She chooses two or three children to go with her on a special trip to the public library every month to return the old books and pick out new ones for the public library tray. By the end of the year, all children will have made this special after-school trip. For many children, it is their first trip to the public library and some children are amazed that you can get books, videos, and other goodies to take home "for free." At the end of the year, the whole class makes a trip to this library again and most children get library cards. The monthly trips with two or three children to the public library and the library-card-getting field trip take extra time and effort, but introducing these children early to a free, unlimited source of reading material makes it worthwhile. When the children have read their own books for about 15 minutes, the teacher chooses several books or parts of books to read to them.

VISITING IN THE PRIMARY CLASSROOMS

The morning is moving on, and we must make it to the primary grades if we are going to see instruction in all four of their blocks. The 2 1/4 hours designated for reading/language arts in the primary classes is divided into four blocks of 20 to 40 minutes each. These four blocks represent the major approaches to literacy instruction: guided reading, self-selected reading, writing, and working with words.

> There is no one best way to teach children to read and write. The different approaches each have strengths, and some children have strong learning preferences for one approach over the other. By providing instruction in each of the four major approaches, we provide four roads to the goal of literacy for all and maximize the possibility that all children will arrive there.

The first class we enter has just finished their working with words block. Activities in this block are designed to help children learn to (1) recognize and spell automatically the high-frequency words that occur in almost everything we read and write and (2) look for patterns in words so that they can decode and spell less-frequent words they have not been taught. A word wall of high-frequency words written on various colors of construction paper catches our eye as soon as we enter. Five words are added to this wall each week, and the children engage in a five-minutes daily clapping/chanting/writing activity to practice these important words.

As we enter, the children are sorting words they have made in their Making Words lesson: From these words in the pocket chart, the teacher picks up *at* and says, "Who can come and hand me three words that rhyme with *at?*" A child handed her the words *sat, rat,* and *cat.* She then has someone find the word that rhymes with *rot—cot,* the word that rhymes with *oats—coats,* and the word that rhymes with *coast—roast.* The children spell the rhyming words and decide that these words all have the same letters from the vowel on. The teacher reminded the children that words that have the same spelling pattern usually rhyme and that this is one way many good readers and writers read and spell words.

"What if I were writing and wanted to write *boats.* Which of the rhyming words we made today would help me?" The children decide that *boats* rhymes with *oats* and *coats* and would probably be spelled *b-o-a-t-s.*

"What if I were writing about foods I liked and wanted to spell *toast,* what rhyming words would help?" The children decide that *toast* rhymes with *roast* and *coast* and would probably be spelled *t-o-a-s-t.* Likewise, they decide how the rhyming words they have made would help them to spell *flat* and *shot* if they wanted to write these words.

The ability to decode and spell unfamiliar-in-print words is worthless if children don't use the strategies they know while reading and writing. By emphasizing common spelling patterns and helping children use the patterns they sort for to spell a few other words, children learn how to use familiar patterns to spell words they need in their writing. In teaching, we often get what we teach. Transfer needs to be taught!

Although the four blocks can be done in any order, the teacher in this classroom follows the working with words block with the guided/shared reading block. On some days they do a shared reading in a big book in which the teacher reads the book first and then the children join in on subsequent rereadings. On other days, the teacher supports the reading of the children in basal readers, literature collections, or trade books of which they have multiple copies. For today's lesson, the teacher chooses *The Carrot Seed* (Ruth Krauss, Harper, 1945). As often as possible, she tries to find things for the children to read that tie in to the science or social studies unit they are studying. *The Carrot Seed* is perfect for their current Seeds and Plants unit.

The teacher displays a copy of *The Carrot Seed* and points to the title. "What word do we see here that we just made in our Making Words lesson?" she asks. The children quickly identify the word *carrot.* The teacher then points to the word *seed* and asks the children to look at the picture on the cover of the book and think about what the boy is doing and what word the letters *s-e-e-d* might spell. The children realize that the boy is planting something and using the picture clue and what they know about letters and sounds are able to figure out the word *seed* and read the title of the book, *The Carrot Seed.*

The teacher and the children then look at all the pictures in the book and talk about what is happening. The teacher makes sure to introduce orally key vocabulary as she talk about the pictures. Next, the teacher assigns reading partners who will read the story together and tells them that after they read the story, they will act it out. Cheers from the children let us visitors know that acting out the story is a popular activity in this classroom.

As the partners finish reading, the teacher hands them index cards, indicating the part they will play in the story reenactment. She then gathers the children around her and they retell the story with emphasis on what the main characters would do. The child who had gotten the "seed" card would be put on the floor and lie there, motionless. The "carrot" would be pulled from the ground and wheeled away by the little boy. The mother and the father and the big brother and then everyone would shake their heads and say, "It won't come up!" The little boy would plant and sprinkle and pull weeds and finally proudly wheel the carrot away.

Space is cleared in the center for a "stage" and *The Carrot Seed* is acted out. This is a low-budget, off-off Broadway production that lacks props, costumes, and rehearsal, but no one seems to care. The children get into their roles and the story is retold with the events occurring in the correct sequence. The only complaints are from those children who had to be part of the "everyone" but who wanted starring roles. The teacher assures them that there are no little parts and that they would act it out again tomorrow and perhaps their luck would be better!

As we leave this classroom, the teacher begins her daily math/science time. On some days, she finds it impossible to integrate the two, so the class does only one or divides the hour between the two. Most days, however, the teacher finds that doing science and math together is a natural integration. Today, she hands out containers filled with various kinds of seeds. She then leads the children in a variety of counting, sorting, predicting, classifying, and weighing activities with the seeds. The children work in groups at their tables, sorting the seeds by putting the ones that are alike together, estimating and then counting to see how many of each type of seed they have and graphing to show which seeds they have more and less of. The teacher gives out simple balance scales and has the children predict which seeds weigh the most and the least. They then weigh the different seeds and determine that it would take "more than they had" of the tiniest seeds to weigh as much as one of their largest seeds. The children are particularly amazed by how tiny carrot seeds were.

Integration can take many forms and is a key component in classrooms where time is used efficiently. Separating all the subject areas is a peculiarly American phenomenon. Primary classrooms in many other countries don't have separate time blocks, textbooks, and grades for separate subjects. Reading, writing, and math are skill subjects and need some content to make them real to children. That content can often be found in our science and social studies curricula. Integration of two or more subject areas maximizes learning and time.

Next door in another primary classroom, the children are in the writing block. This block always begins with the teacher writing something on the overhead as the children watch. They watch and listen as she thinks aloud about what to write.

"I always have so many things I want to write about on Mondays. I could write about going shopping this weekend and finding my car with a flat tire when I came out of the store. I could write about the funny movie I watched on T.V. I could write a list of different kinds of seeds I ordered from the seed catalog this weekend." The teacher decides on a topic and begins to write. As she writes, she models for them how she might sound spell some words. She stops and says a word aloud slowly and writes down the letters she can hear. She also looks up at the word wall occasionally and says, "I can spell *many* because we just put it on our word wall" and "I will look at *some* on our word wall because *some* is not spelled the way you would think it should be."

The writing minilesson takes approximately ten minutes, and the children are then dismissed from the big group to go to their own writing. Children are at various stages of the writing process. Five children are working at the art table, happily illustrating their books. When asked why they got to make books, they proudly explain that you had to write three pieces first. Then, you had to pick the best of the three and get a friend to be your editor— just like we do for the teacher at the overhead. Then, you go to the editing table and the teacher helps you edit it and you copy it in one of these books (holding up stapled, premade, half-sheet construction-paper covered book).

> Sound spelling is a powerful tool for children. It allows them to write ideas that go far beyond the words they can spell correctly. As children sound spell, they are using whatever letter-sound knowledge they have. A child who represents *motorcycle* as *modrsikl* is not in danger of spelling *motorcycle* like this forever. There is the danger, however, that spelling *they* as *thay* may become automatic and thus more permanent because *they* is used so frequently in writing. Things that we do the same way over and over become automatic, which means we do them without any conscious attention. When we have a word wall of high-frequency words that the children practice daily and refer to while writing, most children become automatic at spelling correctly these highly frequent, often irregularly spelled words. (For a readable, sensible discussion of sound spelling, see Regie Routman's "The Uses and Abuses of Invented Spelling" in the May 1993 *Instructor.*)

Four children are at the editing table with the teacher, who is helping them do a final editing of their pieces. Four other children, two identified as learning disabled, work at another table with the learning disabilities teacher who has just arrived in the room. She works with each of the four children in turn as they edit their pieces. A few pairs of children are helping each other edit before proceeding to the editing table. The other children are working away on their first drafts.

The classroom is a busy working place. At a signal from the teacher, the children once again gather on the floor and the Monday children line up behind the Author's Chair. (All the children are designated by a day of the week and on their day, they get to share.) The first child reads just two sentences of a new piece begun today. He calls on various children who tell him that they like the topic (dinosaurs) and give him ideas for what he might like to include. One child suggests a good dinosaur book for him to read. The second author reads a completed piece and calls on children who tell him they like the way he has stayed on the topic (his new baby sister) and ask questions ("What's her name?" "Does she cry all night?" "Is this the only sister you've got?"). The third and fourth children read unfinished pieces and get praise and suggestions. The final author proudly reads the book she has just "published" with technical assistance from the Title 1-funded paraprofessional who is assigned to the "publishing room" in the school and laminates the children's stories and binds them into books.

After the writing block, this class of children goes to lunch and we head next door to another primary classroom where the children are just returning from lunch. Most of the children go to their places for some "quiet time." Seven children join the teacher at the back table to read some "fun" books. The teacher had formed this after-lunch bunch when she realized that many children were not fluently reading the books and stories she was using during the morning guided reading block. These children read with partners and, in this manner, they are able to enjoy, discuss, and act out the stories. She knows from the observations she made and wrote on the file-folder labels that many children are not really at their instructional level in these materials. They depend on their partners to help them figure out many words. The teacher knows that while they enjoy being included in the activities, they need to read easier selections. To develop their reading fluency and to learn to figure out unfamiliar words independently, she needed to provide them with some reading materials in which they could recognize almost all the words.

> To grow in their reading ability, children must read materials in which they can recognize at least 95 percent of the words and understand most of what they are reading. This concept of instructional level is still valid. Teachers need to be concerned about children not working on their instructional level in classroom materials and find ways to provide instructional level reading opportunites. Administrators need to work to ensure that support for such classroom libraries is at hand.

She decided to use the fifteen minutes after lunch to provide some easy reading to meet the needs of children for whom the material read during the guided reading block was really too hard. Further, she decided that she wanted some "good reading models" in the group that came to be called the after-lunch bunch. Each day, the children come in from lunch and look to see if they are in the after-lunch bunch. Every child finds his or her name there at least once a week, but the children whose need for continued easy reading had instigated the formation of this group find their names three or four (but not five) days a week. By including all the children, but the still-at-risk readers more often, the teacher is able to provide for the needs of the weaker readers without having the after-lunch bunch viewed as a "bottom group."

Each day, the children find their names on the after-lunch bunch list and join the teacher and read something together. The teacher uses a variety of materials—stories from old basals, multiple copies of easy library books, and so on—but always chooses material in which the lowest achieving readers can read almost all the words. Generally, she leads the children to talk about the book or story by looking at the pictures and talking about what is happening, then lets each child read it by himself or herself, and then leads a brief meaning-oriented discussion of the story. If there is time, she has the children read selected parts orally. Before the children start to read, she reminds them of the strategies they know for figuring out an unfamiliar word:

1. Put your finger on the unknown word and say all the letters.
2. Use the letters and the picture clues.
3. Try to pronounce the word by looking to see if it has a spelling pattern or rhyme that you know.
4. Keep your finger on the word and read the other words in the sentence to see it it makes sense.
5. If it doesn't make sense, go back to the word and think what would make sense and have these letters.

The combination of easy reading in which they know most of the words and some reminders and support as they try to apply the strategies they are learning to unfamiliar words is helping the lowest achieving children become independent readers. Having a few good readers in every after-lunch bunch provides models for expressive oral reading and discussion. The short after-lunch bunch sessions are generally enjoyable for all the children and the teacher.

Using three reading groups has been our major attempt to address the various reading levels of children. The lack of success for this three-group system is evident when we realize that most children in the bottom groups never achieve grade-level reading and that most high-achieving readers can read way beyond the materials usually used in the top reading group. Children simply do not come in three convenient levels. Many teachers are now trying to organize their instruction to use a whole class, flexible group and cooperative group/partner arrangements. The after-lunch bunch extra reading time is just one example of how teachers use a variety of instructional groupings to meet the needs of their diverse children.

Next on the schedule is the self-selected reading block. The teacher has arranged books in several plastic dishpans and has put one on each of the five tables. Tray one contains books related to the science unit—seeds and plants. Tray two contains some old favorites such as *Are You My Mother?*, *One Fish, Two Fish,* and *Robert The Rose Horse.* Tray three contains books the children have written and class-authored books. Trays four and five are a motley collection of library books—both easy and hard. A tray is put on each table, and children select books from that tray. Exclamations of, "Oh, good, we got the science books today," and "I told you it would be our turn for the oldies but goodies today," demonstrate that the trays are rotated on a schedule so that all the children get chance to read all the books and don't see the same books every day.

The children eagerly read the books, by themselves or with a friend. The teacher walks around with labels on the clipboard, talking with children about their reading and asking them to read a page to her. She makes notes about what different children are reading and how well they are reading. She notes their use of phonics their attempts to figure out unknown words, their fluency, their self-correction, and other reading behaviors. She also asks them what they like about the book they are reading and, sometimes, suggests another book they might like. After approximately 20 minutes of self-selected reading, the teacher signals the Monday children to line up by the Reader's Chair (the Author's Chair recycled). The other children settle in on the floor and listen as the Monday children read or tell about a favorite page in a book they had read.

Next, the teacher sits in the Reader's Chair and reads a book to the students. Today, she reads an informational book with many pictures of seeds and the plants that grow from them. She also shows them a seed catalog that she has brought from home, quickly flipping through it and pausing briefly just to show a page or two of the illustrations.

As we make our way to the intermediate wing, we notice all the second-grade teachers with a special reading teacher and a special-education teacher huddled and busily planning in a second-grade teacher's classroom while the second graders participate in special classes (art, music, physical education, and library).

Becoming School arranged the schedules of the special subject teachers—art, music, P.E.—so that for one hour each week, they took all the children at a particular grade level, thus providing a dependable hour of grade-level team planning time each week. The support teachers (bilingual, remedial, special education, speech) who work with children at that grade level keep that hour free and join the classroom teachers to plan coordinated instruction.

■ VISITING IN THE INTERMEDIATE CLASSROOMS

We arrive in the intermediate wing and work around the lunch schedule of the different classes. As we enter one classroom, the teacher is reading an article that appeared in the Sunday paper to the class. The teacher begins each afternoon by reading aloud from a variety of real-world sources. On Mondays, the teacher usually brings in the newspaper and shares some of the more interesting tidbits with the children. Other days, the teacher reads from informational books, magazines, joke and riddle books, pamphlets, and so on. This teacher is determined to have his students see reading as an essential part of their real world.

We see a Big Word Board. The words displayed on this board are related to the unit topic for the week. This week's unit is on pollution, and the words on the Big Word Board are:

pollution	environment	recycle	renewable
pollutants	environmental	conservation	combustion
resources	chemicals	fertilizers	pesticides

In addition to the unit-connected Big Word Board on which the words change week-ly, there is also a Word Wall of frequently misspelled words. The teacher began the Word Wall at the beginning of the year with words he knew many of the children would mis-spell. The first five words added to the wall were:

they   *were*   *friend*   *from*   *said*

As the year went on, he was alerted to words many children were misspelling in their first-draft writing and added words the children evidently needed.

When children are writing, they are encouraged to use sound spellings and whatever resources they have for spelling words—unless the words are on the Big Word Board or the Word Wall. The teacher insists that these words—which are so readily accessible—be spelled correctly, and students' eyes can be seen going to the Big Word Board or the Word Wall when they are writing.

This week, the topic being studied is pollution. The children have watched a video that showed some of the most serious sources of pollution and have begun filling in some information on a data chart graphic organizer.

Environment Pollution			
Where	Causes	Possible Solutions	Our Area
Air			
Water			
Soil			
Land			

The video described some general pollution problems but was not specific to the geo-graphic area in which the school was located. Their homework assignment was to inter-view two adults about pollution in the local area and determine what these adults think the most significant problems are. The students share what they found out through their interviews/research. Most had talked with someone about the problem and were surprised to learn how high the level of concern was. The teacher shares some newspaper articles from local sources, and more information—particularly in the last column, Our Area—is added to the data chart.

Homework assignments such as this engage the children in meaningful commu-nication with adults for real purposes. All children can be successful at this, and it increases their personal involvement and motivation for the topic under study.

Next, the teacher gives out a list of local businesses. Included on the list are stores and fast-food restaurants that the children go to regularly. He then taught a supported writing lesson in which he demonstrated how to write a list of questions to ask to find out what, if anything, the business is doing about recycling. As the children watch, he writes his list of questions to ask his brother, who works at a car dealership.

After writing his questions, he lets pairs of students decide who or what business they would interview and helps them construct a list of questions to ask. Getting answers to these questions will be another homework assignment.

As we enter the next classroom, the children are having their Everybody Read Time. They read from any book they choose. Many children have a book at their desk that they are in the middle of reading. Other children choose a book from the trays of books that rotate each day to different tables. Each tray is filled with a variety of books, including some high-interest, low-vocabulary books and informational books with lots of pictures. Children are designated by days of the week, a fifth of the class for each day. On Monday, the Monday people can read anywhere and anything in the room—including newspapers, magazines, joke books, the newspaper board, and so on. On the other days, they stay at their seats and read. In this way, everyone gets a chance to "spread out" and read anything one day each week, but most of the class is seated quietly at their desks reading books, magazines, or other materials.

As the students in this classroom settle down to read, we go next door where the class is reading a basal reader selection about a family homesteading in Iowa. Before reading, the teacher began a Then and Now Chart, and the children brainstormed some of the differences they thought would exist in their lives if they were transported back to the prairie of the 1800s. When the students finish reading, they reconvene and discuss what they had read and complete the chart. The teacher has them vote on whether they would rather live "then" or "now." "Now" wins hands down!

Discussion of what is read is a sharing of ideas and opinions. Discussion is what we engage in with a friend or airplane seatmate when we notice they are reading a book we have just read. Teachers lead discussions, helping the children take turns and adding to their ideas when appropriate. Discussion is not questioning. Questioning is an activity teachers do to "make sure children read it and got it right." If after children read, teachers usually ask a lot of questions, children focus their attention on remembering. If after children read, teachers usually engage them in discussion, children focus their attention on understanding and deciding what they think. Questioning fosters remembering. Discussions foster comprehension.

In the next classroom, the teacher is beginning her Writing block. Each day, the teacher models how to think of topics and writes a short piece on the overhead. She tries to write a variety of pieces so that children see that writing can take many forms. She tells the children that she used to write a lot when she was their age—most of her writing was for herself and she didn't let anyone else see it. They know that she used to keep a diary and write in it every night. Sometimes, she writes in her diary the way she did when she was their age. They think that it is hilarious when she writes like an intermediate-aged child. She doesn't read aloud what she is writing, except when she is sound spelling a word. Then, she says the word very slowly—exaggerating the sounds. The children are always eager to see "what she will write today."

Once the teacher finishes her piece, attention turns to the editing checklist:

Our Editing Checklist

1. There is a title.
2. Every sentence makes sense.
3. Every sentence begins with a capital and ends with a punctuation mark.
4. People and place names have capital letters.
5. Words that might be misspelled are circled.
6. The writing stays on the topic.
7. Things people say have commas and quotes (She shouted, "Help!").

As each editing convention the children have learned is mentioned, the class reads the teacher's piece and helps the teacher fix what they think needs fixing. She circles the words she sound spelled so that she will remember to check these in a dictionary or get some help with them if she publishes this piece. The children decide that her piece stayed on the topic well but that some additional capital letters and punctuation marks are needed.

For years, we taught language conventions (e.g, puctuation, capitalization) from a language book and had children practice these skills on worksheets. Transfer from these isolated activities to children's writing was often minimal. When the language conventions are integrated into the teacher's writing demonstrations, children learn to read the teacher's writing, their own writing, and each other's writing to fix these, children learn to produce good, readable pieces.

After this writing minilesson, the teacher takes the children who are publishing a piece this week to the back table, and the other children pursue their own writing. Some children begin new pieces. Others continue writing on an already-begun piece. Some children look in books to help them get ideas and for words they want to spell. The Word Wall and Big Word Board are also looked at as children need spelling help. They can be heard, saying words very slowly and listening for the sounds they want to represent as they sound spell some words just as their teacher did.

Every day at 2:10, the teacher reads to the class from a chapter book, choosing those of high interest to children at this age but varying genres so that the children are exposed to a variety of types of literature. In selecting books, the teacher also incorporates books that provide an introduction to this multicultural society we have created. This week she is reading *Get On Out of Here, Philip Hall* (B. Greene, 1981, Dial). When she finishes each book, there are always many children who want to read it for themselves. She has those who want it put their names on little slips of paper. She then pulls one slip (without looking) and hands the book to that lucky child. The other slips are then pulled and used—in the order pulled—to make a waiting list—just like they do at the library. This procedure is perceived as fair by the children, and there are always waiting lists for the chapter books the teacher has read aloud. Even the children who could not have read the book by themselves can often read and enjoy it once they have listened to it read aloud. Whenever possible, the teacher tries to read aloud a book by an author who has written similar books or a book that is one of several in a series. Children on the waiting list for the book read are often delighted to get a similar book to read in the meantime.

Given all that there is to accomplish, intermediate teachers can't usually do everything every day in the same way that primary teachers can. In addition, intermediate-aged children need larger blocks of time to pursue reading, writing, and research. Not everything can happen every day, but all the important components should happen regularly. Here are the time-allocation guidelines a teacher of at-risk intermediate children might follow:

Every day (no matter what):

1. Teacher reads to the class from a chapter book.
2. Teacher reads something to the class from a newspaper, magazine, riddle book, joke book, book of poetry, or other "real world" source.
3. Children read something they choose from a large and varied selection.
4. Children learn more about the topic they are studying.
5. Children do a Word Wall activity with high-frequency, commonly misspelled words and/or with topic-related big words.

Two or three times a week:

1. Children participate in Guided Reading/Thinking activity.
2. Children participate in Guided Writing/Thinking activity.
3. Teacher models topic selection and writing a short piece.
4. Children write on a topic of their own choice.
5. Children work with words—looking for patterns, learning how to chunk and decode big words, and so on.

Once a week:

1. All children share something they have written.
2. All children share something they have read.
3. One-third of the class revises, edits, and publishes a piece of writing.
4. Children read to their little buddies.
5. Children do research related to topic.

The intermediate classroom in which at-risk children become readers and writers is not a traditional classroom. Traditional classrooms must change—and the needed changes are fairly radical. One thing that must change is the way grades are determined. Grades must be based on effort and not on some notion of grade level and "the tests in the teacher's manuals." This is difficult for everyone to accept because there is a need to maintain some kind of standards. But no one works if they know that they will fail anyway.

The schedule must change. In some intermediate classrooms, time is allocated to a dozen different subjects every day. Even the language arts are broken down into reading, writing, spelling, language, handwriting, and study skills. Then there is math science, social studies, P.E., music, art, foreign language, and computers. Instruction becomes small, isolated segments when separate subjects are presented every day. This choppy, fragmented scheduling is antithetical to understandings of how people learn. We learn as we work with information, applying what we are learning to solve problems and achieve goals. In classrooms in which intermediate-aged children are transformed from at-risk to literate, teachers do whatever is within their power to help children make connections. They take whatever time is allocated and create a schedule that allows for as much integrated learning as possible.

The final needed change relates to how the teacher and children work with one another. The intermediate classroom that succeeds will not be one where the teacher teaches the whole class all the time, nor can it be one where children are assigned to static reading groups based on achievement levels. Intermediate-grade children span a range of reading and writing proficiency and instruction that treats them all the same or that arbitrarily divides them into three groups can not meet their diverse needs. The intermediate classroom in which many at-risk children are learning and growing more literate is one where various flexible learning arrangements are used. Children read, write, edit, and research with partners and in small groups. Teachers who succeed with at-risk older children spend a great deal of time early in the year role playing and modeling cooperative ventures and make a "working together" atmosphere a top priority in their classrooms. They have a "We're all in this together" and a "United, we stand, divided we fall!" attitude and they work with children to help them learn how to work with one another.

The next class we visit is getting ready for the students' regular Tuesday afternoon visit with their kindergarten buddies. Every Monday, after lunch, some kindergartners bring some favorite books from the kindergarten. A Post-it Note™ is attached to each book with the name of the kindergarten child who would like to have that book read to him or her tomorrow. The books are quickly distributed to the "big buddies" who then practice reading that book in preparation for tomorrow's reading. Some children record their reading to hear how they sound. The children eagerly read the books, which include such classics as *Are You My Mother? The Little Red Hen,* and *Caps for Sale.* The teacher sits with one boy who is a very hesitant reader and who needs her help to successfully read this book tomorrow. She leads him to look through the pictures, predicting what will happen and so on, in the way she wants him to with his little buddy tomorrow. As they look at the pictures, she supplies words and phrases needed so that he can successfully read the book. She then reads and enjoys it with him. She praises him for his reading and asks him to read it with her once more as soon as he arrives at school tomorrow so that he will be able to read it with expression and enthusiasm.

AFTER SCHOOL

School is ending. As we make our way to the media center, we pass the classroom of one of the teachers we have observed. She is busily attaching the Monday children's anecdotal comment labels to each child's folders. She then puts a clean sheet of labels on her clipboard. She puts the initials of each Tuesday child on several labels so she will remember to take note of their progress and problems tomorrow. She also puts the initials of several other children and a few words—"solves math problems?"; "using self-correction strategies?"; "using strategies taught for figuring out unknown words?" "Really reading during Self-selected Reading?"—on several other labels that will remind her tomorrow to observe some problem areas she was concerned about for particular children. She then sits at her desk and completes her quickwrite summary for the focal child of the day. The quickwrite is composed on the Macintosh computer in her classroom, printed, and stored on a disk and in the child's evaluation folder. This allows easy access to both copies, and the computer version can be edited and used in the six-week summary report to parents.

As the school day officially ends, some children head home and other children head for their afternoon enrichment/remediation classes. A variety of activities and "clubs" meet on different afternoons. Most special teachers begin or end their day an hour after the classroom teachers do, and they, with paraprofessionals, parent volunteers, and community organizations, run an extended day program until 5:30. Today several classroom teachers and other staff members meet after school to discuss case studies of school reform they found in the book *No Quick Fix: Rethinking Literacy Programs in America's Elementary Schools* (Allington & Walmsley, 1995). These teachers are exploring early intervention designs to even better meet the needs of at-risk children.

We settle down to meet with the administrator and other staff members. Having seen it in action, we know that it is possible to have such a total school effort to promote the literacy development of all children, but we have a million questions about schoolwide issues that go beyond reading and writing and about where you start.

SUMMARY

A school tour can be a useful vehicle for better capturing the possibilities for reorganizing elementary schools. But tours of different schools reveal the differences that emerge as a result of differences in students, communities, and professional staff. Our school tour was not meant to reflect a one-best-way vision of what elementary schools might be but rather to attempt simply to picture a school better that reflects some of the basic themes of this book.

At this time, you may find it useful to take a tour of your own school. Think about the key themes presented in this book. Take notes as you walk or talk quietly into a small tape recorder. What do you see as you tour? Are classrooms rich with print? Are children actively reading and writing? Do you see teachers reading to children? Do you see teachers demonstrating the thinking processes used in reading and writing? Is instructional time being well used? Are parents involved in classroom-support activities?

After the tour, sit and compose a quickwrite on what you observed. Spend no more than five to ten minutes. But save your summary. Later it will prove useful for noticing changes that are occurring. A single walking tour can provide much information, but repeated tours, with longer stays in various locations and chats with a variety of people (including little people) provide even better information. The key questions are; What do you want to see more of? What do you want to see less of in this school?

Getting Started

S o where to start? We began this book by noting that schools that work are collections of classrooms that work. The starting point for creating schools that work is the classroom. If school restructuring is considered a process of improving classroom instruction to enhance student learning, the primary goal is clear. A clear sense of what needs to be accomplished is absolutely critical because lack of a clear purpose has undermined or untracked many previous reforms (Cuban, 1990).

School change is driven by individual change, although as enough individuals change, the larger system changes also. The popular literature on school change is peppered with words like "systemic reform," "structural realignment," and "institutional change processes." But a decade of efforts by federal, state, and local education agencies to map and mandate change illustrates a central problem—all mandates must ultimately be translated and acted on by individual teachers.

In this final chapter we review some recent findings about how to create schools that work better for all students, but especially for students traditionally placed at risk of school failure. We begin by discussing the importance of school culture since schools differ in the dominant beliefs and attitudes of the professional staff about the need for change. Next we review the basis for the current emphasis on shared decision making and site-based management of change. We have elected to focus on these approaches because they seem to be the current dominant vehicle for fostering change and because a variety of evidence points to the potential of such approaches for improving schools. We close the chapter with a series of recommendations for getting the change process started.

School Culture and Teacher Ownership

A culture is usually thought of as a group of people with a shared belief system and common rituals, practices, and customs. As we have trekked through schools across the country over the past 25 years, we have been struck by just how different school cultures can be. For instance, differences in the beliefs of teachers and administrators, differences in school cultures, seem to account for the differences in responses to children who find learning to read difficult. In some schools many of these children are retained in grade or placed in transitional-grade classrooms owing to professional beliefs that time will foster the maturity essential for learning to proceed. In other schools, such children participate in an intensive, early-intervention program designed to accelerate literacy development because the professional beliefs, the culture of those working in that school, see learning difficulties not as a problem of a child's immaturity but as an instructional problem. Other schools may classify these same children as handicapped and provide services through a special-education program and not actually expect the child to ever attain literacy competence because they believe the child has damaged cognitive processes that preclude normal literacy development. Finally, some schools don't do much to or for these children because the dominant belief system expects one-third or more of the children to remain behind their peers in literacy development. In each of these schools, a dominant set of professional beliefs account for the rituals and practices that children experience.

The research on teaching indicates that professional beliefs drive educational decisions about how school personnel respond to children experiencing difficulty in school. In fact, once we identify the belief system of the school, the culture, we can relatively easily predict the responses a school will have created. Teacher beliefs can also be shaped by their school's culture. When new teachers, especially inexperienced teachers, arrive at a school, they adopt the prevailing belief system and join the dominant culture. The culture of schools must often change to create schools that work better for all children. How teachers and students think about and value learning, how they go about the day-to-day routines and rituals, determines how schools work. For instance, in some schools, teachers work collaboratively and watch each other teach, talk, and puzzle through instructional problems together, while in other schools teachers are congenial with each other but are rarely collegial (Barth, 1990). There is a difference between being friendly and being professionally supportive and helpful. Some school cultures support collegiality and others support congenial isolationism.

> Timar (1994) discusses the federally funded Title 1 program, which provides monies to support the education of disadvantaged children:
>
> "The program developed its own culture, one that favored uniformity and procedural regularity over innovation, experimentation, and the exercise of professional judgment. Schools could be sanctioned for not following the rules, but they could not legally be sanctioned for failing to teach students" (p. 53).

The Cultures of Learning

Most schools set student learning and achievement as the primary goal, or mission, of the institution. However, schools differ in how they view teaching and learning and what the actual goals are. For instance, some schools offer a very competitive environment with much ado made over the few high-achieving students, with academic honor rolls prominently displayed, and with broad programs for the few "gifted" students. The academic emphasis is on who will be the "best" with less emphasis on educating all students well and little emphasis on educating the lowest achieving students to high levels of understanding. Other schools seem to focus more on the lowest-achieving students and bringing their academic performance up to some minimum level with less emphasis on the "gifted" students. In both of these types of schools, progress toward academic goals is often measured primarily (if not solely) by student performance on standardized tests, and a primary task for teachers and administrators is the rank-ordering of children according to perceived academic "ability."

Other schools emphasize social development of students. These schools emphasize self-esteem, getting along with peers and adults, and minding one's behavior. Often in these schools, less concern is evident for student achievement than for their social conformity. Students are often evaluated for "citizenship" as well as academics, but the emphasis still remains on ranking students against a common standard of behavior and achievement.

Finally, some schools emphasize student learning and independence. These schools focus less on identifying academic winners and losers while still focusing on learning. They view social development more from a perspective of individual responsibility and less from a conformity model. They still consider achievement test scores (which are expected to show continuing growth), but they weigh other evidence of learning as well. These schools do not define learning solely by test scores, but test scores play a useful role. Here, other evidence of learning is routinely gathered and considered when reviewing student academic development. For instance, the school might collect and organize annual data on student reading habits outside of school, on library usage, on independent projects, and on service activities of children. In addition, student work might be collected and organized into developmental portfolios so that teachers can more easily judge qualitative improvements in student work across time. Reports of progress focus less on ranking the child with peers and more on motivation for learning and acquiring more complex strategies and understandings.

A school's culture affects how students perceive learning. When learning is seen as primarily a matter of "ability," student effort is undermined (at least in those children who see themselves as having low ability). When we make much of rank-ordering children by achievement, we undermine student effort. Students who start school "ahead" remain ahead and those who start "behind" remain behind even when both work hard. When you work hard and still remain behind, there is little motivation to continue to work hard. In competitive-emphasis cultures students often see each other (and themselves) as either winners or losers, and in most cases only the "winners" care to continue playing the game.

In addition, competitive cultures foster teacher competition, and this creates a resistance to collaboration. In one school we visited, the administrator proudly announced that he rank-ordered teachers each year based on their students' standardized test performances and posted the results in the teachers' lounge. In another school system, the superintendent told us that he released to the local newspaper the ranked-ordered performance of students on state exams for each teacher and had warned teachers, "You can't hide. Every parent and taxpayer will know who is doing their job." In these schools, teachers narrowed their curriculum focus and worked simply to produce high scores on the standardized tests. No teacher wanted to be "saddled" with low-achieving students, and teachers admitted pushing to retain or classify these students as handicapped. Teachers also worked in isolation, keeping "good ideas" to themselves in an attempt to gain an advantage over their colleagues. Neither school had good test results, though both had large numbers of students who did not take the tests because they had been retained or classified as handicapped. Worse yet, neither school produced real readers and writers.

School Cultures and Goals

Ames and Ames (1991) describe two types of broad educational goals: ability goals and task goals. Ability goals focus on a student's demonstration of achievement compared to other students. Task goals focus on student improvement compared to past performance or some standard. When schools emphasize ability goals, most students seek to avoid challenging tasks and avoid working cooperatively because the goal is to achieve the highest ranking possible. In schools where task goals reflect the school culture, students are more likely to take on challenging tasks and more likely to work hard at improving because the goal is not outstripping classmates but learning a skill, strategy, or content.

When task goals are emphasized, teachers tend to think and talk differently about students. Rather than describe students in rank-order terms ("Jimmy is one of my slowest students"), teachers are more likely to discuss what students are learning and accomplishing ("Jimmy is working on developing clearer summaries of materials he reads"). When task goals are emphasized, teachers often anguish over giving required grades because, traditionally, grades have been the school's official rank-ordering of students among their peers. But when low-achieving students work hard, make good progress, and still rank below many of their peers, the traditional ability-goal orientation of school report cards forces teachers to assign average or lower grades to students who have been working hard and developing new understandings and skills. This creates a situation that is unlikely to motivate continued effort by these students.

At this point, it should be clear that teachers develop or maintain particular beliefs as a result of participating in a particular school culture. When a school district mandates rank-order comparisons of students on report cards or fosters rank-ordering of teachers on students' standardized test scores, it is not surprising to find (1) little teacher collaboration, (2) little student cooperation, (3) a focus on low-level learning tasks such as those found on standardized tests, (4) low motivation for school work among lower-achieving students, and (5) an avoidance of academic risk-taking by all involved. In schools where the culture emphasizes rank-ordering teachers or children, it is difficult to foster thoughtful literacy, real academic work, collaborative teaching and learning, instructional experimentation, and shared decision making.

Changing School Culture

Rowan (1990) discusses two broad strategies that have been suggested for improving schools. He calls the first *control* strategies. Common throughout the 1980s, control strategies involve developing an elaborate systems of rules, regulations, and mandates designed to standardize the instruction offered in schools and thereby improve student achievement. For instance, some states have mandated the use of particular instructional materials, the amount of time to be spent teaching different subjects, and the skills to be mastered at each grade level linked to student promotion policies. Many states fostered a competitive atmosphere by publicly rank-ordering schools on achievement and rewarding some schools (Blue Ribbon schools, for example) and penalizing others (New York state's "deficient schools" listing). Some school districts went further with mandates for the number of instructional groups, the pacing of schedules for completing curriculum units, and daily homework assignments. Rowan concludes that accumulated evidence indicates that control strategies can work to change teacher behavior, but the most common changes identified seemed not to be changes that actually benefited students or enhanced higher-order learning. Thus, after a decade or more of relatively futile attempts to improve schools through increased control strategies, many states are now experimenting with the second broad set of strategies.

The use of *commitment* strategies involves reducing bureaucratization while fostering professional independence and decision making. The goal is to increase educator involvement in the instructional process. Proponents of commitment strategies argue that teachers take more professional responsibility for educating children when they have ownership of the instructional plan and management is moved from afar and toward decision making on the "shop floor." Motivation to improve is higher when the improvements are locally defined. The evidence on the strength of commitment strategies is less fully developed than that available for control strategies, but early evidence suggests that commitment strategies enhance teacher collegiality and collaboration and that this can have a positive impact on the instructional process and student learning.

> Michael Fullan notes that "systems have a good track record for keeping things the way they are. Systems don't have a good track record for changing things. Individuals have that track record. It's individuals, working, first of all, despite the system, and, secondly, connecting with other kindred spirits, that will begin to develop the critical mass that changes the system." (From Fullan's address at the 1994 meeting of the Association for Supervision and Curriculum Development in Chicago.)

Shared Decision Making

In a study of shared decision making in two schools that enrolled large numbers of at-risk children (between 75 and 95 percent of children received free- or reduced-price lunches), Ames and Ames (1994) found that providing a four-day focus session for instructional leadership teams (selected teachers and the principal) fostered an initial team building. The sessions were organized around student achievement and instructional process information and school climate data gathered before the sessions began. Each team was given standardized test data that had been disaggregated to show how well different groups of students were performing (boys versus girls, economically advantaged versus disadvantaged, and breakdowns by ethnicity). Teams were also provided with data from measures of the degree of experimentation that teachers felt were encouraged, the quality of instructional support, the teachers' satisfaction with the curriculum, the presumed potential of students, and so on. Teams were guided through a process of examining these data and asked to identify school strengths and weaknesses and translate these findings into specific goals and action plans.

Teams were also introduced to a framework for analyzing instructional aspects of the school programs. This framework focused on the tasks that children were assigned, common student groupings for instruction, the amount of time that was allocated for various instructional activities, common evaluation activities used to assess students and teachers, and an inventory of how teachers and students were offered recognition.

Finally, teams were asked to develop a plan to share the results of their analyses with their schools' faculty and enlist the cooperation of all teachers in implementing changes they had identified as needed. Shared decision making in these schools worked more smoothly and resulted in earlier and greater improvements in instructional processes. Collegial and collaborative efforts among faculty improved, and the goals set for student rose. In short, this study provides good evidence that shared decision-making activity can foster shifts in school culture and lead to improved educational processes.

Difficulties in Implementing

Implementing shared decision making is not easy because it involves substantially shifting the traditional roles and responsibilities of nearly everyone involved. Often, early efforts toward shared decision making go off track, and the process loses focus on instructional efforts. One reason for emphasizing school data in the study above was the perceived need to keep participants' attention focused on the process of instructional improvement. Without the data focus, the deliberations became entrenched in discussions and debates of more trivial elements of the schooling process and the focus on instructional improvement was lost. Implementing shared decision making will require work, but the potential it holds for improving the process of education is enormous.

On some sites, parents and community members are included on shared decision-making teams. In these cases, the decision-making process changes even more dramatically. As noted in Chapter 9, involving parents and community members in schools has a powerful potential to broaden support for teaching and learning, but adding parents and community members will almost always require even more training for all participants.

Different states have developed different plans for implementing shared decision making. In some cases, schools have been mandated to implement this commitment strategy. Not surprisingly, when the process is mandated, the effort is seldom a faithful implementation of the commitment focus. In other states, the school teams' authority have been left largely unspecified. When state or school district officials retain broad authority, the process of shared decision making often seems pointless. Unless teams have real authority, the decisions they are allowed to make are usually only trivial decisions. When teams are given authority over the school budget, the curriculum, and the organization of time across the school day, it is common to see substantial involvement in the shared decision-making process.

Finally, even when school teams have substantial authority, two issues—access to information and power status—seem almost always problematic. The problem of information access is often simply a matter of personnel having little experience or awareness of school cultures other than their own. Most teachers have narrow bands of experiences since they have only taught, for instance, in a single school district and often at one grade level in a single school building. Most administrators have relatively limited experiences as well. They do not have a rich array of school cultures, experiences in schools quite different from their own, to draw on when contemplating change. In addition, most schools are ill-equipped to become research libraries where staff can call up articles, books, monographs, or videos in a search for available options to traditional practice at the school. Most schools do not have listings of contact persons in other schools using different curriculum plans or different organizational schemes.

The changing nature of power and authority under shared decision-making plans is another area that is often problematic. Even when the team's authority is described quite explicitly, reforming traditional lines of authority is difficult. In other words, school administrators and teachers (and parents too, in some cases) have to unlearn one set of power and communication relationships and then relearn (or create) new processes and procedures. Shifting to collaborative models for reorganizing a school has proven difficult for many school administrators. Often they have been largely ignored in developing legislation and regulations governing shared decision making. They may still be held accountable for what occurs in their schools but now have less authority in the running of the school.

Roland Barth (1990) comments on the traditional authoritarian school administration: "An inevitable consequence of this patriarchal model of leadership—aside from a certain amount of order and productivity—is the creation of a dependent relationship between principal and teacher" (p. 133). The dependent relationship fosters teachers who never explore alternatives and rarely reflect on their practice or the outcomes of their practice. Instead, they just "do what they're told" and leave it at that. In such situations it is unlikely that schools will improve much because teachers become dependent on being told precisely and specifically what they should be doing. No school administrator ever has time to observe, diagnose, intervene, demonstrate, and educate every teacher in the building. Unless teachers develop greater independence, our schools will remain largely as they are today.

Architect as the Metaphor for the School Administrator

There seems to be a needed shift in the metaphor we use to describe school administrators' roles. Perhaps replacing the metaphor of the school administrator as manager or CEO with the metaphor of architect would be the most appropriate (Cushman, 1992). Architects have particular expertise and they have authority, but architects work with clients to create structures that best meet clients' goals and needs. Architects come with ideas, plans, sketches, visions but they do not come to the initial meeting with a fully detailed set of completed blueprints. Architects also delegate most of the actual work needed to construct the building; architects do not hammer, saw, measure, and so on. Architects listen to the client and the contractor about ideas and solutions to particular problems. Architects function quite differently from plant production managers and CEOs.

Under shared decision-making plans, a school administrator's authority derives less from a hierarchical organizational structure and more from teacher assignment of certain authority to the position. One strategy that seems particularly useful is for the school administrator to observe and monitor continually the effects of the changes being implemented. One principal, for instance, observes for inconsistency with the team-developed instructional plan. If higher-order learning is the established goal, then a teacher using worksheets would be asked how that assignment fit into the overall philosophy of the school. In another case, the principal collects student assessments and teacher summaries of learning progress from classroom teachers. These are presented monthly to the school team and serve as a basis for continuing discussion of whether the elected change is accomplishing the intended goal.

Another principal reports her job is primarily to nudge folks in particular directions. She says, "My job as a leader is to stay at the cutting edge of things in education and to make sure teachers see things, hear them, and talk about them. . . . People come to you with ideas and you can help them. Sometimes you can best help by offering a creative alternative, keeping the person moving in a positive direction. . . . My teachers laugh at me because I'm always making them an offer they can't refuse—but if I do, I try to make it really a better idea" (Cushman, 1992).

Administrators Might Teach

In Rochester, New York, one aspect of the planned move to shared decision making involved school administrators assigned to teach for part of every day. Under the plan, administrators would teach one to two hours daily, in an area of their choice. Some school administrators became co-teachers in classrooms. Others worked with a particular group of children before, during, or after school. A few took over a classroom to free up one teacher who took on some of the leadership tasks in the building. Still others rotated through the building, serving as a sort of substitute teacher, so that teachers could visit each other's classrooms. Involving administrators in the practice of teaching was seen as useful for several reasons:

- The experience allowed administrators to talk with some greater sense of practice in team sessions.
- Such participation reduced the us/them nature of discussions in team sessions.
- It communicated the value held for teaching.
- Teaching provided administrators with the "classroom" view of problems.

Evaluation of Administrators and Teams by Teachers

One final aspect of the shift to shared decision making is teachers evaluating administrators. Perhaps first suggested in the joint proposal developed by the National Education Association and the National Association of Secondary School Principals, the process offers teachers regular opportunities to give administrators feedback on administrator performance. We think giving administrators regular feedback on perceived performance, feedback from teachers, parents, and, perhaps, community members, is a good idea. Without some sustained feedback loop, it is difficult to know how adequately one's performance is perceived.

We would also suggest that shared decision-making teams be evaluated. The evaluation would be done by teachers (and parents) who do not serve on the team. If authority is to be truly shared, so must the evaluation of results.

How to Begin

Creating schools where all children become readers and writers will not be a simple task. Across the entire history of American education some students have been shortchanged. In some cases educational policy denied some children access to their neighborhood schools because of their skin color. In other cases students were denied access because of their immigrant status. Other children were denied access because they had a handicapping condition or were considered "uneducable" or too expensive to educate. Today, the rights of all children to access to our schools are protected under one or more legal statutes and civil rights acts. At the same time, our society is demanding higher academic performance from students—all students. The changing economy and a changing society work to up the ante for schools. Today, schools are expected to teach a more diverse group of children and to bring the performance level of all students to standards historically held for only a few. None of this will be achieved with the schools we have (Allington, 1994). Those schools were organized to educate well only a minority of the children and no at-risk children were in that minority.

So how to begin? In the remainder of this book we offer a brief guide for initiating change in your school regardless of the current status of issues such as shared decision making. We draw heavily on our experiences and observations (many of which are supported by other observers of change) in this final section.

When 30 teachers and administrators sat down to discuss school reform, the talk wandered at first around the barriers to reform. Early on, however, a shift from reactive to proactive talk occurred, and the group developed a list of aspects of the school day they could largely control (Capital Area School Development Association, 1992).

Curricula	Assignment of staff
Relationships between staff	Student evaluation
Expectations for students	Celebration of success
Selection and training of staff	Impetus for change
Standard setting	Community awareness
Opportunities for parent input	Research on practices
Governance	Vision
Responses to criticism	

Recreating Your School

Too often when someone says that schools cannot be changed they mean they are not interested in changing the traditional school culture or not interested in taking on the work required. While current educational policies and practices do often provide an excuse for passivity, an abundance of excuses can be called up to maintain the status quo. But schools will change. We can help shape that change, or we can be told what changes are to be made.

If Not You, Who?

Creating a school that works better for all children starts with you. Waiting for the state education agency or the district superintendent to develop the appropriate plan, allocate the needed money, schedule the necessary professional development, and so on will ensure that your school will look pretty much next year like it does this year and like it has for the last few years. Schools that work for all children are not the product of a state-mandated school improvement plan nor the result of a federal program grant nor a plan developed and mandated by district office personnel. Schools are changed by the people who work in those schools. Others outside the school can help the change process but those people do not do the changing that needs to be done.

To change a school we need to change the culture of that school. Without changing the prevailing beliefs and practices, it is virtually impossible to change the school programs and the educational outcomes. We hope that this book has had an impact on your beliefs and provided you with some educational options to consider. So if you do not initiate the change process, who will?

If Not Here, Where?

Every school we have ever worked in had good reasons from people as to why that school was not the most appropriate school to implement the change process. They perceived other schools to have a more adventurous faculty, a more experienced administrator, better faculty relations, better community support, fewer problem students, more space, and so on. No school that needs changing is ever the perfect place to initiate change.

If change does not begin in this school, where will it begin? It may be that other schools seem to be in a sorrier state and more in need of change. It may be that other schools seem to have better resources to support change. But the school you work in is the school you can change. As Madeline Cartwright, principal of the James G. Blaine Elementary School in Philadelphia, said, "Don't talk about systems, or cities, or other schools. Say, I'm going to make *this* school a better place for teachers, I'm going to make *this* school a better place for parents, I'm going to make *this* school a better place for children. Say, I'm going to sweep up that one block. Not all the blocks in Philadelphia. Not all the blocks in America. This one block. That's what we did at Blaine" (Cartwright, 1993).

If Not Now, When?

There never seems to be a good time to initiate the change process. It always seems as though the schedule this year is already full, that the money needed is not readily available, that the school personnel will need to be better prepared, that student achievement is not really that bad, that at least everything is basically under control. We have never worked with a school that took up the challenge of change because it was a "slow" year and initiating substantial change was needed to keep faculty busy. There never will be a better time to begin than right now, while the ideas and arguments presented in this book are still fresh in your mind.

Beginning the process of creating a school where all children become readers and writers does not mean that tomorrow everything will be topsy-turvy. Beginning the process is the most important step, but it is only the first step. Beginning to change, according to Sergiovanni (1991), starts with taking stock of the current situation.

Taking Stock

In workshops we often ask school administrators to identify three aspects of their schools they would nominate for some national excellence recognition (we also ask teachers to identify three things about their classrooms they would like to present at a conference). Every school (and classroom) should have some feature that deserves recognition. This might be student attendance records, handicapped access to the physical plant, the print-rich kindergarten program, a parent-run after-school technology program, a locally developed literature-based science theme, a video-based portfolio system, the professional-development strand, a performing arts efforts, or almost any aspect of the school or schooling process.

Many school administrators find it difficult to complete this assignment. The same is true when we give this assignment to teachers. When we ask for a listing of three school problems, however, we find that many administrators have difficulty confining the listing to three issues! Nonetheless, we pursue the listing of exemplary practices with school administrators because every school has its strong points (though it seems we do not reflect on these nearly enough).

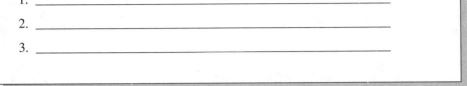

What aspects of your school would you nominate for a state or national recognition program? What about your school would you like featured on a local television program? What would you like to share with other educators and with the public? List three aspects of your school you would nominate.

1. _____

2. _____

3. _____

What are the most positive aspects of the current school culture (remembering that culture encompasses beliefs and practices)? What are the high points, the aspects of the school that could withstand scrutiny? What are the assets of the school? Every school has some model families, model classrooms, model teachers, model students. We begin the change process by identifying the assets that can be drawn on to initiate and support change.

But taking stock also involves an honest status report of current school culture and student outcomes. Throughout this book we have offered a number of data-gathering procedures for taking stock. One powerful focus for this phase is to examine the school experiences of a single cohort of children (who entered kindergarten together) and to identify how the school responded to the risks children faced. How many children who arrived for kindergarten at risk of school failure have had that risk ameliorated and are now active, achieving students? How many students that arrived at risk are still at risk or are experiencing school failure?

Another way of considering the current school culture is to identify how many children in a cohort are truly well prepared for middle school after their six- or seven-year stay in the elementary schools. In other words, are all children ready to go to middle school and are they equipped academically to function with the independence generally considered appropriate for early adolescents? Are there children who seem ill-equipped for the demands of middle school? If we examined kindergarten entrance records of a cohort about to go off to middle school, could we identify those children most likely to be deemed unready for the transition? Has the school reduced the risks for at-risk children? Are fewer children at risk today than when they began school?

If we were to examine these students' achievement records by gender, ethnicity, and family socio-economic status, would we find a pattern of performance differentiation? Would those records show that poor children were just as likely to be ready for middle school as their more advantaged peers? Would we find that more boys had been retained or more often identified as handicapped than girls? Does the reading achievement of minority students equal that of other students? Has the school achieved the goal of educating well all children, regardless of their gender, ethnicity, or family status or income?

Finally, what are the real strengths of the faculty? Remember that good schools are collections of good classrooms. Every school has some superb teachers. Every school has teachers willing to take a risk, to experiment, to change. Every school we have worked in has had teachers chafing under the current system and eager for change. Every school we have worked in has had teachers who knew precisely what change was needed to make the

Will we reduce the risk for children as they progress through our schools? Will this young man in the Author's Chair be ready for middle school?

school work better for all children. These teachers might not have had a comprehensive plan, but they could identify practices that needed to be altered to better serve children at risk.

Setting the Stage for Change

A central question then is, How do we build on the existing strengths of the school? How can teachers who are eager to change be encouraged to take that step? We believe that a good first step is to encourage more diversity in educational practice within the school. Barth (1990) notes that tightly prescribed instructional practices that constrain instructional diversity in a school also work to constrain reflection and discussion of educational practices. When teachers pursue different strategies for meeting the needs of children there is a basis for professional discussion of practice. When everyone simply follows a mandated plan, there is little reason to talk. When school administrators attempt to monitor closely compliance with mandated instructional practices, teachers rarely speak openly about their concerns or the weaknesses of the mandated system. One first step in creating a school that works better for all children is to foster diversity in classrooms. It is important to remember that it is not only children who differ but also teachers. There can never be one best way to serve the needs of all children and no one best practice that all teachers can use effectively.

Sharing Instructional Practices

Celebrate the diversity that emerges and work to ensure that teachers develop greater shared knowledge of the instructional diversity across the school. Barth (1990) tells of holding faculty meetings in individual classrooms rather than in the library or some other common location. At the beginning of each meeting he had the classroom teacher take five to ten minutes to provide a tour of the classroom and the instructional program, emphasizing on the components were considered most successful or unique. Much like the exercise we prescribed earlier for school administrators, this process required teachers to reflect on their teaching and identify those practices they most wanted to share with colleagues. Over time, of course, this strategy fostered much shared knowledge of instructional practices and fostered discussion among the personnel about the existing diversity that became obvious.

Sergiovanni (1991) notes that the supervisory function of school administrators has three potential purposes:

- *Quality control*—Basic monitoring of school functions through visiting classrooms; talking with teachers, students, and parents; reviewing curriculum plans, materials, and lessons;
- *Professional development*—Working to understand what teachers need to teach and what they need to learn to grow and develop professionally; and
- *Teacher motivation*—Nurturing motivation and commitment to teaching as a career, to the school, and to students.

He offers the 80/20 rule for school administrators: When more than 20 percent of supervisory time and money is spent in evaluating for quality control or less than 80 percent of supervisory time and money is spent on professional improvement and enhancing motivation, the quality of schooling suffers.

The point is that it is difficult to be collaborative and collegial without much shared knowledge of instructional practices. It is also difficult to experiment, to take risks, if the school culture emphasizes uniformity and standardization of instructional practices. The first step in breaking down the mutual invisibility that occurs in schools where teachers work largely in isolation from one another is to create settings where diversity is welcomed and where awareness of instructional practices is fostered. A final step in this process is recognizing teacher learning as well as experimentation. "What have you learned from this? About this? As a result of this?" are all good queries that foster reflective discussion of practices.

We also advise that the school administrator work to communicate instructional practices to parents and the larger community. Feature one teacher in the weekly newsletter—a brief article on that week's classroom activity (or upcoming activities) is sufficient. Make sure parents understand that while the basic curriculum goals are met by all teachers, every fourth-grade teacher does not teach exactly the same things. Point out that each teacher has different interests and expertise and these differences are reflected in aspects of their instruction.

Setting Goals

Often, goal statements, or mission statements, are seen as the initial step in the change process. We disagree. In our experience, the typical goal-setting process results in a broad, vague, and pleasant sounding statement that suggests nothing in particular except that the school hopes to do better. Instead of engaging in what can become an extended process of developing a high-minded statement, we would suggest that the first step is fostering experimentation and collegiality.

Our advice to schools has long been "look long, start easy." The look long advice is meant to convey the notion that change takes time. It seems useful to think about the school three years from now rather than the school tomorrow. What would you like to see happening more often three years hence? What would you like to see happening less frequently? Everything cannot change at once, so pick the important changes. Since every school is unique with a particular staff, a particular set of students, particular parents, particular resources, and so on, there is no one change that everyone can start with. But opening up a dialogue among the school staff is critical, and that is often the first goal we set.

The start-easy advice simply means go with the easiest changes first. As we have repeatedly noted, good schools are collections of good classrooms. Which classroom teachers are the most likely to be willing to experiment? Which grade levels will be most likely to share ideas during grade-level team meetings? Which teachers will open up their classrooms to other teacher-observers? Which teachers would agree to observe others? In an ideal world, change would be agreed on by three-quarters of the faculty, much as in the Accelerated School model. But some schools we have worked in that most needed changing were unlikely candidates for achieving such a vote. But every school we have ever worked in had one or more teachers who wanted change and was willing to work for change. Those are the teachers we advise beginning with.

What things would you like to see more frequently in your school? Less frequently? Perhaps an increase in writing activity during the school day? What would you reduce or eliminate to create the space needed for more writing activity? Perhaps less low-level seatwork? Maybe fewer whole-class interrogation sessions after a reading assignment? Would others in your school agree with your lists? Creating such lists often provides a clearer focus for planning and evaluation.

It is a delicate balancing act, however. School administrators cannot just offer public recognition for these teachers and wish everyone else would become more like them! In fact, applauding these teachers' work may simply backfire as other teachers feel the sting of not being included in the rank-ordering of the "best" teachers. Instead, school administrators must convey to the change-agent teachers that their efforts are appreciated and that further experimentation will be supported. The most useful strategy we know for communicating the message about these classes is to focus broadly on the results. The focus cannot be confined to standardized test scores because, for one, those scores are available only once a year in most schools and, second, test scores have a very narrow focus. Instead, we encourage focusing on student performances in writing, in reading literature, in science or social studies. For instance, create an area in the foyer for students to display their work—not just the work of one or two of the "best" students but a display of the work of a whole class. Imagine a display of the essays that every child in a fourth-grade classroom wrote after completing an oral history project, or a video of a class production of a play they developed from a piece of literature, or detailed site maps of different plots of land around the school with every plant indicated by genus and species (and maybe even indications of the insects and animal life observed on the plots), or a display of writing or reading portfolios for a whole class for the fall semester. In other words, put the experimentation on display.

Encourage teachers to display projects in the hallways outside their classrooms. At the Park Terrace Elementary School, we saw several classroom displays arranged on small tables, hallway walls, and the floor. These displays were seen by virtually everyone in the school as they traversed the halls. You could see children stopping to study the displays as well as other teachers (and parents and visitors like us). At this school, teachers also report back to the whole faculty when they visit another school or attend a professional conference or participate in a districtwide committee. The school environment makes it difficult to ignore the learning going on by both children and the adult staff.

Resistors, Wet Blankets, and Other Common Beasts

Whenever schools attempt to change, to move forward, we can expect to find teachers who, at best, are skeptics and, at worst, actively resist and work to undermine change. So what to do with these teachers? First, realize that skepticism is a normal response. For most of this century, American schools have been under attack by a variety of reformers. In our own educational experiences we have lived to see children's literature return to center stage after roughly 30 years of being confined somewhere off stage. We have seen open schools, open-space schools, nongraded schools, promotion standards, manipulative math, and hands-on science rise and fall in popularity just in our careers. Many teachers have also seen all this change trumpeted, attended all the training workshops, worked to implement the new ideas, only to see all of it washed away in the next rush to reform. So why not be skeptical?

The only solution we know for skeptical colleagues is demonstrating the idea's workability and even modestly improved results. Most of the skeptics we have encountered, and that is a fairly substantial number, ask only to be left to their own devices, at least for now. If we implement change around them and if that change produces good results, most skeptics become, first, curious and then experimental. Our goal has been to entice skeptics into the change process. We neither ignore them nor attempt to convert them aggressively. But we do try to get them to watch what is going on.

We think that touting reforms too soon, too loudly, and too aggressively can actually work against the likelihood the change will ever succeed. Too often reformers have trumpeted one quick fix after another, from one state commissioner of education to another, from one superintendent to another or from one principal to another. But there are no quick fixes to the difficulties that beset American education today. In fact, many of the difficulties we face are the result of attempted quick fixes. Thus, we argue for a slower pace of implementation. We argue for trying things on a small scale before jumping in wholeheartedly. We argue for letting reforms stand on their results and for modesty in our claims.

A Parting Word

We have avoided creating a name or an acronym for our school-change efforts. There is something particularly attractive (and particularly American) about a five-step process or a three-point plan. But in our combined 50 years of experience in elementary schools, we have uncovered a few truths. First, creating schools that work for all children takes time, energy, and initiative. Second, no two schools are ever alike, so each school must develop its own plan on its own schedule. Third, every school can improve itself, but not every school does. Fourth, honestly and openly examining how change benefits children is the surest way to create better schools. Fifth, and finally, good schools are collections of good teachers, and creating schools where all children become readers and writers is simply a matter of figuring out how to support teachers in their efforts to develop the reading and writing proficiencies of every student.

Madeline Cartwright, the principal of Blaine Elementary School in Philadelphia, offers her advice: "People would say, 'Aw, your so-called solutions are simple.' Yes they are. If the child has no clean clothes, you get him clean clothes. . . . If you know parents have to go to work in the morning, why wait until 8:45 to open school doors? Open the school at 7:30, and if you haven't got your own people there to watch the kids, find others. . . . Someone must do these things for the children. If a child's hungry, someone must feed him. If he's dirty, someone must wash him. If his clothes need laundering, someone must clean them. . . . We had children for whom no family or agency was taking care of such needs. So we did it. . . . The age we live in demands that we extend such efforts. We speak of how we want to help children, but then we allow ourselves to be tangled in bureaucratic nonsense and help never reaches those who need it" (p. 153). In addition to adding a washer and a dryer to the school-equipment inventory, Ms. Cartwright also provided every child with a personalized book bag, set up a fund where any child could get money for field trips or school supplies, organized parents as school helpers, and began a myriad of other "common sense" initiatives!

References

Abbott, C., Yudd, R., & Gutman, B. (1992). *An evaluation of the Chapter 2 inexpensive books distribution program.* Washington, D.C.: U.S. Department of Education, Office of Policy and Planning.

Adams, M. J. (1990). *Beginning to read: Thinking and learning about print.* Cambridge, Mass.: MIT Press.

Afflerbach, P. (1993). Report cards and reading. *The Reading Teacher, 46,* 458–465.

Allington, R. L. (1983). The reading instruction provided readers of differing abilities. *Elementary School Journal, 83,* 548–559.

Allington, R. L. (1991). The legacy of "slow it down and make it more concrete." In J.Zutell & S. McCormick (Eds.), *Learner factors/teacher factors: Issues in literacy research and instruction* (pp. 19–30). Chicago: National Reading Conference.

Allington, R. L. (1993). *Regulatory and fiscal influences upon the organization of literature-based reading programs.* Paper presented at the annual meeting of the American Educational Research Association, Atlanta.

Allington, R. L. (1994). The schools we have. The schools we need. *The Reading Teacher, 48,* 14–29.

Allington, R. L. (1994). What's special about special programs for children who find learning to read difficult? *Journal of Reading Behavior, 26,* 1–21.

Allington, R. L., & Broikou, K. (1988). Development of shared knowledge: A new role for classroom and specialist teachers. *The Reading Teacher, 41,* 806–811.

Allington, R. L., & McGill-Franzen, A. (1989). School response to reading failure: Chapter 1 and special education students in grades 2, 4, & 8. *Elementary School Journal, 89,* 529–542.

Allington, R. L., & McGill-Franzen, A. (1992). Unintended effects of educational reform in New York state. *Educational Policy, 6,* 397–414.

Allington, R. L., & McGill-Franzen, A. (1993). Placing children at risk: Schools respond to reading problems. In R. Donmeyer & R. Kos (Eds.), *At-risk students: Portraits, policies, programs, and practices* (pp. 197–218). Albany, N.Y.: State University of New York Press.

Allington, R. L., & McGill-Franzen, A. (1994). Reading and the mildly handicapped. In T. Husen & N. Postlewaite (Eds.), *The international encyclopedia of education.* New York: Pergamon.

Allington, R. L., & McGill-Franzen, A. (1995). Flunking: Throwing good money after bad. In R. L. Allington & S. A. Walmsley (Eds.), *No quick fix: Rethinking literacy programs in America's elementary schools.* New York: Teachers College Press.

Allington, R. L., & Walmsley, S. A. (1995). *No quick fix: Rethinking literacy programs in American elementary schools.* New York: Teachers College Press.

Ames, R., & Ames, C. (1991). Motivation and effective teaching. In B. F. Jones & L. Idol (Eds.), *Educational values and cognitive instruction: Implications for reform.* Hillsdale, N.J.: L. Erlbaum.

Ames, R. & Ames, C. (1994). Creating a mastery-oriented schoolwide culture: A team leadership perspective. In M. Sashkin & H. Walberg (Eds.), *Educational leadership and school culture.* Berkeley, Calif: McCutchan.

Ames, C., with Khoju, M., & Watkins, T., (March 1993). *Parents and schools: The impact of school-to-home communications on parents' beliefs and perceptions.* Report no. 15, Center on Families, Communities, Schools, and Children's Learning. Baltimore: Johns Hopkins University.

Anastopoulos, A. D., DuPaul, G. J., & Barkley, R. A. (1992). Stimulant medication and parent training therapies for attention deficit-hyperactivity disorder. In S. E. Shaywitz & B. A. Shaywitz (Eds.), *Attention deficit disorder comes of age.* Austin, Tex.: Pro-Ed Publications.

Anderson, L. W., & Pellicier, L. O. (1990). Synthesis of research on compensatory and remedial education. *Educational Leadership, 48,* 10–16.

Anderson, R. C., & Pearson, P. D. (1984). A schema-theoretic view of basic processes in reading comprehension. In P. D. Pearson (Ed.), *Handbook of reading research* (pp. 255–291). White Plains, N.Y.: Longman.

Applebee, A. N. (1991). Literature: Whose heritage? In E. Hiebert (Ed.), *Literacy for a diverse society: Perspective, practices, and policies.* New York: Teachers College Press.

Barth, R. (1990). *Improving schools from within: Teachers, parents, and principals can make the difference.* San Francisco: Jossey-Bass.

Barton, P. E., & Coley, R. J. (1994). *Testing in America's schools.* Princeton, N.J.: Educational Testing Service.

Beck, I. L., & McKeown, M. G. (1993). Why textbooks can baffle students and how to help. *Learning: A Newsletter from the National Research Center on Student Learning, 1,* 2–4.

Beck, L. G., & Murphy, J. (1993). *Understanding the principalship: Metaphorical themes, 1920s–1990s.* New York: Teachers College Press.

Becker, J. (1992). Power corrupts. *Child and Youth Care Forum, 21,* 71–73.

Birman, B. (1988). How to improve a successful program. *American Educator, 12,* 22–29.

Blalock, G. (1991). Paraprofessionals: Critical team members in our special education programs. *Intervention, 26,* 200–215.

Bond, G. L., & Dykstra, R. (1967). The cooperative research program in first-grade reading instruction. *Reading Research Quarterly, 2,* 5–142.

Borg, W. R. (1980). Time and school learning. In C. Denham & A. Lieberman (Eds.), *Time to learn.* Washington, D.C.: National Institute of Education.

Brophy, J. (1987). Synthesis of research on strategies for motivating students to learn, *Educational Leadership, 45,* 40–48.

Brown, R. G. (1991). *Schools of thought: How the politics of literacy shape thinking in the classroom.* San Francisco: Jossey-Bass.

Bruner, C. (1991). *Thinking collaboratively: Ten questions and answers to help policy makers improve children's services.* Washington, D.C.: Education and Human Services Consortium.

Canter, L. (1989). Assertive discipline: More than names on the board and marbles in the jar. *Phi Delta Kappan, 71,* 57–61.

Canter, L., & Canter, M. (1990). *Parents on your side: A comprehensive family involvement program for teachers.* Seal Beach, Calif.: Canter Associates.

Capital Area School Development Association (1992). *A view from the inside: School reform.* Albany, N.Y.: State University of New York at Albany.

Cartwright, M. (1993). *For the children: Lessons from a visionary principal.* New York: Doubleday.

Chamot, A. U., & O'Malley, J. M. (1994). *The CALLA handbook: How to implement the cognitive academic language learning approach.* Reading, Mass.: Addison-Wesley.

Clay, M. M. (1990). The Reading Recovery programme, 1984–88: Coverage, outcomes and Education Board district figures. *New Zealand Journal of Educational Studies, 25,* 61–70.

Clay, M. M. (1993). *Observation Survey of Early Literacy Achievement.* Portsmouth, N.H.: Heinemann.

Coles, G. (1987). *The learning mystique: A critical look at learning disabilities.* New York: Pantheon.

Coley, R., & Goertz, M. (1990). *Educational standards in the 50 states: 1990.* Research report no. 90–15. Princeton, N.J.: Educational Testing Service.

Comer, J. P. (1980). *School power: Implications of an intervention project.* New York: The Free Press.

Comer, J. P. (1988). Educating poor minority children. *Scientific American, 259,* 42–48.

Cooley, W. (1993). The difficulty of the educational task: Implications for comparing student achievement in states, school districts, and schools. *ERS Spectrum, 11,* 27–31.

Cuban, L. (1990). Reforming again, again, and again. *Educational Researcher, 19,* 3–13.

Cummins, J. (1994). The acquisition of English as a second language. In K. Spangenberg-Urbschat & R. Pritchard (Eds.), *Kids come in all languages: Reading instruction for ESL students* (pp. 36–63). Newark, Del.: International Reading Association.

Cunningham, P. M. (1995). *Phonics they use.* 2d. ed. New York: HarperCollins.

Cunningham, P. M., & Allington, R. L. (1994). *Classrooms that work: They can all read and write.* New York: HarperCollins.

Cunningham, P. M., Hall, D. P., & Defee, M. (1991). Non-ability-grouped, multi-level instruction: A year in a first grade classroom. *Reading Teacher, 44,* 566–571.

Cushman, K. (September 1992). The essential school principal: A changing role in a changing school. *Horace: Newsletter of the Essential Schools, 9,* 1–8.

Daneman, M. (1991). Individual differences in reading skills. In R. Barr, M. L. Kamil, P. B. Mosenthal, & P. D. Pearson, *Handbook of Reading Research.* Vol. 2 (pp. 512–538). White Plains, N.Y.: Longman.

Darling, S. (March 1993). Focus on family literacy: The national perspective. *Newsletter of the National Center for Family Literacy, 5,* 3.

DeFina, A. (1992). *Portfolio assessment: Getting started.* New York: Scholastic.

Denham, C., & Lieberman, A. (1980). *Time to learn.* Washington, D.C.: U.S. Government Printing Office (1980-695-717).

Dolan, L. J. (1992). *Models for integrating human services into the schools.* Report no. 30, Center for Disadvantaged Students. Baltimore: Johns Hopkins University.

Dowd, T., & Tierney, J. (1992). *Teaching social skills to youth.* Boys Town, Nebr.: Boys Town Press.

Downs, A. (1993). Breathing life into the past: The creation of history units. In M. Tunnel & R. Ammon (Eds.), *The story of ourselves: Teaching history through children's literature.* Portsmouth, N.H.: Heinemann.

Dreikurs, R., Grunwald, B. B., & Pepper, F. C. (1982). *Maintaining sanity in the classroom: Classroom management techniques.* New York: Harper & Row.

Duffy, G. G. (1993). Rethinking strategy instruction: Four teachers' development and their low achievers' understandings. *Elementary School Journal, 93,* 231–247.

Dyer, P. C. (1992). Reading Recovery: A cost-effectiveness and educational-outcomes analysis. *ERS Spectrum, 10,* 10–19.

Edmonds, R. (1981). Making public schools effective. *Social Policy, 12,* 56–61.

Education Research Service (1991). *Culturally sensitive instruction and student learning.* Arlington, Va: Author.

Educational Testing Service (1991). *ETS Developments, 37,* 6–7.

Edwards, P. A. (1989). Supporting lower SES mothers' attempts to provide scaffolding for books. In J. B. Allen & J. Mason (Eds.), *Risk makers, risk takers, risk breakers: Reducing the risks for young literacy learners* (pp. 222–248). Portsmouth, N.H.: Heinemann.

Epps, S., & Tindal, G. (1987). The effectiveness of differential programming in serving students with mild handicaps: Placement options and instructional programming. In M. Wang, M. Reynolds, & H. Walberg (Eds.), *Handbook of special education: Research and practice* (pp. 213–248). New York: Pergamon.

Farr, R. (1992). Putting it all together: Solving the reading assessment puzzle. *Reading Teacher, 46,* 26–37.

Fielding, L. G., & Pearson, P. D. (1994). Reading comprehension: What works. *Educational Leadership, 51,* 63–68.

Fielding, L. G., Wilson, P. T., & Anderson, R. C. (1986). A new focus on free reading: The role of trade books in reading instruction. In T. E. Raphael (Ed.), *The contexts of school-based literacy* (pp. 149–160). New York: Random House.

Fischer, M. (1990). *Fiscal accountability in Milwaukee public elementary schools: Where does the money go?* Milwaukee: Wisconsin Policy Research Institute.

Fisher, C. W., & Berliner, D. C. (1985). *Perspectives on instructional time.* New York: Longman.

Fractor, J. S., Woodruff, M. C., Martinez, M. G., & Teale, W. H. (1993). Let's not miss opportunities to promote voluntary reading: Classroom libraries in the elementary school. *Reading Teacher, 46,* 476–484.

Fullan, M. (1991). *The new meaning of educational change.* New York: Teachers College Press.

Gambrell, L., Wilson, R., & Gannt, W. (1981). Classroom observations of task-attending behaviors of good and poor readers. *Journal of Educational Research, 74,* 400–404.

Gamoran, A. (1986). Instructional and institutional effect of ability grouping. *Sociology of Education, 59,* 185–198.

Gardner, H. (1993). *Multiple intelligences: The theory in practice.* New York: Basic Books.

Gelzheiser, L. M., Meyers, J., & Pruzek, R. M. (1992). Effects of pull-in and pull-out approaches to reading instruction for special education and remedial reading students. *Journal of Educational and Psychological Consultation, 3,* 133–149.

General Accounting Office (1993). *School-linked human services: A comprehensive strategy for aiding students at risk of school failure* (report 94–21). Washington, D.C.: Health, Education, and Human Services Division.

General Accounting Office (1994). *Elementary school children: Many change schools frequently, harming their education* (report 94–45). Washington, D.C.: Health, Education, and Human Services Division.

George, P. S. (1988). *What's the truth about tracking and ability grouping really?* Gainesville, Fla.: Teacher Education Resources.

Glasser, W. (1986). *Control theory in the classroom.* New York: HarperCollins.

Glasser, W. (1990). *The quality school: Managing students without coercion.* New York: HarperCollins.

Goodlad, J. I. (1983). *A place called school: Prospects for the future.* New York: McGraw-Hill.

Goodlad, J. I., & Lovitt, T. C. (1993). *Integrating general and special education.* New York: Merrill.

Goswami, U., & Bryant, P. (1990). *Phonological skills and learning to read.* East Sussex, U.K.: Erlbaum Associates.

Guice, S., & Allington, R. L. (1994). Using literature in reading programs. *School Administrator, 6,* 41.

Haladyna, T. H., Nolan, S. B., & Haas, N. S. (1991). Raising standardized achievement test scores and the origins of test score pollution. *Educational Researcher, 20,* 2–7.

Hall, D., Prevatte, C., & Cunningham, P. (1995). Eliminating ability grouping and reducing failure in the primary grades. In R. L. Allington & S. A. Walmsley (Eds.), *No quick fix: Rethinking literacy programs in America's elementary schools.* New York: Teachers College Press.

Harp, L. (March 17, 1993). Study details how districts, schools divvy up money. *Education Week, 22,* 1 & 21.

Hasselriis, P. (1982). IEPs and a whole language model of language arts. *Topics in Learning and Learning Disabilities, 14,* 17–21.

Hayes, D. P., & Grether, J. (1983). The school year and vacations: When do students learn? *Cornell Journal of Social Relations, 17,* 56–71.

Henker, B., & Whalen, C. K. (1989). Hyperactivity and attention deficits. *American Psychologist, 78,* 216–223.

Herrick, S. C., & Epstein, J. L. (1991). *Improving school and family partnerships in urban elementary schools: Reading activity packets and newsletters.* Baltimore: Center for Disadvantaged Students, Johns Hopkins University.

Hiebert, E. H., & Taylor, B. (1994). *Getting reading right from the start: Effective early literacy interventions.* Boston: AllynBacon.

Hillocks, G. (1986). *Research on written composition: New directions for teaching.* Urbana, Ill.: ERIC Clearinghouse on Reading and Communication Skills.

Hodgkinson, H. (1993). American education: The good, the bad, and the task. *Phi Delta Kappan, 74,* 619–623.

Hoffman, J. V., Roser, N. L., & Battle, J. (1993). Reading aloud in classrooms: From the modal to a model. *Reading Teacher, 46,* 496–503.

Hopfenberg, W. S., & Levin, H. M. (1993). *The accelerated schools: resource guide.* San Francisco: Jossey-Bass.

Hyde, A. A. (1992). Developing a willingness to change. In W. T. Pink & A. A. Hyde (Eds.), *Effective staff development for school change* (pp. 171–190). Norwood, N.J.: Ablex Publishing.

Jachym, N., Allington, R. L., & Broikou, K. A. (1989). Estimating the cost of seatwork. *Reading Teacher, 43,* 30–37.

Johnson, D., & Johnson, D. (1993). *Teaching students to be peacemakers.* Edina, Minn.: Interaction Books.

Johnston, P. H., & Allington, R. L. (1991). Remediation. In R. Barr, M. L. Kamil, P. Mosenthal, & P. D., Pearson (Eds.), *Handbook of Reading Research.* vol. 2 (pp. 984–1012). New York: Longman.

Johnston, P. H. (1992). *Constructive evaluation of literate activity.* New York: Longman.

Johnston, P. H. (1992). Nontechnical assessment. *Reading Teacher, 46,* 60–62.

Johnston, P. H., Allington, R. L., & Afflerbach, P. (1985). The congruence of classroom and remedial reading instruction. *Elementary School Journal, 85,* 465–478.

Knapp, M. S. (1991). *What is taught, and how, to the children of poverty: Interim report from a two-year investigation.* Menlo Park, Calif.: S.R.I. Inc.

Knight, S., & Stallings, J. (1995). Implementing the Accelerated School model in an urban elementary school. In R. L. Allington & S. A. Walmsley (Eds.), *No quick fix: Rethinking literacy programs in America's elementary schools.* New York: Teachers College Press.

Koretz, D., Stecher, B., Klein, S., & McCaffrey, D. (1994). The Vermont portfolio assessment program: Findings and implications. *Educational Measurement, 13,* 5–16.

Kozol, J. (1991). *Savage inequalities: Children in America's schools.* New York: Crown.

Kuykendall, C. (1992). *From rage to hope: Strategies for reclaiming black and Hispanic students.* Bloomington, Ind.: National Educational Service.

Langer, J. A., & Allington, R. L. (1992). Curriculum research in writing and reading. In P. W. Jackson (Ed.), *Handbook of research on curriculum* (pp. 687–725). New York: Macmillan.

Lara, J. (1994). Demographic overview: Changes in student enrollment in American schools. In K. Spangenberg-Urbschat & R. Pritchard (Eds.), *Kids come in all languages: Reading instruction for ESL students* (pp. 9–21). Newark, Del.: International Reading Association.

Lareau, A. (1989). *Home advantage: Social class and parental intervention in elementary education.* Philadelphia: Falmer.

Lawson, C. (October 4, 1990). In Missouri, the 12-hour playday. *The New York Times,* sec. C, pp. 1 & 6.

Leinhardt, G., Zigmond, N., & Cooley, W. (1981). Reading instruction and its effects. *American Educational Research Journal, 18,* 343–361.

Leithwood, K. A. (1990). The principal's role in teacher development. In B. Joyce (Ed.), *Changing school culture through staff development* (pp. 71–88). Alexandria, Va.: Association for Supervision and Curriculum Development.

LeTendre, M. J. (1991). The continuing evolution of a federal role in compensatory education. *Educational Evaluation and Policy Analysis, 13,* 328–344.

Levin, H. M. (1987). Accelerated Schools for disadvantaged students. *Educational Leadership, 44,* 19–21.

Little, J. W. (1993). Teachers' professional development in a climate of educational reform. *Educational Evaluation and Policy Analysis, 15,* 129–151.

Lloyd-Jones, R. (1977). Primary trait scoring. In C. R. Cooper & L. Odell (Eds.), *Evaluating writing.* Urbana, Ill.: National Council of Teachers of English.

Lyons, C. A., & Beaver, J. (1995). Reducing retention and learning disability placement through Reading Recovery. In R. L. Allington & S. A. Walmsley (Eds.) *No Quick Fix: Rethinking literacy programs in America's elementary schools.* New York: Teachers College Press.

Lyons, C. A., Pinnell, G. S., & DeFord, D. (1993). *Partners in learning: Teachers and children in Reading Recovery.* New York: Teachers College Press.

Martin, A. (1988). Screening, early intervention, and remediation: Observing children's potential. *Harvard Educational Review, 58,* 488–501.

Martin, J. R. (1992). *The school home: Rethinking schools for changing families.* Cambridge, Mass.: Harvard University Press.

McGill-Franzen, A. (1992) *Shaping the preschool agenda: Early literacy, professional beliefs, and public policy.* Albany, N.Y.: State University of New York Press.

McGill-Franzen, A. (1992). Early literacy: What does "developmentally appropriate" mean? *Reading Teacher, 46,* 56–58.

McGill-Franzen, A. (1993). "I could read the words!": Selecting good books for inexperienced readers. *Reading Teacher, 46,* 424–426.

McGill-Franzen, A. (1994). Compensatory and special education: Is there accountability for learning and belief in children's potential? In E. H. Hiebert & B. M. Taylor (Eds.), *Getting reading right from the start: Effective early literacy interventions.* Boston: Allyn-Bacon.

McGill-Franzen, A., & Allington, R. L. (1991). Every child's right: Literacy. *Reading Teacher, 45,* 86–90.

McGill-Franzen, A., & Allington, R. L. (Dec. 13, 1993). What are they to read? Not all kids, Mr. Riley, have easy access to books. *Education Week,* 26.

McGill-Franzen, A., & Allington, R. L. (1993). Flunk 'em or get them classified: The contamination of primary grade accountability data. *Educational Researcher, 21,* 19–22.

McLaughlin, M. W., & Yee, S. M. (1988). School as a place to have a career. In A. Lieberman (Ed.), *Building a professional culture in schools* (pp. 23–44). New York: Teachers College Press.

Mehan, H., Hartweck, A., & Meihls, J. L. (1986). *Handicapping the handicapped.* Stanford, Calif.: Stanford University Press.

Meisels, S. J. (1993). Doing harm by doing good: Iatrogenic effects of early childhood enrollment and promotion policies. *Early Childhood Research Quarterly, 7,* 155–174.

Mergendoller, J., Bellsimo, Y., & Horan, C. (1990). *Kindergarten holding out: The role of school characteristics, family background, and parental perceptions.* Novato, Calif.: Beryl Buck Institute for Education.

Michelson, N. (1993). *Wanderers: Selecting books for independent reading.* Paper presented at the National Reading Conference, Charleston, S.C.

Millsap, M.A., Moss, M., & Gamse, B. (1993). *Chapter 1 implementation study: Final report.* Washington, D.C.: Office of Policy and Planning, U.S. Department of Education.

Morphett, M., & Washburne, C. (l931). When should children begin to read? *Elementary School Journal, 31,* 496–503.

Morrow, L. M. (1991). Promoting voluntary reading. In J. Flood, J. Jensen, D. Lapp, & J. Squire (Eds.), *Handbook of research on teaching the English language arts* (pp. 681–690). New York: Macmillan.

National Association for the Education of Young Children (1986). NAEYC position paper on developmentally appropriate practice in early childhood programs. *Young Children,* September, 3–29.

National Commission on Excellence in Education (1983). *A nation at risk.* Washington, D.C.: Author.

National Education Commission on Time and Learning (1994). *Prisoners of time.* Washington, D.C.: U.S. Government Printing Office.

Nicholson, T. (1991). Do children read words better in context or in lists? A classic study revisited. *Journal of Educational Psychology, 83,* 444–450.

Osborn, J. H. (1989) Summary: Improving basal reading programs. In P. Winograd, K. Wixson, & M. Lipson (Eds.), *Improving basal reading instruction.* New York: Teachers College Press.

Palestis, E. (1993). Prize-winning family involvement in New Jersey. *Education Digest, 58,* 14–17.

Payzant, T. W. (1994). Comprehensive school services in San Diego. In C.E. Finn & H. Walberg (Eds.), *Radical education reforms.* Berkeley, Calif.: McCutchan.

Pearson, P. D. (1993). Teaching and learning to read: A research perspective. *Language Arts, 70,* 502–511.

Peterson, R. & Eeds, M. (1990). *Grand Conversations: Literature Groups in action.* New York: Scholastic.

Piper, T. (1993). *And then there were two: Children and second language learning.* Portsmouth, N.H.: Heinemann.

Pressley, M., Wood, E., & Woloshyn, V. E. (1992). Encouraging mindful use of prior knowledge: Attempting to construct explanatory answers facilitates learning. *Educational Psychologist, 27,* 91–109.

Rayner, K., & Pollatsek, A. (1989). *The psychology of reading.* Englewood Cliffs, N.J.: Prentice Hall.

Reid, M.K., & Borkowski, J.G. (1987). Causal attributions of hyperactive children: Implications for teaching strategies and self-control. *Journal of Educational Psychology, 79,* 296–307.

Richardson, V. (1990). Significant and worthwhile change in teaching practice. *Educational Researcher, 19,* 10–18.

Rigg, P. (1989). Language experience approach: Reading naturally. In P. Rigg & V. G. Allen (Eds.), *When they don't all speak English: Integrating the ESL student into the regular classroom.* Urbana, Ill.: National Council of Teachers of English.

Rosenholtz, S. (1989). *Teachers' workplace: The social organization of schools.* New York: Longman.

Rowan, B. (1990). Commitment and control: Alternative strategies for the organizational design of schools. In C. B. Cazden (Ed.), *Review of research in education* (pp. 353–389). Washington, D.C.: American Educational Research Association.

Rowan, B., & Guthrie, L. F. (1989). The quality of Chapter I instruction: Results from a study of twenty-four schools. In R. E. Slavin, N. Karweit, & N. Madden (Eds.), *Effective programs for students at risk* (pp. 195–219). Boston: Allyn-Bacon.

Schrag, J. A. (1993). Restructuring schools for a better alignment of general and special education. In J. I. Goodlad & T. C. Lovitt (Eds.), *Integrating general and special education* (pp. 203–228). New York: Merrill.

Schrag, P., & Divoky, D. (1975). *The myth of the hyperactive child.* New York: Pantheon.

Sergiovanni, T. J. (1991). *The principalship: A reflective practice perspective.* Boston: Allyn-Bacon.

Sharpe, M. N., York, J. L., & Knight, J. (1994). Effects of inclusion on the academic performance of classmates without disabilities: A preliminary study. *Remedial and Special Education, 15,* 281–287.

Shepard, L. A., & Smith, M. L. (1989). *Flunking grades: Research and policies on retention.* Philadelphia: Falmer.

Shepard, L. A., & Smith, M. L. (1990). Synthesis of research on grade retention. *Educational Leadership, 47,* 84–88.

Simon, P. (1993). Testimony supporting Senate bill 266: The Elementary and Secondary School Library Act of 1993. *Congressional Record—Senate,* S924, January 28.

Sizer, T. (1988). *Horace's compromise: The dilemma of the American high school.* Boston: Houghton-Mifflin.

Slavin, R. E. (1993). Preventing early school failure: Implications for policy and practice. In R. E. Slavin, N. Karweit, & B. Wasik (Eds.), *Preventing early school failure: Research, policy, and practice* (pp. 206–231). Boston: Allyn-Bacon.

Slavin, R. E., Karweit, N. L., & Wasik, B. A. (1993). *Preventing early school failure: Research, policy, and practice.* Boston: Allyn-Bacon.

Slavin, R. E., Madden, N. A., Karweit, N. L., Livermon, B. J., & Dolan, L. (1990). Success for all: First-year outcomes of a comprehensive plan for reforming urban education. *American Educational Research Journal, 27,* 255–278.

Slavin, R. E., Madden, N. A., Karweit, N. L., Dolan, L., & Wasik, B. A. (1992). *Success for all: A relentless approach to prevention and early intervention in elementary schools.* Arlington, Va.: Educational Research Service.

Slavin, R. E., Madden, N. A., Karweit, N. L., Dolan, L., & Wasik, B. A. (1994). Success for all: Getting reading right the first time. In E. H. Hiebert & B. M. Taylor (Eds.), *Getting reading right from the start: Effective early literacy interventions* (pp. 125–147). Boston: Allyn-Bacon.

Smith-Burke, M. T. (1989). Political and economic dimensions of literacy: Challenges for the 1990s. In S. McCormick & J. Zutell (Eds.), *Cognitive and social perspectives for literacy research and instruction* (pp. 1–18). Chicago: National Reading Conference.

Smith, R. C., & Lincoln, C. A. (1988). *America's shame, America's hope: Twelve million youth at risk.* A report prepared for the Charles Stewart Mott Foundation by MDC, Chapel Hill, N.C.

Snow, C., Barnes, W., Chandler, J., Goodman, I., & Hemphill, C. (1990). *Unfulfilled expectations. Home and school influences on literacy.* Cambridge, Mass.: Harvard.

Stanovich, K. E. (1986). Matthew Effects in reading: Some consequences of individual differences in the acquisition of literacy. *Reading Research Quarterly, 21,* 360–407.

Stanovich, K. E. (1991). Word recognition: Changing perspectives. In R. Barr, M. L. Kamil, P. B. Mosenthal, & P. D. Pearson (Eds.), *Handbook of Reading Research*. Vol. 2 (pp. 418–452). White Plains, N.Y.: Longman.

Stevens, R. J., Madden, N. A., Slavin, R. E., & Farnish, A. M. (1987). Cooperative and Intergrated Reading and Composition: Two field experiments. *Reading Research Quarterly, 22,* 433–454.

Stiggins, R. J., Frisbie, D. A., & Griswold, P. (1989). Inside high school grading practices: Building a research agenda. *Educational Measurement: Issues and Practice, 26,* 5–14.

Stoddard, A. J. (1957). *Schools for tomorrow: An educator's blueprint.* New York: Fund for the Advancement of Education.

Strickland, D. S., & Walmsley, S. A. (1993) *School book clubs and literacy development: A descriptive study.* Final report to the M. R. Robinson Foundation: Executive summary.

Swanson, J. M., et al. (1993). Effect of stimulant medication on children with attention deficit disorder: A review of reviews. *Exceptional Children, 60,* 154–162.

Sweet, A. P. (1993). *Transforming ideas for teaching and learning to read.* Washington, D.C.: Office for Educational Research and Improvement, U.S. Department of Education.

Teale, W. H., & Sulzby, E. (1991). Emergent literacy. In R. Barr, M. L. Kamil, P. B. Mosenthal, & P. D. Pearson (Eds.), *Handbook of Reading Research*. Vol. 2 (pp. 418–452). New York: Longman.

Tharp, R. G., & Gallimore, R. (1988). *Rousing minds to life: Teaching, learning, and schooling in a social context.* New York: Cambridge.

Tierney, R. J., & Shanahan, T. (1991). Research on the reading-writing relationship: Interactions, transactions, and outcomes. In R. Barr, M. L. Kamil, P. B. Mosenthal, & P. D. Pearson (Eds.), *Handbook of Reading Research*. Vol. 2 (pp. 246–280). New York: Longman.

Timar, T. (1994). Federal education policy and practice: Building organizational capacity through Chapter 1. *Educational Evaluation and Policy Analysis, 16,* 51–66.

Vandegrift, J. A., & Greene, A. L. (1992). Rethinking parent involvement. *Educational Leadership, 50,* 57–59.

Vasquez, O. A. (1993). A look at language as a resource: Lessons from La Clase Magica. In M. B. Arias & U. Casanova (Eds.), *Bilingual education: Politics, practice, and research.* Chicago: University of Chicago Press.

Veatch, J. (1959). *Individualizing your reading program.* New York: Putnam.

Walmsley, S. A. (1992). Reflections on the state of elementary literature instruction. *Language Arts, 69,* 508–514.

Walmsley, S. A. (1994). *Children exploring their world: Theme teaching in elementary school.* Portsmouth, N.H.: Heinemann.

Walp, T., & Walmsley, S. A. (1995). Scoring well on tests or becoming genuinely literate: Rethinking remediation in a small, rural school. In R. L. Allington & S. A. Walmsley (Eds.), *No quick fix: Rethinking literacy programs in America's elementary schools.* New York: Teachers College Press.

Walters, K., & Gunderson, L. (1985). The effects of parent volunteers reading first language (L1) books to ESL students. *Reading Teacher, 39,* 66–69.

Weber, R. (1991). Linguistic diversity and reading in American society. In R. Barr, M. L. Kamil, P. B. Mosenthal, & P. D. Pearson (Eds.), *Handbook of Reading Research.* Vol. 2 (pp. 97–119). New York: Longman.

Whalen, C. K., & Henker, B. (1992). Social impact of stimulant treatment for hyperactive children. In S. E. Shaywitz & B. A. Shaywitz (Eds.), *Attention deficit disorder comes of age.* Austin, Tex.: Pro-Ed Publications.

Will, M. (1986). *Educating students with learning problems: A shared responsibility.* Washington, D.C.: Office of Special Education and Rehabilitation Services, U.S. Department of Education.

Willinsky, J. (1990). *The new literacy: Redefining reading and writing in the schools.* New York: Routledge.

Willis, S. (September 1993). Are letter grades obsolete? *ASCD Update, 35,* 1 & 8.

Winfield, L. F. (1991). Lessons from the field: Case studies of evolving schoolwide projects. *Educational Evaluation and Policy Analysis, 13,* 353–362.

Zigler, E. F., & Finn-Stevenson, M. (1989). Child care in America: From problem to solution. *Education Policy, 5,* 313–329

Name Index

Subject Index

Volunteers, 77–78

Word(s)
    Big Word Board, 231
    fluency, 49
    high-frequency, 225–226, 228
    -search puzzles, 119
    working with, 25
Writing, 227–228
    approaches, 55–58
    assessment, 133–134
    checklists, 135
    evaluation of, 124
    genres of, 166

    observations of, 131–132, 136
    opportunities, 51–53
    prior knowledge and, 43–45
    samples and scales, 132–134, 133*f*
    second language learners and, 211–212
    standardized tests and, 129
    student self–evaluations, 136–137
    teacher as model of, 223
    as thinking, 133–134
        versus skill and drill, 41–43
    through demonstration, 45–47
    time allocated for, 38, 132, 155, 235
    time engaged in, 119–121
    traditional seatwork activities and, 120